Film·ol·o·gy

A MOVIE-A-DAY GUIDE
to a Complete Film Education

Chris Barsanti
Senior Writer for Filmcritic.com

Aadamsmedia
Avon, Massachusetts

To Marya

Published by
Adams Media, a division of F+W Media, Inc.
57 Littlefield Street, Avon, MA 02322. U.S.A.
www.adamsmedia.com

ISBN 10: 1-4405-0753-8
ISBN 13: 978-1-4405-0753-3
eISBN 10: 1-4405-1036-9
eISBN 13: 978-1-4405-1036-6

Printed in the United States of America.

10 9 8 7 6 5 4 3 2 1

Library of Congress Cataloging-in-Publication Data
Barsanti, Chris.
Filmology / Chris Barsanti.
    p. cm.
ISBN 978-1-4405-0753-3
1. Motion pictures—Catalogs. I. Title.
PN1998.B32 2010
791.43'75—dc22
        2010038519

Interior images © 123RF.com

This book is available at quantity discounts for bulk purchases.
For information, please call 1-800-289-0963.

Introduction

In the darkness at the movies, where nothing is asked of us and we are left alone, the liberation from duty and constraint allows us to develop our own aesthetic responses.

—PAULINE KAEL

This quotation is a fine way of saying that nobody needs to tell you how to feel about the movies. You like, love, despise, or feel ambivalent about a film based on what you were thinking and feeling while the images were flickering across your retinas. That being said, how do you decide what to watch in the first place?

According to the Motion Picture Association of America, roughly 550 films were released in the United States in 2009, and more than 600 the year before. Now, even if you followed part of director Richard Linklater's advice for learning how to become filmmaker (watch three films a day, every day), it would take months just to catch up on that year's films. Since this doesn't leave much time to hold down a job, people have to be selective about what they watch.

That's where this book comes in. Think of it as a guide pointing the way to 365 of the most thrilling, the most inventive, the most affecting, the most *most* films that have ever been made.

The world of cinema is rich and varied almost beyond description, with an array of fascinating stories and settings (not to mention continually innovating ways for visualizing them) that stands up to the greatest works of world literature. Just about every aspect of cinematic art is represented in these pages, from revolutionary avant-garde experiments to drop-dead-funny comedies to harrowing tales of bloody combat and stranger-than-fiction true stories that have to be *seen* to be believed (and sometimes you won't believe them even then).

For somebody who spends much of his time viewing and writing about films, it's exhausting to see the same "great" films hauled up for praise again and again in those "Top 10" or "100 Greatest" lists that show up in so many magazines and television film tributes. So I made a concerted effort to include films that might not always make those lists. Nothing against Michael Curtiz's wartime romance *Casablanca* (it's included here) but his twisted noir *Mildred Pierce* is every bit as good, if not better. Steven Spielberg's *Jaws* and *E.T.* are regularly lauded as classics, but what about his fever-dream of a war film, *Empire of the Sun*? Bette Davis and Joan Crawford's *What Ever Happened to Baby Jane?* is correctly thought of as a camp classic, but the lesser-known documentary *Grey Gardens* (about two faded socialites living in a falling-down mansion) is just as memorable and dramatic.

There's not a film in here that doesn't deserve at least one viewing; love them or hate them—you won't easily forget them.

Genre Key

Action		Horror	
Animation		Musical	
Avant-garde		Mystery	
Comedy		Non-fiction	
Crime		Romance	
Drama		Science-fiction	
Family		War	
Fantasy		Western	
Foreign			

I Am Cuba

YEAR RELEASED: 1964
DIRECTOR: Mikhail Kalatozov
WHO'S IN IT: Luz María Collazo, José Gallardo, Sergio Corrieri

"The most terrifying thing in life is life."

Russian director Mikhail Kalatozov's oddball, impressionist epic is pure sensation, cinematic poetry in its rawest form. Made just five years after the Cuban Revolution, as Soviet propaganda, *I Am Cuba* was buried in the Mosfilm archives for three decades after only a few screenings.

The film includes four story lines stitched together by narration, forming a portrait of Cuba before and during Castro's revolution. In the first story line, we see Maria (Luz María Collazo), a peasant woman forced to earn money being groped by grotesque, wealthy Americans in tacky Havana clubs. Next, a farmer (José Gallardo) is tossed off his land by the American corporation United Fruit. In the third sequence, students riot in the streets, hurling Molotov cocktails and charging en masse at ranks of police. In the final segment, war comes to a peasant family in the hills.

Though the film is shot in black and white, you'll remember it in color. The street-fighting action is so vivid and electrifying, the scenery so verdant and lush, that your mind paints in what it doesn't see. Kalatozov's dynamic camerawork creates some of the most thrilling and emotive moments ever witnessed onscreen, more than filling the spaces left by the sparse screenplay.

In one justly celebrated, breathtaking scene, the viewer follows the camera's view as it climbs up a building and walks through a rooftop cigar factory before flying out into space over a passing funeral procession for a revolutionary. It's a showoff move, but astounding nonetheless, like the film as a whole.

Historically Speaking

January 1, 1959, was the date of the overthrow of Fulgencio Batista by Cuban revolutionaries, whose exploits are explored in *I Am Cuba*.

Man with the Movie Camera

YEAR RELEASED: 1929
DIRECTOR: Dziga Vertov
WHO'S IN IT: Mikhail Kaufman, Elizaveta Svilova

"An experimentation in the cinematic transmission of visual phenomena."

Dziga Vertov, the man identified in this dazzling film's credits as "the author of the experiment," isn't innovating for its own sake. He's trying for a whole new kind of cinema, and it's nearly as groundbreaking now as it first seemed back in 1929.

This richly imagined carnival of silent imagery tells story after small story, linked by little except the plucky figure of the cameraman, who trots through the film capturing everything he can. Vertov's vision is a pulsating, spinning vortex of daily life in an industrial nation. In his raw openness to the randomness of existence, Vertov actually delivers a powerful rebuke to the totalitarian system he was working under.

Some scenes of spewing smokestacks and grungy-faced laborers hint at the kind of broad-shouldered Soviet propaganda his fellow filmmakers were putting out. Vertov's eye (itself a repeated visual motif) trains instead on smaller subplots: a woman getting dressed, commuters packed into the streets, buses flowing out of garages for the day's work, a mother giving birth. Vertov cuts back and forth across this action (even showing his editor at work creating the film itself), building tiny dramas linked by little except that they are all part of one thrilling day. It's a rich and chaotic tumult, and dazzling to behold.

Though a visual treat, this silent film is definitely best viewed with audio. Check out the 1995 release, which features a clanging, playful, Danny Elfman–esque score by silent-film specialists the Alloy Orchestra, following notes left by Vertov himself.

> **Everyone's a Critic**
> Dziga Vertov's Soviet filmmaking comrade Sergei Eisenstein despised this film, calling it "purposeless camera hooliganism."

The Lord of the Rings: Fellowship of the Ring

YEAR RELEASED: 2001
DIRECTOR: Peter Jackson
WHO'S IN IT: Elijah Wood, Ian McKellen, Viggo Mortensen

"One ring to rule them all, one ring to find them, one ring to bring them all and in the darkness, bind them."

There had been rumors for years about a project to film J. R. R. Tolkien's fantasy trilogy, but it seemed doomed never to happen. Disney tried, but Tolkien (born this day in 1892) was not a fan of the company (given what they did later to his friend C. S. Lewis's books, you can see why). John Boorman took a run and ended up doing *Excalibur* instead. Ralph Bakshi's rotoscope animated 1978 version was less than impressive. So when little-known Australian director Peter Jackson signed on, fans were excited but nervous. It turned out that they didn't have anything to worry about.

As the clouds of war gather in the fantasy world of Middle-earth, the scattered societies of elves, humans, dwarves, and hobbits band together in an expedition to hurl a magic ring—the source of the Dark Lord Sauron's power—into the chasm of Mount Doom. Jackson pulls together the motley heroes with charm and grace, cutting out swaths of the book without lessening its mythic drama. A twinkle-eyed Ian McKellen stands out as the grumbling wizard Gandalf, while the sidelines are packed with great supporting players, from an ethereal Cate Blanchett as the Elven queen Galadriel to Viggo Mortensen as the scruffy but kingly warrior Aragorn. Although Jackson's penchant for massive battle scenes lost its vigor in the increasingly long-winded series, his ability to turn great fantasy writing into thrilling fantasy film is at its peak here.

Lost and Found

The extended cut of *The Fellowship of the Ring* adds about a half-hour of material and stands as a rare example of a director's cut that seems more necessary than self-indulgent.

Snow White and the Seven Dwarfs

🖥️ 🏰 👨‍👧

YEAR RELEASED: 1937
DIRECTOR: David Hand
WHO'S IN IT: (voices of) Adriana Caselotti, Lucille La Verne

"Magic mirror, on the wall, who is the fairest one of all?"

It's difficult to think of Walt Disney's first full-length film as revolutionary, but that's what it was. The idea of taking animation, then best suited to the shorts played before the real movie, and hauling it out to feature length could have been the folly that sank a visionary upstart like Walt. That clearly didn't happen.

The Snow White tale is a curious one to launch such a gamble. As many a comedian has noted: naive princess lives in a house with seven small bachelors? If you stop to think about what's happening, then like any fantasy, it all falls apart. But, like the best fantasies, the story is gripping and elemental enough that most viewers rarely bother with such considerations.

Snow White herself is a lovely vision, her alabaster skin unearthly pale against the dark forest background. The dwarves are a curious bunch—seven kinds of comic relief. While they have the film's attention with all their marching and music, it's the witch who grabs your eye. Her deep and inexplicable malevolence is what powers the film.

While the film was a great international hit, and helped pay for Disney's new animation studio in Burbank, it didn't pave the way for more of the same. Disney thereafter stuck mostly to fairy-tale sources that could be more easily scrubbed up. No more poisoned apples for him.

Production Notes

Before hitting on *Snow White*, Walt Disney considered making his first feature a full-length Mickey Mouse *Steamboat Willie* cartoon.

Princess Mononoke

YEAR RELEASED: 1997
DIRECTOR: Hayao Miyazaki
WHO'S IN IT: (voices of) Gillian Anderson, Billy Crudup, Claire Danes, Minnie Driver

"Cut off a wolf's head and it still has the power to bite."

Japanese animator Hayao Miyazaki had been garnering accolades in his home country for years. When he came up with this dazzling work of fantasy, Western audiences realized what they had been missing.

The film is set during Japan's Muromachi era, around the fifteenth century, a time when the country was starting to creep into modernization and (in Miyazaki's vision, at least) the gods of the wilderness were being killed off. In Miyazaki's world, the gods aren't ephemeral spirits but living, breathing creatures who might have unworldly powers but can still be killed.

The smoggy, industrial city of Iron Town, ruled by the greedy Lady Eboshi, is clearing forests for fuel to power its smelting furnaces. This causes conflict with the creatures of the forest. Among them is a human girl, San, raised by wolves and eager to take revenge on Eboshi. Somewhere between the factions is Prince Ashitaka, on a quest to figure out why a demonic boar tried to destroy his village.

Miyazaki builds slowly to the great confrontation between humankind and nature with a patient sense of timing. One of his most adult-oriented films, this is also his biggest, with a fantasy universe rivaling the greatest of literature. The most expensive *anime* yet made, all the money is on the screen in gorgeous, multilayered compositions and characters drawn with the scrupulous care and vivid drama that the story demands.

Production Notes

Miramax Films hired American stars to handle *Princess Mononoke*'s dubbed English dialogue, and fantasy author Neil Gaiman retooled the translated dialogue.

The Talented Mr. Ripley

YEAR RELEASED: 1999
DIRECTOR: Anthony Minghella
WHO'S IN IT: Matt Damon, Gwyneth Paltrow, Jude Law

"Don't you just take the past, and put it in a room in the basement, and lock the door and never go in there?"

Tom Ripley (Matt Damon, showing why he's a movie star) is a bathroom attendant in 1950s New York. A chance encounter based on a lie gets him an introduction to shipping magnate Herbert Greenleaf (James Rebhorn). Greenleaf soon offers a proposal to Tom: Go to Italy, where the lazy, unambitious heir to the Greenleaf fortune, Dickie (Jude Law), is whiling away his days with girlfriend Meredith (Gwyneth Paltrow), and convince Dickie to return to New York and his familial duties. Tom, who pretended to know Dickie from Princeton, agrees. He's a blank without a past, uncomfortable in his own skin, and eager to take on a role.

In Italy, Tom sticks out, nervous and pale. A convivial liar, he worms into Dickie and Meredith's confidence. Finding out that Dickie has no desire to return, Tom sets about becoming his new best friend and living the high life of hot jazz and sharp clothes. The friendship turns quickly into Tom's stealthy romantic obsession, one that uncoils into sociopathic violence.

A psychological horror film done up like a nostalgic travelogue, this chilly and precise adaptation of Patricia Highsmith's cult novel has more astounding performances than it knows what to do with. You'll also hear a lush score by Gabriel Yared, and feel the spirit of Alfred Hitchcock wafting through each murderously tense scene.

In Homage

Author Patricia Highsmith was particularly enamored of Tom Ripley, making him the star of five of her novels.

Carlito's Way

YEAR RELEASED: 1993
DIRECTOR: Brian De Palma
WHO'S IN IT: Al Pacino, Sean Penn, Penelope Ann Miller

"Remember me? Benny Blanco from the Bronx?"

Brian De Palma's masterpiece starts at the end, with would-be retired gangster Carlito Brigante (Al Pacino) getting shot in the gut and hauled away on a stretcher. As he slides along to his death, he thinks back, daring us to get sucked into it enough to forget about the film's foregone conclusion.

We meet Carlito as he's getting released from prison on a technicality wrangled by his lawyer, David Kleinfeld (a wonderfully snakelike Sean Penn). It's the 1970s in New York and Carlito, a Puerto Rican kid from the Bronx who rose high in the underworld before being sent away, is determined to go straight. At first it looks possible. He hooks back up with his old girlfriend, Gail (Penelope Ann Miller), and gets a legal job running a nightclub. But then he notices that Kleinfeld has started acting just like his gangster clients, no matter how much Carlito warns him against coming late to the game ("You can't learn it at school").

For once, all of De Palma's tricks—the soaring cameras, gimmicky action scenes—come together in a taut work that leaves most gangster films in the dust. Screenwriter David Koepp's tight compacting of the two novels by New York judge Edwin Torres (born on this day in 1931) helps, as does Pacino's wearied and wizened performance. When the plotlines race together at the end, you'll be afraid to blink for fear of missing something.

It's not only the best De Palma ever did, it's the best almost *anybody* ever did.

Ugetsu

YEAR RELEASED: 1953
DIRECTOR: Kenji Mizoguchi
WHO'S IN IT: Masayuki Mori, Machiko Kyô, Sakae Ozawa, Kinuyo Tanaka

"I see death in your face."

Ghosts walk the earth in Kenji Mizoguchi's haunted masterwork, based on a pair of stories by Japanese author Akinari Ueda, with additional material from Guy de Maupassant. Set during the sixteenth century, the story focuses on two couples whose husbands' greed for money and glory leads to supernatural trouble.

Unfortunately for their wives, rural brothers-in-law Genjurô (Masayuki Mori) and Tobei (Sakae Ozawa) think the world owes them wealth and samurai glories. After Tobei's attempt to join a roaming band of samurai fails miserably, the four are forced to leave for town and pawn their few belongings. Along the way, each man is given the chance by phantoms to live out his fantasies, leaving their wives at the mercy of ghosts and bandits. Lessons are learned, but not before it's too late for them to do any good.

Mizoguchi's film is more than a well-honed ghost story. Its vision of a chaotic landscape where chance and cruelty rule the human condition is penetratingly dramatic and exaggerates the haunting qualities of its supernatural elements. The film is spectacularly beautiful to boot (it was nominated for a costume design Oscar), existing on a slippery plane of foggy surreality that evokes both Cocteau's *Beauty and the Beast* and Kurosawa's *Throne of Blood*.

Production Notes

The Chinese legend known as "the lewdness of the female viper" that provided partial inspiration for *Ugetsu* has been filmed at least twenty times in China and Japan.

The Good, the Bad and the Ugly

YEAR RELEASED: 1966
DIRECTOR: Sergio Leone
WHO'S IN IT: Clint Eastwood, Eli Wallach, Lee Van Cleef

"In this world there's two kinds of people, my friend: Those with loaded guns and those who dig. You dig."

This movie is exactly what people think of when they imagine a typical Clint Eastwood flim. He's grizzled and lean in this Civil War–set saga of dust, treachery, and standoffs. He acts like a mythic hero who long ago stopped believing that his life was going anywhere good. Known as "Blondie," he is one of three men trying to claim a treasure in gold coins. Ostensibly, Blondie is the "Good" one of the title, but that's only because the others are so much more demonstrably immoral. There is the Ugly, Tuco (Eli Wallach, having a grand time), who is as low as they come, and also the Bad, Angel-Eyes (Lee Van Cleef), a thin blade of a villain. They all know how to use a pistol, and have ample opportunity to do so.

Sergio Leone's story is one of betrayals and showdowns, much like his first two Eastwood Westerns—*A Fistful of Dollars* (1964) and *For a Few Dollars More* (1965)—known as "spaghetti Westerns" for being made by Italians (though shot mostly in Spain). The difference here is that his characteristic knot of tough, tense confrontations is drawn out to epic proportions. Leone zooms in on the little details (a twitching eyebrow, a hand poised over a pistol), building to nerve-rattling peaks of near-hysteria. The whole thing is monumentally ludicrous, but that's part of the fun.

Grey Gardens

YEAR RELEASED: 1975
DIRECTORS: Albert Maysles, David Maysles
WHO'S IN IT: Edith Bouvier Beale, Edith "Little Edie" Bouvier Beale, Brooks Hyers

"Mother wanted me to come out in a kimono, so we had quite a fight."

East Hampton is a place of repressed wealth and privilege. Or, as Edith "Little Edie" Bouvier Beale puts it in this scintillating documentary from Albert and David Maysles, "they can get you for wearing red shoes on a Thursday; it's a nasty Republican town."

By the time the Maysleses' camera wandered into their lives, Little Edie and her domineering mother, "Big Edie," had spent decades in the crumbling East Hampton estate of Grey Gardens. They lightly claw at each other, Little Edie going on about her great dreams and Big Edie passive-aggressively tearing her down. Practically shut-ins, they live in decay and filth while animals roam the once-beautiful mansion.

One factor giving this cult documentary resonance is the Edies' aura of high society glamour. As cousins of Jackie Kennedy, they would be expected to live in far different circumstances, but their funds are surprisingly meager. It's a testament to the Maysleses' humane impulses that their film never devolves into a freak show, though that's definitely how it's seen by some hard-core fans. The women are content to wander around the house and the overgrown grounds. Little Edie rambles charmingly about her theories on life and Big Edie sings "Tea for Two." Their existence would seem unlivable to most, but the filmmakers take them on their own terms, thus handing back some of the dignity that life has stolen from them.

In Homage
Grey Gardens' cult status inspired a 2006 Tony-winning Broadway musical, a 2006 collection of additional footage titled *The Beales of Grey Gardens*, and a dramatic film with Drew Barrymore and Jessica Lange broadcast on HBO in 2009.

The Magnificent Seven

YEAR RELEASED: 1960
DIRECTOR: John Sturges
WHO'S IN IT: Steve McQueen, James Coburn, Yul Brynner

"We deal in lead, friend."

This film is pretty much what you would expect to see if you handed the story of *The Seven Samurai* to a big-name postwar Hollywood director, let him hire just about any almost-famous star he could find, and said, "Keep it honest. But make it more fun." And that is a compliment.

In the movie, a small Mexican village keeps getting attacked by vicious bandits, who make off with all the food the farmers have grown. A few farmers hire some gunslingers to help. Of the seven, tight-lipped stalwarts Vin (Steve McQueen) and Chris (Yul Brynner) basically run the show. The others are given room to run as well, particularly Britt (James Coburn), who complements his six-gun with a lightning-quick knife. As the bandit leader Calvera, Eli Wallach is an early version of his cackling Tuco in *The Good, the Bad, and the Ugly*.

Director John Sturges is smart enough to get his crew together and stay out of their way. The resulting mix is an addictive one, with sharply cut-together action scenes alternating with mellow comedic relief, all of it backgrounded by Elmer Bernstein's soaring and oft-imitated score. While William Roberts's by-the-numbers screenplay lacks the sociological shading of Kurosawa's original, *The Seven Samurai* (any surprise there?), the vivid humanity of all the characters more than compensates.

Casting Call

James Coburn was a huge fan of *The Seven Samurai*, seeing it seven days in a row. He heard about John Sturges's remake at the last minute and ultimately played a role based on his favorite character from the original.

JANUARY 12

WALL-E

🖥 👽 👪

YEAR RELEASED: 2008
DIRECTOR: Andrew Stanton
WHO'S IN IT: (voices of) Ben Burtt, Elissa Knight, Jeff Garlin, Sigourney Weaver

"Eeee . . . va?"

W*all-E* is a robot love story. Yet Andrew Stanton's lovely, hopelessly tear-jerking sci-fi story managed to fulfill the long-trumpeted promise of the Pixar animation studio.

In the movie, Earth is a rusting wasteland of discarded junk, the remains of a madly consumerist society that escaped to the stars. The last resident is one lone robot, WALL-E, who skitters happily around the mountainous heaps of waste, compacting trash and occasionally singing and dancing along to his old VHS tape of *Hello, Dolly!* He falls in love with a sleek, white, egg-shaped little bot, EVE, who arrives on a spaceship looking for life forms. When she finds a living plant, completing her mission, she zooms back into space with WALL-E holding on desperately. They come to a star liner that holds what's left of humanity: blobby, lazy beings floating around on hovering easy chairs. The plan is for humanity to return to Earth, but the ship's artificial intelligence has other directives.

Much of this exquisitely designed film is dialogue-free but it doesn't matter for a second. The animators lavish so much attention on WALL-E's rattletrap adorability that he instantly becomes a kind of precious object that viewers want to protect from any harm. Although the *Silent Running*–inspired story presents a pretty grim dystopia (and a view of humanity that's far from charitable), this is a love story, filled with sentiment that seems not at all sloppy.

And the Winner Is . . .
WALL-E was nominated for six Oscars (including a nod for screenwriting, rare for an animated film), but only won for best animated feature.

Rashômon

YEAR RELEASED: 1950
DIRECTOR: Akira Kurosawa
WHO'S IN IT: Toshirô Mifune, Machiko Kyô, Masayuki Mori, Takashi Shimura

"Dead men tell no lies."

The setting is medieval Japan during a time of war, and the story changes drastically depending on the teller. Two men and a priest sit in a ruined gatehouse to escape the rain, telling tales. What is certain is that at some point, a woman of noble carriage (Machiko Kyô) was raped in the woods and her samurai husband (Masayuki Mori) was murdered. Also involved is a bandit (Toshirô Mifune), who is a combination of murderer, rapist, inveterate liar—or none of the above. At one unnerving point, the story is told by a dead person via a medium. The absolute truth becomes a will-o'-the wisp, flickering just past the point of recognition and leading the storytellers into confusion and despair.

Akira Kurosawa's most elegant film, one that spread like wildfire among international audiences, is a modernist fable about truth and perception that plays like a mystery. The story seems so simple on the surface, but as he burrows into the specifics, the filmmaker's wiliness becomes more apparent. Watch how the noblewoman's story shades from outrage to guilt or how the bandit glides from gloating brutishness to wild romanticism. This triangle of people becomes a spinning top of stories, flinging out one variation after another until long after it becomes clear that even the witnesses to this strange tragedy may not know what actually happened.

Auteur, Auteur

Akira Kurosawa was frequently derided in his home country as being "too Western" in style. His distributor for *Rashômon* wasn't terribly impressed by the film and actually had to be persuaded by the Venice Film Festival to submit it; the film became a sensation.

Body Heat

YEAR RELEASED: 1981
DIRECTOR: Lawrence Kasdan
WHO'S IN IT: William Hurt, Kathleen Turner, Richard Crenna

"You shouldn't wear that body."

Ned Racine (William Hurt) is an attorney you might like to have a drink with, but you wouldn't want him poking around in your finances. A small-timer in the Florida seaside town of Pine Haven, Ned pals around with prosecutor Peter Lowenstein (Ted Danson, sharp as a tack) and detective Oscar Grace (J. A. Preston), whose friendship may prove helpful once Ned runs into Matty Walker (Kathleen Turner).

A looker with a husky voice and penchant for wearing garments even more revealing than the sultry weather requires, Matty is married to wealthy and possibly crooked businessman Edmund Walker (Richard Crenna). Once Ned and Matty start sleeping together, his flexible morality and her general femme fataleness ensures that Edmund's not going to survive. Ned thinks it shouldn't be a problem, though, since he has everything planned out so perfectly. Only he hadn't.

For his directorial debut, screenwriter Lawrence Kasdan—who recusitated prewar serial adventures with *Raiders of the Lost Ark*—looked back to another bygone genre. Unlike most noir retreads, however, this actually works. One reason is that Kasdan focuses more on character and plot than mood. While the hot, sticky weather makes for an effective backdrop to all the lawbreaking and lovemaking, it's less important than the double and triple twists that keep coming, and the smoky, innuendo-laden dialogue between Matty and Ned. Keep an eye peeled for a very young Mickey Rourke as a guy who knows something about explosives—very handy.

Production Notes

When the producers of *Body Heat* became nervous about hiring an untested director, George Lucas—whom Lawrence Kasdan (who was born on this day in 1949) had cowritten *The Empire Strikes Back* for—stepped in to reassure them.

High Noon

YEAR RELEASED: 1952
DIRECTOR: Fred Zinnemann
WHO'S IN IT: Gary Cooper, Grace Kelly, Lloyd Bridges

"The commandments say 'Thou shalt not kill,' but we hire men to go out and do it for us."

This is the film that helped change the whole idea of what Westerns were. Gary Cooper is Will Kane, unsmiling marshal of a small frontier town that definitely doesn't deserve him. The film begins after ten in the morning and will continue in roughly real-time until the great showdown that everyone came to see. There are three outlaws waiting at the rail depot for the noon train bringing murderer Frank Miller (Ian McDonald). When Miller gets there, the four are going to find Kane and use him for target practice, as revenge for his sending Miller to jail. While everybody knows what is coming, nobody seems willing to help Kane out of his predicament. Instead, the townspeople pressure Kane to get out of town. Kane's Quaker wife (Grace Kelly, too glam for the frontier) is the loudest of these voices. And while Kane wears a tight-jawed grimace of worry through almost every moment of the film, he doesn't waver in resolve to keep his noon appointment.

Zinnemann cuts the expected Western window-dressing, leaving out barroom brawls or Apache ambushes, boiling it all down to one cleanly executed confrontation. The leads are all as quietly effective as the film itself, which strikes a graceful note throughout. Viewers are left to consider what they might have done in Kane's place.

Courting Controversy

High Noon's screenwriter, Carl Foreman, had been a member of the Communist Party in the late 1930s and early 1940s. During the filming of *High Noon*, he was called to testify before the House Un-American Activities Committee, where he refused to "name names." After being blacklisted in Hollywood, Foreman moved to England and didn't return to America until 1975.

She's Gotta Have It

YEAR RELEASED: 1986
DIRECTOR: Spike Lee
WHO'S IN IT: Tracy Camilla Johns, Tommy Redmond Hicks, John Canada Terell, Spike Lee

"Please, baby, please, baby, please."

Tracy Camilla Johns plays Nola Darling, a woman who's juggling a trio of suitors, each with one desirable feature. There is Jamie Overstreet (Tommy Redmond Hicks), the solid and dependable businessman who she might marry, if logic was the only thing that mattered. Greer Childs (John Canada Terell) is the pretty boy, the eye candy with the nice body. Lee himself plays the funny one with the huge, black Run-DMC glasses, Mars Blackmon, who gets what he wants by sheer force of will; he doesn't mind begging.

Shot in Brooklyn over twelve days for $175,000, the film was a deservedly huge hit. Its slick look and pungent mix of eroticism and humor were in very short supply during the mid-1980s, as were films made by and starring African Americans. It also—surprisingly for Lee, whose later work was frequently derided as sexist—presented an impressively independent-minded woman in the lead, apologizing neither for her desires nor her demands to choose the right man for her.

This black-and-white indie comedy was not Spike Lee's first film. The most notorious of his early short films was *The Answer*, a twenty-minute film about an unemployed African American screenwriter who's hired to write a remake of D. W. Griffith's infamous 1915 love letter to the Ku Klux Klan, *The Birth of a Nation*.

Historically Speaking

On this day in 1865, General Sherman issued Special Field Orders No. 15, a temporary plan that provided forty acres of free land to freed slave families, who were also often given some of the Union Army's surplus mules. This became the inspiration for Spike Lee's production company's name: 40 Acres and a Mule.

The Red Shoes

YEAR RELEASED: 1948
DIRECTORS: Michael Powell, Emeric Pressburger
WHO'S IN IT: Moira Shearer, Anton Wallbrook, Marius Goring

"The dancer who relies on the doubtful comforts of human love will never be a great dancer."

Michael Powell and Emeric Pressburger's gaudy and dazzling fable starts with the curtain going up on a new ballet at London's Covent Garden. The guards can't contain a mad crush of students waiting to get to the cheap seats.

One student, Julian Craster (Marius Goring), discovers that his music professor, who composed the ballet, has actually stolen some of his own work. He goes to the head of the ballet, Boris Lermontov (Anton Walbrook), and is hired. Lermontov has Craster compose music for a new ballet he is basing on Hans Christian Andersen's tale about a dancer whose red shoes refuse to stop dancing, eventually resulting in her death.

The dancing girl who will fill those legendary red shoes onstage is initially, like Craster, an outsider trying to win Lermontov's approval. Once Victoria Page (Moira Shearer, a heartbreaking vision) is cast for the new ballet, it becomes unclear—given Lermontov's dictatorial impulses—whether she has won or lost. Once the ballet, a swooning architecture of circuslike wonder and fantastical dancing prowess, premieres, it's clear that the audience has won.

With a backstage drama that frequently devolves into madness, Powell and Pressburger's film is rife with overblown passions. This is visible in the wide-eyed performances (particularly Walbrook's, with his Vincent Price–like haunt and devilish air), highly operatic plot, and the filmmakers' eye for dramatic angles and lush colors.

In Homage
The Red Shoes played for 110 straight weeks in New York alone.

Notorious

YEAR RELEASED: 1946
DIRECTOR: Alfred Hitchcock
WHO'S IN IT: Cary Grant, Ingrid Bergman, Claude Rains

"Miss Huberman is first, last, and always not a lady."

One of Hitchcock's last great black-and-white pictures—see the restored version, as Ted Tetzlaff's luminous cinematography is a thing of beauty—this espionage picture is, strangely for Hitchcock, more about the people than the plot. Certainly there's a great story, but it's almost a distraction from the business at hand, which is watching Cary Grant fall in love with Ingrid Bergman despite, and even because of, her character's scandalous nature.

Grant is T. R. Devlin, an American secret agent tasked with foiling a Nazi plot in Rio de Janeiro. Bergman plays Alicia Huberman, a depressed borderline alcoholic who seems to sleep around. Devlin recruits Huberman, whose father was a convicted spy, to marry one of his old colleagues, Sebastian (Claude Rains), to infiltrate the Rio operation. Devlin sees that she's a lost soul and possibly in love with him, and so manipulates her into harm's way.

Ben Hecht's script is filled with winking hints about Huberman's promiscuity. When Devlin finally lashes out at his superiors and stands up for Huberman's damaged beauty, it's not just a great romantic moment, but also a powerful feminist statement.

Hitchcock and Hecht packed the film with enough beautiful scenery (Sebastian's gothic mansion in Rio, particularly) and innuendo-laden dialogue that they could never be accused of making a message film. But this is a spy story *and* a love story. With meaning.

Casting Call
The height discrepancy between Claude Rains and Ingrid Bergman was so notable that Hitchcock had to put the short actor in elevated shoes.

Strangers on a Train

YEAR RELEASED: 1951
DIRECTOR: Alfred Hitchcock
WHO'S IN IT: Farley Granger, Ruth Roman, Robert Walker

"My theory is that everyone is a potential murderer."

In your classic postwar Hitchcock (after *Rope* and before *The Birds*), a sporting and very British manner of murder can appear to be not necessarily the best thing in the world—but also not the worst.

Case in point is this deft delivery from a Patricia Highsmith novel in which a perfectly blameless woman is murdered and we're not tempted to feel at all bad about it (Highsmith relished dispatching dull or distasteful innocents). Tennis champ Guy Haines (Farley Granger) meets dissipated playboy Bruno Antony (Robert Walker, quipping and campy cruel) on a train, and they get to talking about their troubles. Guy wants to marry a senator's daughter but is stuck with his slutty wife (Laura Elliott), while Bruno resents his father. Bruno suggests that they'll "criss-cross"—he'll kill Guy's wife if Guy kills Bruno's father. It's only after Bruno actually commits his murder that Guy realizes he wasn't joking, and now Bruno wants him to do the same.

Hitchcock keeps a sense of humor (though not as light as his next film, the fun but gimmicky *Dial M for Murder*) without devolving into self-satire. The sequence in which Bruno commits his murder at an amusement park is wire-tight, one of the greatest in the director's portfolio. Walker is especially memorable as the psychopath who doesn't understand why annoying people *shouldn't* be murdered.

In Homage

In Danny DeVito's odd, not unfunny comedy *Throw Momma from the Train* (1987), the director played a stunted man-child inspired by *Strangers on a Train* to bump off his overbearing mother.

Eraserhead

YEAR RELEASED: 1976
DIRECTOR: David Lynch
WHO'S IN IT: Jack Nance, Charlotte Stewart, Allen Joseph, Jeanne Bates

"We got chickens tonight, strangest damned things!"

Henry (Jack Nance, a shell-shocked Buster Keaton type in teased wig and ill-fitting suit) is "on vacation," but it's more like a forced tour of a blasted war zone. He lives in a wretched apartment in a bleak industrial neighborhood where the sounds of palpitating machinery are always audible. His girlfriend, Mary (Charlotte Stewart) just gave birth to . . . something. The not-baby is a horrid creature that wails day and night before transforming into something even more hideous. The dark-haired temptress who lives across the hall seems more interested in the baby than she should be. Terrible sounds issue from the radiator. Meanwhile, Henry has bad dreams.

To explain what happens in David Lynch's first film is to miss the point. Freudian anxiety is the name of the game. A pervasive atmosphere of unease frequently turns into horror, particularly concerning the monstrous, fluid-spewing child.

You can spot Lynch's many obsessions here in their first incarnations, before they sprouted in his later works. There's the haunting stage with luxuriously draped curtains, long and threatening hallways, jet-black spaces whose evil is signaled by the soundtrack's fearsome, low thrumming, and a noir-ish impression of omnipresent threat. All this is wrapped inside a sleekly designed, black-and-white, silent film–style package, which somehow makes it more disturbing.

And people think *The Shining* is terrifying.

Everyone's a Critic

When *Variety* first reviewed *Eraserhead* in 1977, its response to David Lynch (born on this day in 1946) was dismissive at best, calling it a "sickening bad-taste exercise" and adding that "commercial potential for the nonsensical b&w feature is minimal."

Drugstore Cowboy

YEAR RELEASED: 1989
DIRECTOR: Gus Van Sant
WHO'S IN IT: Matt Dillon, Kelly Lynch, William S. Burroughs

"There is no demand in the priesthood for elderly drug addicts."

Gus Van Sant's breakout druggie road film stars Matt Dillon in a role that finally allowed him to break free from the countryboy-rebel shtick he'd been stuck in since the early 1980s.

Underground filmmaker Van Sant and Daniel Yost based their screenplay on a then-unpublished semiautobiographical novel by James Fogle, who was then serving time for drug-related crimes. In their story, Bob Hughes (Dillon) is the head of a loosely organized quartet of drug addicts who wander a rainy Pacific Northwest in the early 1970s. Their specialty is knocking over pharmacies. In between jobs they hole up and do what junkies do.

In these moments, Van Sant is great at catching the rhythms of the family-like group, with the slightly older Bob and his wife Dianne (Kelly Lynch) acting as parents to the younger and considerably dimmer couple, Rick (James LeGros, loveably clueless) and Nadine (Heather Graham). After establishing this idyll in which the gang thinks they've got the system licked, tragedy intervenes and not long after, it's every junkie for himself.

The film has a rainy and blue quality to it, with the Portland, Oregon, locations looking as though it's been decades since the sun has shone. In this narcotic fog, several supporting players easily make themselves noticed. Max Perlich astounds as a sniveling junkie with the eyes of a feral dog, and James Remar stands out playing the narcotics cop who's on Bob's case like a disapproving father. Most memorable is William S. Burroughs, the beatnik author who literally wrote the book on junkies, playing an addict priest who drifts through the film like a dark and defeated angel.

The Cabinet of Dr. Caligari

YEAR RELEASED: 1920
DIRECTOR: Robert Wiene
WHO'S IN IT: Werner Krauss, Conrad Veidt, Friedrich Feher

"There are spirits everywhere."

Although cited as an early horror film, Wiene's experimental silent classic is more a psychological mystery told in the spirit of a German fairy tale—the kind featuring dark forests and no escape. The film begins with Francis (Friedrich Feher), a tortured soul sitting on a bench and mooning over his wife (who wanders catatonically past, not recognizing him), and eager to tell the story of what befell them.

When the film shifts into Francis's story-mode, Wiene jettisons all laws of visual perspective and reality. His town of Hostenwall is a Dr. Seuss–like creation, the buildings climbing up a hill on top of each other like overeager children. The doors and windows come slashing in at odd angles like daggers. Tramping Hostenwall's streets is Dr. Caligari (Werner Krauss), who runs a carnival sideshow featuring Cesare (Conrad Veidt, born on this day in 1893), a "somnambulist" (sleepwalker). Dressed in black like a proto-goth teen and possessed of a murderously balletic grace, the blank-faced Cesare appears to be Caligari's remote weapon—people who have upset Caligari start turning up dead, including Francis's best friend.

Wiene's visual style is surprisingly active for this era of silent film, frequently cutting to close-ups that emphasize his cast's impressively emotive performances. Poetic and savage, clever and cruel, this is a film of grand design that remains unique—no matter how often Tim Burton cribs from it.

Everyone's a Critic

One critic called *The Cabinet of Dr. Caligari* "the first significant attempt at the expression of the creative mind in the medium of cinematography." A dissenter claimed that "it leaves a taste of cinders in the mouth."

Jules and Jim

YEAR RELEASED: 1962
DIRECTOR: François Truffaut
WHO'S IN IT: Jeanne Moreau, Oskar Werner, Henri Serre

"You said, 'I love you,' and I said, 'Wait.'"

Imagine Paris in that tranquil time before World War I. Best friends Jules (Oskar Werner) and Jim (Henri Serre) do everything together, particularly enjoying the city's many beautiful women. The two fall in love with Catherine (Jeanne Moreau, casually captivating), but she marries Jules. World War I sends the two to fight on different sides of the barbed wire (Jules being Austrian and Jim a Frenchman). Afterward, the men have a hard time resuscitating the casual ease of their prewar friendship.

The deeply romantic film has many hallmarks of the growing-up-artistic roman à clef—such as womanizing and a gallantly comprehensive regard for all creative expression. Though the film achieved a certain small infamy for its loose attitude toward lovemaking among the bohemian set, Truffaut isn't really interested in shocking or titillating. The film is truly about these two men and their friendship. When they meet for the first time after the war, Truffaut shows the two embracing, freezing the shot for a moment, hinting that this might be the real love story.

The film is one of Truffaut's jauntiest, particularly in its prewar scenes, which buzz and jump with the adrenaline of those who are young and in love with art and the city. Georges Delerue's lush score remains one of the greatest ever recorded, flawlessly matching the film's mood of nostalgic and lovesick joy.

Courting Controversy

Jules and Jim's mild depiction of a love triangle was condemned by the Catholic League of Decency, which said the film was "alien to Christian and traditional natural morality." The condemnation garnered the film even more publicity.

Safe

YEAR RELEASED: 1995
DIRECTOR: Todd Haynes
WHO'S IN IT: Julianne Moore, Peter Friedman

"We are one with the world who created us, we are safe, and all is well with our world."

There's a comedy inside writer/director Todd Haynes's masterful second feature, even if it does come wrapped in many layers of symbolic, Kubrickian spookiness. This may make it the world's first and (it's safe to predict) only comedy about multiple chemical sensitivity.

Carol White (Julianne Moore) is one of those outwardly smiling and inwardly hyperventilating California housewives whose day can be sent into a tailspin by having the wrong piece of furniture delivered. Carol begins to exhibit strange symptoms (weight loss, nosebleeds) and can't figure out why. She tries out various alternative-health regimens, but her anxiety only increases. A television commercial asks, "Are you allergic to the twentieth century?" Carol enrolls in the advertised institution, a healing retreat in New Mexico, whose guru soothingly stokes residents' fears of invisible chemicals, promising vague cures for vaguer problems, and making out like a bandit.

Moore, a gifted and little-used comedienne, portrays Carol as hopelessly questing and naive, a tabula rasa picking up nearly any suggestion. Her and Haynes's skill is such that her story is treated as quiet satire of a brand of sheltered suburbanite and not outright mockery.

Once the film shifts to New Mexico, what had been light tweaking turns deadly serious. As Carol lets herself be dragged into increasingly ludicrous "treatments" (she is eventually fitted with a kind of space suit), a low hum of horror fills the picture. Even though Haynes's mockery of this facile New Age bunk is spot-on, he doesn't respond to the central concern: what *is* wrong with her? The question hangs out there, disconcertingly unanswered—maybe it's the twentieth century, after all.

Battleground

YEAR RELEASED: 1949
DIRECTOR: William A. Wellman
WHO'S IN IT: Van Johnson, John Hodiak, Ricardo Montalban

"That dream's against regulations, soldier."

It's good that many veterans were involved in the production of this sterling World War II combat film, because civilians would have just mucked it up. Starting in December 1944, we join a worn-out platoon of the 101st Airborne, who, many long months after D-Day, look like they need a year's worth of hot showers and large meals. They're in France for some long overdue R and R, but get tossed into the snowy breach when the Battle of the Bulge begins. Off they go, exhausted and grumbling, to hunker down in snow-covered foxholes and wonder from which foggy treeline the next attack will come.

Given the time period, the gore is kept to a minimum, but that doesn't minimize the film's frightening realism. Director William Wellman was a veteran of World War I and he ensured that the film was packed with men who served (many extras were 101st Airborne vets) and that the sensibility matched the average grunt's. The humor is a knowing and bitingly cynical brand—far from apple-pie patriotism—that you would expect from men who know each moment could be their last and are more interested in small concerns (keeping a rare egg uncracked) than greater issues of strategy. The cast is superb, particularly a young Ricardo Montalban. It's a rebuke not just to more sanitized war films of the period but also to all those filmmakers of later years who thought that they had invented the "realistic" war film. *Battleground* raked in millions at the box office and earned six Oscar nominations, winning two (for screenplay and cinematography).

Historically Speaking

This movie is a good one to watch on January 25, as on that date in 1945, the Battle of the Bulge finally came to an end.

Dangerous Liaisons

YEAR RELEASED: 1988
DIRECTOR: Stephen Frears
WHO'S IN IT: Glenn Close, John Malkovich

"When it comes to marriage, one man is as good as the next."

A period film that acts nothing like *Masterpiece Theater*, Stephen Frears's arsenic-laced tragicomedy of manners set in eighteenth-century France shows that performers in powdered wigs can still wow audiences with emotion and drama.

It's hard to understand why Pierre Choderlos de Laclos's scandalous novel of sexual intrigue had never been adapted to English before Christopher Hampton turned it into a popular play and then wrote the screenplay. The Marquise Isabelle de Merteuil (Glenn Close) summons her partner in scandal, the serial seducer Vicomte Sébastien de Valmont (John Malkovich), to her side with a mission.

To avenge a slight, Merteuil wants Valmont to bed the virginal Cécile de Volanges (Uma Thurman), promised in marriage to a former lover of Merteuil's. Valmont declines because it would be too easy ("she'd be on her back before you'd unwrapped the first bunch of flowers"); plus, he has his own game to play. Of more interest to Valmont is winning, and then throwing over, Madame de Tourvel (Michelle Pfeiffer), legendary for her Christian virtue. Valmont eventually agrees to help Merteuil, unaware of the deeper game being played.

Frears opens the play with gilded sitting rooms and manicured gardens, but keeps attention on his leads, who feint and parry with cruel delight like two cats playing with the same mouse before turning on each other. Their games turn deadly with tragic swiftness, bringing an unforgettably dramatic conclusion to what had seemed like fun and games.

> ### In Homage
> A year after *Dangerous Liaisons*, Milos Forman released his version of Laclos's story, called *Valmont*. Though it starred Colin Firth and Annette Bening, *Valmont* was promptly ignored in favor of Frears's adaptation.

Sophie's Choice

YEAR RELEASED: 1982
DIRECTOR: Alan J. Pakula
WHO'S IN IT: Meryl Streep, Kevin Kline, Peter MacNicol

"I was sent to Auschwitz because they saw I was afraid."

This lavishly produced Alan J. Pakula film features a fresh-faced Southern boy curiously nicknamed Stingo (Peter MacNicol, blank-slate innocent) who moves into a Brooklyn boarding house, intent on becoming a writer. Upstairs are a raucous couple who become his best friends. Nathan (Kevin Kline) is a will-o'-the-wisp genius, a moody Jewish biologist and researcher who likes to play dress-up, get madly drunk, and generally be the life of the party—when not wrecking it. Sophie (Meryl Streep) is a Polish ex-Catholic with a nimbus of blond hair and a concentration camp tattoo on her arm. She has a wounded-bird beauty that attracts Stingo, particularly when she's suffering after one of Nathan's frequent rages in which he makes dark insinuations about how she survived the camps when so many Jews did not.

Pakula's drama (he also wrote the screenplay, adapting William Styron's National Book Award–winning novel) begins as a thwarted romance, with Stingo trying to find his place in this glamorous trio. Then it teases out facts about Sophie's past, the family she lost to the Nazis, and her wasting illness. Pakula turns the screen over to Kline (crafting that volatile mix of kindness and devilish clowning in his first major role) and Streep (frequently speaking directly to the screen, *acting* with every inch of her body) and lets them rip. It's a tear-sodden journey, but one worth taking, with a slightly off-putting narration the only sour note. The film was nominated for five Oscars, winning one for the young Streep, already a three-time nominee.

Historically Speaking

This was the day in 1945 when the Auschwitz concentration camp—where the character of Sophie was interred—was finally liberated from the Nazis by elements of the Red Army.

F for Fake

YEAR RELEASED: 1973
DIRECTOR: Orson Welles
WHO'S IN IT: Orson Welles, Oja Kodar

"For the next hour, everything you hear from us is really true and based on solid fact."

For years, Orson Welles was almost as bad at finishing films as he was at paying restaurant and hotel bills. That makes it all the more incredible that this film about fakery and frauds—strung together out of odds and ends—came together with such ingenious perfection.

In this film about truth and deception, Welles is master of ceremonies. First we have Welles, speaking right to the camera, playing around in a Paris train station, doing magic tricks, and joking with his gorgeous muse (his longtime companion Oja Kodar). As exhibit A, he stitches together a story using footage from a documentary somebody else shot on infamous art forger Elmyr de Hory and his biographer Clifford Irving, who was also unmasked as having forged an autobiography of Howard Hughes. Exhibit B is an entertaining story about an art forger, Picasso, and yet more lies.

Welles had a knack for understanding the limits of his own talents. He was aware that some skillful editing, the soothingly authoritative purr of his voice, and the flash of Kodar's legs was all the misdirection he would need. He winks and quips, ruminating on veracity and authenticity. Does it matter if a Matisse is "fake"? Look at the magnificent Chartres Cathedral, Welles asks in a monologue of heart-stopping poetry, "it is without signature." This is all flimflam of the highest order from a skilled charlatan, but not without a certain powerful truth.

Historically Speaking

On January 28, 1972, Clifford Irving confessed to forging a supposed autobiography of Howard Hughes just as it was to be published with much fanfare. The controversial incident (recounted in Lasse Hallström's 2006 film *The Hoax*) resulted in Irving spending fourteen months in federal prison for fraud.

Badlands

YEAR RELEASED: 1973
DIRECTOR: Terrence Malick
WHO'S IN IT: Martin Sheen, Sissy Spacek

"He was handsomer than anybody I'd ever met. He looked just like James Dean."

Kit (Martin Sheen) is the guy with no future at the center of Terrence Malick's debut, a beautifully blank-souled film about a purposeless murder spree in the wide-open Great Plains. Kit falls for Holly (Sissy Spacek), though she's just a kid (fifteen to his twenty-five). She reciprocates, liking Kit's irresistible James Dean way. What he doesn't like is her father, who's not happy about the relationship. So Kit does what makes sense to him: he kills Holly's father and takes Holly on a murderous joyride.

Malick's film (which he also wrote) is inspired by the true story of Charles Starkweather, who went on a killing spree in the late 1950s with his much younger girlfriend. The filmmaker isn't interested in exploring Kit's reasons for it. Like Starkweather, he is a guy with no internal compass; he operates on pure instinct. There is a phenomenal emptiness to the landscape Kit and Holly inhabit, with the gaping skies, dead-dull towns, tightlipped attitudes, and a faraway sense of celebrity in the movie gossip rags that obsess Holly. In the closing scenes, when Kit is caught, he seems to the cops more star than criminal, void of meaning but eye-catching nonetheless.

Sheen is flinty here like he has rarely been since, while Spacek trades cleverly on her witchiness. The film has a cold beauty to it (shot by Tak Fujimoto years before he went to work for John Hughes) that even a great visualist like Malick could never recapture.

In Homage
Quentin Tarantino later lifted Holly's dreamy narration style wholesale for Patricia Arquette to use in *True Romance*.

Bloody Sunday

YEAR RELEASED: 2002
DIRECTOR: Paul Greengrass
WHO'S IN IT: James Nesbitt, Tim Pigott-Smith

"They're not civvies, they're terrorists, mate."

Before being handed the *Bourne* franchise, Paul Greengrass made this sober, jarring re-creation of the January 30, 1972, "Bloody Sunday" massacre during which British paratroopers fired on demonstrators in Derry, Northern Ireland, killing thirteen. Although the quasi-documentary methods that Greengrass used here had been seen before (see Peter Watkins's films), they had rarely been utilized with such bristling clarity and urgency.

On the morning of the Derry march, we eavesdrop on both sides of the divide. Politician and civil rights activist Ivan Cooper (James Nesbitt, Oscar-worthy) is dashing about with the rushed good humor of the professional organizer, telling everyone to keep things peaceful. Meanwhile, the British "paras" assigned to arrest all the "hooligans" they can find are itching for payback.

The march begins peacefully but both sides are angry: the mostly Catholic marchers for mass internments and the British soldiers for the heavy losses they'd been taking from recent IRA attacks. Shots are fired—it isn't clear who fired first—and the paras advance as though attacking enemy soldiers and not civilians.

Greengrass, who also wrote the film, isn't shy about picking a side here. Although trying hard to show *why* the paras were so trigger-happy, once his cameras follow them into the massacre zone (screaming, unarmed men and women being systematically picked off), a burning outrage is inevitable. As in his masterful *United 93* (2006), Greengrass shows here how one can film historical traumas for high drama without exploiting them for cheap thrills.

> ### Casting Call
> One of the younger Derry marchers in *Bloody Sunday* is played by Declan Duddy, whose uncle Jackie was the first person killed on Bloody Sunday.

Winter Soldier

YEAR RELEASED: 1972
DIRECTOR: Winterfilm Collective
WHO'S IN IT: Rusty Sachs, Scott Camil, John Kerry

"I didn't like being an animal."

Early in 1971, a group of Vietnam veterans testified at a Detroit hotel for three days about the horrors they had seen committed by fellow Americans. The blistering results, filmed by a collective that included future *Harlan County U.S.A.* (1976) director Barbara Kopple, were turned into a film available only sporadically until 2005. It needs to be seen.

A rough assemblage of grainy black-and-white footage, the film isn't pretty to look at, but that fits the subject. Over two dozen soldiers, now a mostly shaggy-haired and disaffected group (with the exception of future Senator John Kerry, who appears briefly to interview one of the other vets), come forward one after another to talk about the memories that are burned in their heads. With numbing repetition, they talk of widescale butchery of Vietnamese civilians, gunned down sometimes just for sport, or captured guerrillas being viciously tortured or hurled blindfolded out of helicopters. The picture it presents is that of a brutalizing system of routine, racist violence visited upon a country by a demoralized military obsessed with one thing and one thing only: the body count. It verified things that until then had mostly been heard about by whisper and rumor.

The title comes from a line by Thomas Paine—"The summertime soldier and the sunshine patriot will in this crisis, shrink from the service of his country"—the idea being that in contrast the "winter soldier" is one who stands tall and tells the unvarnished truth.

Courting Controversy

During the Winter Soldier testimony, which began on January 31, 1971, a band of neo-Nazis paraded outside the hotel, carrying signs that read "Jane Fonda is a Communist" and "Howard Johnsons Harbors Reds."

It Happened One Night

YEAR RELEASED: 1934
DIRECTOR: Frank Capra
WHO'S IN IT: Clark Gable, Claudette Colbert

"I come from a long line of stubborn idiots."

Ellie Andrews (Claudette Colbert) is two stereotypes rolled into one: a pampered rich girl and a virtual prisoner of her ultra-wealthy father, who has the servants do everything but cut her food. Ellie shocks her father with a surprise marriage to an aviator and runs off to meet him in New York. On the night bus with her is just-fired Peter Warne (Clark Gable, born on this day in 1901), a sarcastic newsman. Peter finds out who Ellie really is, and though her father is offering a recapture reward, Peter does his best to keep the clueless dame out of trouble on the way.

Capra's romantic screwball comedy is rightly considered the best the genre has to offer. It enshrines two of the genre's most favored plotlines (the sniffy princess and wiseacre rogue falling in love, and the problem-plagued road trip), and Colbert and Gable are so well cast that they practically saunter away with the film.

The film was nominated for and won five Oscars (for Colbert and Gable, as well as for picture, adapted screenplay, and director). It also inaugurated the most fertile period of Capra's career, with *Mr. Deeds Goes to Town*, *Lost Horizon*, *Mr. Smith Goes to Washington*, and *Meet John Doe* following in rapid succession.

Courting Controversy

It Happened One Night, with its sheet hung between the unmarried characters' beds, was one of the first films to follow Hollywood's so-called Hays Code's standards for onscreen moral conduct.

February 2

Groundhog Day

YEAR RELEASED: 1993
DIRECTOR: Harold Ramis
WHO'S IN IT: Bill Murray, Andie MacDowell

"People like blood sausage. People are morons."

This film achieved some initial notoriety then just kept hanging around, slowly infecting an entire culture's collective unconscious. Harold Ramis's most immortal work turns a simple comic premise into a romantic/philosophic reflection on time, love, and life itself. It has Bill Murray in rare form and a story that would make sci-fi author Philip K. Dick jealous. In short, we're far from Murray and Ramis's film *Stripes*.

Phil (Murray, beautifully deadpan) is a Philadelphia weatherman whose level of interest in humanity is on par with the effort he puts into his job. A particularly irksome annual assignment is to truck up to the little town of Punxsutawney each February 2 to watch the ritual unveiling of the weather-forecasting groundhog—also named Phil. This year, the human Phil's got a pretty, new producer, Rita (Andie MacDowell) accompanying him. They stay overnight to shoot the early morning segment on Groundhog Day, but they're forced to stay over again because of weather. The next morning, Phil wakes up and discovers that it's February 2 again, only everybody else seems to be living it for the first time. This happens every morning, and it's never explained.

In the script that he cowrote, director Ramis finds a multitude of nooks and crannies in which to play comic-philosophical games. As Phil begins to grasp the enormity of the trap he's in ("I was in the Virgin Islands once. I met a girl. We ate lobster, drank piña coladas. At sunset, we made love like sea otters. *That* was a pretty good day. Why couldn't I get *that* day over . . . and over?"), he goes through the stages of grief, soaring from gloomy panic to giddy, suicidal carelessness to wizened acceptance. That Ramis can locate both the humor and the meaning in Phil's daily struggle to win the love of Rita isn't just impressive; it's close to a miracle.

Auteur, Auteur

Harold Ramis once joked that because of *Groundhog Day*'s broad-based religio-philosophical popularity, he is welcome in every ashram, synagogue, and church in the country.

Trust

YEAR RELEASED: 1990
DIRECTOR: Hal Hartley
WHO'S IN IT: Adrienne Shelly, Martin Donovan

"I had a bad day at work. I had to subvert my principles and kowtow to an idiot."

High schooler Maria Coughlin (Adrienne Shelly) is nonchalant when delivering the news of her pregnancy to her parents, who take it more seriously. She slaps her father, who dies of a heart attack, and is then thrown out by her mother and dumped by her jock boyfriend. Meanwhile, the older though not more mature Matthew Slaughter (Martin Donovan) is having his own problems. At his job, he mashed a supervisor's head into a vice. His father, even more rage-prone than Matthew, erupts in biblical fury. The stage is set for Matthew and Maria to meet and figure out how to reconstruct their thoroughly wrecked lives, together if possible.

Writer/director Hal Hartley debuted a year earlier with the smart, dour indie *The Unbelievable Truth* and refined his style in this arthouse comedy where danger lurks around every corner. Hartley's mismatched lovers are a study in antisocial attitudes, with Maria's belligerent tartiness set against the brainy Matthew's perfectionist fury.

The dialogue is fast and angular, chopped up with Hartley's stew of cool non-sequiturs and spasms of violence. Shelly and Donovan (the latter of whom became to Hartley what De Niro once was to Scorsese) keep up with ease. Her bracing bombshell smarts mesh with his self-educated arrogance—the two might be having a ball, but you would hate to run into them on a night out.

Auteur, Auteur

Adrienne Shelly became a director of small-budget romantic comedies like the sleeper hit *Waitress* (2007). After Shelly was murdered in 2006, Cheryl Hines, who had a role in *Waitress*, directed Shelly's last script, the dark comedy *Serious Moonlight* (2009).

FebRuARY 4

Night of the Living Dead

YEAR RELEASED: 1968
DIRECTOR: George A. Romero
WHO'S IN IT: Duane Jones, Judith O'Dea

"Now get the hell down in the cellar. You can be the boss down there, but I'm boss up here."

Before zombies starting showing up in the big-budget horror remakes pumped out during the 2000s, they were creatures of the drive-in. There were many cheap-o variations on the theme, often coming from cut-rate Italian splatter factories (the *giallo* films of the 1970s). For years, however, the only film that mattered, zombie-wise, was this smart, no-budget, black-and-white stunner from George A. Romero.

Brother and sister Johnny (Russell Streiner, uncredited) and Barbra (Judith O'Dea) are visiting their father's grave when a ghoulish-looking man attacks Johnny. Chased by other zombies, Barbra gets to a farmhouse, where she discovers a partially eaten corpse. A young man, Ben (Duane Jones), shows up to help fight zombies. They find more people hiding in the basement. After that, the fight against the flesh-eating hordes outside becomes almost secondary to the fight for control inside. They hear reports about the dead rising from graves all over the East Coast—nobody knows why.

If Romero's story were just about battling zombies, it would have remained a cult oddity, but its focus is more on the survivors and the prejudices they reveal. By casting an African American man as Ben, seemingly the sole survivor with any sense of logic or heroism, Romero makes a larger point than many well-meaning social dramas could. The social critique in the final scene carries a loathsome scare that's more unsettling than a week's worth of *Friday the 13th*s.

Everyone's a Critic

Night of the Living Dead was denounced for its violence by *Variety:* "In a mere 90 minutes this horror film [raises doubts] about the moral health of filmgoers who cheerfully opt for this unrelieved orgy of sadism."

The Truman Show

YEAR RELEASED: 1998
DIRECTOR: Peter Weir
WHO'S IN IT: Jim Carrey, Laura Linney, Ed Harris

"Good afternoon, good evening, and good night."

What if everything we see has been constructed specifically for our benefit? That's the fantasy behind this subversive, thoughtful Peter Weir film.

Truman Burbank (Jim Carrey, tamed but still featuring that face-cracking grin) lives a regular and pretty enviable life. He has a good job, a beautiful house in a beautiful town, a great best friend, and a gorgeous (though occasionally distant) wife. Problems do arise, such as why does something get in his way every time he tries to leave town, and what *is* that weird, light-like object that dropped out of the sky?

It *was* a light that almost hit him, because his entire town is a giant television studio where every moment of his day is broadcast as one of the most popular shows ever made. Everyone he knows is an actor (even the man who played his dead father, whom he thinks he spots one day as a homeless guy who is quickly hustled away) and every event in his life has been choreographed for ratings.

If Andrew Niccol's script just satirized reality television, it would have fallen flat. But because he makes it about the truth being slowly unveiled to Truman, the drama comes alive; it's like watching a man being born again in slow motion.

And the Winner Is . . .

The Truman Show was nominated for three Oscars—director, screenplay, and supporting actor (Ed Harris)—but didn't win any.

Glengarry Glen Ross

YEAR RELEASED: 1992
DIRECTOR: James Foley
WHO'S IN IT: Al Pacino, Jack Lemmon, Alec Baldwin

"I made $970,000 last year. How much you make? You see pal, that's who I am, and you're nothing."

This movie takes place in an office of real-estate salesmen, one more miserable than the next. A few play down the pressure as though it's no sweat, like Ricky Roma (Al Pacino), who we first see in a bar roping a dope (Jonathan Pryce) with his slick line of patter. Others have a thinner confidence, like Dave Moss (Ed Harris, prickly and bullying), or are simply reeking of desperation, like Shelley "The Machine" Levene (Jack Lemmon), who needs money for his daughter's operation.

Into this cage of backstabbing and swagger comes Blake (Alec Baldwin, as purely distilled aggression), who's been asked by the bosses to give the boys a dressing-down. The resulting speech isn't just the highlight of Baldwin's career and a font of ready-made quotations ("ABC: Always Be Closing"), it's the cold, cruel heart of David Mamet's screenplay—which, curiously enough, he added for the film; it doesn't exist in his original play. As the salesmen scramble to put up sales, the screws tighten with a swift mercilessness.

Director James Foley's filmography is a mixed bag, with guilty-pleasure genre flicks like *Fear* (1996) existing alongside some quality noirs like *After Dark, My Sweet* (1990) and outright embarrassments such as *Who's That Girl?* (1987). Nothing, in short, that would indicate he had the ability to pull off a solid actor's piece like this. But the ensemble does top-notch work across the board, with actors like Lemmon given the chance to stretch muscles they hadn't used in a while and those like Pacino tamping down their excessive ways.

Historically Speaking

The original play *Glengarry Glen Ross* premiered on February 6, 1984, in Chicago.

Great Expectations

YEAR RELEASED: 1946
DIRECTOR: David Lean
WHO'S IN IT: John Mills, Alec Guinness, Martita Hunt

"Keep still, you young devil, or I'll slit your throat!"

On the Thames marshlands, a young boy, Pip, is accosted by a scarred, old escaped convict, who orders Pip to bring him food and a file (for his manacles), or he'll cut out Pip's liver. Pip does as he's told, only to see the convict rearrested. Later, Pip is summoned to batty old Miss Havisham (Martita Hunt), who has remained in her wedding dress ever since being left at the altar. She likes having him around, so Pip plays in Havisham's dusty, cavernous old castle. He endures the taunts of her imperious and pretty young ward, Estella (Jean Simmons), whom Pip falls in love with.

Several years later, the adult Pip (John Mills) receives a mysterious summons. He moves to London and becomes a gentleman of leisure, all of it paid for by Havisham—but Estella (Valerie Hobson) is no more enamored of him than before. And then his past comes calling.

Charles Dickens's absurdities are taken at face value by director David Lean, who plays the cobwebby Havisham scenes for gothic camp and foretells the expansive skies of his later films in the opening marshland scenes. The older Pip is something of a wet blanket, but a chipper Alec Guinness perks things up as his comrade in idle wealth. The blithe cruelty of Estella—brought up by Miss Havisham "to wreak revenge on all the male sex"—packs a punch as well. This film is grandly entertaining and utterly unashamed of its frequent silliness.

In Homage
Alfonso Cuarón's 1998 *Great Expectations* has Ethan Hawke in the Pip role, Gwyneth Paltrow as Estella, Robert De Niro as the convict, and Anne Bancroft as the Miss Havisham stand-in.

FEBRUARY 8

The Lives of Others

YEAR RELEASED: 2006
DIRECTOR: Florian Henckel von Donnersmarck
WHO'S IN IT: Sebastian Koch, Ulrich Mühe, Martina Gedeck

"Hope always dies last."

In stories about totalitarianism, we are rarely asked to feel sympathy for the agents of oppression. Florian Henckel von Donnersmarck's intensely empathic story about a conscience-stricken East German surveillance operative doesn't just come at its story from an unexpected angle; it also stands as one of the decade's most unforgettable films.

The great Ulrich Mühe plays the Stasi (the East German secret police, which was established on February 8, 1950) agent, Hauptmann Gerd Wiesler. Wiesler is tasked with spying on a theater director, Georg Dreyman (an intense Sebastian Koch). Wiesler works dilligently in Dreyman's attic only to find out that the mission was invented because a sleazy government minister is trying to steal away Dreyman's beautiful girlfriend. Although the mouse-like Wiesler seems one of the state's most purely devoted servants, this discovery unravels his universe. In reaction, Wiesler decides to do what he can to help the man he spends most of his waking hours listening to.

Director Donnersmarck plays the tension like a master, making every creak of the floorboards as potent as a thunderclap, and coaxing whole novels worth of emotions out of Mühe's slightest shifting of position or widening of the eye. It's a character study as thriller, set in a landscape of drab apartments and empty streets populated by living ghosts who all seem to be either spied upon or in the act of spying.

And the Winner Is . . .
The Lives of Others won the Oscar for best foreign film in 2007. The only other German films to take this prize were *The Tin Drum* (1979) and *Nowhere in Africa* (2002).

FEBRUARY 9

Crouching Tiger, Hidden Dragon

YEAR RELEASED: 2000
DIRECTOR: Ang Lee
WHO'S IN IT: Chow Yun-Fat, Michelle Yeoh, Zhang Ziyi

"Only by letting go can we truly possess what is real."

Sword-fighting becomes infinitely more interesting once it's liberated from gravity. Director Ang Lee knew this when he turned a famous Chinese *wuxia* (martial arts) novel into a magical brand of Asian epic.

In the late eighteenth century, near the end of Emperor Qianlong's reign, veteran warrior Li Mu Bai (Chow Yun-Fat) is tasked with retrieving the magical Green Dynasty sword. He's aided by Yu Shu Lien (a regal Michelle Yeoh), another formidable warrior. The two have been in unacknowledged love for years.

The wild card here is Jen Yu (foxlike Zhang Ziyi), the spoiled, willful daughter of the district governor who has just purchased the Green Dynasty sword. Jen has a secret from her past, in which she fell in love with a charming bandit. With him as her inspiration, she decides to skip her arranged wedding and takes off with the sword, making the job of the two older warriors that much more difficult.

The ease with which Lee commands the *wuxia* film—while still giving it his own stamp of casual humor and sharply calibrated performances—remains breathtaking. Even more so are the acrobatic fight scenes, where the characters clamber up walls and fly between the trees. Peter Pau's glossy cinematography and the misty, wooded scenery add to the fairy-tale mood, where peril and intrigue is the order of the day and anything seems possible.

And the Winner Is . . .

Crouching Tiger, Hidden Dragon was nominated for ten Oscars, winning four.

Election

YEAR RELEASED: 1999
DIRECTOR: Alexander Payne
WHO'S IN IT: Reese Witherspoon, Matthew Broderick

"Dear God, I know I don't believe in you, but since I'll be starting Catholic school soon, I thought I should at least practice."

A teenage terminator, Tracy Flick (Reese Witherspoon) is either her high school's greatest future alumni success or its worst nightmare. Whatever she is, her teacher, Jim McAllister (Matthew Broderick, playing wonderfully against type), loathes Tracy's robo-efficiency and puts his efforts toward eliminating it.

Flick being no threat to McAllister is a central joke of this cool, vicious comedy. He justifies his antipathy by fixating on the school presidential elections, for which she is campaigning with frightening efficiency, all bouncing ponytail and curt little smiles. The script (adapted from Tom Perrotta's novel) could have played it off as a joke. But the lurking truth seems darker, as though Flick reminds him that she'll smilingly bludgeon her way to a great job far away from Omaha's Carver High, while he'll still be stuck there. McAllister has nothing much to keep him going—his marriage is a dud and even a cringing attempt at an affair goes terribly wrong.

There is a shockingly real, biting cruelty to Payne's comedy, which he lavishes on all the major characters. While McAllister's crusade is too ugly to be entirely sympathetic, Flick is more than just annoying; she's a corporate bully in larva form. Payne's later films like *About Schmidt* (2002) and *Sideways* (2004) were more popular than this classroom war story, but they didn't have anything like its brave, angry wit.

And the Winner Is . . .
Election was nominated for an Oscar in the best adapted screenplay category, but lost to John Irving for *The Cider House Rules*.

Forbidden Planet

YEAR RELEASED: 1956
DIRECTOR: Fred M. Wilcox
WHO'S IN IT: Walter Pidgeon, Anne Francis, Leslie Nielsen

"Monsters from the subconscious . . . of course."

Fred M. Wilcox's science-fiction film landmark is pitched as *The Tempest* in space, with Prospero stuck on a distant planet visited by human astronauts in the twenty-third century.

A spaceship crew rockets toward the planet Altair-4, hoping to find out what happened to the ship *Bellerophon*, not heard from since landing there twenty years ago. They receive a mysterious warning telling them to land at their own peril. Not wanting to make the film unnecessarily short, they land, and find the *Bellerophon's* sole survivors: Dr. Morbius (Walter Pidgeon) and his curious daughter Altaira (Anne Francis). Morbius tells them everyone else was killed off by mysterious creatures. The rescue ship's Commander John Adams (Leslie Nielsen, in the kind of role he has been mocking for years) thinks something fishy is going on. Due to genre demands, he's also attracted to Altaira, no matter how spooky she acts. Also due to genre demands, the hulking Robby the Robot gets more screen time than some human characters.

Though nobody's idea of a masterpiece, the film's alien planet that could well have a mind of its own has since been echoed all across the genre, from *Solaris* to *Star Trek*. The idea of the researcher who is overly enamored of alien intelligence (think of the android Ash in *Alien*, talking about how he admires the beastly species' "purity") has also been oft repeated. Almost as influential was the film's score (credited as "electronic tonalities"), which used the high, wavering alien tones of the electronic musical instrument theremin to create the unearthly sound that for decades afterward became cinematic audio shorthand for all things not earthly.

Requiem for a Dream

YEAR RELEASED: 2000
DIRECTOR: Darren Aronofsky
WHO'S IN IT: Ellen Burstyn, Jared Leto, Jennifer Connolly, Marlon Wayans

"You make me feel like a person."

Darren Aronofsky's film of Hubert Selby, Jr.'s novel is a tour of purgatory that exhilarates as much as it terrifies. Set in Brooklyn's Brighton Beach, it follows several addicts demolishing their lives and souls just as fast as possible.

Sara Goldfarb (a fearless Ellen Burstyn) is a retiree who spends most days watching television. After receiving a phone call telling her that she's going to be on a television show, Sara becomes obsessed with being able to fit in a red dress and turns to weight-loss pills. Her son, Harry (Jared Leto), is a less-reputable addict, hustling for his fix on the street with his junkie buddy Tyrone (Marlon Wayans) and girlfriend Marion (Jennifer Connolly).

Over a summer, fall, and winter, everybody's lives devolve from bad to desolate. Sara's addiction leads to hallucinations, while Harry and Tyrone's drug-dealing plans go torturously awry, and Marion is forced to sell her body. Aronofsky—who showed in his smart, gnomic debut *Pi* (1998) how to turn imagery to otherworldly ends—signals the characters' deterioration with visuals and whip-fast editing that warp, distort, and stun. Watching the film can be akin to entering a whirlpool, with the dizzying camerawork and haunting, widely copied score by Clint Mansell and the Kronos Quartet furthering the bleak desperation.

It can't be enjoyed, per se—but it can't be missed, either.

And the Winner Is . . .

For her stunning performance in *Requiem for a Dream*, Ellen Burstyn was nominated for an Oscar and a Golden Globe, losing both awards to Julia Roberts for *Erin Brockovich*.

Vertigo

Q

YEAR RELEASED: 1958
DIRECTOR: Alfred Hitchcock
WHO'S IN IT: James Stewart, Kim Novak

"One final thing I have to do, and then I'll be free of the past."

San Francisco has rarely been this beautiful, or this haunted. Alfred Hitchcock—who lived nearby—shot the film not in the expected dark, dank tones, but in rich, hazy Pacific sunlight. It makes the proceedings even more like a dream.

James Stewart plays guilt-ridden detective Scottie Ferguson, whose fear of heights causes the death of a cop during a rooftop chase. When a friend asks Scottie to tail his wife Madeline (Kim Novak, born on this day in 1933), Scottie takes the job. She wanders distractedly around the city, then takes an unexpected jump into the bay. Scottie leaps in to save her, and after that, he becomes just as obsessed as she is.

Madeline's obsession is death, particularly the suicide of an ancestor. Scottie's obsession is more basic: Madeline. It becomes even more pronounced after he is unable to stop her from hurling himself from a tower to her death. Later, Scottie can't stop reliving her, forcing another woman to transform herself *into* Madeline, his ghost.

Like Hitchcock's more interior films, *Vertigo* dances with the ridiculous. Its script (based on a novel by Pierre Boileau, whose books also inspired *Eyes Without a Face* and *Diabolique*) lays out the story's psychological precepts as though quoting from a textbook. But the film's cyclical obsessions (assisted by Bernard Hermann's memorable score) cast a uniquely spectral kind of shadow.

In Homage
Paul Verhoeven's *Basic Instinct* (1992) is something of a takeoff on *Vertigo*. The San Francisco setting, the story in which an icy blond is chased by a troubled detective, and the score all echo Hitchcock's film. (The delirious violence and acrobatic sexuality was all Verhoeven, however.)

Picnic at Hanging Rock

YEAR RELEASED: 1975
DIRECTOR: Peter Weir
WHO'S IN IT: Rachel Roberts, Dominic Guard

"We shall only be gone a little while."

It's St. Valentine's Day, 1900. The girls at Appleyard College in Victoria, Australia, are beside themselves. Besides celebrating the holiday (poems are recited, the saint's statue held aloft, roses proffered), it's also the day that the girls are let out of their cloistered grounds to picnic at the picturesque peak of Hanging Rock. The day begins with laughter and ends in panic: three girls and one teacher missing. People go searching, and many theories are proffered, but no explanation comes forward. It's as though the landscape—a great, expansive thing of seductive beauty surrounding this small, barely civilized settlement—has swallowed them whole.

There is a hint of the horror film in Peter Weir's mystical mystery. Against nature's raw power Weir juxtaposes the stuffy armor of late Victorian society, the overstuffed corsets, and frilly, impractical dresses. Somewhere in between is the joy of the Valentine's Day rituals and the girls' joy, which moves quickly into hysteria. Dario Argento explored a similarly cloistered horror a couple years later in *Suspiria* (albeit with far more bloodshed).

Weir's moody, ghostly film was one of a number of Australian films in this decade, such as Nicolas Roeg's *Walkabout* (1971), Weir's own *The Last Wave* (1977), and Fred Schepisi's *Chant of Jimmie Blacksmith* (1978), that saw civilization as precariously perched in a beautiful, but definitively hostile, landscape.

Historically Speaking

Although *Picnic at Hanging Rock*'s opening credits assure us these disappearances happened, there doesn't appear to have been any such incident. The film's basis was a 1967 Joan Lindsay novel, which presented itself as based on historical fact.

Naked

YEAR RELEASED: 1993
DIRECTOR: Mike Leigh
WHO'S IN IT: David Thewlis, Katrin Cartlidge, Lesley Sharp

"I sent off for one of those linguistic packages, 'Talk Shite in a Fortnight.' It's all going very well. I haven't quite got the hang of the transitive verbs yet."

Like a comet plummeting to the ground that will annihilate everything in its path, Johnny (David Thewlis) is a force of nature. He talks, and talks, and talks, until those around him go quietly mad as he ties them in rhetorical knots. He's probably mad himself, but nobody's been able to lock him up yet. Maybe nobody has dared to try.

In writer/director Mike Leigh's lacerating drama of midnight terrors and existential mysteries, Johnny appears almost out of nothingness, the same place he's rocketing toward. We first see him in a dark alleyway, apparently raping a woman. He steals a car and heads for London, planning to hole up with former girlfriend, Louise (Lesley Sharp). When Johnny shows up, though, Louise isn't there. He starts talking with Louise's none-too-bright, drug-addict roommate Sophie (Katrin Cartlidge), starting the seduction that will end in another violent assault. Afterward he'll head out into the grimy London night, conferring with every lowlife he can find and looking for the deepest, rankest, most immoral point of existence he can find.

Johnny speaks with a deep-rooted liar's confidence about everything from Nostradamus to the butterfly effect. It doesn't add up to much but a bleak and intellectually inconsistent view of the universe, articulated by a demon seemingly conjured from Thewlis's unconscious. His titanic performance made almost every other actor in the 1990s appear to recede into insignificance.

Hard-Boiled

YEAR RELEASED: 1992
DIRECTOR: John Woo
WHO'S IN IT: Chow Yun-Fat, Tony Leung

"When I'm a Triad, the cops want to kill me and when I'm a cop, everyone wants to kill me."

When John Woo said goodbye to Hong Kong, he did so with a bang; thousands of them, in fact. Before he and his star Chow Yun-Fat decamped for Hollywood, though, they did their best to burn the place to the ground.

Chow plays Tequila, one of those loner cops who always gets his man. In the eye-popping shootout in a crowded restaurant that opens the film (complete with civilians and gangsters falling like ten-pins), Tequila slides down a long banister, pistol in each hand blazing away, a match cocked in his mouth; and he makes it look *easy*. His mirror opposite (doubling being a Woo trademark, along with the fluttering doves and armies of expendable extras) is Tony, played with strikingly wounded sensitivity by Tony Leung. Tony is an undercover cop who gets his moral compass realigned after teaming up with Tequila to take down the bad guys.

Woo's early career in comedy becomes more apparent as the film goes on. The firefights become delirious self-parody, as though Woo is shutting the door on that part of his career and wants to leave no rounds unfired. The conclusion is a forty-minute pitched battle between cops and gangsters inside a hospital filled with patients. A scene where Tequila leaps out a window with a baby in his arms as a massive fireball blooms behind him in slow motion just about sums it all up.

Auteur, Auteur

Woo went on to a decent Hollywood career with projects that were forgettable (*Broken Arrow*, 1996), memorable (*Face/Off*, 1997), and in between (*Windtalkers*, 2002), but none achieved the giddy glee of *Hard-Boiled*'s bullet-riddled free-for-all.

Brick

$\mathcal{Q}$

YEAR RELEASED: 2005
DIRECTOR: Rian Johnson
WHO'S IN IT: Joseph Gordon-Levitt, Nora Zehetner, Meagan Good

"When the Upper Crust does shady deeds, they do them all over town, and the pitch is, they got these little symbols so they can tell each without word getting around."

The most engrossing noir of the modern era has no private eyes and hardly even any adults. The plot is murky and all the characters (mainly high schoolers) speak in an invented language that there's no glossary for. Yet none of those factors keep writer/director Rian Johnson's first film from being a mesmerizing experience.

The incomparable Joseph Gordon-Levitt stars as outsider Brendan Frye. When Brendan looks into the disappearance of his ex-girlfriend Emily (Emilie de Ravin), he quickly uncovers an elaborately organized and intricately hierarchical criminal underworld. Brendan's one friend, known only as The Brain (Matt O'Leary), provides clues that lead to a mysterious boss, The Pin (a wraithlike Lukas Haas). In between Brendan and the Pin are a pair of fatales (Nora Zehetner, Meagan Good) and plenty of guys eager to use Brendan's face to stop their fists.

Johnson's hook is that everything is discussed with clipped diction, using a dense lexicon of slang that's a mix of the imaginary (stoners are "reef worms") and anachronistic (cops are "bulls"). His otherworldly universe shares a sensibility of intelligent suburban surreality with Richard Kelly's *Donnie Darko* (2001), but its razor-sharp, sarcastic characters seem to have dropped straight out of director Howard Hawks's world (no surprise that Johnson had his cast watch films like *His Girl Friday* for clues on the kind of energy he wanted).

Shot for a half-million bucks with zero studio support, *Brick* is plucky, ingenious filmmaking of the rarest kind. Hawks would approve.

FEBRUARY 18

The Breakfast Club

YEAR RELEASED: 1985
DIRECTOR: John Hughes
WHO'S IN IT: Judd Nelson, Anthony Michael Hall, Molly Ringwald, Ally Sheedy, Emilio Estevez

"Eat. My. Shorts."

Teen comedy or therapy session? Earnest drama about American adolescents, or the wacky escapades of misfits killing time one slow Saturday? Whatever it is, writer/director John Hughes's bid for seriousness deserves watching—or revisiting, even if only to see how your reactions to it and the characters change as you age.

A cross-section of high schoolers spend Saturday detention testing each other's limits, probing for weaknesses, categorizing, and defining. Hughes's unsurprising motive is to tear down the stereotypes and make them all see each other as people.

It all comes back to the parents. The mumbly nerd (Anthony Michael Hall) has a quasi-suicide attempt because of grade pressure. The jock (Emilio Estevez) bullies to impress his old man. The stuck-up princess (Molly Ringwald) cuts class because her parents fight over her, while the basket case (Ally Sheedy) gets ignored by hers. The burnout (Judd Nelson, the spark that lights this fire) pulls pranks because his dad uses him as an ashtray. They bicker and flail and cast about, unifying in a cloud of pot smoke.

Though the Psych 101 analysis borders on the facile, Hughes's ode to alienation still appeals for its drive to break kids out of the boxes that most teen films spend their time constructing.

Auteur, Auteur

The original name for *The Breakfast Club* was *Detention*, and it was supposed to be John Hughes's directorial debut. Producer Ned Tanen let Hughes direct *The Breakfast Club*, as long as he shot *Sixteen Candles*—a raucous comedy that Hughes wrote in just two days—first. Both films starred his muse, Molly Ringwald, who shared a birthday (February 18) with Hughes.

The Proposition

YEAR RELEASED: 2006
DIRECTOR: John Hillcoat
WHO'S IN IT: Guy Pearce, Ray Winstone, Danny Huston

"Australia. What fresh hell is this?"

The greatest moment in John Hillcoat's grisly, propulsive Australian Western comes in a quiet front yard. The local law man, Captain John Stanley (Ray Winstone), and his wife Martha (Emily Watson) are expecting trouble, as is their aborigine servant, who simply walks out into the wide-open plains, but not before removing his shoes and socks, utterly foreign objects to aborigines. This scrupulously detailed scene speaks volumes about the clash of cultures.

Most of the film is not so delicate. Goth-rock deity Nick Cave's screenplay is an ultraviolent Western revenge epic that mocks these European settlers' pretenses to "civilization." Arthur Burns (Danny Huston), a madman on the loose, is wanted by Stanley for massacring an entire family. Stanley, who has jailed Arthur's brothers Mikey (Richard Wilson) and Charlie (Guy Pearce), gives Charlie a proposition: capture Arthur in nine days and you'll both get pardons. If not, we'll hang Mikey on Christmas. Charlie rides into the wilderness to betray Arthur, a demented messiah who would be equally at home in a Joseph Conrad novel or Werner Herzog film. The bullets fly with abandon in the unbridled landscape, captured in opulent wide-screen by cinematographer Benoît Delhomme. The cast is uniformly sublime; watch for John Hurt as a half-mad bounty hunter with a taste for biting wordiness.

Hillcoat garnered more attention a few years later when he tried with middling success to film Cormac McCarthy's postapocalyptic novel *The Road*; this lesser-known film is far more worthwhile to seek out.

Historically Speaking

Although Westerns are more associated with America than Australia, the first feature-length film made in Australia (and possibly the world) was *The Story of the Kelly Gang* (1906), about Australia's most infamous outlaws.

The Right Stuff

YEAR RELEASED: 1983
DIRECTOR: Philip Kaufman
WHO'S IN IT: Sam Shepard, Scott Glenn, Ed Harris

"Our Germans are better than their Germans."

Before America ever seriously thought about venturing into space, the sound barrier had to be broken. In 1947, test pilot Chuck Yeager (Sam Shepard) does it with staggering nonchalance. Afterward, the best pilots in the country descend on Edwards Air Force Base to test newer planes. Later, this ultra-competitive band becomes the first group to be put through the wringer to determine whether they have what it takes to be astronauts. Once the *Mercury* 7 program begins in earnest, it's seen as a race with the Soviets for dominion over space itself, and little is allowed to stand in the way. Before long, however, technology and history begin leaving the original band behind, with a new group selected for the next target: the Moon.

Nothing in director Philip Kaufman's career indicated that he would have been the man to bring Tom Wolfe's incredible history of the early space program to the screen. A well-regarded Western, *The Great Northfield Minnesota Raid* (1972), and a quasi-comic remake of *Invasion of the Body Snatchers* (1978) were the highlights of his body of work. But somehow Kaufman was able to rope together one of the greatest collections of steel-jawed American actors since they stopped making Westerns—most notably Ed Harris, whose intensely humane portrayal of John Glenn is possibly the best work he's ever done—and send them barreling through a vividly shot, three-hour-plus, improbably funny, and immaculately detailed historical epic. In the process, Kaufman nearly bankrupted the production company but scooped up eight Oscar nominations and four wins.

Historically Speaking
On February 20, 1962, John Glenn officially became the first American to orbit Earth.

The Wild Bunch

YEAR RELEASED: 1969
DIRECTOR: Sam Peckinpah
WHO'S IN IT: William Holden, Ernest Borgnine, Robert Ryan

"If they move, kill 'em!"

The film that will forever be the one most associated with Sam Peckinpah's name, this end-of-an-era Western is so filled with weaponry (grenades, machine guns) that it almost deserves to be called a war film. Just before World War I, a gang of outlaws decides that the Wild West isn't dead yet, so they rob a bank in Texas and hightail it to Mexico, where they indulge in one last job: stealing weapons from a U.S. Army train for a renegade Mexican general. When things turn south, the bunch takes revenge in one of the bloodiest shootouts in film history.

Savagery is Peckinpah's staple theme, and he deploys it right from the outset, cutting from boys laughing at fighting scorpions to the bank robbery in which civilians are mowed down like wheat. By the final shootout, Peckinpah has whipped up the film into a frenzy, with seemingly half the Mexican army being annihilated in his trademark slow-motion, blood-gushing manner.

Somewhere inside all this is a story, meaningful at times, about the tides of change, and the increasing mechanization of what used to be the frontier. The bunch hides out in lawless Mexico, since that most closely resembles the world they once knew, but even there it's clear there is no place for them anymore. What else to do, then, but shoot it out?

Lost and Found

Warner Bros. cut about ten minutes of footage from the initial release of *The Wild Bunch*, which was restored in a 1995 rerelease. Interestingly, given all the uproar about the film's over-the-top violence, none of the cuts were made in the action scenes.

Belle de Jour

YEAR RELEASED: 1967
DIRECTOR: Luis Buñuel
WHO'S IN IT: Catherine Deneuve, Jean Sorel

"You are sweet and fresh, just the way they like them."

If it were just a film about a bourgeois housewife leading a secret life as a prostitute, it wouldn't work. But Luis Buñuel's phantasmagoric allegory on societal hypocrisy operates on levels that have little to do with the lusty fascination that drew scandalized audiences to the film when it opened. Buñuel knew what he was doing, of course, putting the cool, chic Catherine Deneuve in the starring role—frequently naked—but he was aiming for something deeper.

When Séverine Serizy (Deneuve) hears about a woman in her upscale circle who moonlights as a prostitute, she is interested. After getting the address of a brothel from a shady friend of Pierre's, she starts working there in the afternoons, gaining the nickname "Belle de Jour" (Beauty of the Day) from the Madame (Geneviève Page). Sexually withdrawn from her husband, Séverine finds freedom in the debasement of whoring. Buñuel doesn't make things that easy, of course, having one of her clients, a deformed vampiric gangster, become overly enamored of her.

Buñuel, the canny old surrealist, plays games with the audience throughout. He stocks the screen with wealth and beauty, lovingly photographing Deneuve's Yves Sant Laurent wardrobe even as he slips in the self-hating fantasies and troublesome childhood memories that undergird her schizophrenic soul. In this lush dreamscape, true desires are dangerous, all leading back to trauma. It's textbook Freud in designer outfits, and you can't tear your eyes away from it.

Production Notes

The name Madame Anais gives Séverine in *Belle de Jour* is a play on *belle de nuit*, a French term for "prostitute."

Near Dark

YEAR RELEASED: 1987
DIRECTOR: Kathryn Bigelow
WHO'S IN IT: Adrian Pasdar, Jenny Wright, Lance Henriksen

"You people sure stay up late."

In a small Oklahoma town, the brash young Caleb Colton (Adrian Pasdar) hits on a woman, Mae (Jenny Wright), whom he spots seductively licking a cone outside an ice-cream parlor. Caleb gives her a ride in his truck, but when he tries to get a kiss, she bites his neck instead and runs off. Since his truck won't start, he tries walking home. Feeling sicker and sicker, he stumbles along, pained by the rising sun. Then an RV roars up and hands pull him inside: now he's with Mae's undead coven. They give him one week to figure out how to be a vampire.

Instead of the serene figures of Anne Rice's imagination, these vampires are more like a band of outlaws from an old Western. In fact, their leader, Jesse Hooker (Lance Henriksen), is old enough to have fought for the Confederacy; "we lost," he quips. Also on board are the gleefully homicidal Severen (Bill Paxton, brilliantly playing the fool) and Homer (Joshua John Miller), who appears to be barely a teenager but acts much older.

Kathryn Bigelow films with a quick fury rarely witnessed in horror films, which prefer to skulk about in dark, limited spaces. She showcases her skill as an action director in two astounding sequences, one in a honky-tonk that the vampires turn into a slaughterhouse, and the other in a motel room surrounded by police who blast holes in the walls, letting in deadly rays of sunlight (a nice quotation from the end of *Blood Simple*).

Vibrantly mixing up ideas from Western, horror, and chase films, Bigelow's hybrid vampire thriller remains a guilty pleasure from the pre-*Twilight* era.

Once

YEAR RELEASED: 2006
DIRECTOR: John Carney
WHO'S IN IT: Glen Hansard, Markéta Irglová

"Take this sinking boat, and point it home."

The oldest of premises, a musical about musicians making music, gets an electrifying workout in this no-budget charmer from Ireland that also features some of the most exquisite music ever recorded for film.

A tall, bearded guy (Glen Hansard) is playing guitar on the streets of Dublin. He's belting it out, pounding away on his guitar as though it is the last song he'll ever play. A Czech immigrant (Markéta Irglová, Hansard's real-life bandmate) likes what she hears and wants to talk to him about music. They have an immediate rapport that isn't romantic and isn't just friendship; it's two people who just belong together.

The story evolves fitfully and by happenstance, though you never want to complain, as the leads are so eminently watchable. There is a swapping of love stories—he has an ex-girlfriend who took off for London, while she has an estranged husband back in the Czech Republic. They play some songs and decide in short order that it's time to make an album.

But for a few minor plot points, that's the film. Without any big dance numbers or dramatic tension, and clearly shooting on the cheap, John Carney stitches together a hugely enjoyable film with little more than a pair of effort-lessly charming leads (*more* charming for their amateur status) and a book of fantastic, heart-rending songs. In fact, on February 24, 2008, "Falling Slowly" won an Oscar for best original song.

Casting Call

Originally, the lead in *Once* was supposed to be played by Cillian Murphy. But when he dropped out, the filmmakers replaced him with Glen Hansard, who was already familiar with the story because he'd been working on the music.

The End of the Affair

YEAR RELEASED: 1999
DIRECTOR: Neil Jordan
WHO'S IN IT: Ralph Fiennes, Julianne Moore, Stephen Rea

"I hate you, God. I hate you as though you existed."

Graham Greene: great to read, tough to film. The key? Understand the indelible sadness of Greene's fiction, the impossibility of happiness, and the dour seduction of infidelity, and remember that God, inscrutable God, is always watching, though he's not going to help.

A chronicle of atheism wrapped in a story about a torrid affair and laced with the torment of war, Neil Jordan's adaptation of Greene's novel retains the author's true spirit while injecting it with some doomed movie-star glamour. Ralph Fiennes (steeped in self-loathing) plays Greene's protagonist, Maurice Bendrix, a British novelist having a steamy affair with the married Sarah (Julianne Moore) and despising them both for it. Most of the film takes place in 1946, two years after Sarah broke off the affair. An obsessed, jealous Maurice hires a Dickensian private detective (Ian Hart) to follow her in order to see whether she's still cheating on her weak-willed husband, Henry Miles (Stephen Rea, all in mild, gray tones). Unable to come to terms with separation from her, Maurice seems to desire evidence of her depravity.

Jordan's film is two parts romantic minefield and one part theological battle-ground, set against a fog-bound, ration-book, postwar London backdrop, where memories of the Blitz are still fresh. It's a compelling but bleak world, where Maurice's anguished, blasphemous protests have a terrible logic.

And the Winner Is . . .

The End of the Affair was nominated for two Oscars, best actress for Julianne Moore and cinematography for Roger Pratt, losing to Hilary Swank (*Boys Don't Cry*) and Conrad L. Hall (*American Beauty*).

The Hustler

YEAR RELEASED: 1961
DIRECTOR: Robert Rossen
WHO'S IN IT: Paul Newman, George C. Scott, Jackie Gleason

"Even if you beat me, I'm still the best."

Paul Newman was already in his mid-thirties when he took the role of pool hustler Fast Eddie Felson, but in Robert Rossen's jazzy, downbeat drama, he acts like some punk kid. Wiry and arrogant, Eddie's a guy who lights up the world when he's on a streak, but hauls it down to the pits when he's not. In the epic pool hall battle between Eddie and the legendary Minnesota Fats (a spry Jackie Gleason, who reportedly did most of his own pool-shooting) that occupies much of the film's first half-hour, we see Eddie as the ugly loser who doesn't know when to quit. As the bankroll guy Bert Gordon (George C. Scott) tells Eddie from the sidelines where he works the odds with hawk-like vigilance, "You're a born loser." Given that Eddie was $18,000 up before letting Fats wear him down, it's hard to argue.

Rossen's film, based on a 1959 novel by Walter Tevis, seems initially to be a play on differing notions of winning and losing, but later turns into more of a character examination. *The Hustler* received nine Oscar nominations, winning two, one for the sharp-as-a-pin black-and-white CinemaScope by Eugene Shuftan, who had just shot *Eyes Without a Face* the year before. Look for the real Jake "Raging Bull" La Motta as a bartender in the opening scene.

> **Production Notes**
> Real-life pool hustler Rudolph Wanderone insisted that he was the inspiration for Minnesota Fats; Walter Tevis always denied this. Wanderone, who adopted the name Minnesota Fats for himself anyway, played pool against *The Hustler*'s technical advisor, Willie Mosconi, in an ABC *Wide World of Sports* match in 1978. Wanderone lost.

The Grapes of Wrath

YEAR RELEASED: 1940
DIRECTOR: John Ford
WHO'S IN IT: Henry Fonda, Jane Darwell

"Seems like the government's got more interest in a dead man than a live one."

Coming off a couple of ripping crowd-pleasers, *Stagecoach* and *Drums Along the Mohawk*, John Ford filmed John Steinbeck's Pulitzer-winning novel of social protest. While a daunting project, Ford succeeded, crafting a large-scale epic that is also intensely, astoundingly personal.

Like thousands of other families suffering in the Dust Bowl, the Joads of Oklahoma are forced to head west, fighting the resentment everyone seems to feel for these dusty, desperate "Okies." There are two stars here. First is Ma Joad (Jane Darwell), the indefatigable matriarch who will move heaven and earth to keep her family fed and housed. Second is Tom (Henry Fonda), just paroled from prison after serving four years for a barroom murder. If Ma is the family's heart and mind, he is its hands, the lean and forceful man of action who will lead them to the promised land—failing that, California. If that means fighting back with deadly force when a cop tries to hassle him for no good reason, then so be it.

This is about as close to socialist rabble-rousing as Hollywood ever came, though one couldn't call it propaganda (Ford, among the most conservative of directors, wouldn't have signed on for that). Gregg Toland's striking cinematography is part expressionist and part documentarian, deeply influenced by the haggard tragedy of Dorothea Lange's Works Progress Administration Dust Bowl photography.

Courting Controversy

The Grapes of Wrath was shown in Warsaw Pact countries as an example of hardships wrought by the capitalist system. (Though the film was pulled from Yugoslavia, as even the Joads looked more prosperous than most Yugoslavs.)

His Girl Friday

YEAR RELEASED: 1940
DIRECTOR: Howard Hawks
WHO'S IN IT: Cary Grant, Rosalind Russell

"Walter, you're wonderful, in a loathsome sort of way."

No newspaper job was ever as much fun as it's portrayed in *His Girl Friday*—in fact, no job, period, has ever been this much of a gas. Precious few films, either. Cary Grant is at his scalpel-witted best as Walter Burns, the editor of a big Chicago newspaper who's desperate not to lose his ace reporter and one-time wife, Hildy Johnson (Rosalind Russell). To keep Hildy on the job and stop her from marrying a strictly dullsville insurance salesman, smart-alec and workaholic Walter sets her loose on a killer story (a cop shooting, politics, the whole bit) that he hopes will reignite her passion for reporting and for him.

The result is a breathless hour-and-a-half comedy that comments on everything from gender politics to the corruption of the press. The motormouth dialogue is crammed into nearly every available second. The crackerjack lines often run right over the other, delivered with greyhound speed by Grant and a steely Russell, both of them apparently ad-libbing with abandon. The peerless result is not just one of the greatest comedies of all time, but an honest-to-goodness ode to the *joie de vivre* of America's shamelessly exuberant yellow-journalist past.

In Homage
His Girl Friday is based on the 1928 smash hit Broadway play *The Front Page* by crack Chicago newspapermen Ben Hecht and Charles MacArthur. It was filmed several times, most recently by Billy Wilder in 1974 with Walter Matthau and Jack Lemmon, but Hawks's version is widely acknowledged as by far the greatest.

Sweeney Todd: The Demon Barber of Fleet Street

YEAR RELEASED: 2007
DIRECTOR: Tim Burton
WHO'S IN IT: Johnny Depp, Helena Bonham Carter

"You, sir? How about a shave?"

Benjamin Barker (Johnny Depp), an honest barber, married a woman who caught the fancy of a crooked judge who falsely convicted Barker and shipped him off to hard labor in Australia. Calling himself Sweeney Todd, Barker returns to London like the spirit of vengeance, sharpening his razors and figuring that there are some people in this world who could use a very close shave.

Stephen Sondheim made the mass-killer Sweeney the subject of a 1979 musical that featured wall-to-wall murder and mayhem. The popular, stripped-down 2005 Broadway revival had a classic 1930s Universal horror film sensibility that makes its translation to film utterly logical. Though Tim Burton had seemed on autopilot for years, Sondheim's cleverly wrought lyrics and an exquisitely horrifying screenplay by John Logan represented a near-perfect marriage of artist to material.

Depp stalks the sooty alleyways of London in a Bride of Frankenstein fright wig and long black coat, fury seeping out of every pore of his body. His partner in murder is Nellie Lovett (Helena Bonham Carter, mad as the proverbial hatter), who runs the pie shop downstairs and doesn't mind getting some free, fresh-meat fillings for her pies. The whole affair reverberates with pitch-black humor and bloodletting amidst the belted-out songs. Few films are this frightening *and* this catchy.

Historically Speaking

Sweeney Todd's first appearance in print was in the 1846 "penny dreadful" serial *The String of Pearls*. When a London theatrical adaptation, subtitled *The Fiend of Fleet Street*, opened a year later it was advertised, with little supporting evidence, as "Founded on Fact." It wasn't until March 1, 1979, that the *Sweeney Todd* musical opened on Broadway in the United States.

King Kong

YEAR RELEASED: 1933
DIRECTORS: Merian C. Cooper, Ernest B. Schoedsack
WHO'S IN IT: Fay Wray, Robert Armstrong, Bruce Cabot

"It was beauty killed the beast."

The misunderstood monster with a heart of gold has never been better presented than in this surprisingly effective early special-effects classic. In fact, the rampaging ape ultimately is given more humanity than any of the ant-like people he destroys. Filmmaker Carl Denham (Robert Armstrong) is looking for a place to shoot his movie and figures that Skull Island is as good a place as any. If the swarms of angry natives weren't bad enough—to say the film is retrograde in its treatment of the islanders is to be generous—there are also prehistoric creatures hunting down his crew and menacing his leading lady, Ann Darrow (Fay Wray). A fifty-foot ape proves particularly troublesome, even having the boldness to fall in love with Darrow. A showman to the end, Denham doesn't miss a trick. He cages up Kong and ships him back to New York for display as "The Eighth Wonder of the World." Problems ensue with the Empire State Building and buzzing biplanes.

The massive set for the Skull Island natives' fortress stood for years afterward and was ultimately burned down as an Atlanta stand-in for *Gone with the Wind*. The movie's legacy was longer-lived, spawning sequels in 1976 and 2005, neither of which was in the least bit necessary.

Auteur, Auteur
One of *King Kong*'s uncredited directors, Merian Cooper, met the film's producer Ernest Schoedsack after World War I, in which both served as pilots. The two men traveled the world in search of adventures that would inspire their idea for the film.

MARCH 3

Mad Max

YEAR RELEASED: 1979
DIRECTOR: George Miller
WHO'S IN IT: Mel Gibson, Joanne Samuel, Hugh Keays-Byrne

"They say people don't believe in heroes anymore."

A young Mel Gibson plays Max, a policeman in a country that looks to be falling apart at the edges. No explanation is provided; we are simply hurled into an opening sequence in which Max has to contend with a hopped-up homicidal hot rodder, Nightrider. Max takes off after him in a car chase that's a demented flurry of crash-zooms, smashed cars, booming engines, and manic editing. After Nightrider dies in a fiery crash, Max's boss warns him that gang-leader Toecutter (Hugh Keays-Byrne) is out for revenge. Max blows it off, not realizing his family is in danger.

While Miller's film comes straight out of the 1970s drive-in school of directing (complete with terribly-dubbed dialogue still used in most circulating versions of the film), there's a vision here that goes beyond the cheap dialogue and occasionally forced situations. By never explaining why exactly the outback is falling to savagery, Miller brings an uncertain fear to the story. With no sense of a greater civilization outside these lonely, criminal-prowled highways, there is no chance of the cavalry coming to the rescue. You get the feeling that once Max's fellow cops are killed or retire, there won't be anybody to replace them.

Miller's next two sequels—*The Road Warrior* (1981) and *Mad Max Beyond Thunderdome* (1985)—were bigger-budget, more clearly delineated affairs. Neither could match the raw intensity of this pulverizing, scruffy debut.

Auteur, Auteur
George Miller, who worked as a doctor to raise money for making *Mad Max*, has said that some of his inspiration for the film came from working on so many car-accident victims in emergency rooms.

Nosferatu

YEAR RELEASED: 1922
DIRECTOR: F. W. Murnau
WHO'S IN IT: Max Schreck, Gustav von Wangenheim

"Nosferatu! That name alone can chill the blood!"

Considering that F. W. Murnau's "Symphony of Horror" is based on the ultimate vampire novel, Bram Stoker's *Dracula*, his groundbreaking silent horror film is surprisingly free of fangs and bloodletting. When most people think of a vampire, they're not imagining Murnau's Graf Orlok (Max Schreck), with his wide bat ears, popped-out eyes, and slow, staggering gait. He wears a cape, at least, so that's something.

In mid-nineteenth-century Bremen, young newlywed Hutter (Gustav von Wangenheim) is sent on a business trip to Transylvania. There, he ignores all the villagers' warnings, continues on to Orlock's spooky castle, and ends up getting bled every night by his host. Eventually Orlok alights for Bremen on a ship whose crew will soon be severely depleted. The only one who can stop him from decimating the town is Hutter's wife, "a woman pure in heart."

Like the zombies that would follow him, Schreck's Orlok is terrifying not for his speed but for his *inevitability*. He nearly glides across floors instead of walking and seems able to power boats by thought alone. More ghoul than seducer, Orlok is like a plague-bearing wind. It's an effective characterization for one of the first true horror films, because, really, who was ever really that *scared* of Dracula?

Murnau subtitled his film a *Symphony of Horror* and its premiere on this day in 1922 was appropriately elaborate. The event was held in the lavishly ornate Marble Hall at Berlin's Zoological Gardens and featured live symphony accompaniment and a fancy-dress ball.

In Homage

Tim Burton paid respect to Max Schreck by naming Christopher Walken's wild-haired villain in *Batman Returns* after him. E. Elias Merhige's 2000 film *Shadow of the Vampire* imagines life on the set of *Nosferatu*, proposing that Schreck's (Willem Dafoe) performance was so truly frightening because he actually *was* a vampire.

Easy Rider

YEAR RELEASED: 1969
DIRECTOR: Dennis Hopper
WHO'S IN IT: Peter Fonda, Dennis Hopper, Jack Nicholson

"They're not scared of you. They're scared of what you represent."

Since Dennis Hopper's first directing job reportedly came about because Peter Fonda, a standing member of producer/director Roger Corman's counterculture B-movie factory, wanted to do a road movie with him, it's little surprise that *Easy Rider* is something of a mess. Terry Southern (*Dr. Strangelove*) had a hand in writing a screenplay, but not much appears to have survived. Most of the dialogue takes place around campfires between motorcycle travelogue shots scored to a rock soundtrack that reflects the time the film was made (much of it passé, but the Jimi Hendrix still stands up). The film is mostly filled with long silences punctuated by pot-mumbling between hyper Billy (Hopper) and mellow Captain America (Peter Fonda). A plotline becomes more apparent after the men pick up a small-town lawyer, George Hanson (Jack Nicholson, the film's true antihero), who actually seems to know how to carry on a conversation, but the story is basic as can be: heading to Mardi Gras.

The film's surprise success could have signaled many things: the arrival of a brave new artistic voice in Hopper, the vogue for biker flicks, the younger generation's delight in seeing blatantly celebrated drug use. But it instead galvanized a studio system already in disarray (the old-style blockbusters weren't working anymore, and television was hitting them hard) and looking for something to wow audiences. So this film, addle-brained and arbitrarily plotted as it is, ended up being the spark that launched Hollywood's short-lived embrace of experimenting with unproven directors and nontraditional storytelling.

> **Casting Call**
> Dennis Hopper was originally only supposed to be behind the camera for *Easy Rider*, but he stepped in front of it once Bruce Dern backed out of playing Billy.

The Princess Bride

YEAR RELEASED: 1987
DIRECTOR: Rob Reiner
WHO'S IN IT: Robin Wright, Cary Elwes, Mandy Patinkin, Wallace Shawn, Christopher Guest

"I don't think that means what you think it means."

The most quotable comedy of the 1980s wants to have its cake and eat it too. Normally this spells disaster, but Rob Reiner's desire to poke fun at fairy tales and romance while still celebrating them succeeds in every way.

William Goldman, a screenwriter better known for thrillers (*Marathon Man*) and Stephen King adaptations (*Misery*), had been trying to film his tongue-in-cheek fantasy novel for years. He got lucky, since Reiner is a jokester but also a softie, *and* he loves the right kinds of classic movies.

In some pretend, faraway land, beautiful blond Buttercup (Robin Wright) has fallen in love with stableboy Westley (Cary Elwes). He gets kidnapped and apparently killed by "The Dread Pirate Roberts." Later, Buttercup is about to marry an evil prince she doesn't love when she's kidnapped by Roberts himself, who turns out to be Westley, and he's ticked she didn't wait for him.

The rest of the film is a swashbuckling and comedy mix, with heavy emphasis on the latter. Reiner stocks each role with sterling talent, from Christopher Guest's brilliant variation on Basil Rathbone's sadistic nobleman from *The Adventures of Robin Hood* to Wallace Shawn's blustering fool and Mandy Patinkin's revenge-obsessed Spanish duelist.

It ends up somewhere between grand high romance and Monty Python, with just enough of each to make everyone happy.

Auteur, Auteur

In the introduction to the twenty-fifth anniversary edition of his novel, William Goldman wrote that of all the movies he'd ever been involved in he only truly loved two: *Butch Cassidy and the Sundance Kid* and *The Princess Bride*.

Betty Blue

YEAR RELEASED: 1986
DIRECTOR: Jean-Jacques Beineix
WHO'S IN IT: Jean-Hugues Anglade, Béatrice Dalle

"I had known Betty for a week. We made love every night. The forecast was for storms."

Zorg (Jean-Hugues Anglade) doesn't have much going for him, but that doesn't deter Betty (a smoldering Béatrice Dalle) from forming a powerful attachment to him. First there's the nearly nonstop lovemaking. Then Betty finds a manuscript of a novel Zorg has written; this leads her to decide he should move to the city and become a writer. Oh, and she decides to set fire to Zorg's bungalow, being an impetuous type and all.

It's all very *l'amour fou* (mad love), and so by definition hard to take too seriously—but delivered quite convincingly by Dalle and Anglade, two great actors who never quite got their due. Betty is a swirling tempest of passion with seemingly no ability to control her moods. Dalle's exaggerated bombshell looks, those pouty red lips and jet-black hair that made the poster for this film a 1980s college-dorm mainstay, accentuate the feeling of her being less of a character than a pure emotional manifestation. She is the beating heart of the film.

Despite writer/director Jean-Jacques Beineix's predilection for gloss over substance—his 1981 cultish New Wave extravaganza, *Diva*, is a perfect example—the actors' utter commitment to the frequently silly material and Jean-François Robin's astounding cinematography were all part of what helped Beineix win the Oscar for best foreign film.

Lost and Found

The overt sensuality of *Betty Blue* met with problems on its first U.S. release, and it was heavily edited to 120 minutes. A complete director's cut that ran over three hours long came to theaters in 2009.

Chungking Express

◐ ♥ 👤

YEAR RELEASED: 1994
DIRECTOR: Wong Kar-wai
WHO'S IN IT: Brigitte Lin, Tony Leung, Faye Wong, Takeshi Kaneshiro

"People like you are hung up on freshness."

There are two stories here and while they're not really related, in the world of Hong Kong art house impresario Wong Kar-wai, they sort of make sense together. Even if they didn't, it wouldn't matter a bit since the film as a whole is a beautiful ride.

In the first tale, Takeshi Kaneshiro plays police officer 233, who's just broken up with his girlfriend. For reasons that are never made clear, he decides that a good way to get past this pain is to continually buy and eat canned pineapple with an expiration date of May 1, one month after he was dumped. He finds himself attracted to a beauty in sunglasses and a blond wig (Brigitte Lin), who's actually a drug dealer packing a gun that she's not afraid to use.

The second story has another cop, badge number 663 (Tony Leung). He's also suffering from a breakup, but doesn't have the pineapple fetish to fall back on. Instead he becomes friendly with a counter girl named Faye (Faye Wong), who redefines quirky. First there's her habit of sneaking into 663's apartment to rearrange things as some kind of flirtation. Then there's her obsession with "California Dreamin'," which she plays in a near-constant loop and will either be revealed to viewers as musical genius or drive them insane.

Wong presents these stories and characters with no apology for their quirks. It doesn't matter much anyway, since his romantic sensibility and hyperbolic neon-color-drenched visuals achieve a pop romantic delirium that sweeps away all reason before it.

Auteur, Auteur

In the mid-1990s, Quentin Tarantino began his own specialty film distribution company. Rolling Thunder Pictures was established by Miramax Films (which has released nearly everything Tarantino's done over the years) and specialized in new foreign and obscure exploitation films. *Chunking Express*, which hit theaters on this day in 1996, was the company's premiere release.

Paris, Texas

YEAR RELEASED: 1984
DIRECTOR: Wim Wenders
WHO'S IN IT: Harry Dean Stanton, Nastassja Kinski

"I knew these people. These two people. They were in love with each other."

A man in ragged clothes with stubble and a thousand-yard stare comes walking out of the desert. He takes a drink of water from a plastic jug and looks at his sun-bleached surroundings. He walks on. It's been four years since he disappeared into the desert.

He is Travis (Harry Dean Stanton in his most iconic role), one of those lost men of mysterious, violent depths whom playwright Sam Shepard specializes in. Shepard wrote the screenplay for this spare, serene ode to the West. An all-American art film by a foreigner, it's a fascinating mix, with Wenders and cinematographer Robby Muller shooting the vast Western skies and long, arcing highways with the reverent love only a foreigner could bring.

Shepard's screenplay is long on spacious silence and short on dialogue until the end, where he delivers in one of film history's greatest soliloquies. Much of the film before that is set up as a mystery, with Travis's brother trying to return him to Los Angeles, where he has been raising Travis's son, Hunter. The two are reacquainted, awkwardly at first. But when Travis decides to hit the road again, Hunter feels the call as well.

Wenders layers a painterly quiet over the film, until Travis's eight-minute "I knew these people" speech, in which the dam bursts and all the buttoned-up pain and hurt seem about to rush out of the screen. It's a long moment that actors dream of getting to play and audiences dream of being able to watch.

In Homage

The wide-open American spaces of *Paris, Texas* were particularly inspirational for musicians. It was supposedly Kurt Cobain's favorite film and the band Travis named themselves after Harry Dean Stanton's character. U2 has also said that the spirit of their album *The Joshua Tree*, released on this day in 1987, was heavily influenced by the film's Western landscapes.

The Killer

YEAR RELEASED: 1989
DIRECTOR: John Woo
WHO'S IN IT: Chow Yun-Fat, Sally Yeh

"Life's cheap. It only takes one bullet."

Surviving in Hong Kong is hard for an assassin, particularly if he has a code of honor (and what film-world assassin doesn't?). That's the dilemma presented in John Woo's explosive action extravaganza, which showed the whole world that two guns is always better than one.

Jeffrey (the great Chow Yun-Fat) is a hired killer with a meticulous way of doing business. During the shootout that opens the film, an innocent, beautiful young singer, Jennie (Sally Yeh), is blinded. Wracked with guilt, Jeffrey quits the business, but not before taking on one last job in order to pay for an operation for Jennie. As any film criminal should know, the last job is never the last job. Later Jeffrey will stand in a church, side by side with a detective who understands him better than anybody, as wave after wave of Triad gunmen come after the two in an apocalyptic firefight.

Audiences used to Hollywood action films that had become progressively slower and more stupid over the years were knocked back in their seats by Woo's exuberantly over-the-top film. His Sam Peckinpah–esque use of slow motion and exquisitely choreographed shootouts created violent ballets that acted as perfect counterweights to the melodramatic sincerity of the leads' male bonding. The mixture was near perfect, and remains so today.

In Homage

For years, there were rumors of a Hollywood remake of *The Killer*. Sylvester Stallone was suggested as the star at one point, and then there was a plan to have Walter Hill direct and Richard Gere and Denzel Washington star. Nothing ever came of these plans, which was likely for the best.

THX 1138

YEAR RELEASED: 1971
DIRECTOR: George Lucas
WHO'S IN IT: Robert Duvall, Maggie McOmie

"If you feel you are not properly sedated, call 348-844 immediately. Failure to do so may result in prosecution for criminal drug evasion."

The future, sometime. For reasons unknown—environmental catastrophe, nuclear war—the human race now lives underground in a blank world of complete surrender where everyone wears white jump suits, has shaved heads, and are spoken to constantly by unseen voices, who tell them when to take their medications. It's a steady diet of pills and nothingness in an underworld of anonymous drones shuffling down white corridors.

Robert Duvall is worker THX 1138, who doesn't want to take his pills anymore. He discovers an illegal attraction to his roommate LUH 3417 (Maggie McOmie)—sex is strictly regulated, as in Orwell's *1984*—which is further complicated by the unwanted advances on 1138 from worker SEN 5421 (Donald Pleasance). THX goes on the run, not knowing where there is to run to.

George Lucas's anti-Hollywood cohort Francis Ford Coppola produced, and there's a line that can be drawn from this film to Coppola's similarly bleak *The Conversation* (1974). To realize that this was Lucas's first feature (based on his dialogue-free student short, *Electronic Labyrinth THX 1138 4EB*) is to behold his truly awesome talent. The film is a wonder of design and mood, the splintered screen humming with ever-present machinery and computerized tones, and the abstracted white-on-white sets pushing the dislocation even further.

It's a furious, frightening attack on the dehumanization of society that eclipsed almost everything else Lucas did afterward.

Production Notes

George Lucas shot the chase scenes for *THX 1138* in San Francisco's still-unfinished BART subway tunnels.

The Great Dictator

YEAR RELEASED: 1940
DIRECTOR: Charlie Chaplin
WHO'S IN IT: Charlie Chaplin, Paulette Goddard

"We've just discovered the most wonderful, the most marvelous poisonous gas. It will kill everybody."

In his first sound film, Chaplin plays a Jewish barber (looking and acting just like the Tramp of earlier films) serving in World War I, who ends up in the hospital with amnesia. Coming out of his coma, the barber discovers that the nation has been taken over by anti-Semitic stormtroopers worshipping their Hitlerian dictator, Adenoid Hynkel (also Chaplin, same mustache).

Chaplin's comedy is sometimes difficult to watch, particularly once the barber is sent off to a prison camp. (Chaplin said in his autobiography that had he known what was actually going on in the concentration camps, he never would have made the film.) Aside from that questionable note, and some inappropriately slapstick moments, this is some of Chaplin's most biting comedy. His earlier comedies, for all their often overrated social critique, drifted toward the sentimental, whereas Chaplin's depiction of Hynkel as a froth-mouthed, gibberish-spewing clown has more edge than anything else dared in Hollywood at the time. Some poorly handled speechifying near the end dulls the potency of the satire somewhat.

Surprisingly, the adoption of sound works to Chaplin's advantage, his soft, light voice and fussy manner nicely pitched for the script's deadpan humor, which foreshadowed both Monty Python and Mel Brooks. German protestations or not, the film went over very well in America, and would be Chaplin's last great success.

Production Notes

Halfway through production of *The Great Dictator* in 1939, Britain declared war and filming was halted. Chaplin put a lot of his own money into a project seen as too serious for a war-jittery public; his risk would pay off handsomely.

Boogie Nights

YEAR RELEASED: 1997
DIRECTOR: Paul Thomas Anderson
WHO'S IN IT: Mark Wahlberg, Burt Reynolds, Julianne Moore, Heather Graham

"I'm gonna be a great big bright, shining star."

That hardest of things: a serious movie about a very silly subject. Paul Thomas Anderson's bid for the big time—his first film, *Hard Eight* (1996), was a critical hit but had limited exposure—throws almost everything into the mix without seeming desperate.

Mark Wahlberg stars as Dirk Diggler, a porn star at the industry's swinging height in the late 1970s. An innocent soul with the air of a wide-eyed farm kid in the big city for the first time, Dirk is part of a swirl of characters orbiting around the sex-film factory run by Jack Horner (Burt Reynolds, in a brief but dazzling return to form). There's the troubled Amber Waves (Julianne Moore) and the serenely happy Rollergirl (Heather Graham), as well as Don Cheadle, John C. Reilly, and a small city's worth of other actors given the chance for glory in Anderson's wide-open epic.

The story is all dizziness and speed as Anderson sends it hurtling from guilt-free idylls in the California sun to ugly ruin. There's a suicide. Drugs. A nerve-jangling scene set to Night Ranger's "Sister Christian." The 1980s loom like a dark machine, and the triumph of mass-produced and plotless porn signals the end of a more carefree era. Anderson, with his dazzling camera techniques and broad cast of characters, can sometimes here be accused of doing too much. But it beats the alternative.

Production Notes

To ensure the verisimilitude of *Boogie Nights*, Paul Thomas Anderson hired porn star Ron Jeremy as a consultant for the shoot and gave other adult-film actors cameos throughout.

Paris Is Burning

YEAR RELEASED: 1990
DIRECTOR: Jennie Livingston
WHO'S IN IT: Pepper LaBeija, Sandy Ninja, Octavia St. Laurent, Venus Xtrava-ganza, Dorian Corey, Paris Duprée

"I went to a ball, I got a trophy, and now everybody wants to know me."

It's a three-strike situation, we hear at the beginning of Jennie Livingston's epochal documentary, when you're African American, male, *and* gay. Since the world is not prepared to accept those fitting that description, it seems, they had better find their own ways of getting by. If that means creating a fantasy persona to escape that sense of not belonging, so be it.

Livingston's film was released in 1990, the same year as Madonna's single "Vogue." It was a fitting serendipity, given that Ms. Ciccone had lifted the dance style from the same uptown Manhattan drag parties, or balls, that Livingston was filming back in 1987, well before vogueing had crossed over. The dance itself is something else, both spiky and fluid, a liquid chain of aggressively graceful poses set against an invisible mirror or rival.

But that's only a small part of what Livingston's funny, deeply moving film is all about. She's documenting the culture of these balls, where the men gather to perform in a variety of competitions with confoundingly specific titles (schoolgirl, town & country, luscious). It all seems to come down to a desire for "realness," the ability to pass unnoticed into a different look, a different life. The barriers of class and race appear implacable, with one interviewee, Venus, saying quite simply, "I would like to be a spoiled, rich, white girl." Unlike previous generations of (mostly white) drag queens, Livingston's subjects take the big-haired divas of the small screen (*Dynasty*) as their models—no Judy Garland or Marilyn Monroe for them. It's fantasy as survival: "You left a mark on the world if you just get through it."

Reservoir Dogs

YEAR RELEASED: 1992
DIRECTOR: Quentin Tarantino
WHO'S IN IT: Harvey Keitel, Tim Roth, Michael Madsen

"Let me tell you what 'Like a Virgin' is all about."

When it was first released, all anybody could discuss about Quentin Tarantino's debut film was its violence. That was before *Hostel* and *Saw* and *Grand Theft Auto* and a thousand other bloodbaths. Even then, though, what was most surprising about this crime film wasn't necessarily the violence but the talking.

We see a gang of bank robbers in black suits and black ties having breakfast. But instead of talking strategy, they're debating the subtext of Madonna songs. This rambling, obscene discussion shifts into a debate over tipping, ended when their boss growls, "Cough up a buck, you cheap bastard."

With the exception of later flashbacks, the rest of the film is situated inside a warehouse where the men gather after their botched robbery. Inside that void space, the robbers—identified only by color-coded signifiers—bark and growl and snap at each other, trying to figure out who the rat is. Guns are drawn and there is some business with a severed ear. But in the main, this is a character-based theater piece, with blood.

The Tarantino aesthetic, with its ironic use of trash culture and extreme verbosity, became a hallmark for indie cinema in the 1990s. While this well ran dry fast, Tarantino did manage to find a new way to create genre films that were neither straight-to-video trash nor predictable, big-budget oversimplifications.

Auteur, Auteur

Supposedly, Quentin Tarantino had a hard time pronouncing Louis Malle's *Au revoir, les enfants* (1987) while working in an L.A. video store, which is where he came up with the name for *Reservoir Dogs*.

The Conformist

YEAR RELEASED: 1970
DIRECTOR: Bernardo Bertolucci
WHO'S IN IT: Jean-Louis Trintignant, Stefania Sandrelli

"He'll be a typical intellectual, disagreeable and impotent."

Bernardo Bertolucci's flashback-riddled arthouse thriller with a dense political backdrop and sensual demeanor is many things at once, all of them engrossing.

Marcello Clerici (*Z*'s Jean-Louis Trintignant, frighteningly opaque), the conformist, just wants to go along with the social order (being Italian and of a certain age, that means becoming a churchgoing, married Fascist) but isn't sure how exactly to do that. In his childhood during World War I, his family's wealth keeps him isolated. A key moment with the family chauffer involving a gun and an inappropriate advance establishes Marcello's schizoid, detached, repressed nature.

In order to belong, Marcello joins the burgeoning Fascist movement and marries the beautiful Giulia (Stefania Sandrelli). Never mind that he doesn't have a political bone in his body and his heterosexuality is ambiguous at best. A true test of Marcello's nature comes when a Fascist group that he belongs to orders him to assassinate one of his college professors.

While Bertolucci stutters the film with flashbacks and philosophical and psychological allusions, Vittorio Storaro's shimmering cinematography creates a dream-world of lush darkness and grand, soaring interior spaces. As the man who isn't fully there, Marcello is continually dwarfed by his surroundings.

Two years later, Bertolucci shocked those audiences who liked to be shocked with the sexually explicit *Last Tango in Paris*, but that was a fraction of the film this one is—while *The Conformist* is a film *about* emptiness, *Paris* is simply empty.

And the Winner Is . . .

The Conformist was nominated for a best adapted screenplay Oscar. But Bertolucci (born on this day in 1940) wouldn't win an Oscar until 1988, when he took home two for *The Last Emperor*.

Escape from New York

YEAR RELEASED: 1981
DIRECTOR: John Carpenter
WHO'S IN IT: Kurt Russell, Lee Van Cleef

"Call me Snake."

The thing to remember about this great John Carpenter sci-fi adventure is that at the time, New York's image was that of a crime-infested urban battleground. Keep this in mind when you consider that Carpenter's pre-Giuliani film, set in 1997, imagines the whole island of Manhattan as a maximum-security prison.

The comic-book script starts with a one-two punch. The president's plane is shot down, but the chief executive's escape pod lands him in Manhattan. Who can get him out? None other than the scruffy, eye-patched Snake Plissken (Kurt Russell, as many boys' ideal of what a hero should look like), an ex-special forces operative and bank robber who gets a poisoned carrot dangled in front of him by police chief Bob Hauk (Lee Van Cleef): rescue the president and get a full pardon. Oh, and do it in twenty-four hours, otherwise these microscopic explosives we injected you with will turn you to bloody mush.

A prime example of genre filmmaking done with smarts and efficiency, not to mention a stellar cast of character actors (particularly Harry Dean Stanton and Ernest Borgnine) this film kicked off Carpenter's most successful period. Soon after, he shot a remake of Howard Hawks's Antarctica alien thriller *The Thing* (1982) and Stephen King's *Christine* (1983). An unfortunate 1996 sequel, *Escape from L.A.*, tried to rekindle the same magic; it didn't take.

Production Notes

New York didn't look run-down enough for the filmmakers when shooting *Escape from New York*, so they used the next best thing: St. Louis. Among those who worked on the special effects was a young James Cameron.

Bull Durham

YEAR RELEASED: 1988
DIRECTOR: Ron Shelton
WHO'S IN IT: Kevin Costner, Susan Sarandon, Tim Robbins

"Sometimes you win, sometimes you lose, sometimes it rains."

Sports films that are even passable are few and far between—mostly they're a wasteland of cliché. Fortunately, writer/director Ron Shelton spent enough time in minor-league baseball to pick up a feel for the sweat and magic of the game. His hero, Crash Davis (Kevin Costner, having a field day), is a journeyman catcher starting to think about retirement. One character says about Crash, "He's different. . . . I actually saw him read a book without pictures once." This attracts Annie (Susan Sarandon, in full bloom), a poetry-spouting groupie for Crash's newest team, the Durham Bulls (a real team founded this day in 1904 as the Durham Tobacconists). But she ultimately shacks up with the Bulls' hot young pitcher, "Nuke" LaLoosh (Tim Robbins), who's being groomed for the majors and who Crash is supposed to mentor. Nuke isn't the brightest—he mistakenly assumes that Annie reading Walt Whitman to him is foreplay—but he's uncomplicated. The love triangle makes for some fantastically prickly verbal sparring, frequently at Nuke's expense, and a surprisingly resonant eroticism.

The sense of baseball as joyful ritual has never been better explored on film. Via Crash, Shelton treats the game with reverence and love but without the sepia-toned lugubriousness of *The Natural* (1984) or *Field of Dreams* (1989). The result is delicate, literate, dirty-minded, and truthful.

> **Auteur, Auteur**
> Ron Shelton played as an infielder in the Baltimore Orioles' minor-league farm system from 1967 to 1972, eventually rising to AAA level.

The Sixth Sense

YEAR RELEASED: 1999
DIRECTOR: M. Night Shyamalan
WHO'S IN IT: Bruce Willis, Haley Joel Osment, Toni Collette

"Do you know why you're afraid when you're alone? I do."

There is no hokier plot than giving dead spirits messages for the living. The belief that these spirits are simply waiting on the other side to communicate with those they left behind scares as much as it reassures—that's probably why it's proved so popular. That writer/director M. Night Shyamalan found a singular way to handle this formula is evidence of his talent. But the astounding confidence with which he handled this moody, haunting film is something altogether different.

Malcolm Crowe (Bruce Willis, taking the rare chance to do some acting) is a psychologist who is surprised to find a patient in his house one night waving a pistol and looking haunted. He shoots Crowe and kills himself. Afterward, Crowe seems hardly himself but continues to work. One new case, a young child, interests him. Cole Sear (Haley Joel Osment) tells Crowe that he has the ability to see and talk to dead people. It's a terrible gift, what with the deads' habit of showing up unexpectedly; you can see why Sear looks as though he hasn't slept in a year. Without disturbing the film's carefully constructed, churchlike ambience (Philadelphia, shot in wintry gloom by Tak Fujimoto), Shyamalan turns the film from a straight ghost story into one where Sear actually *wants* to talk to these ghosts, no matter how terrifying; he just wants to help.

Knowing the twist ending doesn't ruin the film at all. The director's handle on his material is so assured and powerfully dramatic that the much-parodied twist fast becomes the last thing you think about.

MARCH 20

Inside Man

YEAR RELEASED: 2006
DIRECTOR: Spike Lee
WHO'S IN IT: Denzel Washington, Clive Owen, Chiwetel Ejiofor, Jodie Foster

"Pay strict attention to what I say because I choose my words carefully and I never repeat myself."

The heist film seemed dead and buried by the time Spike Lee got around to making one, but he showed that there was life in the old genre yet. Having Clive Owen there to play the lead bank robber (a study in cool, wise control) and Denzel Washington as his NYPD adversary helped, but Lee still fought an uphill battle against predictability.

Owen starts the film with a speech; listen to his every word, as he implores, but you still won't fully get what he's talking about until the very end. There's a deep secret in the bank that he's robbing, which is bringing undue attention from highly placed people. (A steely Jodie Foster shows up as a woman whose work seems to be frightening those less well connected than she.) Washington's Detective Frazier senses the mystery and tries to puzzle it out in interrogations done *after* the heist that Lee intercuts throughout.

For the first piece of pure entertainment Lee ever directed, he could hardly have done better. Russell Gewirtz's script relies on trickery, not gunplay, to keep the audience goosed; the pointed lack of violence seems a deliberate jab by the filmmaker at his lazier contemporaries. The scenes have a New York crackle and buzz, helped along by Washington's I-own-the-city stride and Terence Blanchard's throwback 1970s score.

Production Notes

Inside Man was originally to have been directed by Ron Howard, who instead shot *Cinderella Man*. Similarly, Martin Scorsese was to direct the film *Clockers* (1995) before Lee (born on this day in 1957) took it over.

MARch 21

Metropolis

🌍 👤 👽

YEAR RELEASED: 1927
DIRECTOR: Fritz Lang
WHO'S IN IT: Brigitte Helm, Rudolf Klein-Rogge, Gustav Fröhlich

"There can be no understanding between the hand and the brain unless the heart acts as mediator."

Fritz Lang's gigantic silent film about a rebellion in a sprawling factory-city of the future is frequently cited as one of the early greats of cinematic science fiction. Truth be told, it's less science fiction than it is quasi-Nordic mythology transplanted to a modernist fever-dream.

High above the city, where John Frederson (Alfred Abel) rules, there appears to be order. However, his son Freder (Gustav Fröhlich) has a vision about the problems facing the city, in which the workers—seen throughout as long, shuffling lines of ant-like nonentities—lose what little is left of their humanity. A war is brewing in the city's dark underworld, where the masses are torn between Maria (Brigitte Helm), a saint-like preacher of Christian protest, and the violent message of her robot lookalike created by the evil inventor with the Wagnerian name Rotwang (Rudolf Klein-Rogge).

The story isn't the thing here, though, particularly its resolution, where a surprise solution wraps things up all too neatly. Lang's gothic morality tale prefigures everything from George Orwell to *Blade Runner*, producing one of film's most potent nightmares about the industrial revolution's potential for dehumanization. The massive sets of Lang's future-city (beyond anything that the European film industry had seen at that point) depict factories and skyscrapers as *hungry*.

Lost and Found

In 2008, footage from *Metropolis* assumed lost—and containing entirely new subplots—was discovered in the archive of Buenos Aires' Museo del Cine.

The English Patient

YEAR RELEASED: 1996
DIRECTOR: Anthony Minghella
WHO'S IN IT: Ralph Fiennes, Juliette Binoche, Kristin Scott Thomas

"You speak so many bloody languages, and you never want to talk."

Ralph Fiennes took over movie screens in 1996 as Count Laszlo de Almásy, playing the lover of a woman who could never be his and a poetic-minded explorer of great, wild spaces. Grandeur was long missing from the big screen, killed off by everything from special effects to encroaching cynicism. Anthony Minghella's planet-sized version of Michael Ondaatje's novel was like a flare going up in a darkened plain, reminding people of how films could be.

The story is told in flashback from the bedside of a near-death burn patient. He is Lazlo, an explorer in North Africa who fell in love with the wife (Kristin Scott Thomas) of a fellow explorer in the early days of World War II. In between segments unfurling brightly around this doomed desert affair, we see Lazlo in the present day being attended to in a falling-down Tuscan villa by a nurse, Hana (Juliette Binoche, finally coming into her own), who reads to him from his beloved Herodotus. Jealousy and desire intersect, with the pains of the past slowly catching up with both Lazlo and Hana.

Minghella's rich canvas is painted over beautiful landscapes, from the serene sands of Egypt to the cool colonial residences of Cairo and sun-dappled fields of Tuscany. His performers stand tall in these vividly etched spaces. It worked out well for everyone: Fiennes became a movie star, Minghella got his pick of literary projects, and everyone else was treated to the return of cinematic grandeur.

And the Winner Is . . .
The English Patient won nine Oscars, including best picture and director.

Cabaret

YEAR RELEASED: 1972
DIRECTOR: Bob Fosse
WHO'S IN IT: Liza Minnelli, Michael York, Joel Grey

"Leave your troubles outside."

First a book, then a play, then a film, then a musical, then another film, then another musical, the story of a naughty little Berlin cabaret during the declining years of the Weimar Republic has an evergreen quality. Although some Bob Fosse films haven't aged well—see the adventurous but often embarrassing *All That Jazz* (1979)—this version of the decadent exhibition always makes for a good show.

Brian Roberts (Michael York, uptight as ever) is a poor writer who washes up in 1930s Berlin. He mixes poorly with the extravagantly tawdry nightlife's live-fast-die-young ethos until meeting cabaret dancer Sally Bowles (Liza Minnelli), a lightning rod of enthusiasm and bad ideas. In between telling the story of Brian and Sally's love triangle with a wealthy young man of flexible sexuality, Fosse cuts back to the scene at the cabaret, since that's where the film's real action is. A master of ceremonies (Joel Grey, like a possessed, sickly, dirty-minded elf) leers and goggles in between the cynical, catchy numbers. Then Sally comes out in Fosse uniform (black hat, garters) and knocks everyone's socks off.

Though the plot can flag at times, there is never a moment when that could be said about the performances. With Fosse's wicked choreography and Minnelli's tireless energy, the songs provide a biting soundtrack for the country's slide into Nazi barbarism (which began on this day in 1933 with the passing of the second Enabling Act, which gave Adolf Hitler dictatorial powers).

And the Winner Is . . .

Cabaret was the surprise hit at the Oscars in 1973, garnering ten nominations and winning eight—and this was the same year as *The Godfather*.

The Great Escape

YEAR RELEASED: 1963
DIRECTOR: John Sturges
WHO'S IN IT: Steve McQueen, James Garner, Charles Bronson

"We have, in effect, put all our rotten eggs in one basket. And we intend to watch this basket carefully."

In 1944, the Nazis build a new stalag, or prisoner of war camp, to house all of their most incorrigible escapees, a kind of Alcatraz without the great views. Of course, once all those prisoners are together the first thing they do is start figuring out how to escape.

First is Capt. Hilts (a gimlet-eyed Steve McQueen), an escape machine who patiently tests the fencing, looks for blind spots, and for his troubles gets continually tossed into an isolation cell. Capt. Ramsey (James Donald), the leader of the group, starts organizing a digging crew including Lt. Danny "The Tunnel King" Velinksi (Charles Bronson).

James Clavell and W. R. Burnett's entertaining script is adapted from Paul Brickhill's novel. An Australian pilot shot down in 1943, Brickhill based the book partially on his experiences in POW camp Stalag Luft III (which some prisoners really did escape from on March 24, 1944). Although the execution of escapees was a charge brought during the Nuremberg Trials, what viewers take away from the film is a striving sense of heroic daring. This is encapsulated in Sturges's most celebrated scene, in which McQueen (a motorcycle fanatic) jumps his bike over a length of barbed-wire fencing.

John Sturges's breezy World War II caper, one of the last of its easygoing kind, is a spacious ensemble piece, given ample room for his oversized cast to jostle around and play inside. Like in his equally marvelous *The Magnificent Seven* (1960), a life-or-death task is treated with equanimity by a broad range of individuals, each contributing their particular skills toward the common good.

Dancer in the Dark

YEAR RELEASED: 2000
DIRECTOR: Lars von Trier
WHO'S IN IT: Björk, Catherine Deneuve

"In a musical, nothing dreadful ever happens."

Before *Chicago* (2002) made it safe again for Hollywood musicals, Danish cinematic revolutionary Lars von Trier went ahead and did his own. He cast Björk as Selma Jezkova, a young Czech immigrant living in the Pacific Northwest in the early 1960s. Björk (about two-thirds of the reason the film works) plays her as part sweet naif and part alien being, with a way of looking at people as though she's not quite sure they're really there but is nevertheless interested. Selma lives in a trailer with her son and works a grueling factory job; also, she's going blind and painstakingly saving money for a preventative operation.

Selma's hard life has only one relief: musicals. She's constantly going to the movies with her friend Kathy (Catherine Deneuve) and even wins a role in an amateur production of *The Sound of Music*. Her musical-mad spirit turns reality into big, clanging song-and-dance numbers, and von Trier obliges by staging them wherever he can with his hand-held digital cameras—in one especially thrilling number, Selma and the dancers cavort on a railroad bridge.

Dancer in the Dark is a rebellious mix of modern, nervy agitation and silent-film melodrama that never rests on convention. This film is a musical done as gothic noir, with a gun in hand and song in the heart.

And the Winner Is . . .

Dancer in the Dark won the Palme d'Or and best actress (Björk) at the Cannes Film Festival. It also received an Oscar nomination for Björk's song "I've Seen It All." It was on March 25, 2001, that Oscar nominee Björk walked the red carpet in the infamous "swan dress" and mimed laying an egg.

The Godfather: Part II

YEAR RELEASED: 1974
DIRECTOR: Francis Ford Coppola
WHO'S IN IT: Al Pacino, Robert Duvall, Diane Keaton, Robert De Niro, John Cazale

"This . . . is the life . . . we've chosen!"

It's become a cliché to say that the second *Godfather* beats the first, but watch it again and you'll see that it's true.

The story picks up in the late 1950s, a few years after the first film's assassination campaign left Mafia chieftain Michael Corleone (Al Pacino) nearly without rivals. Echoing the real-life Mafia's westward drift in the postwar years, Michael has decamped to Nevada. When we first see him, Michael's lavish Lake Tahoe estate is flooded with guests, many powerful politicians among them, to celebrate his son's First Communion. That night gunmen try to kill Michael and his wife Kay (Diane Keaton). After telling his consigliere Tom Hagen (Robert Duvall) to take care of his family, Michael leaves town to handle some business. Meanwhile, flashbacks follow Michael's father Vito (Robert De Niro, playing a younger Marlon Brando) from a vendetta-scarred Sicilian childhood to New York's teeming immigrant ghettos.

Where *Part II* improves on the first film is in its more clinical approach. Without Brando's familial godfather providing the illusion of the mafia as honorable rogues, Pacino's colder, corporatized leader strips away the nostalgia. Also, the film's broader historical scope—even decamping for pre-revolutionary Cuba—and wider range of great performances (John Cazale as Michael's weak-willed brother is especially heartbreaking) give it an epic breadth and texture few other American films have ever achieved.

Lost and Found

A 1977 television broadcast called *The Godfather Saga* combined the stories of the first two films into one continuous chronological story and included about fifteen minutes' worth of new material.

Inglourious Basterds

YEAR RELEASED: 2009
DIRECTOR: Quentin Tarantino
WHO'S IN IT: Brad Pitt, Mélanie Laurent, Christoph Waltz, Michael Fassbender, Diane Kruger

"We ain't in the prisoner-takin' business; we in the killin' Nazis business. And cousin, business is a-boomin'."

After a brief spate of interest in war films during the 1990s sparked by *Saving Private Ryan* and *The Thin Red Line*, Hollywood returned to the notion that they were simply not good for business. Then Quentin Tarantino showed up and proved that wasn't necessarily true.

As ringleader of this carnival, Tarantino is having almost too good a time, and that sensation rubs off on everybody involved. The story is crowded but the gist is: A young French Jewish woman, Shosanna (Mélanie Laurent), escapes the butchery of her family by SS Col. Hans Landa (Christoph Waltz, an evil genius of an actor) and flees to Paris. Lt. Aldo Raine (Brad Pitt) leads a commando unit of Jewish GIs whose mission is simple—terrorize the Nazis by scalping as many of them as possible. The "Basterds" head toward Paris, where word is there's going to be a meeting of German brass. Landa will be there, too, as well as Shosanna.

This isn't a war film, per se. We're in the "guys on a mission" territory of *Where Eagles Dare* (1968), with skullduggery and quick shootouts in small spaces. The language-obsessed Tarantino warps the genre, though, with myriad details that make it his own, particularly the many lovingly crafted tension-filled confrontational scenes, where each syllable of multilingual dialogue counts.

It's all movie-mad, with music and plots ripped from a thousand other films, and absolutely unconcerned about violence overkill. But the vivid intelligence and sharp humor are what's remembered. Long a denizen of fantasy, Tarantino collides here with history—and the resulting explosion is incandescent.

The Man with the Golden Arm

YEAR RELEASED: 1955
DIRECTOR: Otto Preminger
WHO'S IN IT: Frank Sinatra, Kim Novak, Eleanor Parker, Darren McGavin

"The monkey never dies."

Frank Sinatra is wire-taut in this film, in which he plays dope fiend and backroom card dealer Frankie Machine. Frankie is back in Chicago after getting clean and learning to play drums, determined to change his ways. Everything conspires against him, particularly his needy wheelchair-bound wife, Zosch (Eleanor Parker), who cripples him with guilt just as his drunk driving crippled her. Though there's a ray of light in the downstairs dancehall girl, Molly (Kim Novak, angelic), who is Frankie's true love, more visible in the foreground is his old dealer, Louie (Darren McGavin), who doesn't see why one little fix would be so bad.

That director Otto Preminger could even make a major film about a heroin junkie in the mid-1950s is incredible. So we can forgive the film's weaker elements, like the obviously back-lot Chicago sets. Preminger's flair for the baroque is in full swing here, particularly with Arnold Stang's comic-relief street twerp Sparrow and Parker's full-on gargoyle act (oddly enough creating the one character who feels true to the gutter-dwelling inhabitants of Nelson Algren's masterful source novel). Sinatra digs deep, particularly in the scene where he tells Molly to lock him in a room so he can detox, and not to let him out no matter how much he begs. The righteously low and threatening jazzy score is by Elmer Bernstein at the height of his talent; it's perfectly married to Saul Bass's oft-imitated jagged animations in the famous title sequence.

Courting Controversy

According to Gene D. Phillips's *Exiles in Hollywood*, Nelson Algren was not pleased with Hollywood's version of his novel, saying, "The novel was Algren; the movie was Preminger."

Jesus of Montreal

YEAR RELEASED: 1989
DIRECTOR: Denys Arcand
WHO'S IN IT: Lothaire Bluteau, Gilles Pelletier

"The text's a bit dated."

Although its point of view is more challenging to mainstream Christian theology, Denys Arcand's allegory about a modern-day Christ figure received only a fraction of the controversy as Martin Scorsese's *The Last Temptation of Christ*, released the previous year. Maybe the religious scolds figured because it was a Canadian film, nobody would notice.

In any case, Arcand's story makes for bracing drama. Father Leclerc (Gilles Pelletier) asks brooding actor Daniel (Lothaire Bluteau, a fiery presence with the dark visage of a prophet) to help update his church's tired Passion play. Daniel does so with a vengeance, rounding up a cast of starving actors and researching all the latest theories on the history of Jesus. The play he presents horrifies with its anti-orthodox, Gnostic-inspired presentation, and Daniel's fired, though the play is a hit.

At that point, Arcand's film, which has been flirting with New Testament parallels, shifts into a full-fledged Christ allegory. Daniel, unhinged, begins to see his life pulled away from him by powers beyond his control. Soon he's raving in the underground city, in the grip of a fervor he can't understand. A Christ-figure for the new millennium, Daniel is as loved, hated, and misunderstood as the man whose legacy he tries to excavate from beneath the layers of organized religious beliefs.

Bracingly written and passionately acted, Arcand's film is one of a very few films that has not only tackled a religious subject with honesty and bravery but made forceful drama out of it at the same time.

And the Winner Is . . .

Jesus of Montreal was nominated for the best foreign film Oscar, though it lost to the overbearingly (but inarguably effectively) schmaltzy *Cinema Paradiso*.

Killer of Sheep

YEAR RELEASED: 1977
DIRECTOR: Charles Burnett
WHO'S IN IT: Henry Gayle Sanders, Kaycee Moore

"I'm not poor. I give things away to the Salvation Army sometimes."

You have never seen anything like this movie. *Killer of Sheep* is set in Los Angeles' Watts neighborhood, where bleak poverty is a fact of life but there's still joy to be had. One of the most important American films of the last several decades, Charles Burnett's black-and-white debut is a spare and wounding story.

Stan (Henry Gayle Sanders) puts in long hours at the slaughterhouse dismembering animals (filmed in unblinking detail) to support his wife and children. Other than that, there isn't that much of a plot to hang on to. Fortunately, it doesn't matter.

Burnett filmed over the course of two years, and the resulting film is one of patches of imagery sometimes roughly hurled together. His eye is extraordinary, however, particularly with the many scenes of children playing in the neighborhood's dusty vacant lots. They run with carefree abandon, dangerously flinging themselves from one rooftop to the next, in stark contrast to the adults in their midst, who worry about money, money, money. It's hard not to see parallels between the shots of the sheep that Stan herds into the killing room and these kids, as though hinting at a painful, dangerous future they can't even imagine.

Burnett shoots with a tough authenticity that recalls the Italian neorealists or the grimmer works of Robert Bresson (*Pickpocket*, in particular). His gift for poetic imagery is further complemented by the soundtrack of Dinah Washington and Paul Robeson songs, whose swelling moodiness brings the whole roughly assembled piece together in a kind of sad harmony.

Production Notes

Although *Killer of Sheep* would later be regarded as one of the most seminal American movies—it was added to the National Registry of Films by the Library of Congress in 1990—for almost thirty years it was only rarely screened, mostly due to the expense of clearing music rights for its soundtrack. The film finally received a proper theatrical release on March 30, 2007, thirty years later.

Annie Hall

YEAR RELEASED: 1977
DIRECTOR: Woody Allen
WHO'S IN IT: Woody Allen, Diane Keaton

"They're always giving out awards. Best Fascist Dictator: Adolf Hitler."

In this rightfully beloved, antiromantic comedy, Woody Allen plays Alvy Singer, a death-obsessed neurotic who can't imagine life outside his New York bubble. Sound familiar? That's mostly because this was the first of Allen's long Manhattan period, which followed his zanier sex comedies like *Sleeper* (1973). This one set the template for what came to be known as typical "Woody Allen" films.

Singer can't relax; movie posters even tagged the film "a nervous romance." He also can't stop analyzing his relationship with ex-girlfriend Annie Hall (Diane Keaton, whose birth name was Hall and whose nickname was Annie), whose casualness about everything makes him even more stressed. Singer goes so far as to chase her out to California (cue the scene of a miserable Allen driving in Los Angeles, like a turtle without its shell). Though he can't get Annie out of his mind, he doesn't seem able to get her back into his life either.

Around this story Allen riffs on everything from intellectual pretensions to anti-Semitism and the woefulness of life. It all begins with a direct address by Singer, telling the old joke about the two old women at a Catskills resort. One says, "Boy, the food in this place is really terrible." The other responds, "Yeah, I know. And such small portions." That's how Singer feels about life: "Full of loneliness and misery and suffering and unhappiness, and it's all over much too quickly."

If that joke doesn't do it for you, watch a different film.

> **And the Winner Is . . .**
> *Annie Hall* won four Oscars (including best picture), beating out *Star Wars* in multiple categories.

The Rocky Horror Picture Show

YEAR RELEASED: 1975
DIRECTOR: Jim Sharman
WHO'S IN IT: Tim Curry, Susan Sarandon, Barry Bostwick

"Don't dream it; be it."

This is not a film like any other: meaning, do not watch it with the same expectations you bring to most other films. If you should choose to do so, it will become rapidly apparent just what a cheap, slapdash piece of work this is, which takes all the fun away.

In this rock musical about a cross-dressing mad scientist from the Planet Transsexual (yep), Brad (Barry Bostwick) and Janet (Susan Sarandon) are straight-laced newlyweds who show up at a remote castle looking for help with a flat tire. A trio of lewd, half-zombified servants bring them to the cross-dressing master of ceremonies, Dr. Frank-N-Furter (Tim Curry). Frank introduces the squeamish pair to some suggestive dances. After a few more songs, he's bedded Brad and Janet, murdered a couple of people, and set himself up for a great, mascara-streaked aria.

Unlike most films that end up as repeat midnight fare at rundown arthouses, this mock-sci-fi musical is actually *not* horrible (it's not *Showgirls*, in other words). The direction is crude at best, and the plot is stitched together, Frankenstein-fashion. But the songs, a mash-up of ballads and danceable rock numbers, make the whole thing hum along. Still, it works best when seen with a crowd hurling obscenities and objects at the screen; failing that, there's a DVD release with an audio commentary track that will do the trick.

Production Notes

The Rocky Horror Picture Show began as an experimental stage show in London in 1973. A live revival has since been performed around the world, including a couple stints on Broadway. Its first midnight screening at New York City's Waverly Theatre took place on April 1, 1976.

This Is England

YEAR RELEASED: 2007
DIRECTOR: Shane Meadows
WHO'S IN IT: Thomas Turgoose, Stephen Graham, Joseph Gilgun

"Do you consider yourself English, or Jamaican?"

A young boy growing up semi-feral falls under the sway of a racist skinhead; it sounds like a supreme downer. But writer/director Shane Meadows takes the hard-edged elements and spins them into something transcendent.

Thomas Turgoose, one of the decade's great discoveries, plays twelve-year-old Shaun. He lives with his mother (his father died in the Falklands War in 1982) in the kind of grim Northern England town where factories are shutting down and the remaining unions are thoroughly battered by Thatcherism. A chance encounter with some older local skinheads results in Shaun being taken under the wing of the kindly Woody (Joseph Gilgun, marvelous). They dress him in skinhead garb—shiny Dr. Marten boots, natty Ben Sherman shirts, suspenders—and all seems well.

Then the gang's old friend Combo (a magnetic Stephen Graham) shows up, fresh out of prison with his head full of white supremacist rhetoric that doesn't play well with Woody; a schism results. Shaun takes up with Combo, who indoctrinates his protégé in a violently anti-immigrant neo-Nazi mindset. The battle for Shaun's soul is a drag-out affair with plenty of scars for all concerned.

Tough-minded on the outside, Meadows's autobiographical modern classic has a warmly flickering soul underneath as touching as it is antisentimental. Meadows's sociological exactitude, exhibited in earlier films like *A Room for Romeo Brass* (1999), creates a vivid portrait of this embattled punk subculture, but never forgets the lost boy at its core.

> **Casting Call**
> The casting director for *This Is England* could only convince Thomas Turgoose to audition by giving him a five-pound note. The second audition cost a tenner.

Chicago

YEAR RELEASED: 2002
DIRECTOR: Rob Marshall
WHO'S IN IT: Renée Zellweger, Catherine Zeta-Jones, Richard Gere

"Give 'em a show that's so splendiferous, row after row will grow vociferous."

Even if Rob Marshall's razzle-dazzle extravaganza about murder and mayhem in Jazz Age Chicago didn't have a deep thought in its pretty little head, this would still be a hell of a show. Roxie Hart (Renée Zellweger) is a wannabe singer and dancer who's got a long way to go before she could even be called a starlet. She also has a temper, which is why she plugged her boyfriend full of holes and thought that a murder rap would be a good way to get press. Roxie ends up in the Cook County Jail with Velma Kelly (Catherine Zeta-Jones), also in for killing a guy.

Since the local press loves murdering vixens, Roxie thinks she has a shot at stardom. All she has to worry about is the death penalty, but for that, she hires the best lawyer in town, Billy Flynn (Richard Gere). The resulting media frenzy and legal battle is waged as blood sport, only with a chorus line.

The musical's rapid march of catchy showstoppers gives it a powerful momentum, and its streetwise, tongue-in-cheek treatment of Roxie's homicidal lust for fame gives everything a darkly funny tone. Rob Marshall directs using the overkill method, exploding flashbulbs, slinky outfits, MTV-style editing, and snazzy sets. This is not always a bad thing—particularly when it comes to hiding Gere's two left feet. *Chicago* was nominated in thirteen Oscar categories and won six, including best picture; it was the first musical to do so since 1968's *Oliver!*

Historically Speaking

On this day in 1924, Roxie Hart inspiration Beulah May Annan killed her lover, claiming they both reached for the gun.

The Trial

YEAR RELEASED: 1962
DIRECTOR: Orson Welles
WHO'S IN IT: Anthony Perkins, Jeanne Moreau, Orson Welles

"To be in chains is sometimes safer than to be free."

Josef K. (Anthony Perkins) wakes up to find some curious, dark-suited men searching his room, asking oblique and vaguely accusatory questions. He will be arrested and tried but never told what his crime is. Everybody he's brought before seems sure of Josef's guilt, though—if he wasn't, why would he keep digging himself further into a hole with every stuttered question? Even the mysteriously powerful Advocate (Orson Welles) who takes Josef's case seems helpless before the power of the blind and baffling law.

In adapting Franz Kafka's novel, director Welles took liberties with the plot, particularly in the ending, which feels more comic absurdist (the executioners hurl dynamite at Josef, who laughs) than the book's bleak conclusion (Josef, stabbed in the heart by his executioner, has the final words: "Like a dog"). But the alienated spirit of his film remains resolutely true to that of the book, an awesome achievement given the prickly and untranslatable nature of Kafka's works.

Welles sets the minutely budgeted film in a generalized Euro-nowhere of office towers and empty lots, pulling off some stunning imagery, particularly those scenes shot in the cavernous Gare d'Orsay, a then-abandoned train station in Paris. Though it disappeared quickly from theaters and is still hard to find today, Welles once called this his best film. He may be right.

Auteur, Auteur

Fellow director Henry Jaglom said that Orson Welles believed *The Trial* was his most autobiographical film. "He and I shared this recurring dream of being in jail and not knowing why," Jaglom said. "He said the difference between us was that in his dream he never got out."

What Ever Happened to Baby Jane?

 LOL!

YEAR RELEASED: 1962
DIRECTOR: Robert Aldrich
WHO'S IN IT: Bette Davis, Joan Crawford

"But you are, Blanche, you are in that chair!"

Without this film, drag queens might have been stuck with only Judy Garland for inspiration. Robert Aldrich's Grand Guignol–type horror-comedy is a nasty piece of work, with *grandes dames* Joan Crawford and Bette Davis going at each other with hysterical abandon like some John Waters adaptation of *Grey Gardens*. The film's view of humanity is low, and the laughs are mostly of shock or incredulity, but that doesn't mean it isn't a treat.

Baby Jane Hudson was a spoiled Shirley Temple type back in the vaudeville days whose popularity wilted as her older sister Blanche's star rose. A mysterious car accident left Blanche crippled and blaming Jane. In the present, wheelchair-bound Blanche (Crawford) is stuck being waited on by an embittered Jane (Davis, the image of malevolence), who takes out her frustrations on Blanche. As Jane's mania increases, she starts cutting Blanche off from the world.

Aldrich revels in grotesquerie and black humor, much of it revolving around *Sunset Boulevard*'s Norma Desmond–like dreamworld that Jane inhabits. His actresses rise to the occasion, with Davis in particular camping it up like this was her final performance. Crawford draws from the same well of grand dignity that served her so well in *Mildred Pierce* (1945). Whether or not one believes the gossip about on-set brawling between the divas, there's no mistaking their characters' simmering, locked-room enmity: this is war.

And the Winner Is . . .

Bette Davis was nominated for the best actress Oscar for *What Ever Happened to Baby Jane?* but Joan Crawford wasn't. Crawford still managed to get onstage, accepting Anne Bancroft's Oscar for her role in *The Miracle Worker* because she was unable to attend the award show.

April 6

Beyond the Gates

YEAR RELEASED: 2005
DIRECTOR: Michael Caton-Jones
WHO'S IN IT: John Hurt, Hugh Dancy, Claire-Hope Ashitey

"Over here, they're just dead Africans."

Coming unfortunately just a year after Terry George's well-meaning but dramatically inert *Hotel Rwanda* (2004), Michael Caton-Jones's film was almost entirely overlooked. It's not just far superior to George's film; it's one of the most searing, unforgettable films ever made about evil in the modern world.

Hugh Dancy plays Joe Connor, an idealistic young Brit working in a church-run school in Kigali, Rwanda. John Hurt is Fr. Christopher, the kind church priest and spiritual heart of the institution. The story stays mostly within the school, so that when the majority Hutu ethnic group begin the massacres of the minority Tutsis on April 6, 1994, viewers have as little information as the refugees huddled inside. Joe and Christopher make the school into a safe zone for panicked Tutsis, while outside the gates, a gang of Hutus gathers, machetes at the ready. The school has only the thin protection of Belgian UN peacekeepers under strict orders *not* to use force. At one point their commander informs Christopher that his men are going to shoot the dogs outside the gates feeding on dead bodies—this (apparently true) moment both encapsulates the world's feeble nonresponse and gives the film its name outside the United States: *Shooting Dogs*.

While it's impossible for a film to put a truly human face on a tragedy, Caton-Jones's brave and unmissable film comes close.

Production Notes

On this day in 1994, President Habyarimana of Rwanda was killed, marking the beginning of the genocide. Unlike *Hotel Rwanda*, which was filmed in South Africa, *Beyond the Gates* was shot in Kigali, using many extras and crew who had lost family and friends in the genocide. Many of them can be seen in the film's closing credits.

April 7

Midnight Cowboy

YEAR RELEASED: 1969
DIRECTOR: John Schlesinger
WHO'S IN IT: Jon Voight, Dustin Hoffman

"You're beginning to smell and for a stud in New York, that's a handicap."

Joe Buck's stated career goal, once he kicks the dust of his small Texas town from his boots, is to go to New York City and make a living as a "stud," thinking that it'll be easy since the city's men are apparently all limp-wristed creampuffs. To the surprise of nobody save Joe, reality proves altogether different. What's surprising is that you actually care what happens to a character this ridiculous.

The sole reason you care is Jon Voight's naive, chastened take on Joe, creating one of his best career performances (the other being *Deliverance*). Director John Schlesinger matches him with another actor coming into his prime, Dustin Hoffman (killing off his college-boy image from *The Graduate*) playing the sickly hustler, Ratso Rizzo, who takes Joe under his lame wing.

At the time the film came out, much of the noise swirling around it had to do with the controversy of its sleazily mercantile sexuality. Hollywood preferred its hookers to be pretty girls whose jobs were left undetailed (*Breakfast at Tiffany's*), not men trolling Times Square for other men.

The film's grime still registers as a portrait of a Dickensian New York where the only social safety net seems to be death. Schlesinger's take on the material can be bludgeoning at times, but even he can't undo the power of the film's wholly unlikely friendship. The image of Joe and Ratso riding the bus together down to Florida, Joe worrying over his dangerously ill friend, is an indelible moment in American film.

And the Winner Is . . .
On April 7, 1970, *Midnight Cowboy* became the first X-rated movie to win the Oscar for best picture.

Silent Running

YEAR RELEASED: 1972
DIRECTOR: Douglas Trumbull
WHO'S IN IT: Bruce Dern, Cliff Potts, Ron Rifkin, Jesse Vint

"You don't think it's time somebody had a dream again?"

In this film, a four-man crew tries to keep from going batty onboard the futuristic space freighter *Valley Forge*. Three of them can't wait to get back to Earth. Doing less well is Lowell (Bruce Dern), who cares for the giant greenhouse domes that are the ship's primary cargo. Although all natural life has died out on Earth, Lowell seems the only one bothered by this. He nurses his plants and eats their fruits (disdained by the others, who prefer their synthetic grub).

Then he's ordered to jettison their greenhouse domes and destroy them with nukes. This is good news to most of the crew except Lowell. Pretty soon it's just Lowell, a couple of helpful droids, and his beloved plants floating among the stars.

Douglas Trumbull made his feature debut with this quiet morality tale. Already having been responsible for the special effects in *2001: A Space Odyssey* (and later *Blade Runner*), Trumbull puts on a convincing visual show, but doesn't always have the best feel for his actors or music (Joan Baez contributed some syrupy tunes to the soundtrack). Dern ably takes up the slack, vividly creating a man who might have the light of a fanatic in his eyes but isn't necessarily *wrong*. What we know of Earth, where poverty has been erased but so has nature, is chilling enough that Lowell's actions make a certain sense. There's a reason his first name is Freeman.

Production Notes

In *2001*, Douglas Trumbull included corporate logos on his space-age designs. He does the same thing in *Silent Running*, where containers in the *Valley Forge*'s cargo hold bear the stamp of Coca-Cola and Dow.

The Searchers

YEAR RELEASED: 1956
DIRECTOR: John Ford
WHO'S IN IT: John Wayne, Natalie Wood, Jeffrey Hunter, Henry Brandon

"Do you know what Ethan will do if he has a chance? He'll put a bullet in her brain."

John Wayne stands framed in a cabin's dark doorway, one arm clasping the other in a hint at weakness. Everyone else has gone inside, to family and life. But still he stands outside. After a moment, he turns and walks away, no place for him in this world after completing the mission that only he would have bothered to finish. He doesn't say anything, which is probably for the best—Wayne might have spoiled it.

Wayne is Ethan Edwards, a Confederate soldier returned from the war to his brother's family just in time for an Indian raid that leaves everyone dead except his niece Debbie (Natalie Wood), who was stolen by an Indian named Scar (Henry Brandon). Ethan spends years chasing Debbie, though it's not clear whether he's doing so because of love, fear of mixed-race relationships (remember his Confederate service), or because he cannot live without a cause.

The film is probably John Ford's greatest, the one that obsessed a generation of movie-school brats. It's Ethan's story that provokes this obsession—his twinned sense of mission and rage, the uncertainty over what he will *do* once he finds Debbie. If the film allowed the viewer to believe that Ethan's search could ever end, one viewing would be enough. But because Ford leaves Ethan stranded between worlds and forever searching, that unresolved tension leads many fans to watch it time and again.

In Homage

Stuart Byron's 1979 article "The Searchers: Cult Movie of the New Hollywood" discusses how *The Searchers* influenced younger directors, from Martin Scorsese to John Milius to George Lucas. Steven Spielberg told Lucas he watched the film twice just while shooting *Close Encounters of the Third Kind*.

The Seventh Seal

🌐 👤 🎭

YEAR RELEASED: 1957
DIRECTOR: Ingmar Bergman
WHO'S IN IT: Max von Sydow, Gunnar Björnstrand, Bengt Ekerot

"I am Death."

Antonius Block (Max von Sydow, born on this day in 1929) is a knight just returned from the Crusades, where he sees black-robed Death (Bengt Ekerot) dispassionately approaching. Block makes him a deal—let's play chess, and if I win, I can keep living.

After apparently defeating Death, Block and his squire Jöns (Gunnar Björnstrand) ride across the plague-ravaged countryside, seeing one discomfiting scene after another: An accused witch is burned at the stake for allegedly bringing the plague. A former seminarian plunders a corpse and announces to a woman who saw him that he must kill her now and there is no God to stop it. A line of flagellants pass by, chanting mournfully. All the while, Block and the squire Jöns's bleak journey is contrasted with the simple domesticated joy of a small family of traveling performers.

Ingmar Bergman's most famous film is also his most overanalyzed. From the opening invocation of the Book of Revelations to the layered-on symbolism and running debate over the existence of God, it's easy to see why—there's enough here for a thousand term papers. It is also a brilliant and thought-provoking film whose reputation for grave self-importance should simply be ignored. Yes, Bergman was tackling the largest of themes here, but its approach is very plainspoken and Nordic. That's why when Block sees Death, he doesn't scream and run, but instead makes a simple offer. Matters of life and death needn't always be so dramatic.

In Homage

The Seventh Seal's chess scene was used as a running gag in *Bill & Ted's Bogus Journey* (1991), in which Death plays Bill and Ted several games, including Clue, Twister, and Battleship.

One False Move

YEAR RELEASED: 1992
DIRECTOR: Carl Franklin
WHO'S IN IT: Bill Paxton, Cynda Williams, Billy Bob Thornton, Michael Beach

"He watches television. I read nonfiction."

Former actor Carl Franklin's blistering directorial debut is a modern-day noir that packs an emotional wallop. Working from a script by Billy Bob Thornton and Tom Epperson, Franklin crafts a suspenseful film in which the two groups of players don't even meet until nearly the end. A trio of murderers fleeing Los Angeles are a triangulated nexus of violent dysfunction: Ray Malcolm (Thornton), a murder-prone redneck; Pluto (Michael Beach), a bespectacled type with the air of a professorial assassin; and Fantasia (Cynda Williams), Ray's girlfriend. Franklin—one of the most exciting of the new wave of African American directors who hit the scene in the early-1990s—neatly handles some mostly unspoken racial subtext in the trio, quietly subverting audience expectations.

The detectives hunting the trio are straight from central casting, so it's a small-town Arkansas sheriff, Dale "Hurricane" Dixon (Bill Paxton, hopelessly gung-ho), assisting them who almost walks away with the picture. Hurricane is more overgrown kid than lawmaker, which his patient, worried wife tries to impress on the detectives he's showing off to. By the time that Ray, Pluto, and Fantasia hit Star City, a film that began in brutal murder has become more interested in the subtle interplay of race and friendship than stolen drugs or murders. The final scene is one of the most touching in modern American film.

Lost and Found

As acclaimed as it was, *One False Move* almost didn't even make it to theaters. Gene Siskel and Roger Ebert, along with other critics, beat the drum for the film so insistently that it was rescued from straight-to-video oblivion.

The General

LOL! 👫

YEAR RELEASED: 1927
DIRECTORS: Buster Keaton, Clyde Bruckman
WHO'S IN IT: Buster Keaton, Marion Mack

"If you lose this war, don't blame me."

Marietta, Georgia, 1861. Train engineer Johnny Gray (Buster Keaton) is smitten with local beauty Annabelle Lee (Marion Mack). He seems to be making progress, but then war breaks out and she pointedly wonders why he hasn't enlisted. Gray tries to join up but is rebuffed since his job is considered too strategically important. A year later, Gray is driving his trusty engine, *The General*, near the front lines. It's a fortuitous location because not only will it give him a chance to foil some dastardly Union spies but also save his beloved Annabelle.

Keaton's hangdog expression maintains an assumption that the entire universe is against him. This was never more true than in this inventive silent comedy, wherein a cabal of enemy soldiers, literal loose cannons, and errant trains—all apparently inspired by a real Civil War incident dated April 12, 1862, and known as the Great Locomotive Chase—consistently refuse to do his bidding. This is a silent film of insanely escalating crises, all handled at the last possible second by Gray's inventiveness and Keaton's own mix of balletic grace and vaudeville cluelessness. It's never easy, however. Gray may be able to leap onto a train and knock three soldiers off it in mere seconds like a kung fu master, but at the end, when he's finally in uniform and wants to kiss Annabelle, those soldiers he has to salute just won't stop marching past and interrupting. That universe never lets Keaton catch a break.

Everyone's a Critic

The General was viciously reviewed at the time of its release, and the public stayed away in droves. After a few decades, however, many critics believed it Keaton's greatest work.

On the Town

YEAR RELEASED: 1949
DIRECTORS: Stanley Donen, Gene Kelly
WHO'S IN IT: Gene Kelly, Frank Sinatra, Jules Munshin

"Somewhere in the world there's a right girl for every boy."

The first collaboration between the formidible directing duet of Stanley Donen and Gene Kelly, and music/writing team of Adolph Green and Betty Comden, this is a rainy-day sort of musical. As in, watch it on a sad and rainy day. If this film doesn't cheer you up, seek help.

It doesn't waste time getting down to business. Three sailors have arrived in New York and they've got one full day to see the town before reporting back to the boat the next morning. There's free-wheeling Gabey (Gene Kelly), nerdy over-planner Chip (Frank Sinatra), and up-for-anything Ozzie (Jules Munshin). They hit the ground singing and then dash for Manhattan as though somebody just announced drinks were on the house. Each sailor ends up making a play for a particular gal they meet while on the town (Gabey and Ozzie being easily dame-distracted, while Chip wants to see the sights), which is what occupies the bulk of the film.

As simple as the story seems, like *Singin' in the Rain*, this is a surprisingly modern work. First, there's the case of the women, who for once get treated with utter respect, and also seem to outclass the men in every way. There is also the fact of Donen and Kelly shooting a musical on location in a bustling city, one of the first times this was ever attempted. Even today, directors prefer to keep their musicals safely on a sound stage, where everything can be managed. Donen and Kelly just let their film rip on the busy New York streets with an energy that can barely be contained.

McCabe & Mrs. Miller

YEAR RELEASED: 1971
DIRECTOR: Robert Altman
WHO'S IN IT: Warren Beatty, Julie Christie

"That man? That man never killed anybody."

This film is a Robert Altman Western, though such a thing seems impossible. As John McCabe, the man in the black derby hat always looking to buy all the boys in the room a drink, Warren Beatty seems initially like the most important man for many miles around. But when Constance Miller shows up, it becomes clear that he knows less than nothing. Miller is Julie Christie under a mop of frizzy hair, wielding a madam's sharp Cockney accent that knifes through all the half-drunk frontier mutter and mumble. Of course, they fall in love, just in time for him to make a very bad decision when a large mining concern makes him an offer he shouldn't refuse.

Shot in British Columbia by Vilmos Zsigmond as a series of beautiful weather-beaten tableaux, the film lets itself be taken over first by the amazing scenery and second by the quiet longing that springs up between McCabe and his new business partner. A number of plaintive Leonard Cohen songs do a good job of holding the film together in its muddled early stretches, where Altman's penchant for overlapping dialogue goes into overdrive.

Sharing a theme of relentless pursuit with the film's rough contemporary *Butch Cassidy and the Sundance Kid*, the end is a kind of waking dream. In it, the increasingly luckless McCabe is chased by mining company mercenaries amid pillowy hills of soft snow. Christie was nominated for an Academy Award, the film's only nomination.

Production Notes

The particularly worn-out look of the film stock in *McCabe & Mrs. Miller* was created by process known as "flashing and fogging" that simulated the look of an old photograph.

Superbad

 LOL!

YEAR RELEASED: 2007
DIRECTOR: Greg Mottola
WHO'S IN IT: Michael Cera, Jonah Hill, Christopher Mintz-Plasse

"I'm sorry that the Coen brothers don't direct the kind of porn I like."

The premise really couldn't be worse. Seth (Jonah Hill) and Evan (Michael Cera) are horny high-school seniors about to graduate, still virgins. By divine Providence they are invited to a party with girls who might actually talk to them. One road-block: dispatched to buy liquor for the party, Seth and Evan rely on their even geekier friend Fogell (Christopher Mintz-Plasse), who has a fake ID. Fogell gets caught in a robbery and spends the night driving around with the world's least responsible cops. This leaves Seth and Evan to find other means of getting booze, which will require ingenuity and a selective morality.

The film is nonstop hormonal overdrive, with Hill playing the pudgy, curly-haired id, his mood accelerating into higher levels of barking hysteria as his chances for potential deflowering fade. Cera perfected his trademark fey elfin neuroticism here, while Mintz-Plasse's nasally nerd is unleashed upon the suburban streets with a cop car, too many beers, a loaded pistol, and no worries.

As the high point of the Judd Apatow–produced comedy boom of the mid- to late 2000s, *Superbad* creates something gleeful and fresh from an idea more appropriate for some standard-issue 1980s teen titillation comedy.

Director Greg Mottola brings it all together with a keen sense of character and a less sentimental mood than that which afflicts Apatow's bigger films like *Knocked Up*. There is no room here for cheap laughs or crude ogling (despite the X-rated talk, the sensibility is quite caring). Amidst all the vomiting, gunfire, chase scenes, and binge drinking emerges a sweet film about friendship. And Van Halen.

Three Times

YEAR RELEASED: 2005
DIRECTOR: Hou Hsiao-hsien
WHO'S IN IT: Shu Qi, Chang Chen

"When your heart's on fire, you must realize, smoke gets in your eyes."

This stately paced triptych features the same two actors (Shu Qi and Chang Chen) falling in and out of love in three different time periods. The first story takes place in a small-town pool hall in 1966, where a boy falls for a girl just as he's about to leave for the army; he gives chase months later when he returns to find she's moved. This segment's poppy romance is sharply contrasted with the next, set at a brothel in 1911 during Japanese occupation. Here the two play out a mannered, silent film–style drama where a courtesan falls in love with a married man and suffers mightily for it. In the angry, discontented last segment, set in 2005, the unhappy couple are modern Taipei youths, disaffected and confused about love, life, and everything else. It's dysfunctional romance, modern-style, with plenty of talking but no listening.

Hou's film would be worth watching just for the gorgeous visuals, which he composes with impressionistic perfection. But his impressionism also extends to the film's emotions, particularly in the first story where the background of youthful exhilaration and wall-to-wall American pop music (the Platters' "Smoke Gets in Your Eyes" gets as heavy rotation as "California Dreamin'" did in *Chungking Express*). By putting the same actors through three stories, Hou presents three different ways to love, and to lose, all uniquely beautiful.

> **And the Winner Is . . .**
> *Three Times* was nominated for a Palme d'Or at the Cannes Film Festival, Hou Hsiao-hsien's sixth unsuccessful nomination in that category.

High Fidelity

YEAR RELEASED: 2000
DIRECTOR: Stephen Frears
WHO'S IN IT: John Cusack, Iben Hjejle, Jack Black, Todd Louiso

"What came first? The music or the misery?"

Star, producer, and cowriter John Cusack made this adaptation of Nick Hornby's London-set novel a clear labor of love. The film mines its immature male protagonists' pop-culture obsessions for good-natured laughs while also pinpointing said obsessions as the primary cause of their arrested adolescence. As Laura (Iben Hjejle, spryly intelligent), tells her newly ex-boyfriend Rob (Cusack), "You haven't changed so much as a pair of socks since I've met you." In a fit of teenage-worthy vanity, Rob lists his five worst breakups (for this culture vulture, it's all about the list), telling Laura she'd be lucky to break into the top ten. Deep down, he knows she's the best he'll ever have, but it'll take him most of the film to realize that.

Rob introduces viewers to his legacy of relationship self-destruction, as well as his world of record geekery. Providing a sounding board for Rob's rage are his employees, a matched pair of vinyl freaks, who either blink nervously at human interaction like Dick (Todd Louiso, playing a gentle, sweet soul who looks like a sad android) or drop napalm on differing opinions like Barry (Jack Black, before he became, well, *Jack Black*). Tim Robbins pops by as a terrifying amalgamation of New Age odiousness, and Bruce Springsteen offers Rob wisdom and a few bluesy chords.

The film tweaks its grungy analog subculture lightly, adeptly letting its characters' misery heighten the comedy, not drag it down. Rob's mental catalog of obscure B-sides may have kept him from appreciating his lady, but it definitely prepared him, at least at first, for what happened when she bolted.

Beauty and the Beast

🌐 🏰 👤 👪

YEAR RELEASED: 1946
DIRECTOR: Jean Cocteau
WHO'S IN IT: Josette Day, Jean Marais

"The Beast will devour them all. And we'll marry princes!"

This is the first and last word in fairy-tale film. In a small French town, a family has fallen on hard times. The father tries to pay off debts, and his daughter Belle (Josette Day, brightly burnished) works to keep up the house, even while her sisters act as though they're still rich.

Riding through the forest one dark and foggy night, the father enters an old castle, where he sees living arms holding chandeliers from walls and marble busts whose eyes follow him. In the garden, he picks a rose for Belle. An enraged man-sized beast (Jean Marais) in nobleman's clothing appears. He allows the father to leave, but only if he returns soon. The father falls sick, and Belle volunteers to be the Beast's hostage. Once she's a prisoner in the Beast's magic kingdom, where the mirrors answer questions and jewels can be conjured out of the air, Belle starts to care for the solicitous Beast.

This is what happens when a surrealist films a children's story. The fog is thick and luxurious, the special effects both fantastical and straightforward (when Belle cries over her father's sickbed, the tears come out as diamonds), and a romantic danger is darkly layered over it all. It might not have the songs of Disney's 1991 version, but there is a magical mood here few filmmakers would ever dare to attempt to match.

Production Notes

The months it took to shoot *Beauty and the Beast* were agony for Jean Cocteau, who suffered from a painful skin condition that required penicillin several times a day and reportedly left him feeling as repulsive as his Beast.

The Producers

YEAR RELEASED: 1968
DIRECTOR: Mel Brooks
WHO'S IN IT: Gene Wilder, Zero Mostel

"You have exactly ten seconds to change that look of disgusting pity into one of enormous respect."

Zero Mostel plays scummy producer Max Bialystock, who wheedles money out of little old ladies and uses it to put on some of the worst rubbish ever to hit Broadway. Leo Bloom (Gene Wilder, as frantic as Mostel is exuberant) is Max's new accountant. When Leo shows Max that he raised more for his last show than it cost to put on, Max hits on a scheme: he'll find the worst play ever written, convince his little old ladies to put up a bank vault's worth for it, and once the flop flops, he'll abscond to Rio.

While writer/director Mel Brooks gets a lot of mileage out of Mostel and Wilder's shtick, the film hits a true giggling pinnacle of tastelessness once Max finds the perfect play: "Springtime for Hitler: A Gay Romp with Adolf and Eva at Berchtesgaden." When the musical—equal parts Nuremberg Rally and Vegas floorshow—opens, the audience decides it's a gag, guaranteeing a hit.

Decades' worth of transgressive comedy from *South Park* to Sarah Silverman have dulled some of the film's shock value, but it hasn't taken the edge off of Brooks's tightly wound screenplay (missing the windbag digressions of many of his later films) or Wilder and Mostel's unhinged performances. And the songs are still catchy, and found their way into a musical that opened on Broadway on April 19, 2001.

Auteur, Auteur

Roger Ebert was once in an elevator with Mel Brooks and wife Anne Bancroft when a woman got on and told Brooks that his film was "vulgar." "Lady," Brooks smiled, "it rose below vulgarity."

Close Encounters of the Third Kind

👽 👪

YEAR RELEASED: 1977
DIRECTOR: Steven Spielberg
WHO'S IN IT: Richard Dreyfuss, François Truffaut, Teri Garr

"These planes were reported missing in 1945."

In this lustrous, joyful epic of discovery, a small child wakes up to find that all his toys have come to life. Going to the door, he sees a warm rush of golden light. As his mother gives chase, he disappears, laughing. Roy Neary (Richard Dreyfuss) spots several UFOs one dark night and tries to chase after them; afterward he's afflicted with strange dreams that manifest in a waking compulsion to create a model tower out of every material at hand (mashed potatoes, anything).

Meanwhile, people around the world are having strange experiences of their own. Planes appear that went missing in the Bermuda Triangle decades earlier. A ship materializes in the Gobi Desert. French scientist Claude Lacombe (François Truffaut) tries to link these incidents while Neary's visions are becoming more urgent and drawing him to Devil's Tower in the Black Hills.

It would be easy to dismiss this film as Spielberg nonsense of the most senti-mental kind. And while his vision here is certainly of the optimistic and childlike variety, it's a sentiment that's earned. The sense of daring and epic, oversized won-der that cascades through nearly every frame of this beautifully photographed film (Vilmos Zsigmond, doing wonders yet again), is true to its adventurous optimism from start to finish.

None other than Ray Bradbury called it the greatest science-fiction film ever made. Who are we to argue?

Production Notes

The working title for *Close Encounters of the Third Kind* was *Watch the Skies,* which was the last line of the 1951 sci-fi classic *The Thing from Another World.*

April 21

Short Cuts

YEAR RELEASED: 1993
DIRECTOR: Robert Altman
WHO'S IN IT: Andie MacDowell, Fred Ward, Tim Robbins, Matthew Modine, Tom Waits, Lily Tomlin

"How many clowns can you fit in that car?"

After the surprise success of his murderous star-studded 1992 Hollywood satire *The Player* reminded the industry that he was still a vital filmmaker, Robert Altman had a golden get-out-of-jail-free card. He wisely chose to use it on this vast, sprawling anthology story that threw several Raymond Carver short stories into a Southern California blender of dysfunction and natural disaster.

Starting with a threatening storm of helicopters buzzing over Los Angeles spraying for fruit flies and ending with an earthquake, the film features nearly two dozen characters playing out tangled, interlinked subplots where the predominant emotions are guilt and fear. Moral choices must be made, from the fishermen who discover a dead body but aren't sure they want to cut their trip short to report it, to the woman who accidentally hits a small boy with her car and sends him on his way without telling anybody; weakness prevails.

Something does get lost in the transition from Carver's working-class, small-town East Coast settings to this brown and smoggy city, but Altman makes the stories his own, bringing a sharper edge and a viewpoint that's both funnier and less sympathetic. It was his first film since *Nashville* (1975) to truly show off his gift for creating an ensemble epic. Although none of Altman's later films (with the possible exception of 2001's *Gosford Park*) would really come close to topping it, this was the film that made the whole last stretch of his career possible.

April 22

Duel

🔍

YEAR RELEASED: 1971
DIRECTOR: Steven Spielberg
WHO'S IN IT: Dennis Weaver

"Talk about pollution."

When Steven Spielberg's secretary discovered Richard Matheson's short story "Duel" in *Playboy*, Spielberg was a steadily working TV director (*Columbo*). The story would prove a perfect marriage of material and filmmaker. Though the Matheson-scripted film was produced for American TV, it made waves when it played in Europe and showed that Spielberg could easily graduate to the big screen. (*Duel* wouldn't get a true theatrical release until this day in 1983.) Four years later, he would make *Jaws*.

A man named Mann (Dennis Weaver) starts a long drive through the hot, open California countryside. It all goes fine until he gets stuck behind a slow-moving truck. Sick of all the black exhaust and delay, Mann accelerates around the truck, only to find it then tailing him with a strange fury. Unable to understand what he's done wrong, Mann keeps trying to escape the trucker, who pursues him inexorably across the desert.

Quickly and cheaply shot, Spielberg's film is a tightly compacted exercise in simple tension, with hardly any speaking parts and a villain who's never fully visible. Spielberg employs just enough trick shots and odd angles to keep things off-balance without drawing undue attention to them. While Matheson had deeper topics in mind—there's a substrata of antimodernist rage here, with the exhaust-belching truck and a befouled landscape—Spielberg was simply pitting one man against an implacable foe and seeing who would come out on top.

Everyone's a Critic

In Douglas Brode's book on Steven Spielberg, he writes about the strange scene at the 1973 Taormina Film Festival in Italy, where critics stormed out of a press conference after the director disagreed with their classification of *Duel* as Marxist class satire.

Hamlet

YEAR RELEASED: 2000
DIRECTOR: Michael Almereyda
WHO'S IN IT: Ethan Hawke, Kyle MacLachlan, Liev Schreiber, Bill Murray

"Time is out of joint."

Michael Almereyda went for the jugular when paring down the Bard's text to make his sleek, modern-dress *Hamlet*. It was released four years after Kenneth Branagh's full-text, four-hour opus and clocks in under two hours, but feels like less. Ethan Hawke plays the scion of the family-run, Manhattan-based Denmark Corporation who comes home from college to find his father dead and his mother shacking up with Claudius, the guy Hamlet thinks killed him.

The clipped speed of Almereyda's film has less to do with the modern setting than with his cast and script. Hawke, a onetime mopey heartthrob who was just coming into his own, fully embodies the prince's tragic indecision and murderous self-obsession. Kyle MacLachlan and Liev Schreiber are the definition of stone-cold villainy as, respectively, Claudius and Laertes. More impressively, Bill Murray does a fascinating, wearied take on Polonius's patient counsel to Hamlet ("neither a borrower nor a lender be"). The infamously audacious setting of Hamlet's "To be or not to be" soliloquy in a Blockbuster Video store works fantastically, and not just as a sight gag.

Because of its modernist hipster vibe, Almereyda's *Hamlet* was frequently compared to Baz Luhrmann's *Romeo + Juliet* (1996). Luhrmann's film—a teen-pop variation starring Leonardo DiCaprio and Claire Danes—was by far more successful at the box office. It was also, however, a victim of its own coolness and hasn't aged nearly as well as Almereyda's.

Casting Call

Ethan Hawke was twenty-nine years old when he played Hamlet, the first time an actor that young had played him onscreen. Among earlier film Hamlets, Mel Gibson was thirty-four, Kenneth Branagh thirty-six, and Laurence Olivier forty-one.

The Apartment

YEAR RELEASED: 1960
DIRECTOR: Billy Wilder
WHO'S IN IT: Jack Lemmon, Fred MacMurray, Shirley MacLaine

"That's the way it crumbles, cookie-wise."

At first you see C. C. Baxter (Jack Lemmon) working late on the nineteenth floor of the Consolidated Life Insurance tower, and he appears to be a dutiful drone. Conscientious employee that he might be, there's another reason he lingers at his desk long after everyone else has vacated theirs. He's a bachelor, you see, and some of the company's married executives have taken to using his apartment as a hot-sheet hotel room for after-work romps with their secretarial-pool girlfriends. They string Baxter along with the promise of eventual promotion. While he is a bit put out by all the trouble, it only really bothers him when Mr. Sheldrake (Fred Mac-Murray) starts bringing Fran Kubelik (Shirley MacLaine), the pixie-bright elevator operator Baxter has an eye on. This is the story of how a schlemiel, a schnook, tries to become a real mensch.

Billy Wilder's bittersweet film is premised on a gimmick, but it never interferes with the story, mostly due to his cast. MacMurray deploys the same icy chill that Wilder used to such strong effect in *Double Indemnity* (1944), while MacLaine's take on a bad-luck girl trying to keep her chin up ("When you're in love with a married man, you shouldn't wear mascara") is simply irresistible. Lemmon carries the picture, though, investing even the most prosaic scenes (making phone calls, cooking dinner) with a fussy and birdlike preciseness that rivets the eye; he's a delicate clown.

And the Winner Is . . .
Despite being an uncharacteristically dark (for the time) romantic comedy, *The Apartment* was a huge hit with the public and won five Oscars, including one for the tart screenplay.

Gallipoli

YEAR RELEASED: 1981
DIRECTOR: Peter Weir
WHO'S IN IT: Mel Gibson, Mark Lee

"They're being cut down before they can get five yards!"

The cinematic history of the First World War has been limited, with films like *Grand Illusion* (1937) and *All Quiet on the Western Front* (1930) making it seem the war was confined to the trenches of France. Then came Peter Weir's film about the disastrous Dardanelles campaign (which begain on April 25, 1915), where thousands of Anzac (Australian and New Zealander) troops were hurled against Turkish machine guns in an attempt to force Germany and Austria's ally out of the war. It didn't work, and those nations never forgot, even if much of the rest of the world did.

Some five years in the making, Weir's first true epic opens in the Australian outback as a story of male bonding and sprinting. Two young men, upstanding Archy Hamilton (Mark Lee) and roguish Frank Dunne (Mel Gibson), become friends, bonding over their love of running. They join up, as the war has just started and the news about what's really going on hasn't filtered back yet. Archy ends up in the cavalry, Frank in the infantry. Once on the Gallipoli peninsula in the Dardanelles, Anzac bravery proves no match for British strategic ineptitude.

This film gave Weir his passport to Hollywood for several reasons. The warm friendship he establishes between Archy and Frank feels completely organic, and he delivers the battle scenes with a searing sense of horror and waste. Stitched into the main story line are gracefully handled parallels between the men's youthful sprinting in the outback and the doomed soldiers' sprints out of the trenches into certain death. The final-freeze frame has all the power of Michaelangelo's *Pietà*.

Almost Famous

YEAR RELEASED: 2000
DIRECTOR: Cameron Crowe
WHO'S IN IT: Patrick Fugit, Kate Hudson, Frances McDormand, Philip Seymour Hoffman

"The only true currency in this bankrupt world is what we share with someone else when we're uncool."

One of the most transcendent films ever made about writing and rock 'n' roll is also partially about having your dreams come true and getting your heart broken at right around the same time.

Writer/director Cameron Crowe spent part of his adolescence not wasting time in high school like the rest of us but working for *Rolling Stone* magazine (which first published him in its April 26, 1973, issue). His deeply autobiographical—in spirit, if not always in event—screenplay for *Almost Famous* follows William Miller (Patrick Fugit), a prematurely grown-up fifteen-year-old who talks his mother (Frances McDormand, lovable *and* terrifying), circa 1973, into letting him go on the road with the up-and-coming band Stillwater. He convinces *Rolling Stone* to publish his story, figuring they don't need to know he's in high school. On the road, he falls in love with Penny Lane (Kate Hudson, never again this luminous), one of Stillwater's sprite-like "band aids" (don't call them groupies), and learns how to be a writer. Philip Seymour Hoffman, playing rock journalist Lester Bangs, appears as the funny, wise, profane soul of the film. Steven Spielberg, still running DreamWorks when the film was made, supposedly told Crowe to shoot every page of the script. You'll understand why.

Lost and Found

"The Bootleg Cut" of *Almost Famous* has an extra forty minutes of material. Some of the added details from the tour are worthwhile but overall it's a little flabby. Stick with the original version; it's love incarnate.

8½

YEAR RELEASED: 1963
DIRECTOR: Federico Fellini
WHO'S IN IT: Marcello Mastroianni, Claudia Cardinale, Anouk Aimée, Sandra Milo

"That's how the film ends?"

Guido Anselmi (Marcello Mastroianni) is a famous director getting ready to shoot a new film. Casting is underway, the sets are being built, and expectations are stratospheric. The only problem: he doesn't have any idea what the film is about.

Like most artists, what Guido does best of all is avoid working. This isn't a film about making film; it's about avoidance strategies and delaying tactics. In between lying to his wife Luisa (Anouk Aimée) and mistress (Sandra Milo), Guido tries to hide from the producers and press people who eternally ask those damnable questions about what his film is about. Even when he's finally dragged to a press conference on one of his gargantuan sets, Guido isn't sure what to say.

Although Federico Fellini layered this wandering but groundbreaking film with self-referential tics, even dressing his alter ego Mastroianni (floppy black hat, glasses) as himself, his point about creative stasis is near universal for artists. However, much of the grand, Cinema Italiano window-dressing around that theme—The bombshell women! The clothes! The dreams!—is strictly Fellini. He made it in the immediate aftermath of his international sensation *La Dolce Vita* (1961), whose fiery mix of sin and celebrity created such a demand for another great work from the Maestro that the dreamy abstractions of 8½ were all he could come up with. It was more than enough.

In Homage

8½ inspired the 1982 Tony-winning Broadway musical *Nine*, which was filmed in 2009 by Chicago director Rob Marshall with Daniel Day-Lewis in the Mastroianni role and Marion Cotillard, Penélope Cruz, and Nicole Kidman as the women in his life.

Who's Afraid of Virginia Woolf?

YEAR RELEASED: 1966
DIRECTOR: Mike Nichols
WHO'S IN IT: Richard Burton, Elizabeth Taylor, Sandy Dennis, George Segal

"If you existed, I'd divorce you."

Some of the movie posters read, "You are cordially invited to George and Martha's for an evening of fun and games." Those who had caught Edward Albee's cage match of a play on Broadway could chuckle knowingly, while everybody else (even if they'd heard the advance publicity and *thought* they knew what they were in for) was in for a surprise.

George (Richard Burton) and Martha (Elizabeth Taylor) are a long-married couple who see their union more as combat than cohabitation. On the night we join them (a gothic nighttime opening with full moon and wavering tree branches), they are coming back late from a party, bickering and drunk, when Martha drops the news that they're having guests. Once the couple (Sandy Dennis and George Segal) shows up, George and Martha's claws just get sharper, their verbal digs louder and nastier, as though they're determined to take down everyone with them. Burton is dry and pitch-perfect as the henpecked history professor who's never lived up to his promise, while Taylor plays the blowsy shrew with well-calibrated vulgarity. Gaspingly funny when not horrifyingly cruel (frequently both at the same time), it's a twelve-round bout of open wounds and petty victories, with ugly truths behind every mean-spirited jab.

This was Mike Nichols's first directing job, though you wouldn't know it. He tracks every up and down of George and Martha's match with unerring precision. Screenwriter Ernest Lehman (showing that taste for sour he exhibited a few years before in *The Sweet Smell of Success*) doesn't do much with Albee's play besides present it to the audience for their consideration, which is as it should be. For a whole generation that knows of Taylor and Burton only as gossip-trivia punchlines, this indecently entertaining film is the best proof of why they were once the biggest stars around.

Citizen Kane

YEAR RELEASED: 1941
DIRECTOR: Orson Welles
WHO'S IN IT: Orson Welles, Joseph Cotten

"I expect to lose a million dollars this year. I expect to lose a million dollars next year. You know, Mr. Thatcher, at the rate of a million dollars a year, I'll have to close this place in . . . sixty years."

Put aside all the noise about whether or not *Citizen Kane* is the greatest film ever made. It's simply a towering American drama, capturing the sweep of a great man's life with equal parts humor and pathos. After the death of news baron Charles Foster Kane (Orson Welles, layered in makeup), reporters gather to figure out the mystery of his last uttered word, "Rosebud." The story quickly coalesces around the reason for Kane's success: his newspapers.

Deciding to run a destitute New York newspaper on a whim, the wealthy Kane turns it into a full-bore tabloid extravaganza. As Kane's riches and waistline grow, he turns from precocious to arrogant, alienating amiable old cohorts like Jedediah Leland (Joseph Cotten, whose laid-back insolence outdoes even Welles's). He acquires a trophy wife, and starts believing his own propaganda. The bright-eyed upstart becomes the bloated mogul.

Gregg Toland's raw, theatrical cinematography still seems years ahead of its time, and all aspiring screenwriters should study the wry script. Only twenty-five years old when he made *Citizen Kane*, Welles would spend the rest of his life chasing the success of his first film. Watch it (again, if necessary) to see what an impossible task that must have been.

Historically Speaking

Media mogul William Randolph Hearst, whose powerful chain of newspapers epitomized "yellow," or tabloid, journalism around the turn of the century and is considered to be the inspiration for Charles Foster Kane, was born on this day in 1863.

Meet Me in St. Louis

YEAR RELEASED: 1944
DIRECTOR: Vincente Minnelli
WHO'S IN IT: Judy Garland, Margaret O'Brien

"The fair won't open for seven months, and that's all anybody ever sings about or talks about. I wish they would all meet at the fair and leave me alone!"

It starts in the sultry summer of 1903, still months away from the opening of the World's Fair (which took place on April 4, 1904), but it's all anybody can talk about. The Smith family's amiably grouchy patriarch announces that he's moving them all to New York at the end of the year. Tears well up, but he's father and what he says goes.

Though it sounds like a *horrible* idea for a musical, what follows is like a Technicolor fair in and of itself. Judy Garland (framed beautifully by the director she would marry) plays Esther, the second oldest of the four Smith girls, and she has a crush on the boy who just moved in next door, who seems oblivious to her. While the Hugh Martin and Ralph Blane numbers are mostly solid, a few would have fallen flat were Garland not the one singing them.

Vincente Minnelli stuns with a succession of well-staged songs, from the heady charm of "The Trolley Song" to the melancholy of "Have Yourself a Merry Little Christmas." He plays up the story's society cotillion aspect, filling the screen with frilly outfits, flirtations, and elegant dances, all lit by the nostalgia of a closing era. The film is one of bright candy colors and sweet melodies mixed with wistfulness.

Production Notes

Meet Me in St. Louis began as short stories Sally Benson wrote for the *New Yorker* about growing up in a large St. Louis family.

The Royal Tenenbaums

YEAR RELEASED: 2000
DIRECTOR: Wes Anderson
WHO'S IN IT: Gene Hackman, Anjelica Huston, Ben Stiller, Gwyneth Paltrow, Luke Wilson

"I think we're just gonna to have to be secretly in love with each other and leave it at that."

One of the freshest voices in American film comedy, Wes Anderson gets more out of a blank stare and beat of silence than many filmmakers can from a page of jokes. He knew when to let the silences lengthen and when to insert those spikes of strangeness.

Anderson's third film shows him exploring the great extended-family comedy, with a tale that might have leapt from a lost J. D. Salinger short story. The Tenenbaums, archaeologist Etheline (Anjelica Huston) and rogue lawyer Royal (Gene Hackman), raised three child prodigies who all later crashed and burned. There is Chas the businessman (Ben Stiller), Margot the playwright (Gwyneth Paltrow), and Richie the tennis pro (Luke Wilson). Fluttering around the margins are a drug-addicted writer of Cormac McCarthy–esque Westerns (Owen Wilson), a fuzzy-headed neurologist (Bill Murray) who likes to run experiments on his son, and Royal's Indian manservant, who's also a former assassin (Kumar Pallana).

The plot pivots around Royal, a professionally inconsiderate man who's been estranged from the family for some time but is trying to win back the heart of Etheline—who's busy being romanced by her accountant (Danny Glover). Anderson keeps the film as steadily paced as a great work of literature, with thoughtful attention paid to each and every one of his creations (moments where Royal is showing Chas's overprotected sons how to have fun are especially appealing).

Production Notes

The famously finicky Wes Anderson used the same typeface, Futura, for almost all the signage seen throughout *The Royal Tenenbaums*.

MAY 2

Run Lola Run

○ ♥ ♦

YEAR RELEASED: 1998
DIRECTOR: Tom Tykwer
WHO'S IN IT: Franka Potente, Moritz Bleibtreu

"The ball is round. The game lasts ninety minutes. . . .
Everything else is pure theory."

There never was a more appropriately named film. A woman named Lola has to run. A lot. And fast. If she doesn't, her boyfriend Manni will die. The fact that Manni doesn't seem like that much of a keeper isn't really the point.

A panicked phone call from Manni (Moritz Bleibtreu) to Lola (Franka Potente) establishes the setup. He's a low-level hood who just lost 100,000 marks and needs Lola to come up with that much money in the twenty minutes before his boss shows up, or it's bye-bye Manni. Off she runs, flame-colored hair flapping and a dire cast to her face, like a determined punk Valkyrie.

Writer/director Tom Tykwer spins three different scenarios from that nexus. In each, Lola decides to tap her bank executive father. But he tweaks her actions each time, as though she were a video-game avatar (a sensation highlighted by Tykwer's rapid-fire editing and inclusion of short animated segments) figuring out the best way through a maze. Along the way, Lola runs into various people—a man on a stolen bicycle, a woman in her father's office—whose futures we then glimpse, via a series of Polaroid-like snapshots, before returning to the race.

For a gimmick-laden film, Tykwer quickly dispels the idea that it's only a stunt creation, another fractured narrative trick from a decade whose films were lousy with them. It's genuinely invigorating and surprising throughout, the gimmicks more than balanced by Tykwer's intense interest in his characters. It helps that unlike most speed-obsessed films, Lola isn't running away from something, she's running toward it—love.

The Maltese Falcon

🔍

YEAR RELEASED: 1941
DIRECTOR: John Huston
WHO'S IN IT: Humphrey Bogart, Mary Astor, Sydney Greenstreet, Peter Lorre

"When you're slapped, you'll take it and like it."

Humphrey Bogart's Sam Spade is a character indeed, as Peter Greenstreet's mournful thug says with a throaty chuckle. A San Francisco private detective who doesn't look for work or trouble (both find him), Spade and his partner take a case for Mary Astor's untrustworthy dame. In record time, Spade's partner gets himself killed. This causes Spade roughly half a second of worry before moving on, the first sign that this is *not* a film noir—despite all the angular interiors and sour dialogue—because it has no interest in good or evil.

The somewhat beside-the-point statue of a falcon that Spade ends up chasing becomes the closest thing to a moral statement that this ludicrously enjoyable film has to offer. Instead of morality, one has Spade, laid-back yet always on the ball, not hunting people down so much as letting everybody outsmart themselves. There's Greenstreet's fey, finger-waggling aristocrat, who would be a real villain if he ever roused himself from slumberous languor. Peter Lorre's Joel Cairo, twice as effeminate as Greenstreet, is no more a match for Spade's steel-trap mind than Astor. Bogart unveils the cool but playful heart of the film after Astor has made one of her best pleas, when he says, "Now you *are* dangerous." You can't be sure whether he's worried or just plain amused.

And the Winner Is . . .

When John Huston made *The Maltese Falcon*, he was best known as the son of popular actor Walter Huston, who appeared in a small role. Seven years later, John cast Walter in *The Treasure of the Sierra Madre*, for which he won his only Oscar.

Charade

YEAR RELEASED: 1963
DIRECTOR: Stanley Donen
WHO'S IN IT: Cary Grant, Audrey Hepburn

"There's no law against stealing stolen money."

Alfred Hitchcock hadn't utilized Cary Grant in a thriller since 1959's *North by Northwest*, but fortunately Stanley Donen stepped in to give Grant a prime role in this 1963 film. *Charade* was wholly unlike the frothy musicals Donen was known for, and it gave the nearly sixty-year-old Grant the last great film of his career. It was a gift for Audrey Hepburn (born this day in 1929), as well, but she still had *My Fair Lady* (1964) to look forward to.

Hepburn is "Reggie" Lambert, whose husband has just been mysteriously murdered, leaving her penniless and with some dangerous men hunting around for the $250,000 that he helped some guys steal from the U.S. government some years back. Grant plays Peter Joshua, who Reggie met on her Switzerland ski vacation and now agrees to help her find the lost money and stay alive.

The Peter Stone screenplay is a twisty kind of thriller, with plenty of chases and double-crosses, all adroitly handled by Donen. But it's the film's canny flirtatiousness that makes it such ingenious entertainment. Grant and Hepburn play off each other like the pros that they are, doing everything they can to stay alive but never letting things get overly dour. At one point, Peter is being forced up onto a rooftop by an assailant who wants to push him off. "All right," he grumbles, "but the view had better be worth it."

Casting Call

When director Stanley Donen decided he wanted Cary Grant for the lead in *Charade*, he surprised the actor by showing up at the Bristol nursing home where Grant's mother was living and giving him the script. Grant agreed, adding, "If only Audrey would play the girl."

MAY 5

Paradise Lost: The Child Murders at Robin Hood Hills

YEAR RELEASED: 1996
DIRECTORS: Joe Berlinger, Bruce Sinofsky
WHO'S IN IT: Jessie Misskelly, Jason Baldwin, Damien Echols

"Little kids will be looking under their beds before they go to bed: 'Damien might be under there!'"

On May 5, 1993, the mutilated bodies of three eight-year-old boys were found near the small town of West Memphis, Arkansas. The community was set aflame by the discovery and eager to find the perpetrators. When teenager Jessie Misskelly confessed, the case was almost as good as decided. Jessie, a passing acquaintance of heavy metal-loving Damien Echols and Jason Baldwin, claimed the three had killed the boys in a satanic ritual. Although Jessie seemed easily manipulated (he had an IQ of 73), there was a lack of physical evidence, and the "expert" on satanic killings was nothing of the sort, the odds were quickly stacked against Damien and Jason.

As the law enforcement apparatus grinds into overdrive, Joe Berlinger and Bruce Sinofsky's two-and-a-half hour film delves into all aspects of the case, treating the defendants with the same lack of judgment as everyone else and giving the parents of the dead children the time to speak their minds.

Easily scapegoated outsiders make great suspects in reality as well as in the movies, as is vividly demonstrated in this powerful examination of justice denied. Nevertheless, by the time the film is over, it is hard not to believe that a great injustice has been done. This is a film that becomes a cause.

> **Auteur, Auteur**
> Joe Berlinger originally worked in advertising but later joined famous documentarians David and Albert Maysles at their company, Maysles Films. It was there that Berlinger met his future collaborator, Bruce Sinofsky.

MAY 6

Touch of Evil

🔍

YEAR RELEASED: 1958
DIRECTOR: Orson Welles
WHO'S IN IT: Charlton Heston, Janet Leigh, Orson Welles

"I don't speak Mexican."

A purposefully sleazy piece of work from Orson Welles (born this day in 1915) that shines darkly with all the attributes of the greatest pulp, this film asks audiences to imagine that Charlton Heston can play a Mexican detective named Ramon Miguel Vargas. Once that is digested, the rest of the film goes down just fine.

In its rightfully celebrated opening scene, we see a timed bomb being put into a car's trunk. Then, in an uninterrupted, three-minute-long crane shot, we follow the car rolling through the crummy Mexican border town of Los Robles, paralleling Miguel and his American wife Susan (Janet Leigh). It finally crosses the border and drives out of the camera's view. On camera, the Vargases' kiss until they hear the car explode. The resulting investigation exposes all levels of cross-border corruption.

This film was the last that Welles shot in America (a pregentrification Venice Beach doubling as Los Robles), which is no surprise, given its overwhelmingly dark sense of exhaustion and cynicism. Welles wrote the script from a potboiler by Whit Masterson and cast himself as the venal and utterly corrupted villain Captain Quinlan. He also convinced several name actors to show up for what was considered a low-grade B-movie, including Joseph Cotten, Keenan Wyn, and most vividly, Marlene Dietrich as a whorehouse madam (her bantering scenes with Welles are among the film's best). With or without their inclusion, though, Welles's film stands the test of time.

Lost and Found

For reasons that have never been made entirely clear, Universal dramatically cut *Touch of Evil* down to 93 minutes, infuriating Welles. A restored 111-minute edit, based on a 58-page memo of Welles's, was released in 1998.

The Big Red One

YEAR RELEASED: 1980
DIRECTOR: Sam Fuller
WHO'S IN IT: Lee Marvin, Mark Hamill, Robert Carradine, Bobby Di Cicco, Kelly Ward

"You know how you smoke out a sniper? You send a guy out in the open and you see if he gets shot."

For his last great film, Sam Fuller chose the subject of the 1st Infantry Division, his old unit. But Fuller knew that reality often mucked up a perfectly good story, so he put Lee Marvin's character front and center, relegating his own story to that of a sidekick character, Zab (Robert Carradine). Zab is a struggling novelist whose wiseass narration provides a spine for this sprawling story.

Marvin plays the nameless Sergeant, a survivor of World War I who stuck around long enough to kill more Germans on the second go-round, probably because he couldn't think of anything else to do. The Sergeant and three other men comprising the only members of their squad who *don't* get killed acquire a nickname: the Four Horsemen of the Apocalypse. They trudge from one battle to the next, grinding their way through North Africa, Italy, France, and Germany, losing recruit after recruit in the march of death. It's only at the very end, when they liberate a concentration camp—just as Fuller's unit did on May 7, 1945—that any of it seems to have purpose. This would be Fuller's last film to be properly released, and while it's not his greatest, the film was a fitting capstone to a passionate, idiosyncratic career.

Lost and Found

Heavily cut on its first release, *The Big Red One* was finally put back together in a forty-minute-longer "reconstructed" version in 2005 that gives it a human dimension war epics often lack.

MAY 8

Coraline

YEAR RELEASED: 2009
DIRECTOR: Henry Selick
WHO'S IN IT: (voices of) Dakota Fanning, Teri Hatcher, John Hodgman, Jennifer Saunders, Keith David

"You probably think this world is a dream come true. Well, you're wrong."

In 2009, the world proclaimed James Cameron's *Avatar* the film that finally showed what 3-D could do. Earlier that year, though, another film tested the full-immersion world of 3-D and put Cameron's derivative space opera to shame.

Henry Selick's stop-motion animation adaptation of Neil Gaiman's short, diamond-like novel is a haunted magic house of sinister wonders. It's equally enthralling for adult and child audiences. Coraline Jones (voiced by Dakota Fanning) is a grumpy girl frequently ignored by her busy parents. When she finds a tunnel that leads to an alternate, more fanciful version of her house, where her parents are *much* more attentive, Coraline is tempted to live with them instead. Her new parents aren't really so wonderful, of course, and once she discovers the ghosts of other misled chidren, she needs to escape.

This is a grass-is-always-greener cautionary tale wrapped up inside a Grimmsian fairy tale by way of Hayao Miyazaki's *Spirited Away* (2001). Gaiman's story delivers many dark delights, from a giant beetle blocking Coraline's escape to a slinking black cat who speaks in a frightful deep purr (the great Keith David). In addition to tweaking children's most primal fears, Selick presents an impossibly gorgeous universe of twinkling, starry nights, and nightmare gardens. For once, the third-dimension filmmaking actually propels viewers deeper into this fantasy instead of simply pricking them with occasional "wow" moments.

Coraline is maybe the only film fantasy truly worthy of the name since Cocteau's *Beauty and the Beast* (1946).

In Homage

In addition to Henry Selick's film, *Coraline* has been turned into a video game, graphic novel, and several stage productions. It opened on May 8, 2009, as an off-Broadway musical.

Miller's Crossing

YEAR RELEASED: 1990
DIRECTOR: Joel Coen
WHO'S IN IT: Gabriel Byrne, Albert Finney, Marcia Gay Harden, John Turturro, Jon Polito

"Tommy, look into your heart."

Tom Reagan (Gabriel Byrne) is number-two for Prohibition-era Irish mob boss, Leo (Albert Finney). Tom is worried about their Italian rivals, even if Leo isn't. After the Italian mob's boss, Johnny Caspar (Jon Polito, sweaty-cheeked and ridiculous), ends a meeting with Tom and Leo in a fury, Leo waves off the problem: "C'mon, Tommy, you know I don't like to think." "Well," Tom says, "think about whether you should start."

The double-cross-laden script is heavily indebted to the detective novels of Dashiell Hammett. Yet, while Joel and Ethan Coen juice up the classic gangster flick set pieces (the most memorable involving Leo, a Tommy gun, and a tearjerking rendition of "Danny Boy"), they're more interested in Tom's character. In the performance of a lifetime, the hawk-like Byrne is the classic man apart, the one who knows all the angles and sees how it will all play out. But like a figure out of Greek mythology, nobody believes Tom. Before it's over, he'll have sacrificed his last pretense at humanity, and all for somebody who's not worth it.

The Coens have a fantastic time here, rolling out the slang-laden dialogue and daring you not just to keep track of what's going on, amidst all the blazing guns and their deadly mockery of the stooges surrounding Tom, but also to actually *care* about it. Is it the greatest gangster film of all time? That's certainly possible. Now go watch it again so you can make up your mind.

> ### Auteur, Auteur
> Joel and Ethan Coen suffered writer's block while working on *Miller's Crossing*. To break it, they whipped out *Barton Fink* (1991), about a blocked writer whom many bad things happen to.

To Have and Have Not

YEAR RELEASED: 1944
DIRECTOR: Howard Hawks
WHO'S IN IT: Humphrey Bogart, Lauren Bacall

"You know how to whistle, don't you, Steve? You just put your lips together and blow."

Just because we've seen a story like this before doesn't mean it can't make for perfectly smashing filmmaking. Humphrey Bogart plays another reluctant hero but makes it seem fresh. His Harry Morgan, who runs a charter fishing boat out of the island of Martinique, gets caught in a squabble between some Gestapo and French Resistance fighters. While Morgan is figuring out which side, if any, of the conflict he's going to be on, his eye keeps getting distracted by the sultry, sylph-like Marie Browning (Lauren Bacall), or "Slim," as he calls her.

There is an Ernest Hemingway novel by this same name, but any resemblance to the source novel is mostly cosmetic, which is probably as it should be. With Hemingway's characters being so shorn of emotion, it's hard to imagine what Howard Hawks could have done with them. The result is an easygoing entertainment that has more fun with the romance than it does with the drama about Morgan's smuggling operation. It makes sense, as the war itself was starting to draw to a close and audiences knew it, whereas they didn't know how this particular love story, danger smoking in the background, was going to turn out.

Production Notes
Humphrey Bogart and Lauren Bacall didn't just play lovers in *To Have and Have Not*, they began a real romance on the set. They married the following year and were together until Bogart's death in 1957.

The Adventures of Baron Munchausen

 LOL!

YEAR RELEASED: 1988
DIRECTOR: Terry Gilliam
WHO'S IN IT: John Neville, Sarah Polley

"It's all logic and reason now. . . . No place for three-legged cyclops in the South Seas."

We join Baron von Munchausen (John Neville) in mid-crisis. It's the eighteenth century, and the city he's in is under siege by a huge army of Turks. Inside the walls, a troupe of actors are rehearsing a play recounting his fabled exploits, only they're getting it all wrong. So the slim but aged Baron, powdered wig on and sword at the ready, charges up to the stage to admonish the actors. No, *this* is what happened. . . .

What comes next is a fable-like cornucopia of Gilliam's fully unleashed imagination and the writings of the real Munchausen, an eighteenth-century soldier of fortune and tall-tale storyteller born on May 11, 1720. With the intrepid stowaway girl Sally (Sarah Polley) at his side, the Baron undertakes all manner of adventures, from flying a hot-air balloon made out of women's underpants to the moon to riding atop a flying cannonball.

The effect is a fairy-tale mix-tape, with Gilliam zipping from one tall tale to the next as impatiently as the Baron himself. The filming—in Spain and Italy—was a nightmare (bad luck, bad financing, and a complicated shoot), and given the vast canvas that Gilliam paints, it's not hard to see why. Eric Idle and Robin Williams pop in to take part in the circus, as does Uma Thurman, playing Venus, and Sting shows up in a cameo as a soldier being executed for being so brave that he's demoralizing the other men.

Production Notes
The Adventures of Baron Munchausen underwent legendary production problems, including a last-minute financing cutoff while Terry Gilliam was in the middle of shooting a massive battle scene, no less.

MAY 12

The Philadelphia Story

YEAR RELEASED: 1940
DIRECTOR: George Cukor
WHO'S IN IT: Cary Grant, Katharine Hepburn, James Stewart

"The prettiest sight in this fine pretty world is the privileged class enjoying its privileges."

Tracy Lord (Katharine Hepburn, clenching her jaw like it's a weapon) is a Philadelphia heiress feeling like she just got out of jail, having divorced playboy C. K. Dexter Haven (Cary Grant). He's witty and a gas to be around, but completely unreliable, driving Tracy to marry the respectably boring George Kittredge (John Howard).

Dexter appears at the ceremony to muck things up for his ex with the help of a pair of tabloid journalists he brought along. The two start snooping for scandal while Dexter annoys the bejesus out of Tracy. She needles Dexter every time she can ("You haven't switched from liquor to dope by any chance, have you, Dexter?"), before discovering that she's actually attracted to the tabloid writer, gawky but quick-thinking Mike (James Stewart). Tracy and Mike become epically drunk together. Grant louses about charmingly, Stewart has a grand old time, and Hepburn is hilariously, miserably confused.

The Philadelphia Story had run for years on Broadway by the time George Cukor (fresh off adapting 1939's men-free divorce comedy *The Women*) was brought on. Hepburn originated the stage role of Tracy, so she was an obvious choice despite her reputation as "box-office poison." That didn't prove true for this film, however. It was not only one of the greatest high-society screwball comedies, but also a box-office success that took away two Oscars (actor for James Stewart, and adapted screenplay for Donald Ogden Stewart).

Casting Call

Katharine Hepburn originally wanted to cast Clark Gable and Spencer Tracy for the leads in *The Philadelphia Story*, having never worked with either of them.

Mean Streets

YEAR RELEASED: 1973
DIRECTOR: Martin Scorsese
WHO'S IN IT: Harvey Keitel, Robert De Niro, Cesare Danova

"You don't make up for your sins in church. You do it in the streets. You do it at home. All the rest is B.S., and you know it."

Martin Scorsese was just another film school graduate with a couple of Roger Corman exploitation flicks under his belt when he came out with this enthusiastic but tough-minded story about faith, violence, and the old neighborhood.

Harvey Keitel, fraught with worry, plays Charlie, who's banging around the Little Italy of the 1960s and trying to live righteously. Everything around him leads to sin—and the film makes a point of showing Charlie in church, earnestly praying. But it's difficult, what with his uncle Giovanni (Cesare Danova) being the local mob boss and his best friend being Johnny Boy (Robert De Niro), a street punk psychopath in a pork-pie hat (he likes to blow up mailboxes and blow off loan sharks).

Though the screenplay is clogged with pre-Vatican II, incense-laden guilt, the film is shot with rough abandon. The energy of so much of the action around Charlie (a brew of random fights and bursts of pop music that so many directors would cop from later) works in direct opposition to the twisted stagnation of his soul.

The whole thing looks rough around the edges these days—particularly after seeing how much more skillfully Scorsese manipulated similar elements in *Goodfellas* (1990)—but there remains a palpable thrill in seeing a great director flex his creative muscles as if for the first time.

> **Production Notes**
> Though *Mean Streets* is considered one of the great New York films, Scorsese shot most of it in Los Angeles.

The New World

YEAR RELEASED: 2005
DIRECTOR: Terrence Malick
WHO'S IN IT: Colin Farrell, Q'orianka Kilcher, Christopher Plummer

"Remember, Smith, you came to these shores in chains."

Although it's a singular moment in American history, the founding of Jamestown on May 14, 1607, has never interested filmmakers—apart from *Pocahontas* (1995). In telling the story of what happened after English settlers came in touch with the coastal forest-dwelling Indian tribes, Terrence Malick decided to go the nonmusical route.

A scruffy Colin Farrell plays Captain John Smith, who is scheduled to be hanged for mutiny. Once they're on Virginia soil, however, Captain Newport (Christopher Plummer) pardons Smith. When Smith is later sent upriver to trade with the Indians, he's again nearly executed before the chief's daughter, Pocahontas (the incredible Q'orianka Kilcher), hurls her body onto his, asking that Smith be spared. Out of that spontaneous moment grows their love, albeit one frequently communicated without the benefit of language.

This is really more Pocahontas's film than Smith's, with Malick's focus squarely on Pocahontas and her watching eyes. When later in the film she is taken to England, a trophy to be displayed, it's the stone buildings and manicured gardens that seem alien, not the verdant swamps and forests of Virginia, so soon to be despoiled. There is a lot of one hundred-proof Malick here, with all those swooning, resplendent nature scenes and the wandering plot that seems straight of out of *The Thin Red Line* playbook. But there's also a sense of wonderment that no other film about the early colonies has ever captured, or even tried to.

Production Notes
The Virginia Algonquin tongue spoken by Pocahontas's people was invented for the film, as the actual language had been extinct for two centuries.

Lolita

 LOL!

YEAR RELEASED: 1962
DIRECTOR: Stanley Kubrick
WHO'S IN IT: James Mason, Shelley Winters, Sue Lyon, Peter Sellers

"I want you to live with me and die with me and everything with me."

Professor Humbert Humbert (James Mason) rents a room from Charlotte Haze (a dizzy Shelley Winters), a neurotic, status-seeking mantrap who won't leave the posh, arrogant Humbert alone. He rebuffs her clumsy seductions until he gets an eyeful of her preteen daughter, Lolita (Sue Lyon) sunning in the backyard.

Humbert marries Charlotte to be closer to his obsession. Things seem to solve themselves when Charlotte, horrified at what she's read about Lolita in his diary, runs into the street and is killed by a car. But there remains the question of how Humbert can live with Lolita, as well as what is her connection with local Lothario, Quilty (Peter Sellers)?

Lolita is a strange confection, satirizing both deluded sexual obsessions (at no point does Humbert consider that he's wrong in chasing down Lolita) and pretensions (both of the self-satisfied professional intellectual and the insecure postwar American bourgeois). It makes for odd but compelling comedy, with Sellers's crafty and feline Quilty standing as the just-as-corrupted but more honest degenerate counterpart to Humbert's clueless pretense.

The film was not nearly as titillating as people imagined, but the ad campaign used controversy for all it was worth. Posters emblazoned with the iconic shot of Lyon sucking a lollipop while wearing heart-shaped glasses asked, "How did they ever make a movie of *Lolita*?"

Lost and Found

Vladimir Nabokov's first screenplay draft was 400 pages long. Reportedly, only about 20 percent of Nabokov's Oscar-nominated script was actually shot.

Farewell, My Concubine

🌐 ❤️

YEAR RELEASED: 1993
DIRECTOR: Chen Kaige
WHO'S IN IT: Leslie Cheung, Zhang Fengyi, Gong Li

"I am by nature a girl, not a boy."

In the early 1990s, most Western moviegoers didn't realize China produced any films besides the chopsocky variety. Chen Kaige's tear-jerking, operatic, gender-bending soapy epic changed all that.

In the 1920s, a young boy is delivered to the Peking Opera, a place of glorious creative transformation and brutal training. In adulthood, the boy, Cheng Dieyi (Leslie Cheung) and his best friend Duan Xiaolou (Zhang Fengyi) are still close, though Cheng—whose delicate features mean he is given the female roles in the all-male company—has realized that his chummy feelings for Duan are really romantic ones. Once the glamorous courtesan Juxian (Gong Li) drops in to their lives, the duo becomes an inherently unstable triangle.

The most difficult thing for a Western audience to get past in Chen's film is not the swooning, melodramatic story or its lusciously art-directed look (Chen has a fashion director's feel for powerful colors, and an artist's sense for how to use them emotionally), but the opera itself, with its halting, high-pitched singing and opaque stories. But once the performances are seen as sublimations of their performers' true feelings, any stylistic difficulties quickly fall by the wayside. Chen's sense of tragedy is deeply studied and skillfully used to evoke an almost physical response from the viewer. It's painful, but sweetened by incredible beauty.

Auteur, Auteur

Along with Zhang Yimou (2002's *Hero*) Chen Kaige is one of the most successful of the "Fifth Generation" of filmmakers, those who graduated from Beijing film school right after it reopened after the Cultural Revolution, which had begun on this day in 1966.

Grand Illusion

🌐 💣

YEAR RELEASED: 1937
DIRECTOR: Jean Renoir
WHO'S IN IT: Jean Gabin, Pierre Fresnay, Erich von Stroheim

"I just shot down a Caudron fighter. If they're officers, invite them for lunch."

In this movie, World War I might be going on, but some soldiers aren't suffering too much. A French reconnaissance pilot, working-class Lieutenant Maréchal (Jean Gabin) and an aristocratic officer, Captain de Boeldieu (Pierre Fresnay), are shot down by a German ace, Captain von Rauffenstein (Erich von Stroheim), and greeted like gentlemen in the German officers' club and treated to a fine meal. Since Maréchal was wounded, a German even cuts his food for him. The illusion of war as a grand game is almost unbreakable.

Most of Jean Renoir's immortal war drama takes place in prison camps where the Frenchmen launch countless escape attempts. Although the two sides play at being civilized, the lie becomes harder to maintain. The men are transferred to a mountain fortress where they find that a wounded von Rauffenstein (wedged into a back brace, a portrait of Prussian military righteousness) is their new commandant. Friends or not, Maréchal and his cohorts keep trying to escape.

Renoir is better remembered for his bourgeois satire *The Rules of the Game* (1939), but *Grand Illusion* is the more notable film. He includes sly digs at the high-society warriors with their monocles and fine manners, playing at chivalry while working-class men are slaughtered in the trenches. The other grand illusion is more damning: "Don't delude yourself," is one man's world-weary response to Maréchal's hope that this will be the war to end all wars.

Courting Controversy

Joseph Goebbels called *Grand Illusion* "public cinematograhic enemy number one" and the antiwar film was banned in Germany, Austria, and Italy.

Taste of Cherry

🌍 🎭 👤

YEAR RELEASED: 1997
DIRECTOR: Abbas Kiarostami
WHO'S IN IT: Homayoun Ershadi, Abdolrahman Bagheri

"You want to give up the taste of cherries?"

In order to make *Taste of Cherry*, Abbas Kiarostami underwent three grueling rounds of censorship with the conservative Iranian government. In the film, Mr. Badii (Homayoun Ershadi) drives out of Tehran into the dried-out hills, pulling up alongside strangers and asking them if they'd like to make some money, with little luck. When finally he gives a ride to a young soldier, Badii has time to explain.

Badii has a plan to kill himself but it requires assistance. He wants to take a fistful of sleeping pills and lie down in a predug grave at night. Then, somebody needs to come by in the morning and call his name: if Badii answers, he'll need their help to get out of there. If he doesn't answer, he'll want somebody to bury him. The Kurdish soldier wants no part of this, nor does an Afghan seminarian he gives a ride to later and argues with about theology.

The third man Badii talks with is different. Instead of clumsily debating Badii, Bagheri (Abdolrahman Bagheri) lectures *him* on why his plan makes no sense. Eventually Badii has to make a choice.

Abbas Kiarostami's meditative film is deliberate to a fault, bunching its dialogue together in a few bursts of eloquence. Kiarostami pulls out all the stops at the end, as Badii enjoys the view, his determination perhaps wavering. Saying that what follows is maybe the most splendid sunset ever filmed provides only a hint of the joys contained in this poetic picture.

Performance

YEAR RELEASED: 1970
DIRECTORS: Donald Cammell, Nicolas Roeg
WHO'S IN IT: Mick Jagger, James Fox, Anita Pallenberg

"The only performance that makes it, that makes it all the way, is one that achieves madness."

Chas (James Fox) is a gangland enforcer who spends his days beating the stuffing out of people who owe money and his nights bedding party girls. Things go south, and Chas hides out in a Notting Hill basement, where he falls in with Turner (Mick Jagger), a faded rock idol who's submerged himself in an ill-lit cavern of quasi-paganism, well-fueled with psychedelics and lascivious women. Though they're worlds apart, Chas's endangered circumstances and Turner's vampiric need for his new friend's violent energy allow the barriers to come down. Before long, the two seem to have merged into one, a rock 'n' roll *Persona* (1966).

There are many fragments of genius through Donald Cammell and Nicolas Roeg's half-experimental, half-crime film, even if the whole of it can seem pretentious at times. It's amusing also to behold Jagger's wraith-like Turner, almost a parody of the rock star's late-1960s persona, when he was digging deep into occult practices, William S. Burroughs, and the like.

Cammell and Roeg skirt structure and reality throughout, shooting from odd angles (particularly through mirrors, a persistent theme) and fracturing the soundtrack into an atonal cacophony. Nobody knew much what to make of *Performance* when it was released, and nobody particularly does now, but it maintains an eerie, disturbing edge no matter how many years have passed.

Courting Controversy

Not knowing what to do with Donald Cammell and Nicolas Roeg's genre mash-up, the studio sat on it for a couple years. When it was finally released, the first cut was slapped with an X rating (it was later rated R).

2001: A Space Odyssey

👽 👤

YEAR RELEASED: 1968
DIRECTOR: Stanley Kubrick
WHO'S IN IT: Keir Dullea, William Sylvester, Leonard Rossiter

"No 9000 computer has ever made a mistake or distorted information. We are all, by any practical definition of the words, foolproof and incapable of error."

Stanley Kubrick's science-fiction masterstroke comes in four elegantly photographed sections, all backgrounded by lavish Ligeti and Strauss compositions, and linked by little more than a sense of mystery and awe.

In "The Dawn of Man," ape-like creatures in an African-looking landscape battle over a water hole. A mysterious monolith suddenly appears, thrumming with an eerie sound. After that, one of the apes learns how to use a bone as a weapon, leading to victory over the water hole. Cut to the near future on the moon's surface where astronauts behold another monolith. Nine months later, a spaceship travels to Jupiter, following a radio warning the monolith emitted. The crew notices their computer, the HAL 9000, exhibiting a creeping paranoia.

To try and understand Kubrick's epic is to play a fool's game. Kubrick spent years on research and rewriting with sci-fi author Arthur C. Clarke, and along the way he seemed to have lost touch with the spark of the human, as well as the widely understood nature of story. While this cold touch would make his later films increasingly hard to digest, it worked here. Kubrick's sheer mad devotion delivers a mind-opening spectacle like none that had been seen before, or would be seen again. Comprehension is unnecessary.

Lost and Found

Stanley Kubrick filmed interviews about extraterrestrial life with twenty-one scientists to use as prologue for *2001: A Space Odyssey*. The footage has been lost but transcripts of the interviews were published in 2005.

May 21

Eternal Sunshine of the Spotless Mind

♥ 👽 👤

YEAR RELEASED: 2004
DIRECTOR: Michel Gondry
WHO'S IN IT: Jim Carrey, Kate Winslet

"You want to empty your home, you want to empty your life, of Clementine."

Michel Gondry's elegant distillation of a Charlie Kaufman mind-bending fantasy comedy asks if love is a thing of free will, or a habit that can be kicked?

Joel Barish (Jim Carrey) is a glum sort of guy, lonely but still perturbed if interrupted while reading alone. He plays hooky from work one wintry morning, taking the commuter train out to Montauk. Clementine Kruczynski (Kate Winslet) is a dyed-hair free spirit of fiery moods who strikes up a conversation with Joel. Though opposite personalities, the two hit it off.

Only it's not that simple. Joel and Clementine already knew each other. Their relationship went sour some time ago, and Clementine had a procedure done that literally erased Joel's painful memory from her mind. He did the same. But when the technicians come to erase Clementine, he decides he doesn't want to lose her, so he dashes through his subconscious trying to hide her from the encroaching erasure.

Kaufman's script revels in the same sort of frame twisting he delivered in *Being John Malkovich* (1999), where time comes unglued without warning. He treats an astounding concept (memories erased like pencil drawings) nonchalantly, leaving the film free to explore the emotional collateral damage taking place. It's a wrenchingly heartfelt work, part diehard romantic and part melancholic dirge.

Gondry's direction, similarly, is fantastically skilled without being distracting. The clever, lo-fi, homemade-looking special effects used during the surreal scenes inside Joel's mind have immeasurably more impact for not being purposefully dazzling.

It's a happy accident, a work of genius.

Historically Speaking

Alexander Pope, the poet whose line from his 1717 poem of doomed romance, *Eloisa and Abelard*, provided the title for this film, was born on May 21, 1688.

Z

YEAR RELEASED: 1969
DIRECTOR: Costa-Gavras
WHO'S IN IT: Yves Montand, Jean-Louis Trintignant

"Always blame the USA! Even if you're wrong."

On May 22, 1963, the murder in Greece of leftist politician and doctor Gregorios Lambrakis caused an outrage. So did this fictional variation on that story, with Algeria standing in as the unnamed Mediterranean country where police and military work with nationalist thugs to suppress every hint of liberalism.

A casually heroic Yves Montand plays the Lambrakis stand-in, who arrives in the capital city to deliver an impassioned speech against corruption, militarism, and foreign intervention. With a battalion of riot police standing by, he's fatally clubbed down in a public square. The police and army—a collusion of thick-headed, medal-bedecked toads in uniforms—claim it's an accident, but the acerbic investigating judge (Jean-Louis Trintignant) keeps finding details that don't match their story.

Director Costa-Gavras heightens the film's authenticity not just in its echoes of the Lambrakis case, but also in the haphazard nature of the assassination conspiracy. A fully fictionalized film would have made the conspirators more obviously sinister and invincible, the kind of villains who don't forget anything. But in a police state where the villains think they never have to worry about a real investigation, why bother being *too* careful?

Costa-Gavras directs with flair and imagination and a sense of outrage that doesn't insist on being humorless. It would inform all manner of later conspiratorial thrillers, from *The Parallax View* (1974) to *JFK* (1991).

Historically Speaking

Although *Z*'s setting is never made explicit, there is no doubt that it's meant to be Greece. A note at the beginning of the film states that "any similarity to actual persons or events is deliberate."

Bonnie and Clyde

YEAR RELEASED: 1967
DIRECTOR: Arthur Penn
WHO'S IN IT: Warren Beatty, Faye Dunaway

"We rob banks."

Arthur Penn's frenetic, addictive, criminals-on-the-run film looks to the past while nodding to the rebellious sentiment of the 1960s. Loosely based on real-life Depression-era bank-robbing couple Clyde Barrow and Bonnie Parker (who were killed in a police ambush on May 23, 1934), the film was as potent as anything that had hit American screens in years (what was left of Old Hollywood would be completely blown away by *The Wild Bunch* a couple years later). It sharply divided critics and audiences, much as the gangster flicks of Bonnie and Clyde's era were lambasted for celebrating criminality.

One poster read, "They're young . . . they're in love . . . and they're killers," and that sums up the plot. Warren Beatty is Clyde, a scammer with more guts and luck than brains. He hits the road with Bonnie (Faye Dunaway), a similarly aimless small-town beauty, and they start robbing banks. People who get in their way are killed (as in one jarring shot where a bank employee throws himself onto their getaway car, getting a bullet in the face). Eventually the law closes in for a military-style ambush.

Instead of making a straightforward gangster picture, Penn stylistically pushed the envelope, just as Steven Soderbergh would later do with *Out of Sight* (1998). Penn unleashes a range of New Wave tricks with flickering editing and generally nervous visuals. It all clicks. The film raked in ten Oscar nominations, winning two (supporting actress for Estelle Parsons's hysterical turn as a moll, and Burnett Guffey for cinematography).

Production Notes

Bonnie and Clyde was written by David Newman and Robert Benton for François Truffaut to direct. In their original screenplay, Clyde was bisexual, but perhaps that idea didn't sit well with the studio in the mid-1960s.

Fish Tank

YEAR RELEASED: 2009
DIRECTOR: Andrea Arnold
WHO'S IN IT: Katie Jarvis, Michael Fassbender, Kierston Wareing, Rebecca Griffiths

"You need sortin' out, you do."

In a run-down council estate tower in Essex, England, a family of three women is falling apart. The dyed-blond terror of a mother is all rage and bad dating choices, while the younger daughter has a sailor's mouth and an unearthly gift for aggression. Bouncing out of the banged-up apartment with a headful of adolescent rage is fifteen-year-old Mia (Katie Jarvis, treating acting like a cage match), whose sole release is putting her music on and dancing. It's her dream to be a professional, thinking it's her escape from this cycle of unemployment and hopelessness.

Writer/director Andrea Arnold's near-genius second film is perhaps most impressive in how it treats Mia's dream. *She's not a great dancer.* This would be unheard-of in most films about wayward youth in bad situations; uplifting dramas demand exceptionalism. But while Arnold is a poet of uniqueness (each woman in this family is dysfunctional, but in entirely different ways), she doesn't need to make Mia special in ability, just in spirit and heart.

The story sharpens with the addition of Connor (Michael Fassbender), who starts dating the mother but has eyes for Mia. Arnold understands that Mia's hard shell is brittle, and that once she's broken, there will be hell to pay. The film's final scenes, first vengeful and then heartrending, are nothing less than fearless.

Auteur, Auteur

Like her heroine in *Fish Tank*, Andrea Arnold wanted to be a dancer, and in the early 1980s, she was part of a dance troupe on the British television show *Top of the Pops*.

The Class

YEAR RELEASED: 2008
DIRECTOR: Laurent Cantet
WHO'S IN IT: François Bégaudeau, Franck Keïta, Esméralda Ouertani

"If I start using names to suit all your origins, it will never end."

The classroom genre is such a cringe-worthy one. It's studded with films trading in feel-good parables about how One Teacher Can Make a Difference, so it makes a work like this one from Laurent Cantet all the more invigorating and unsettling. His film's teacher, Mr. Marin, is played by François Bégaudeau, who taught for years in a Parisian middle school and wrote a book about his experiences, which Cantet used as the film's inspiration. Marin is dedicated and tough-minded, but Cantet isn't here to celebrate; he wants to observe.

The film is shot like a documentary, simply hanging around in the classroom, watching the subtle give-and-take. We see each side striving for minute advantages in the power struggle—the white and bourgeoisie Marin trying to keep order, the mostly immigrant students prodding and testing him every moment. In one telling scene, they ask why all the names in his grammar examples sound white: "What's with all the Bills?" They suggest more relevant alternatives: Aïssata, maybe Fatou.

A crisis develops when Marin, exhausted and harried, snaps at a critical moment, and the class—waiting as adolescents will for any sign of weakness—surges. How Marin scrambles back from that precipice and tries to acknowledge an error while maintaining authority is a lesson in fragile diplomacy for his students, as is his gentle admonishment of a naive new teacher ("The Enlightenment will be tough"). There have been films about teachers for decades, but this feels like the first time one mattered.

Stagecoach

YEAR RELEASED: 1939
DIRECTOR: John Ford
WHO'S IN IT: Claire Trevor, John Wayne

"You got to live, no matter what happens."

John Ford's first sound Western, coming after less-remembered films like the William Faulkner–scripted *Submarine Patrol* (1938) and the Irish Civil War drama *The Informer* (1935), spelled a kind of doom for him. It ensured that for the rest of his career, which lasted almost another three decades, Ford would be known as a Western director, for better or for worse. In this case, it was for the better.

The script tracks a disparate group of travelers heading from one frontier town to another. The problem? There's an Apache revolt going on. The solution? John Wayne (born on this day in 1907), who gets his first truly great role here as the rough-around-the-edges but ultimately heroic Ringo Kid. The film has a lot of fun with the stagecoach passengers, throwing a card shark, prostitute, pregnant bride, and outlaw (that's Ringo) together and seeing whether they'll crack under the pressure before the cavalry can come. Although it's a Western, *Stagecoach*'s look resembles Ford's more expressionistic films, with a lot of F. W. Murnau–influenced dark angles that enhance the claustrophobia of the stagecoach rattling on under the blazing desert sun.

Ford does his best to keep the conclusion in doubt until the very end, but he was never one for fussing around. According to Peter Bogdanovich's book on John Ford, the director was asked once why the Indians didn't just shoot the horses pulling the stagecoach. To which Ford replied, "If they had, it would have been the end of the picture, wouldn't it?"

Auteur, Auteur
Orson Welles once said, "John Ford was my teacher. My style has nothing to do with his, but *Stagecoach* was my textbook."

A Boy and His Dog

YEAR RELEASED: 1975
DIRECTOR: L. Q. Jones
WHO'S IN IT: Don Johnson, Susanne Benton, Jason Robards

"War is hell."

Director L. Q. Jones, a tall and spindly character actor with some Sam Peckinpah credits to his name, learned from that bloody-minded filmmaker how to present violence onscreen: without apology. What he added was the humor.

It's the year 2024 and America has been blasted into radioactive dust. Among the survivors are immature tough-guy Vic (Don Johnson, a lifetime before *Miami Vice*) and verbal, literate Blood, his telepathic dog (played by *Brady Bunch* regular Tiger, and voiced by Tim McIntire), who acts as Jeeves to Vic's Bertie Wooster, Gromit to his Wallace.

Watching an ancient, scratched porno film in a refugee camp–like movie theater, Blood sniffs out what he thinks is a woman hiding as a man in the crowd. This is big news, as women are hardly seen anymore, and sexual frustration among the heavily armed, poorly fed male wanderers is high.

The woman turns out to be bait to lure Vic to a sterile underground city whose residents—led by Jason Robards in pancake makeup—live a creepy fantasy of Norman Rockwell Americana. Apparently their men are impotent, and they need Vic's help in that department.

Jones emphasizes the postapocalyptic action much less than the chatty repartee between Vic and Blood, who delight and annoy (mostly the latter) each other a dozen times a day. The striking visuals (done on the cheap) were picked up on by the Hughes brothers for their highly derivative 2010 sci-fi film, *Book of Eli*.

Everyone's a Critic

A Boy and His Dog sparked criticism over what many have seen as a deeply misogynistic attitude, one that wasn't as prevalent in Harlan Ellison's original story.

The Double Life of Veronique

YEAR RELEASED: 1991
DIRECTOR: Krzysztof Kieslowski
WHO'S IN IT: Irène Jacob, Philippe Volter

"I have this feeling that I'm not alone."

There's Veronika and Veronique, both played by the same actress (Irène Jacob). However, despite some ghostly hints to the contrary, and the fact that they both share a birthday, their lives are not the same.

Veronika is a young Polish music student and choir singer with a weak heart and bouts of sadness. Crossing a square, she spots a woman who looks just like her and snaps a photo. Later, she gives a tremendous debut performance, only to suddenly drop dead.

At that moment, the film shifts to Veronique, a Parisian singer who impetuously decides right then to stop her musical career. As Veronique tries to figure out what to do with her life (the bordeom of beautiful women like Jacob would become a specialty of director Krzysztof Kieslowski), she starts receiving packages from a secret admirer.

Kieslowski plays the strings here like a master unworried that somebody will discover his secret—perhaps because there might not be one to discover. It's tempting to either dive into this fantasy conundrum and try to divine the thin threads linking these stories or to dismiss it all as arthouse hokum: a nonstory dressed up with sumptuous camerawork and an operatic score. Both options would be valid, and yet that doesn't address the innate pull this kind of ghost-twin story can have.

It's a mystery without a solution. Not only that, it's a mystery which you won't *want* to be solved.

Auteur, Auteur

After *The Double Life of Veronique* became Kieslowski's first international success, he began his signature "Colors" trilogy—*Blue*, *Red*, and *White*—the last of which was released two years before his death in 1996.

MAY 29

The Silence of the Lambs

🔍

YEAR RELEASED: 1991
DIRECTOR: Jonathan Demme
WHO'S IN IT: Jodie Foster, Anthony Hopkins, Ted Levine

"Well, Clarice? Have the lambs stopped screaming?"

The film that kicked off Hollywood's serial killer obsession and set the template for today's graphically forensic television police procedurals came from an unlikely source. Jonathan Demme had carved out a niche as a singularly nice kind of indie director, with films like the cutting-loose comedy *Something Wild* (1986). It took Demme adapting Thomas Harris's thriller for people to remember that this was a guy who had started out doing Roger Corman B-movie flicks like *Caged Heat* (1974).

The serial killer being chased throughout the film is "Buffalo Bill" (Ted Levine), theoretically the story's raison d'être. But really, it's about Dr. Hannibal Lecter (Anthony Hopkins, all his overacting skills for once perfectly adapted to the material), a genius psychologist and killer who finds a new game to play when rookie agent Clarice Starling (Jodie Foster) asks for help chasing Bill. They've been parodied and copied so frequently now that it's hard to watch them fresh, but the scenes between Starling and Lecter still feel like intellectual combat ("First principles, Clarice. Simplicity. Read Marcus Aurelius.") played out against a ticking clock.

While Demme winds up the action tighter than a drumhead, he never lets the accelerating tension distract from his characters, particularly Foster's Starling, without whose clipped confidence the film would not be half the classic it is. It's a landmark of intelligent mainstream filmmaking from a time when the phrase itself seemed an oxymoron.

In Homage
Thomas Harris published two follow-ups to *Silence of the Lambs*, the sequel *Hannibal* and the prequel *Hannibal Rising*. They were filmed in 2001 and 2007, respectively, though it's unclear why, as both fall far short.

The Passion of Joan of Arc

YEAR RELEASED: 1928
DIRECTOR: Carl Dreyer
WHO'S IN IT: Maria Falconetti, Antonin Artaud

"You are no daughter of God. You are Satan's creature!"

Carl Theodor Dreyer's majestically stark, silent account of the trial and execution of Joan of Arc (which took place on May 30, 1431) is all angle and emotion, with soul-wrenching theological battling thrown in for good measure.

Like many totalitarian regime's crimes, the nineteen-year-old Joan's heresy trial was fully recorded to sadden future generations. Dreyer's first shot is the original records being opened for examination. The spare white courtroom is filled with soldiers, clergy, and judges all eager for a crack at the loathsome heretic in men's clothes. What follows is the expected travesty, but given an immortal power by Dreyer and his leading lady.

Falconetti's Joan is a performance never to be matched. Dreyer frames her close-up—just her wide, lantern eyes, close-cropped hair, and tear-streaked cheeks—as she struggles to make sense of the charges being hurled at her. She looks to heaven while her accusers glare up at her, their sneering faces the very image of bullying contempt. Even the more sympathetic men (including Antonin Artaud as one of the friars) seem abstract figures next to the bruising passion of Falconetti. It progresses from the trial to the torture chamber to the carnival-like execution ground, which erupts in a bloody riot that Dreyer shot with a kinetic fury that makes even the work of experimental silent-era contemporaries like Eisenstein look practically stodgy.

Lost and Found

The Passion of Joan of Arc was censored on first release by authorities nervous about its antireligious stance, a problem exacerbated when the negative burned in a 1928 fire. In 1981, however, an original print was discovered in a closet at a Norwegian mental institution.

The Third Man

YEAR RELEASED: 1949
DIRECTOR: Carol Reed
WHO'S IN IT: Joseph Cotten, Alida Valli, Trevor Howard, Orson Welles

"In Italy for thirty years under the Borgias they had warfare, terror, murder, and bloodshed, but they produced Michelangelo, Leonardo da Vinci, and the Renaissance. In Switzerland they had brotherly love, they had 500 years of democracy and peace, and what did that produce? The cuckoo clock."

Shot in the ruin of postwar Vienna, Carol Reed and Graham Greene's coy, sad drama ostensibly concerns the black market but it's really about friendship. Pulp writer Holly Martins (Joseph Cotten) shows up to bury his late buddy Harry Lime, a guy he always loved, never mind that Lime sucked all attention toward him like a sinkhole. So he's put out first to spot the should-be-dead Lime (Orson Welles) grinning with Wellesian nonchalance from the shadows, and second to discover Lime has been responsible for unforgivable crimes (bad penicillin, disfigured children), with his underground business dealings. So the chase is on, with Martins knowing he has no choice but to bring his resurrected friend to justice.

Greene riffed with good humor on his American innocent abroad, leaving it to Reed to supply the darkness. This is what you remember, of course, if you've seen the film—those striking shots of the cavernous Viennese sewers (you can take tours these days), with Lime on the run. But there's a lot of wonderful texture above ground, too, such as Alida Valli's tragic beauty, and the thinnest remnant of law and order stretched tight over the ruins. Against that backdrop, Greene's good-natured humor carries an icier sting. This was Cotten and Welles's last real collaboration, and in its portrayal the painful truths of betrayed friendship, it's every bit as potent as *Citizen Kane* (1941).

Se7en

YEAR RELEASED: 1995
DIRECTOR: David Fincher
WHO'S IN IT: Brad Pitt, Morgan Freeman, Gwyneth Paltrow

"Ernest Hemingway once wrote, 'The world is a fine place, and worth fighting for.' I agree with the second part."

Morgan Freeman plays Will Somerset, a weary, cynical homicide detective in an unnamed, crumbling, rainy city. In his last week on the job, Somerset is assigned a young new detective, David Mills (Brad Pitt), to break in. The two catch a curious murder on day one: an obese man force-fed until his stomach burst, with *Gluttony* written on the wall. Then another murder, and another, with Somerset putting it together that a killer is basing murders on the seven deadly sins.

Predestination hangs over the film's cloud-covered universe, where the cops bag up the evidence, update their files, and wait for it all to play out. By the time the killer's monstrous plan comes to fruition, viewers, like Mills and Somerset, can only watch in stunned horror.

Far from an exercise in moping, however, Andrew Kevin Walker's script is a finely nuanced look at the detectives' relationship, with Mills's tough optimism banging against Somerset's intellectualized depression. In a marvelous, unexpected scene between Somerset and Mills's wife, Tracy (Gwyneth Paltrow), a teacher downcast about her hellish new home, the detective provides a piercing, surprising look into his past and his soul; it's the finest acting Freeman has ever done. Likewise, director David Fincher's smart take on guilty gloom (later imitated to death) is some of his best work.

Production Notes

After New Line bought Andrew Kevin Walker's script for *Se7en*, they asked him to alter the bleak conclusion. Morgan Freeman, Brad Pitt, and David Fincher stood firm behind Walker's original ending and eventually the studio backed down.

The Graduate

YEAR RELEASED: 1967
DIRECTOR: Mike Nichols
WHO'S IN IT: Anne Bancroft, Dustin Hoffman, Katharine Ross

"I'm a little upset about my future."

Everybody wants a piece of Ben. The college graduate (Dustin Hoffman) is being feted by his busting-with-pride parents and their closest friends, but he wants nothing to do with it. He is pulled this way and that by gooney-faced adults who either provide useless advice meant to be Talmudic in its wisdom ("plastics") or pressure him about his future. Escape comes in the form of family friend, Mrs. Robinson (Anne Bancroft), who asks Ben to drive her home from the party. The affair between Ben and the woman old enough to be his mother—which the film drives home by giving *his* mother a similar haircut and wardrobe—starts up soon after. Their relationship becomes the closest thing to an anchor the drifting Ben has, until he starts dating Mrs. Robinson's daughter, Elaine (Katharine Ross).

One of the great cinematic antiheros, Ben makes an ugly transition from burnt-out overachiever to callous ingrate. Mike Nichols keeps the pressure on throughout, jamming the camera and inquisitive adults into Ben's face, or sticking him at the end of long, lonely hallways. Hoffman's performance progresses subtly from cool disdain to frantic confusion. That he holds his own at all against Bancroft, who cruises across the screen like a cheetah in eveningwear, is even more impressive.

The now-ubiquitous songs by Simon & Garfunkel provide a haunting gloss to the bright-edged cinematography and help reinforce the conclusion's initial euphoria of revolt followed by a painfully slow fade.

Production Notes

When *The Graduate* opened to strong, then stronger, then huge box-office receipts, studios like Universal and Warner Bros. began rethinking their filmmaking strategy, retooling around the idea of attracting younger audiences and hiring younger filmmakers.

Some Like It Hot

YEAR RELEASED: 1959
DIRECTOR: Billy Wilder
WHO'S IN IT: Jack Lemmon, Tony Curtis, Marilyn Monroe

"Nobody's perfect."

The beginning seems like the scrap of an idea from director Billy Wilder's wastebasket. A couple of Chicago musicians, short of gigs and money, become accidental witnesses to the St. Valentine's Day Massacre. Running from the mobsters, the fellas hop a train to Florida, disguised as members of an all-women's band.

Jack Lemmon plays the man calling himself Josephine, a ditzy type who can never find anything in her purse. Tony Curtis hides as Daphne, giving a more refined drag performance. While the two couldn't pass muster on a sunny day in reality, for a movie-length gag, they do just fine. Once they see bandmate Marilyn Monroe, though, the makeup begins to melt.

Going drag doesn't get the boys out of trouble, of course, with the same gangsters they're running from ending up in their Florida hotel. Fortunately, Wilder thought it was funnier to watch Curtis hide his masculinity under those tasteful summer dresses, and to see Lemmon get so in-character that he becomes truly *thrilled* when a daffy older gentleman begins to court Josephine.

Some Like It Hot is often termed the greatest comedy of all time. While this is partly due to the cult of Wilder, the praise is earned, and not just because of the humor. The film is little more than a romp, and one certainly not without sexist attitudes, but it still presents a kind of openhearted tolerance particularly bold for its time.

Casting Call
Originally, Billy Wilder wanted Mitzi Gaynor in the Marilyn Monroe role and Danny Kaye and Bob Hope for the male leads.

Rome: Open City

🌐 💣 🎭

YEAR RELEASED: 1945
DIRECTOR: Roberto Rossellini
WHO'S IN IT: Aldo Fabrizi, Anna Magnani

"How these Italians scream!"

Cinema waits for nobody and no event. World War II had barely concluded, with Italy still covered in rubble (Rome had only been liberated by Allied forces on June 4, 1944), when Roberto Rossellini started filming this neorealist classic. He had no budget and everything was hard to come by, but again, cinema doesn't wait.

Shooting with a rough, quasi-documentary look, Rossellini set his wartime espionage drama in a rundown and occupied Rome, where half-starving residents riot at the bakery and even little children form small partisan bands to strike back at the Nazis and their Fascist cohorts. The action pivots around a partisan group hunted by the Gestapo, focusing particularly on a partisan priest whose grumpy, exhausted-seeming appearance conceals the heart of a true idealist. (Supposedly, the film began as a documentary about a priest who worked with the resistance.) The net begins to close, with the Nazis looking for weak links in the network to exploit. In an otherwise quiet film, the screams of the tortured reverberate with particular horror.

Written by Rossellini along with Sergio Amidei and Federico Fellini, the film takes understandable national pride in the calm heroism of these resisters. But there is universal appeal to the story's immediacy, particularly in the outrages enacted on a suffering populace—the scene in which a woman chasing after her arrested fiancé is gunned down stings so because of its casualness; it's as though this happens every day.

Production Notes

Roberto Rossellini once joked that *Rome: Open City* was "worth more than the persuasion of our Ministry of Foreign Affairs in helping Italy regain its place in the concert of nations."

Ferris Bueller's Day Off

LOL! 👪

YEAR RELEASED: 1986
DIRECTOR: John Hughes
WHO'S IN IT: Matthew Broderick, Alan Ruck, Mia Sara

"How could I possibly be expected to handle school on a day like this?"

It's a beautiful day in the Chicago suburbs, June 5, 1985. The sky is bright, blue, and hopeful, the sun shining, and school feels like even more of a prison than usual. Ferris Bueller (Matthew Broderick, rarely better) is the star of his school and family, and he feels like playing hooky. Given that he's the kind of kid everybody makes excuses for, it doesn't prove hard.

Invited along on this adventure is his best friend Cameron (Alan Ruck), a hypochondriac depressive who's crucial to the plan because his dad has a really cool convertible. Ferris's girlfriend (Mia Sara) is also along for the ride, but she seems to be there mostly to back up Ferris when he's trying to convince Cameron to do something.

They run around town, taking in a Cubs game at Wrigley, checking out the paintings at the Art Institute, and generally enjoying the hell out of being loose in the big city. The most upbeat of John Hughes's high-school films, it has the effervescence of a musical—and even turns into one when Ferris takes the mike for Beatles karaoke during a parade they wander through—and the same giddy disconnect from reality. For reasons unknown, it also became a short-lived television series several years later.

Production Notes

Among the paintings that Ferris and crew check out in the Art Institute of Chicago are Kandinsky's *Improvisation 30 (Cannons)*, Picasso's *Nude Under Pine Tree*, Hopper's *Nighthawks*, and most pointedly, Seurat's *A Sunday Afternoon on the Island of La Grande Jatte*.

Waltz with Bashir

🖥 📖 🍶

YEAR RELEASED: 2008
DIRECTOR: Ari Folman
WHO'S IN IT: Ari Folman, Gadi Erel

"If some details are missing, memory fills in the holes with things that never happened."

Ari Folman's feature-length animated documentary opens with a friend's story about a recurring dream where a pack of vicious dogs gather under his window, eager to get at him. Boaz (Gadi Erel) thinks it's related to something he saw during the Lebanon War, which began on June 6, 1982. Folman also served, but says he doesn't have any dreams. In fact, he can barely remember anything; it's as though an eraser has been dragged across his mind.

The film follows his tracking down of friends, many of whom also served, to see if they can help him unlock the past. As details are pieced together, we see Folman (drawn gloomily with stubble and sad eyes) thrust into a brutal guerrilla war where he can't divine any strategy, only the randomness of ambush and accident. His slow accrual of information leads through battle and terror in the shattered streets of Beirut toward what could be at the heart of his problem: the massacre of Palestinian refugees by Christian Phalangist militias.

Folman dreams that he and some other soldiers plod like sleepwalkers out of the sea toward a wall of skyscrapers while flares drift down, casting everything in a sickly yellow glare. These surreal flashes and Folman's interrogations of himself and others powerfully illustrate the unreliability of memory, and how even the most vivid ones may be invented. Disturbing and emotional, this visually stunning film twins the sad absurdity of *Catch-22* with the tough-minded dedication of the best investigative reporting.

And the Winner Is . . .

Waltz with Bashir was nominated for the best foreign language film Oscar, losing to Japan's *Departures*.

Rio Bravo

 LOL!

YEAR RELEASED: 1959
DIRECTOR: Howard Hawks
WHO'S IN IT: John Wayne, Dean Martin, Ricky Nelson

"A game-legged old man and a drunk, that's all you got?"

John Wayne hadn't strapped on the six-guns since 1956's *The Searchers* when he played sheriff John T. Chance, but his time off didn't hurt him. Chance has arrested a man for murder, the problem being that the convict's brother has plenty of money to toss at the gunmen willing to take a bullet for the boss.

Chance holes up in his town's tiny jail, with only a couple deputies—the alcoholic Dude (Dean Martin, deploying his drunk act for surprising dramatic effect) and the ancient, irascible Stumpy (Walter Brennan)—to back him up. Though Chance picks up some allies like the town hussy, Feathers (Angie Dickinson) and an angel-faced kid (Ricky Nelson), their chances for survival remain awful. Fortunately, Martin and Nelson don't miss the opportunity to harmonize on a couple of tunes.

The bad guys didn't count on Chance and company's resourcefulness, of course, and that inventiveness (and the witty script) is what gives *Rio Bravo* its considerable kick. Director Howard Hawks avoids grandstanding heroisms in favor of terrific scenes where Chance and his compatriots outwit their numerous opponents, whether it's getting the drop on them in a lightning-quick shootout, or discovering that sticks of dynamite turned into primitive hand grenades can even the odds quite nicely. It's professionalism, not bravado, that wins the day. Amidst all this, Hawks still plucks the heartstrings a little. The mostly unspoken friendship between Chance, Stumpy, and Dude is expressed mostly through glares, grunts, and jokes, but you still know these guys would die for one another.

In Homage

Director John Carpenter is one of many who believe that *Rio Bravo* is one of the most perfect films ever made, saying that in one way or another, he's been trying to remake it his entire career.

JUNE 8

The Thin Man

YEAR RELEASED: 1934
DIRECTOR: W. S. Van Dyke
WHO'S IN IT: William Powell, Myrna Loy

"It's putting me way behind in my drinking."

The most enjoyable pair of highly functioning alcoholics ever to grace the screen, Nick and Nora Charles are a debonair pair who like to drink martinis (Nick walks trays of them around a party, inquiring, "Ammunition?") and sass each other. Nick (William Powell) used to be a detective, but after Nora's (Myrna Loy) late father left them a fortune, he doesn't have to work much.

At the start of this film, vaguely adapted from the Dashiell Hammett novel, Nick and Nora are back in New York after four years relaxing in California. Nora finds him in the bar, after which the two of them get down to some serious imbibing and witty repartee. This comes after an overly long murder-mystery setup about a rich inventor of Nick's acquaintance who's missing, with a slew of dubious characters and money-grubbing wives to suspect. Nick isn't interested, but Nora's bored, and even a suave man like Powell can only say no to Loy for so long.

The mystery has nothing to do with how much fun the film is, and in fact just seems to get in the way. Better to hear Nick elucidate to Nora just what his type of woman is ("lanky brunettes with wicked jaws") than to sit through more exposition.

The film was a great hit, appropriately debuting in theaters just a year after Prohibition was ended. Five sequels followed, somehow all less serious than even the mostly frivolous first.

And the Winner Is . . .
Impressively for such a light mystery-comedy, *The Thin Man* was nominated for four Oscars (picture, director, actor, adapted screenplay), but it didn't win any.

JUNE 9

Dead Man

YEAR RELEASED: 1995
DIRECTOR: Jim Jarmusch
WHO'S IN IT: Johnny Depp, Gary Farmer

"Some are born to sweet delight, some are born to endless night."

In Jim Jarmusch's bleakly comic mind-bender of uncommon beauty, Johnny Depp plays a clueless accountant from Cleveland named William Blake who goes out West for a job. Arriving in the town of Machine, Blake finds out from his would-be boss, John Dickinson (Robert Mitchum, in his last role, looking like a biblical prophet) that the job has already been filled. Drunk and looking for consolation, he winds up in bed with a woman, only to have her ex-lover burst in shooting, wounding Blake and killing her. Blake kills the man and escapes. Unfortunately the dead man was the son of Dickinson, who sends a trio of bounty hunters after the slowly dying Blake.

In the woods, Blake finds a lone Indian, Nobody (the excellent Gary Farmer). Captured as a child and sent to England for schooling, Nobody is thrilled to meet someone named for his favorite poet, whose works Nobody recites from memory. The two of them start for the coast, with hunters on their trail and Nobody assuring Blake that he should become "a killer of white men."

The cultural associations come fast and thick, from Nobody's reverent recitations of Blake's apocalyptic works to Depp's Buster Keaton look and downcast demeanor, all of it backed by Neil Young's soundtrack of sheets of windy guitar distortion. While some interactions have the straight-faced humor one associates with Jarmusch, its otherworldly, deathly beauty is entirely separate from anything he has ever created.

Production Notes

Dead Man was the first Western to be filmed in black and white since John Ford's *The Man Who Shot Liberty Valance* (1962).

Homicide

YEAR RELEASED: 1991
DIRECTOR: David Mamet
WHO'S IN IT: Joe Mantegna, William H. Macy

"You know what's called for here? Some of that police work people talk about."

In an unnamed city that could be Chicago but was actually Baltimore (architecture never lies), FBI agents botch the arrest of a suspect. When city detectives are called in to assist, bitch and moan though they do, it's an opportunity they relish. They prowl the squad room, exchanging the kind of bluster that psychs them up for the hunt: "FBI couldn't find Joe Louis in a bowl of rice"—that sort of thing.

But there's a snag. Two of the detectives, Bobby Gold (Joe Mantegna) and Tim Sullivan (William H. Macy, leading-man material well before he was recognized as such) are on their way to make an arrest and embarrass the FBI when they're interrupted. An old Jewish lady was shot dead in her store in an African American neighborhood. Gold gets the case. At first, insecure about his own Jewishness, Gold jokes for the other detectives, making anti-Semitic cracks about the victim's family. Then, feeling guilty, he overcompensates by diving headlong into a conspiracy theory about neo-Nazis and an underground network of anti-Nazi guerrillas. Just enough of it is true to get Gold in way over his head.

By this time, playwright David Mamet had written several screenplays and even directed a couple—*House of Games* (1987), *Things Change* (1988)—but this was the first time he appeared as a real filmmaker. His previous efforts were a little mannered, but here the drama is fluidly captured. Mamet's trademark spiky and profane dialogue is organically woven into the quick-moving plot, and questions of identity and self-hatred flare up in between all the cops-and-robbers action.

The Life Aquatic with Steve Zissou

YEAR RELEASED: 2004
DIRECTOR: Wes Anderson
WHO'S IN IT: Bill Murray, Owen Wilson, Cate Blanchett

"We're in the middle of a lightning strike rescue op, Klaus."

For his *Royal Tenenbaums* follow-up, Anderson created another hideout where his childlike adults can get away from the world. The *Belafonte* is a marine research vessel that's got everything one needs: wine cellar, trained dolphins, and plenty of firearms. (The name is a tribute to Jacques Cousteau, born June 11, 1910, whom the film is dedicated to, and whose boat was named the *Calypso*.)

Steve Zissou (Bill Murray, so deadpan he's nearly tranquilized) is a once-famous marine explorer already fallen on hard times when his partner was eaten by a rare "jaguar shark." He sets out for revenge with the ragtag Team Zissou, which includes an extremely eager young man, Ned Plimpton (Owen Wilson), who might be Zissou's estranged son, and a pregnant Australian reporter (Cate Blanchett).

Much of the film simply slips by, as though seen through Zissou's pot-fogged brain. Even the comparatively action-packed moments—a fantastic, gun-blazing pirate raid set to the blasting guitar of Iggy Pop's "Search and Destroy"—exist inside a dreamlike state. Appropriately, even the humor (and this is a very funny film) comes at the viewer sideways, with most of the jokes taking a second to sink in. Easygoing but never dull, photographed in blissful Mediterranean tones, this is a curiously wonderful comedy that makes you think *every* film should star Bill Murray.

Production Notes

The songs performed in *The Life Aquatic* by Brazilian samba star and sometimes actor Seu Jorge (he had a role in *City of God*, 2002) are all David Bowie covers, only sung in Portuguese with numerous lyrical tweaks by Jorge.

Casino

YEAR RELEASED: 1995
DIRECTOR: Martin Scorsese
WHO'S IN IT: Robert De Niro, Sharon Stone, Joe Pesci

"You only exist out here because of me."

Martin Scorsese explores the cheap thrills of Las Vegas in this ambitious adaptation of Nicholas Pileggi's nonfiction book. Chicago bookie Sam "Ace" Rothstein (Robert De Niro, muted) is sent by the bosses to supervise a huge casino they're skimming oceans of cash from. Nicky Santoro (Joe Pesci), fire to Sam's ice, shows up as muscle, but makes bigger waves than the bosses like. Further complications arise when Sam, in the worst idea of the century, marries beautiful scam artist Ginger McKenna (Sharon Stone).

Scorsese is playing with a broader, flashier canvas than before. Robert Richardson's camerawork dazzles with the glitz of false promises, and the wall-to-wall soundtrack (arias to the Rolling Stones) leaves no room for contemplation. An all-business Sam narrates the inner workings of the casino skim—a seamless crawl into the corridors of money that echoes the famous *Goodfellas* Copacabana steadicam shot—before laying out how and why everything goes wrong.

Pileggi and Scorsese's complex script has fun with the culture clash of the big-city mobsters running wild in the desert. The mobsters bang up against the old-boy network (great cowpoke cameos by L. Q. Jones and Joe Bob Briggs) in a knockdown battle that paved the way for the corporate takeover. This Vegas isn't where dreams are made; it's where they're broken.

Historically Speaking

The names of many real people were changed for *Casino*. Tony "The Ant" Spilotro became Nicky Santoro, Frank "Lefty" Rosenthal became Sam "Ace" Rothstein, and Geri McGee became Ginger McKenna. And Chicago became simply "back home."

The Last Picture Show

YEAR RELEASED: 1971
DIRECTOR: Peter Bogdanovich
WHO'S IN IT: Jeff Bridges, Cybill Shepherd, Timothy Bottoms, Ben Johnson

"Nothing's really been right since Sam the Lion died."

The dust bowl of the 1930s doesn't seem to have let up in the one-horse Texas town of Anarene, circa 1951, with the whole place looking ready to blow away. The local class of high-school seniors has taken a look around and not liked what they've seen. A cocky Jeff Bridges plays Duane Jackson, a popular jock who gets involved with the rich and seductive ice queen Jacy Farrow (Cybill Shepherd, in her debut).

They're all killing time and they know it. The heart and soul of the town, ex-cowboy and pool hall proprietor Sam the Lion (Ben Johnson), is getting older, and people aren't going to the town's second-run theater as much anymore. Once Sam is gone and the theater is closed up, everybody will have to figure out what to do with their lives.

Although the film studiously tries to be true to its setting (particularly in the lonesome country soundtrack), it has several hallmarks of Peter Bogdanovich's long apprenticeship as a film buff (self-conscious film references, shooting in black and white, a stark presentation of sexuality) and was duly praised. Bogdanovich had a strong friendship with Orson Welles at the time, so it's maybe fitting that this picture would prove to be Bogdanovich's *Citizen Kane*. Although his wildly varied career contained some successes, he would never match the artistry or popularity of this sad and lovely film.

Lost and Found
A director's cut of *The Last Picture Show* that Peter Bogdanovich edited in 1999 contained seven minutes of extra footage, mostly extra scenes of Duane and Jacy.

Before Sunrise

YEAR RELEASED: 1995
DIRECTOR: Richard Linklater
WHO'S IN IT: Ethan Hawke, Julie Delpy

"But then the morning comes, and we turn back into pumpkins, right?"

Céline (Julie Delpy) isn't stupid; she just believes she knows what Jesse (Ethan Hawke) is thinking. "It's like some male fantasy," she says, the idea of meeting a beautiful French women on a train, sleeping with her, and never seeing her again. She might be right but that doesn't mean she's going to stop talking to him; they're having too nice a time.

In the hands of most filmmakers, this would be an exercise in patience. A voluble young American meets a smart young French woman on the train from Budapest. He's catching a morning flight from Vienna; she's going on to Paris. They start talking. Too soon, the stop for Vienna comes up. In an inspired moment, he convinces her to get off the train with him to walk around all night until his plane leaves. All just a little too perfect.

As he showed in talk-happy films from *Dazed and Confused* (1993) to *Waking Life* (2001), though, Linklater is the premier American director of amiable, half-meaningful chat. Once it's realized that this is really all there is—just two people, walking and talking through a beautiful day and night in Vienna—viewers can relax and go with it, following the ebb and flow of conversation as though eavesdropping on fascinating strangers.

This film is a romance, make no mistake—they aren't walking around Buffalo in January, after all, this *is* Vienna—but it's a romance for people who normally can't stand the genre.

In Homage

The equally excellent 2004 sequel *Before Sunset* reunited Julie Delpy and Ethan Hawke, several years older and sadder, for another enthralling day of walking and talking, this time in Paris. An uncommon occurrence of lightning striking twice.

Airplane!

YEAR RELEASED: 1980
DIRECTOR: Jim Abrahams, David Zucker, Jerry Zucker
WHO'S IN IT: Robert Hays, Julie Hagerty, Leslie Nielsen, Lloyd Bridges, Peter Graves

"Stewardess? I speak jive."

Airplane! was the bastard creation of three writer/directors, who crafted the comedic equivalent of tossing lit cherry bombs at the movie screen. Stewardess Elaine (Julie Hagerty) is having problems with her boyfriend Ted (Robert Hays), an ex-military pilot still psychologically damaged after a doomed mission in "the war." (It's the 1970s but his memories all look suspiciously like WWII footage.) Ted sneaks onto Elaine's flight for a last-ditch reconciliation, which turns out to be fortuitous when the pilots start dropping from food poisoning.

What Abrahams and the two Zuckers got so right in this superbly unsubtle gagfest was not trying to be too specific in what they were ripping on. While there are pointed references to *Saturday Night Fever* (1977) and *From Here to Eternity* (1953), the film is really goofing on the steady stream of lousy, cast-of-hundreds disaster films that had been lumbering into theaters for the previous decade. So you get the crack contingent of 1950s TV stalwarts (Peter Graves, Robert Stack, Lloyd Bridges) chewing scenery and ripping through the gags with hilariously straight-faced discipline. The chaotic mood is pitched somewhere perfectly between playground silly and standup comic filthy.

Auteur, Auteur

The filmmakers three behind *Airplane!* would reunite for a couple other worthwhile comedies like *Top Secret!* (1984) and *Ruthless People* (1986) before the Zuckers split off for less glorious pursuits, like 1990's *Ghost* (Jerry) and 2003's *Scary Movie 3* (David).

JUNE 16

Battleship Potemkin

YEAR RELEASED: 1925
DIRECTOR: Sergei Eisenstein
WHO'S IN IT: I. Bobrov, Beatrice Vitoldi

"Revolution is war."

The events that Sergei Eisenstein, arguably the Soviet Union's greatest filmmaker, documented in this, his most heralded film, are not pretty. But in the hands of a man whose work seems revolutionary even today, they become heart-racing calls to action.

This sometimes stiff, frequently enthralling piece of silent propaganda deals with an unsuccessful 1905 revolt against Russia's tsars. It starts on the Russian warship *Potemkin*, where the sailors are sick of officer brutality and eating maggot-ridden meat (close-up of squirming maggots, cut to sneering officer). So they mutiny. Sailing into Odessa, the crew lays out for display the body of martyred sailor Vakulinchuk, which brings crowds of people to mourn and agitate against their oppressors. (His actual funeral took place on June 16, 1905.)

Out of nowhere the army marches down a wide flight of steps with robot precision, slaughtering women and children with impunity. Panic explodes while the Cossacks charge and a baby carriage rattles helplessly downward. Later, the *Potemkin* sails off, its newly emancipated crew of comrades ready to do battle, hopelessly outnumbered by an approaching squadron of czarist vessels.

Eisenstein made this silent film just eight years after the 1917 Communist revolution, and his repeated images of striking sailors and proud workers shouting for justice still has a whiff of authenticity. While subtle as a kick in the head, and proto-Stalinist in its ugly worship of machinery and power, the film's electrifyingly quick edits and pungent fury is as palpable today as then. Make sure to watch a version that includes Shostakovich's score.

In Homage
Brian De Palma cribbed from Eisenstein's Odessa Steps sequence for his bravura Union Station shootout in *The Untouchables* (1987).

June 17

All the President's Men

YEAR RELEASED: 1976
DIRECTOR: Alan J. Pakula
WHO'S IN IT: Dustin Hoffman, Robert Redford, Jason Robards, Martin Balsam, Hal Holbrook

"Just follow the money."

When Robert Redford bought the film rights to Bob Woodward and Carl Bernstein's book about the Watergate break-in and cover-up, it could have signaled impending disaster. The combination of serious subject matter and hot young film star could have ended up with truth of the matter jettisoned for dramatic expediency. What happened, shockingly, was that the filmmakers took the story as it was and found their drama in the historic and journalistic record. Amazing.

Redford plays Woodward and Dustin Hoffman is Bernstein, the two *Washington Post* reporters who helped bring down the Nixon White House. Starting with a curious June 17, 1972, break-in at a Democratic office in Washington, DC's Watergate Hotel, Woodward and Bernstein track down leads with the help of code-named source "Deep Throat" (Hal Holbrook), who gives them hints about what lies behind the break-in, imploring them to "follow the money."

As the scope of the conspiracy widens, the two reporters seem almost overwhelmed by it, and they alternately badger and are helped along by their executive editor Howard Simons (Martin Balsam) and managing editor Ben Bradlee (Jason Robards). William Goldman's dialogue-heavy script and Alan J. Pakula's steady direction resolutely refuse to tart up the material; all the actors play it down the middle without melodramatics, yet it's all continually enthralling. The actors run around like real reporters, with bleary eyes and rumpled clothes, notebooks at the ready. And eventually they find the truth.

It's a reminder of a time when journalists could still be heroes.

And the Winner Is . . .

All the President's Men was nominated for eight Oscars, winning four, including one for Jason Robards. It lost best picture to *Rocky*.

Blue Velvet

YEAR RELEASED: 1986
DIRECTOR: David Lynch
WHO'S IN IT: Kyle MacLachlan, Isabella Rossellini, Dennis Hopper

"Frank is a very sick and dangerous man."

Although David Lynch's first two films—*Eraserhead* (1976) and *The Elephant Man* (1980)—were both grotesque in a stately, black-and-white manner, with *Blue Velvet* he set the template for his middle career. Here, Lynch discovered color, plot, and most importantly, violence.

Kyle MacLachlan, who put on his best blank expression for Lynch here and in his TV series *Twin Peaks*, plays Jeffrey Beaumont. After discovering a severed ear on the sidewalk in his supposedly idyllic town of Lumberton, Jeffrey gets sucked in to a world of violence, sex, and (of course) violent sex. Though attracted to blond, wholesome Sandy Williams (Laura Dern, Lynch's female MacLachlan), Jeffrey also falls in lust with Dorothy Vallens (Isabella Rossellini). A nightclub singer with sultry allure, Dorothy is the plaything of psychotic, nitrous-huffing gangster Frank Booth (Dennis Hopper), who's holding her husband and child hostage. Jeffrey wants to make things right. It remains to be seen whether such a thing is even possible in this world.

There is some satire in Lynch's film, a drawing back of the self-satisfied suburban veil to reveal the rottenness underneath (early on, his camera practically burrows into the dirt to find it). It's not the most shocking of revelations, as books and films have been doing the same thing since *Peyton Place*. What gives the film its power is the nightmarish fury with which Lynch unleashes his demons upon the audience. He would try the same kind of sensory assault in later films like *Wild at Heart* (1990) and *Lost Highway* (1996), but the end result is never so memorable (or skincrawlingly strange) as it is here.

There Will Be Blood

YEAR RELEASED: 2007
DIRECTOR: Paul Thomas Anderson
WHO'S IN IT: Daniel Day-Lewis, Paul Dano, Ciarán Hinds

"I like to think of myself as an oilman."

For too long Daniel Day-Lewis was the exquisitely crafted actor whose quiet side had been exploited by well-meaning literary adaptations from *A Room with a View* (1985) to *The Age of Innocence* (1993). After Scorsese unleashed his inner demon in 2002's *Gangs of New York*, he became a performer who raised the hounds of hell with a few choice words.

As oil prospector Daniel Plainview, Day-Lewis is the pure distillation of American greed in this curious and furious film. Plainview has seemingly no interior life, having acquired a son, H. W. (Dillon Freasier), more by accident than on purpose. With predatory determination, he relieves a young preacher, Paul Sunday (Paul Dano), of his oil-rich land for what proves to be a very low sum. Plainview lets nothing get in his way, his eyes betraying only contempt for the human race. At a moment of victory he exults with barbaric glee over the man he's bested, and coins the decade's best catchphrase at the same time: "I. Drink. Your. Milkshake!" (There are even T-shirts.)

The film was a welcome departure for Paul Thomas Anderson, who had followed the overstuffed, adrenalized style of his ensemble films like *Magnolia* (1999) as far as that would take him. Moving in fits and starts to an unearthly soundtrack (by Radiohead's Jonny Greenwood), the story gathers momentum more through the power of its elemental landscape and raw performances than the plot.

Production Notes

Paul Thomas Anderson based *There Will Be Blood* (somewhat) on Upton Sinclair's novel *Oil!* (1927), changing the names and almost all of the plot.

The Adventures of Robin Hood

YEAR RELEASED: 1938
DIRECTOR: Michael Curtiz, William Keighley
WHO'S IN IT: Errol Flynn, Olivia de Havilland, Claude Rains, Basil Rathbone

"You're a bold rascal, Robin. I like you."

Hearing that King Richard, off fighting the crusades, has been taken for ransom, the squirrelly Prince John (Claude Rains) and his right-hand thug, Sir Guy of Gisbourne (Basil Rathbone, one year before donning Sherlock Holmes's deerstalker cap), use that as an excuse to ramp up taxes on the people of Nottingham, torturing and murdering all those who oppose. Who will stop him? Sir Robin of Locksley (Errol Flynn), of course.

Any question about Flynn's status as true movie star is completely erased in the scene where he strides into a banquet at Nottingham Castle, arrogantly mouths off to the dozens of armed Normans, and then daringly escapes (Arrows fly! Swords clash!). Every inch the dashing hero, even in scorching bright green tights, Flynn bounds through this giddy Technicolor adventure without once breaking his grin. His Robin Hood might be furious about injustice, but that doesn't stop him from having a grand time. Flynn's trademark stance here is chest thrust out with hands on hips, all the better to deliver a great bellowing laugh.

Norman Reilly Raine and Seton I. Miller's script emphasizes dashing fun over all, with friendly brawls, giant feasts, some cute scenes between Robin and Maid Marian (Olivia de Havilland), and great sword fights. Rains and Rathbone have a blast camping it up as the hiss-worthy villains. Swashes are buckled. The innocent are avenged. Evildoers are punished. And love conquers all.

Production Notes

Hard-driving Michael Curtiz replaced *The Adventures of Robin Hood*'s mild-mannered first director William Keighley, who had let the film go over budget and over schedule.

Natural Born Killers

YEAR RELEASED: 1994
DIRECTOR: Oliver Stone
WHO'S IN IT: Woody Harrelson, Juliette Lewis, Robert Downey, Jr.

"Do you think anyone actually remembers anything out there in zombieland?"

A psychedelic onslaught that would be laughable if it weren't so ingenious, Oliver Stone's blood-soaked, media-saturated hell-ride through the television-besotted America of the 1990s represents an evil kind of pinnacle in his career.

Building on the bones of a Quentin Tarantino script about young killers on the run, Stone creates a mad, time-skipping carnival in which overkill is just the beginning. Mickey (Woody Harrleson, giddy with bloodshed) and Mallory (Juliette Lewis) are star-crossed lovers who kill her parents—in a scene disconcertingly shot as a sitcom, canned laugh track and all—and go on a murder spree. Serial killers being a national pastime, Mickey and Mallory have chasers, from psychotic cops to fame-hungry tabloid journalists (Robert Downey, Jr., walking away with every scene).

Since his canvas is huge (America in the age of trash media), Stone shoots wide and messy. His *JFK* experiments with changing film stocks and confetti-like editing are paired with a warping music-video surrealism. The mood shifts from slapstick comedy to crazed bloodshed in the blink of an eye, with everything dialed up to eleven all the time. Everyone performs like they're having the time of their lives—see Tommy Lee Jones's greasy, Molière-inspired warden with the farcical moustache.

The ending is a cop-out, but the director's cut alternate conclusion crafts a poetic grandeur out of the horror that preceded it.

Production Notes

Although intended as a critique on violence in America, after *Natural Born Killers'* release there were multiple news stories about thrill-killings committed by young people supposedly obsessed with the film.

Sunset Boulevard

YEAR RELEASED: 1950
DIRECTOR: Billy Wilder
WHO'S IN IT: William Holden, Gloria Swanson, Erich von Stroheim

"We didn't need dialogue. We had faces!"

When we first see Joe Gillis (William Holden, half-caring, half-cynical, all worn out), he's lying face-down in a pool. Dead. "The poor dope," Joe narrates. "He always wanted a pool." Flashing back, Joe is on the run from bill collectors and hides in the driveway of the Hollywood mansion of silent-movie star Norma Desmond (Gloria Swanson, rapturously psychotic). Not exactly overrun with friends these days, the delusional, gargoyle-like Norma takes Joe on to write a screenplay about biblical seductress Salome, which she thinks will be her triumphant cinematic return. He's really a kept man, though, ensuring that once Norma finds out about the girl he's seeing, there will be hell to pay.

It's about the best thing that Billy Wilder ever did. Even *Double Indemnity* (1944) doesn't quite have anything like Norma's gothic fantasies about a fame that no longer exists, or Holden's self-hating smirk, which almost makes you think he knows what's in store for the likes of him. Wilder adds a number of nice Hollywood touches as well, casting the great Erich von Stroheim as Norma's personal assistant (von Stroheim directed Swanson in 1929's *Queen Kelly*) and having a trio of real silent-film stars (including Buster Keaton) play what Joe calls her "waxworks" friends. That touch of authenticity makes Norma's purgatory, as divorced from reality as it is, seem so sadly true to life.

Lost and Found

Charles Brackett and Billy Wilder had planned another beginning for *Sunset Boulevard*, starting with Joe's corpse arriving at the morgue while a man narrates, "Don't be scared. There's a lot of us in here." Joe then answers, "I'm not scared."

Blood Simple

YEAR RELEASED: 1984
DIRECTOR: Joel Coen
WHO'S IN IT: John Getz, Frances McDormand, Dan Hedaya, M. Emmet Walsh

"What I know about is Texas. And down here, you're on your own."

As a first film, it's a career maker; even as a fifth or tenth film, it would be a classic. Somewhere in Texas, country-western bar owner Julian Marty (Dan Hedaya) suspects his much-younger wife Abby (a teenage-looking Frances McDormand) has been cheating on him. After private investigator Loren Visser (M. Emmet Walsh) brings Marty graphic evidence of her shacking up with one of his bartenders, the quiet Ray (John Getz), Marty decides it's time to get rid of the two of them permanently. It's clear a double-cross or two is coming, but the buried-alive thing is something of a shock.

Joel and Ethan Coen's taut script echoes pulp novelists like Jim Thompson, while also giving the giggly Walsh opportunity to show why he was one of the best supporting players out there. The brothers' keen visual artistry was already evident in the film's striking look, which made the most of the Texas setting's wide-open nighttime spaces. It also resulted in a few indelible sequences, particularly the bloody climactic scene where a pursuer blasts holes through a wall after his prey, each bullet sending a shaft of blinding light into a darkened room.

The Coens' next film, *Raising Arizona* (1987), was bawdier but also much more derivative. It took a few more tries before they could reconnect with the originality of their debut.

Lost and Found

Unlike most such re-edits, the Coen brothers' 2000 director's cut of *Blood Simple* didn't include extra footage, and was in fact about three minutes shorter. The Coens facetiously said that they chose to cut out "some of the boring parts."

Dazed and Confused

YEAR RELEASED: 1993
DIRECTOR: Richard Linklater
WHO'S IN IT: Jason London, Rory Cochrane, Matthew McConaughey

"If I ever start referring to these as the best years of my life . . . remind me to kill myself."

Richard Linklater's follow-up to his innovative and nearly formless *Slacker* (1991)—which announced that decade's indie filmmaker crop—is almost as plot-free but infinitely more enjoyable. Structurally it's akin to *American Graffiti* (1973), though not as serious—the upperclassmen still have senior year to look forward to. There's darkness on the edges, but in the meantime, a six-pack and some Foghat tunes will make everything just fine. It's the last day of classes at a high school in a small Texas town in the bicentennial year of 1976—flags are flying. Everyone cruises around, enjoying their freedom. Beer and pot are consumed in epic quantities. Next morning, some friends will drive to Houston to buy Aerosmith tickets for the concert on June 24, 1976. All in a day and night's fun.

Linklater's long, improvisational rehearsal process for his cast of indie stalwarts (Adam Goldberg, Rory Cochrane) and soon-to-explode stars (Ben Affleck, Matthew McConaughey) paid off. His sprawling mass of characters wander, seemingly at random, in and out of the action while still making a vivid impression. McConaughey's sleepy-eyed car fiend who's way too old to be hanging out with these kids ("That's what I love about these high-school girls, man. I get older, they stay the same age") particularly resonates. This is a film, loved by both critics and people just looking for a rowdy comedy, that not only rewards but also demands repeated viewing.

Production Notes

Concerned over the wall-to-wall depictions of drug use, Universal dumped *Dazed and Confused* into theaters with little support. It later became a cult hit.

Network

YEAR RELEASED: 1976
DIRECTOR: Sidney Lumet
WHO'S IN IT: Faye Dunaway, William Holden, Peter Finch

"I don't have to tell you things are bad. Everybody knows things are bad."

A film more imitated and quoted from than sincerely watched these days, Sidney Lumet's scandalous satire is one of the bleakest, most vicious things to come out of the 1970s. It treats its story's tragedy and chaos with little more than a resigned, tearful chuckle.

Peter Finch plays Howard Beale, the TV news anchorman we see charging madly through the rain-pummeled Manhattan streets at the start. Once in the studio, he rants on the air about how horrible everything is in the world and wonders why somebody doesn't do anything about it. Realizing his mental implosion means huge ratings, the network exploits him as much as possible. Max Schumacher (William Holden) and Diane Christensen (Faye Dunaway) are his handlers, a tired old newsman who remembers better days and a shark-like executive who sees nothing but dollar signs ahead. Disorganization reigns as Finch's show is filled with increasingly elaborate stunts, and everything that needed to be said about the advent of reality television is said.

Paddy Chayefsky's script raged boldly against what seemed to be a civilization-wide collapse, from rising crime to the diminishing quality of almost everything. While flirting too much with the apocalyptic, Chayefsky's critique of a media world gone mad for profits is still dead-on. Lumet delivers a potentially hysterical story with rigorous drama and smart humor. He knows that people might shout that they're mad as hell and aren't going to take it anymore . . . but afterwards they'll shut the window and go back to watching whatever rubbish is on television.

M

🌐 🔗

YEAR RELEASED: 1931
DIRECTOR: Fritz Lang
WHO'S IN IT: Peter Lorre

"This won't bring back our children."

This dense chiller by Fritz Lang goes further than almost any other film in eliciting sympathy for the devil. This was stage actor Peter Lorre's first film role (Lang cast him without even a screen test), and after viewing it, there is no way to shake this impression of him.

Lorre (born on this day in 1904) plays Hans Beckert, a meek little man who murders children in the dark alleyways of an unnamed German city, while whistling Edvard Grieg's "In the Halls of the Mountain King" from Ibsen's play *Peer Gynt*. The killings (based supposedly on Peter Kürten, a serial killer who haunted Düsseldorf in 1930) turn the city upside down, and the police solicit help from all corners. The city's criminal element is delighted to help, since police pressure is disrupting business most unpleasantly.

Beckert is no antihero, though Lang dares us to sympathize with him. The film certainly doesn't leave us with the impression that Beckert even enjoys his monstrous acts; he seems as terrified of his own sick compulsion as he is of those chasing him. Once Beckert is tracked down—somebody recognizes his whistling and uses chalk to tag his coat with a large *M*—the city's criminals put him on trial in their own kangaroo court, delighted to be able to pass judgment on somebody.

Auteur, Autuer

Fritz Lang left Germany not long after making *M*, a hunted man in his own way. In 1933, Nazi propaganda minister Joseph Goebbels offered him the lead position at the German Cinema Institute. Lang turned it down and eventually stole out of the country. The job went to Leni Riefenstahl, whose films like *Triumph of the Will* (1935) showed she had no problem celebrating the Nazis.

2046

YEAR RELEASED: 2004
DIRECTOR: Wong Kar-wai
WHO'S IN IT: Tony Leung, Faye Wong, Takuya Kimura, Zhang Ziyi

"Love is all a matter of timing."

The setting of *2046* is a hotel in 1960s Hong Kong. Tony Leung plays Chow Mo-wan, his character from Wong Kar-wai's *In the Mood for Love* (2000). But whereas in that film Chow pined endlessly for a woman always beyond his reach, in this more sensual and strange companion piece, he is getting into one tricky relationship after another, frequently with the women moving in and out of the apartment next door (number 2046). There's the frisky Bai Ling (Zhang Ziyi), a party girl and prostitute; the landlord's daughter, Wang Jing-wen (Faye Wong), who moons over a Japanese boyfriend; and Su Li-zhen (Gong Li), a mysterious gambler he meets in Singapore. While all this is going on, Chow is eking out a living as a science-fiction author and crafting a surreal epic of a futuristic city where people ride a train toward a distant place where they can relive their memories.

Any attempts to make sense out of *2046*'s spider's web of entanglements are doomed to failure. Wong Kar-wai seems to have just roughly outlined his story, then spent years embroidering around it. The sensibility of the better-known *In the Mood for Love* (which this is something of a sequel to) is all here, only more intensely realized: the dark hallways and richly saturated lights, cigarette smoke curling in slow motion, glamorous outfits, and thwarted desires. It is less a story than an intoxicating ballad of tragic love.

Production Notes

Wong Kar-wai took four years and three cinematographers to make *2046* and was still shooting material until just a few days before its Cannes Film Festival premiere.

Blazing Saddles

YEAR RELEASED: 1974
DIRECTOR: Mel Brooks
WHO'S IN IT: Cleavon Little, Gene Wilder, Harvey Korman, Mel Brooks

"Not only was it authentic frontier gibberish, it expressed the courage little seen in this day and age."

In 1974 Mel Brooks released two vaudeville takes on classic Hollywood. *Young Frankenstein*, which spoofed Universal horror films, was very funny, but nothing more. The other was this genre-smashing spoof of Westerns whose sly racial satire reflects the voice of cowriter Richard Pryor, whose stamp can still be felt in the film's more jarringly controversial moments.

A cabal of corrupt businessmen and politicians want to run a railroad right through a peaceful Western town. To make sure nobody will want to live there anymore, the evil Hedley Lamarr (Harvey Korman) sends the town Bart (a dashing, urbane Cleavon Little), the West's first African American sheriff, assuming they'll run him out. The reception, unprintable for the most part, isn't pretty, but Bart makes the best of it. Soon, with the help of gunslinger Jim (an admirably restrained Gene Wilder), he's got the town on his side battling against the anachronistic army of outlaws, bikers, and Nazis Hedley sends their way to finish the job.

The kitchen-sink approach that doomed so many of Brooks's broader comedies works ingeniously here, from Madeline Kahn's role as Lili von Shtupp, a goony Marlene Dietrich spoof, to Brooks's appearance as a Yiddish-speaking Jewish-Indian chief. Brooks's nonsensical impulses ultimately can't be contained and the whole affair busts out of the Old West into modern-day Hollywood. It's all gleefully tasteless in the best possible way.

Courting Controversy

Richard Pryor's split from Mel Brooks during the production of *Blazing Saddles* left Pryor bitter, believing that he never received proper credit for his contributions.

The Man Who Knew Too Much

🔍

YEAR RELEASED: 1956
DIRECTOR: Alfred Hitchcock
WHO'S IN IT: James Stewart, Doris Day

"Don't you realize that Americans dislike having their children stolen?"

In this spy thriller, Hitchcock takes a rare excursion to an exotic locale, setting up in beautiful Morocco, where a vacationing American family gets sucked in to killer intrigue.

Dr. Ben McKenna (James Stewart) is touring Morocco with his wife Jo (Doris Day, perfectly matching Stewart's wholesome straightness) and son Hank (Christopher Olsen). They make friends with one Louis Bernard (Daniel Gelin), who seems normal enough to Ben. Jo has her suspicions, confirmed when a fatally wounded Louis comes to them in a bustling market and whispers of a murder. But Ben and Jo can't tell anybody because soon after Hank is kidnapped, they're told not to let out the secret, or else.

One of Hitchcock's lightest and most purely entertaining works since *The 39 Steps*, there is little psychological backdrop to what's going on, which is perhaps why the film receives less critical attention than, say, *Vertigo* or *Psycho*. But the classic moments keep coming. The shot in the market with the makeup peeling off Louis's slackened face is one of Hitchcock's most indelible, while the climactic scenes in London—where an assassination has been timed to coincide with a cymbal crash at a Royal Albert Hall concert, and Jo tries to find Hank by brightly singing "Que Sera Sera" (the song won the Oscar that year)—are a nerve-wrattling blast. This is a Hitchcock film you could watch with the kids, which isn't a criticism.

In Homage

The Man Who Knew Too Much is the one instance of Hitch revisiting his own work. He shot his first version in black and white in 1934 with Leslie Banks, Edna Best, and Peter Lorre, but that one is barely remembered these days.

Harlan County U.S.A.

YEAR RELEASED: 1976
DIRECTOR: Barbara Kopple
WHO'S IN IT: Lois Scott, Florence Reese

"If I get shot, they can't shoot the union out of me."

In the summer of 1973, the coal miners of Brookside, Kentucky, decided to join the United Mine Workers of America. Their employer, Duke Power, refused to sign the contract, so the miners went on strike on June 30. Documentarian Barbara Kopple recorded what happened next.

The film begins underground, with the soot-streaked miners hunched in dark caverns, doing the work that powers the nation. Kopple interviews the strikers but more often just records strategy meetings and the picket lines. She has a particular affinity for the women's auxiliaries of miners' wives who help block the road to the mine that "scab" replacement workers are trying to use. Several of the women have long memories from the 1930s, when the county was known as "Bloody Harlan." Footage from that time shows lines of armed soldiers, mounted machine guns, and running street battles. The "feudal" system the miners were fighting then doesn't seem to have changed, with the presence of squint-eyed "gun thugs" who stare menacingly at the strikers, fingering their triggers. Shots are fired, the camera crew attacked. This is labor warfare.

In a film exploding with immediacy, Kopple doesn't pretend not to side with the workers. But given what she shows of their employers' ugly tactics, it's hard to blame her. A recurring song has a chorus that says it plain: "Which side are you on?" With profit-hungry thuggery on one side and serf-like conditions on the other, it's an easy question to answer.

And the Winner Is . . .

Harlan County U.S.A. reportedly out-performed *Rocky* and the first remake of *King Kong* at one Boston theater where they were all playing. It went on to win the Oscar for best documentary.

The Triplets of Belleville

YEAR RELEASED: 2003
DIRECTOR: Sylvain Chomet
WHO'S IN IT: (voices of) Jean-Claude Donda, Michel Robin, Monica Viegas

"Swinging Belleville rendevouz . . ."

This film is best described as a chase with musical interludes, and as such is a free-wheeling, foot-tapping delight. In comic–book artist Sylvain Chomet's singularly strange animated fantasia, a story of sorts is concocted somehow out of a bicyclist, his dedicated mother, a lazy dog, and three Jazz Age singers with catchy rhythms and witchlike eyes.

There is little dialogue throughout Chomet's film, but with a storytelling style that harkens back to early Walt Disney films and the silent cinema, none is needed. Madame Souza is a squat, determined little old lady who wants nothing more than for her odd son, Champion, to be happy. She buys him a dog, Bruno, but that doesn't help. Thinking he might have an interest in racing, she buys him a bicycle, which works. Champion becomes so enamored of the sport (though keeping his gloomy disposition) that he enters the Tour de France. Unfortunately, he does so just in time to be kidnapped by some gangsters.

With a panting Bruno at her side, Souza chases after Champion and his kidnappers, following them to a city that seems to be New York. Along the way, she also encounters the Triplets of Belleville themselves, a song-and-dance group who hum and sing like starlets from a 1930s film, with a jazzy, Django Reinhardt–esque musical score backing up their catchy little ditties.

And the Winner Is . . .

The Triplets of Belleville received Oscar nominations for best foreign film and best song, somehow losing in the latter category to a forgettable Annie Lennox number from *The Lord of the Rings: The Return of the King.*

Unforgiven

YEAR RELEASED: 1992
DIRECTOR: Clint Eastwood
WHO'S IN IT: Clint Eastwood, Morgan Freeman, Gene Hackman

"You'd be William Munny out of Missouri, killer of women and children."

A prostitute in a raw Western frontier town has her face viciously slashed; the other prostitutes, flushed with vengeance, offer a reward for the killing of the assailant. They get a brash young wannabe calling himself the Schofield Kid (Jaimz Woolvett), as well as retired gunslinger William Munny (Clint Eastwood, haggard of face, voice, and soul) and his old partner Ned Logan (Morgan Freeman, sublime). Also looking for the reward is contract killer English Bob (Richard Harris), shadowed by a smug penny novelist (Saul Rubinek) busy mythologizing the Old West's bloody and antiheroic reality.

What should be an easy job becomes rife with thorny moral and practical complications. When the hired guns finally locate their target, Schofield, who claims to have killed five men, can't finish him off; neither can Ned, realizing he can't return to his old ways. Munny—a legendarily nasty killer once reformed by his now-dead wife—does the job, unleashing his old, ugly self. Once a feckless sheriff takes his revenge, Munny visits a whirlwind of fury upon the town.

This thoughtful, doom-laden script by David Webb Peoples (*Blade Runner*) provided the pinnacle of Eastwood's career as actor and filmmaker. His William Munny is burnt-out and bleak, offering up knowing lines like "we've *all* got it coming, kid." He's the ugly soul of the Old West and the nation itself. Eastwood even makes sure to include a fluttering American flag in the background as Munny announces, "I'll come back here and kill all of you."

And the Winner Is . . .
Unforgiven was nominated for nine Oscars, winning four, including Best Picture.

July 3

Magnolia

YEAR RELEASED: 1999
DIRECTOR: Paul Thomas Anderson
WHO'S IN IT: Julianne Moore, William H. Macy, Tom Cruise

"This is something that happens."

There is so much teeming life, pain, love, hate, and poetry coursing through this film's veins that it is almost as though its creator is trying to show off just how much he can wrangle into a single work. Like Robert Altman, to whom this film and its predecessor *Boogie Nights* caused Paul Thomas Anderson to be endlessly compared, writer-director Anderson doesn't see the point of one story when a whole batch of them (preferably interlinked in a dozen small ways) would be better.

Among his cast of characters careening through the Southern California night are William H. Macy, playing a former champion of kids' quiz shows, a dying Jason Robards, Tom Cruise as a snake-oil salesman of the men's motivational variety, and a druggie played by Melora Walters, who is the object of attraction for sadsack cop played by John C. Reilly.

There is a lot more going on around the edges, and it doesn't tie together in the taut but sometimes hysterical way of *Boogie Nights*. Anderson had figured out how to replace physical violence with the emotional variety, and the gaping wounds are much bloodier. It's shot like a dream and includes, short though it is, the best evidence of what a great actor Cruise really could have been. It's a great American film—one of the decade's most memorable—and infinitely rewarding, no matter what you think about that plague-storm of frogs.

In Homage

During the filming of *Prairie Home Companion* (2007), Robert Altman was apparently so sickly that the film's insurer demanded a backup director; this turned out to be Paul Thomas Anderson, perhaps repaying a debt for inspirations received.

On the Waterfront

YEAR RELEASED: 1954
DIRECTOR: Elia Kazan
WHO'S IN IT: Marlon Brando, Eva Marie Saint, Karl Malden, Lee J. Cobb

"The only arithmetic he ever got was hearing the referee count up to ten."

This is a film many people have seen a few seconds of in some classic-film clip show—usually those scenes of Marlon Brando bemoaning his sad, pathetic lot in life. The film is a story about dockside corruption whose protagonist (Brando) is a punchy ex-fighter and all-around galoot living on the wrong end of the New York waterfront. The film that waits on the other side of those oversampled moments isn't quite a masterpiece, but it's a shining example of American drama with soul, grit, and a purpose; three commodities always in short supply.

Brando's ex-fighter Terry Molloy does odd errands and enforcement work for the local labor/crime boss, Johnny Friendly (Lee J. Cobb, menacing as always). When he inadvertently helps Friendly's boys rub out a friend on the suspicion that he was going to squeal to the Crime Commission, Molloy starts having pangs of conscience. Joining him in the fight are Edie Doyle (Eva Marie Saint), whose brother was killed by Friendly, and Father Barry (Karl Malden), a reformist priest. Watching the battered and bruised Molloy try to resuscitate some glimmer of dignity in his disappointing life constitutes much of the film's drama. Director Elia Kazan's stark direction and Budd Schulberg's hard-nosed script provide the rest.

And the Winner Is . . .

Budd Schulberg based his script on an earlier draft by Arthur Miller, itself inspired by a 1949 Pulitzer Prize–winning *New York Sun* investigation of New York waterfront racketeering. Schulberg won an Oscar for it, one of eight that the film raked in.

Two-Lane Blacktop

YEAR RELEASED: 1971
DIRECTOR: Monte Hellman
WHO'S IN IT: James Taylor, Dennis Wilson, Warren Oates

"Color me gone, baby!"

There is something in this plot-less film for almost everyone *not* to like, and yet its reflective sense of beauty and wandering poetry make it a work of wonder. A man credited as the Driver (James Taylor, yes, *that* one) and his sidekick, the Mechanic (Beach Boy Dennis Wilson) are heading east in a dirty-gray '55 Chevy looking for street-racing action like pool hustlers. They run up against a man (Warren Oates) named in the credits for his showoff car, a tarted-up yellow GTO. He's spoiling for a race, so they give it to him—first one to Washington, DC, wins the other's car. The race itself is an understated affair. The Driver and Mechanic don't seem worried, even helping G.T.O. out when he has engine problems. The film ambles gracefully along, taking in the breathtaking countryside in a way that's beautiful without being postcard-ready.

Nobody talks much, but for G.T.O., which makes sense. Oates, giving a fidgety and touchingly vulnerable performance, is the only real actor here. Their Zen-like devotion to the drive is all. It ends not in fame or destruction, but almost as a dream, the Driver still going, and the filmstrip literally burning away before your eyes. Universal, hoping for another *Easy Rider*, hated this film and dropped it as soon as it could. Audiences weren't much friendlier, though it grew in later years to become a cult classic.

Production Notes

Screenwriter Rudy Wurlitzer recalled for Brad Stevens's book on Monte Hellman that the director "flew me out to L.A., put me in a hotel, sat me down with a bunch of car magazines, told me to keep to the general idea of a race across the country."

July 6

The Manchurian Candidate

YEAR RELEASED: 1962
DIRECTOR: John Frankenheimer
WHO'S IN IT: Frank Sinatra, Janet Leigh, Laurence Harvey, Angela Lansbury

"They can make us do anything, Ben, can't they?"

This is one of the last movies in which Frank Sinatra bothered to actually act. Here, he plays Ben Marco, a Korean War veteran with a recurring nightmare: he sees Medal of Honor winner Raymond Shaw (Laurence Harvey, vaguely zombie-like as always) placidly following Communist orders to murder American soldiers. Marco starts to realize that there actually is a plot afoot in which Shaw has been brainwashed to carry out political assassinations whenever he hears a particular trigger phrase. Since Shaw's parents are well-connected political figures, this puts him in close proximity to people with power whom the Reds might want to eliminate.

The story is somewhat half-cocked and more than a little insane, based on a thin tissue of Cold War rumors about Red Chinese mind-control techniques and a post-McCarthy era hangover in which the idea of well-buried enemies seemed quite plausible. But the film works due to a multiplicity of factors, among them John Frankheimer's chisel-like direction, which brings perfect comic timing to a thriller plot, and George Axelrod's script (based on Richard Condon's novel), which flings out red herrings and nonsequiturs like confetti. Although the performances are all top-notch, Angela Lansbury, as Shaw's status-seeking wicked witch of a mother who shamelessly (almost gleefully) manipulates her son into unspeakable acts, is a thing of malevolent genius.

Courting Controversy

Given *The Manchurian Candidate*'s volatile depiction of a brainwashed gunman and planned political assassination, the film was pulled from theaters after the killing of John F. Kennedy.

Bicycle Thieves

🌍 🎭 👨‍👧

YEAR RELEASED: 1948
DIRECTOR: Vittorio De Sica
WHO'S IN IT: Lamberto Maggiorani, Enzo Staiola

"If you don't have a bike, forget it."

The desperately underemployed Antonio Ricci (Lamberto Maggiorani) lives with his family on the outskirts of Rome. He snags a job hanging up posters, but finds out it requires a bicycle; his is still at the pawnshop. His wife, Maria (Lianella Carell), puts up their fine linens to get it out of hock. One day on the job, and his bicycle is stolen.

Devastated by this news, which could mean destitution for his family, Antonio sets out with his son Bruno (Enzo Staiola) to scour Rome, about two-thirds of whose population appears to ride exactly identical models. Though the odds stacked against him are incalculable and Bruno becomes less and less amenable as the day wears on, Antonio shows no sign of giving up.

Vittorio De Sica's film has many hallmarks of a heartwarming humanist tale, from the loving and somewhat hapless father to the inarguably cute kid, to the charming sights of old Rome. Though tagged as "neorealist," as though it were a hardboiled docudrama, the film in fact has more in common with Frank Capra (but for the ending). De Sica produces an immortal kind of drama here, and also captures some great, memorable location work around Rome, particularly in the bustling streets and the department-store-sized pawn shop, whose cavernous size says more about the economic state of postwar Italy than all the hard-etched desperation in Maggiorani's face.

Technically Speaking

Vittorio De Sica's (born on this day in 1902) *Bicycle Thieves* was inexplicably first released in America as *The Bicycle Thief*. Not only is that title an incorrect translation, but it also misreads the entire point of the film's poignant conclusion.

July 8

Roman Holiday

YEAR RELEASED: 1953
DIRECTOR: William Wyler
WHO'S IN IT: Audrey Hepburn, Gregory Peck

"You're not what I would call trouble."

In Rome on a goodwill tour, the youthful Princess Ann (Audrey Hepburn) has had enough of official visits and state functions. After being sedated by her entourage, she steals out into the streets and promptly collapses on a bench. Seasoned American journalist Joe Bradley (Gregory Peck) has an attack of conscience while walking by, and brings her to his cramped apartment to sleep it off. Realizing he's sitting on top of a gold mine of a story (beautiful, media-beloved princess goes renegade), Joe calls in a photographer friend, and they tour Rome for a day, the two men pretending they have no idea who Princess Ann is.

William Wyler shot everything on location in Rome or at the legendary Cinecittà Studios (still a rarity at the time for Hollywood), and the city looks nothing short of ravishing. Hepburn, in her first starring role, dazzles with a playful optimism that stops just short of seeming immature. Wyler shoots her lovingly, but also deftly wields her talent for comedy (as he would later in his underrated 1966 heist flick *How to Steal a Million*).

Though a fairy tale in conception (it's hard to swallow that the Princess Diana–famous Ann could wander the streets unrecognized), the film grounds itself in reality at important moments. The drawn-out tension of the final press conference scene, when Joe has the opportunity to divulge everything, is masterfully handled, highlighting the gulf between the classes without losing the film's romantic spirit.

And the Winner Is . . .

Roman Holiday made a star of Audrey Hepburn and secured ten Oscar nominations, winning three. The screenplay award wasn't presented to the blacklisted writer Dalton Trumbo until after his death in 1993.

July 9

Once Upon a Time in China

YEAR RELEASED: 1991
DIRECTOR: Tsui Hark
WHO'S IN IT: Jet Li, Rosemund Kwan, Yuen Biao

"No matter how good our kung-fu is, it will never defeat guns."

In director's Tsui Hark's lightning-paced marital-arts masterpiece, Jet Li is introduced as the real-life nineteenth-century Chinese hero Wong Fei-hung. Portrayed by Jackie Chan in his popular *Drunken Master* films as a well-meaning goof who also happened to be an unbelievable martial arts master, Li's Fei-hung is something else entirely: a standup icon of Chinese national pride.

As in Chan's films, Fei-hung's dilemma here is to protect his homeland from encroachment by marauding white colonial forces and the traitorous Chinese who do business with them. Fei-hung runs afoul of the local Cantonese gangsters during a fight that he didn't mean to get involved in, and so earns the enmity of not only the gangsters and the police but the Westerners who are involved in an ugly slave-labor racket. All of this, though, is merely preamble for the dizzying final warehouse fight scene in which Fei-Hung and the villainous Iron Robe Yim (Yee Kwan Yan) spend most of their time atop ladders.

Li had been studying martial arts since the age of eight but only appeared in a few films; this film made him a star, and it's easy to see why. Not only does Tsui consistently shoot him in glorious widescreen as the savior of a nation, but Li's engaging presence makes an impression right from the start. Small and assassin-lithe, delicately powerful and deadly serious, Li starred in five sequels to this deservedly popular film.

Historically Speaking

The real Wong Fei-hung was a doctor, martial arts master, and folk hero who was born on this day in 1847, and lived in Canton province. Somewhere between 100 and 200 films have been made about him, some even approaching reality.

July 10

Inherit the Wind

YEAR RELEASED: 1960
DIRECTOR: Stanley Kramer
WHO'S IN IT: Spencer Tracy, Fredric March, Gene Kelly

"Contempt of conscience, sentimentality in the first degree."

In this film of the Broadway dramatization of the 1925 Scopes evolution trial (which begain on July 10), Clarence Darrow has been renamed Henry Drummond (Spencer Tracy) and William Jennings Bryan is Matthew Harrison Brady (Fredric March). The trial's theme of antiscientific religiosity has been left unchanged.

As in the Scopes trial, a high-school teacher in a small, conservative town is charged with breaking the law forbidding the teaching of evolution. The case becomes an ideological showdown. The famously free-thinking Drummond shows up for the defense. Brady, a showboating down-home populist, argues for the prosecution and also endures the withering scorn of Drummond. Commenting and cackling from the sidelines is E. K. Hornbeck (Gene Kelly, utterly apt), a Baltimore journalist and stand-in for the real-life H. L. Mencken (whose newspaper covered Darrow's fees in the Scopes trial), who can't get over all the dumb, God-fearing rubes.

Though often derided (not always incorrectly) as a ham-fisted deliverer of preachy liberalism, Kramer deftly handles two characters who keep the film from being a glorified history lesson. First is Claude Akins's villainous Reverend Jeremiah Brown, a dangerous and possibly insane rabble-rouser. Second is Kelly's portrayal of Hornbeck, who despite an unfortunate conclusion where he's lambasted by Drummond, is the gleeful, happily cynical heart of the film. It's fun to see a bright-eyed dreamer like Kelly using his powers for darkness instead of light.

In Homage

Inherit the Wind has been remade three times for television, most recently in 1999 with Jack Lemmon playing Drummond, George C. Scott as Brady, and Beau Bridges as Hornbeck.

July 11

Adventureland

YEAR RELEASED: 2009
DIRECTOR: Greg Mottola
WHO'S IN IT: Jesse Eisenberg, Kristen Stewart, Martin Starr

"They don't like people like me where I'm from."

Finding his comparative literature and Renaissance studies degrees don't go far in the Pittsburgh job market, James Brennan (Jesse Eisenberg) gets a position at the Adventureland amusement park. It's easy, but as his similarly overeducated friend Joel (Martin Starr) notes, "We *are* doing the work of pathetic, lazy morons."

It wouldn't be a summer film (one of the greatest, in fact) without romances, one fully wrong-headed and the other painful in a way that seems wholly worth it. James has an immediate connection with the quiet, darkly mannered Em (Kristen Stewart), who, unbeknownst to him, is seeing an older, married man. Lisa P. (Margarita Levieva), the gum-popping vixen, is distracting eye-candy. James and Em's relationship is a dance you can't *not* watch; Eisenberg has a shy way of reconnoitering a situation before rushing in at exactly the wrong moment, while Stewart plays it just out of reach, with a world of hurt in her eyes.

Writer/director Greg Mottola delivers the rare one-wild-summer story that doesn't resort to trite summations. The alt-rock soundtrack sings of beautiful alienation while the camera captures the lazy summer rhythms: those long nights of restless driving and endless talk. You don't have to have lived through the 1980s or loved the Replacements and the Velvet Underground to latch on to this film like a life preserver, but you do have to have been in love in the worst, most painful way.

Auteur, Auteur

Greg Mottola based his script for *Adventureland* on his experiences working in a low-end amusement park when he was younger. It wasn't exactly a Disneyland, he explained later—more a place where you could get knifed.

July 12

Freaks

YEAR RELEASED: 1932
DIRECTOR: Tod Browning
WHO'S IN IT: Wallace Ford, Harry Earles, Daisy Earles

"We accept you! We accept you! One of us! One of us!"

This film is a horror film that is rooted in sweetness, and it is all the more hair-raising for it. It follows a traveling circus, where there is a hierarchy of performers. There are the "normal" performers, your strong men and beautiful acrobats. And then there are your "freaks," the Siamese twins, the man with no legs, and the little people. One of the little people, Hans (Harry Earles) is in love with the beautiful full-size Cleopatra (Olga Baclanova). She and her lover, the strongman Hercules (Henry Victor), string Hans along to get some money out of him. When Cleopatra discovers that Hans has recently inherited a large fortune, she decides to marry him for it, but the wedding party turns into a mockery. Revenge is in the air.

This short, vivid fable owes its power to both the story's simplicity and the tenderness with which director Tod Browning treats his outcasts. It was a daring move on Browning's part, first in casting real people with real deformities as the freaks and then in making them sweeter and more human than anyone else. He shoots them all as he would any other circus performers, catching them in small moments that highlight their differences (the Siamese twin who lights up when her twin is kissed). The protective love that little Frieda (Daisy Earles) shows for Hans is one of prewar Hollywood's most romantic stories.

Casting Call
Freaks' Hans and Frieda were played by siblings Harry and Daisy Earles, who appeared in a number of films, including *The Wizard of Oz*, and worked for decades in the circus.

July 13

Fast Times at Ridgemont High

 LOL!

YEAR RELEASED: 1982
DIRECTOR: Amy Heckerling
WHO'S IN IT: Sean Penn, Jennifer Jason Leigh, Judge Reinhold

"Awesome! Totally awesome!"

Remembered mostly for its sterling soundtrack (Go-Go's, Tom Petty) and stoner class-clown catch phrases ("hey bud, let's party!"), Amy Heckerling's high-school romp—based on an investigative book by Cameron Crowe (*Say Anything*)—has slightly more serious intentions in mind. There *is* still the matter of a bikini-wearing Phoebe Cates climbing out of a pool in slow-motion, though.

The film's episodic plot follows one high-school year, in the Valley. Mike Damone (Robert Romanus) is a would-be ladies man who scalps concert tickets and gives horrible advice to his timid buddy, "Rat" Ratner (Brian Backer). Brad Hamilton (Judge Reinhold) is a senior who works at a burger joint and thinks he's got life by the tail, only to have it all collapse on him. His younger sister, Stacy (a painfully shy Jennifer Jason Leigh), is the most affecting character of all, as she looks for love in all the wrong men. The life of the party is the fully baked surfer Jeff Spicoli (Sean Penn, playing an amalgam of the surfers he grew up with), who pops up occasionally to spout off.

As she showed in her Valley Jane Austen comedy, *Clueless* (1995), Heckerling has a gift for the rhythms of teen life, its wandering boredom and fears of an unknowable future. She brings an honesty to Stacy's scenes of romantic disappointment as well as a suspicion that everything may not turn out all right for these kids after the prom.

Production Notes

Cameron Crowe was twenty-two when he went undercover as a student at the Southern California high school (possibly in San Diego) he called "Ridgemont."

July 14

Persona

YEAR RELEASED: 1966
DIRECTOR: Ingmar Bergman
WHO'S IN IT: Bibi Andersson, Liv Ullmann

"Is it really important not to lie, to speak so that everything rings true?"

It's hard to say what Bergman was up to with this groundbreaking, eye-opening work. In a moment that must have been unnerving for her audience, actress Elisabeth Vogler (Liv Ullmann) froze onstage in the midst of a performance as the child-murdering Medea, appearing to smile as though it were all a great joke. Afterward, having seemingly lost the power of speech, Elisabeth is sent to a remote island with a nurse, Alma (Bibi Andersson), in the hope that the one-on-one attention will return her to the land of the living.

The film opens with a blitzing cacophony of imagery (corpses, a silent comedy, a film projector) pointedly reminding viewers that what they're watching is manufactured, not real. Then, after delving into an intensely dramatic and Jungian study of two personalities in conflict, Bergman pulls back again, showing the filmstrip itself breaking and burning a hole in the screen.

By the film's end, Bergman has merged real and unreal to such a degree that one stops even asking which is which, all the better to enjoy the dynamic performances from Andersson and Ullmann, the former cycling between zealous obsession and furious rage, while the latter watches in frustrating but finely tuned silence. In one of *Persona*'s most famous scenes, Bergman merges a shot of their faces into one, to the point where they become indistinguishable.

Casting Call

By the time of *Persona*, Bibi Andersson had not only starred in numerous Ingmar Bergman films, but the two of them had also been romantically involved. While shooting *Persona*, Liv Ullmann and Bergman also became lovers.

July 15

Seven Samurai

YEAR RELEASED: 1954
DIRECTOR: Akira Kurosawa
WHO'S IN IT: Takashi Shimura, Toshirô Mifune, Yoshio Inaba

"The farmers have won. Not us."

As humane and thoughtful as it is thrilling, *Seven Samurai* is everything a film should be. In a Japanese village during the chaotic 1600s, farmers hire samurai to defend them from bandits. They have little to offer but food, leading the village elder to smile grimly: "Find *hungry* samurai."

Kurosawa introduces each samurai in vivid vignettes. In the lead is Kambei (Kurosawa's stalwart, Takashi Shimura) first seen bravely rescuing a kidnapped young boy. Wizened but not cynical, Kambei knows the odds against his band (the bandits number at least forty), but also knows that jobs are rare and these villagers are like sheep before wolves. Of the other samurai, the most memorable is the braggart Kikuchiyo (Toshirô Mifune, at his effusively clowning best), who turns out not to be a samurai at all but the son of a farmer. This revelation sets up one of the film's most memorable scenes, when Kikuchiyo lambastes his fellow samurai for looking down on the villagers as cowards, asking them who had inspired villagers' fearful behavior. "You did!" he admonishes them.

Kurosawa's build-up to the final confrontation is deliberate but never slow. The strategy sessions are carefully laid out and relationships well illustrated, so that by the time the bandits make their appearance, the full measure of what is at stake weighs on each slashing of a sword, each hissing of an arrow.

Auteur, Auteur

In *Akira Kurosawa: Interviews*, the director explains that after making his powerful humanist drama *Ikiru* (1952), "I wished in my next project, quite naturally, to make a lighter, more lively film, a simple and detached one . . . so I made *The Seven Samurai*."

Akira

YEAR RELEASED: 1988
DIRECTOR: Katsuhiro Ôtomo
WHO'S IN IT: (voices of) Mitsuo Iwata, Nozomu Sasaki

"What did you people do to my head?"

World War III came early to the graphic novel world of Katsuhiro Ôtomo's *Akira*, which Ôtomo adapted for this frenetic film. The movie dramatically condensed his novel's sprawling plot but kept its core spirit of energetic ultraviolence intact.

On July 16, 1988, a nuclear blast decimated Tokyo. When the story begins, it's thirty-one years later, and the city of Neo-Tokyo has sprouted from the ruins and around the vacant crater left behind. In the new city, the schools are a graffiti-covered wasteland and teen biker gangs rule the night. One night, Kaneda (Mitsuo Iwata) and his boys—including Tetsuo (Nozomu Sasaki), a younger tagalong, are battling a rival gang. Tetsuo rides his bike into a strange-looking old man, after which there's an explosion. Tetsuo is whisked away to a hospital by an army helicopter. He begins to have headaches and nightmares, as well as the first signs of awesome telekinetic powers somehow related to the old man he ran into and a secret government research program. As Tetsuo begins a power-mad, homicidal rampage across Neo-Tokyo, the army mobilizes to stop him and prevent another holocaust.

The film was a sensation when it was exported in 1988, presenting a darker and more mature side of Japanese animation than had been seen before. It also plugged in to legions of sci-fi fanboys excited to see the film version of what they'd been reading in cyberpunk fiction. Plenty of other *anime* have played on the specialist circuit since then, but none had this film's explosive impact.

Lost and Found
Though *Akira*'s critical acclaim set it apart from most anime imports, most editions still have a distracting dubbed English dialogue track instead of subtitles.

The Devil's Backbone

YEAR RELEASED: 2001
DIRECTOR: Guillermo del Toro
WHO'S IN IT: Fernando Tielve, Eduardo Noreiga, Marisa Paredes, Federico Luppi

"What is a ghost? A tragedy condemned to repeat itself over and over?"

Director Guillermo del Toro's invigorating haunted-house story is set during the Spanish Civil War in 1939 at an isolated orphanage school called Santa Lucia. A new boy, ten-year-old Carlos (Fernando Tielve) arrives at the school, where a huge, unexploded bomb is stuck in the courtyard, too dangerous to be moved. It's a reminder of an attack years before, and of the death of a child named Santi, who was murdered the same night and his body dumped into a pool in the basement. At night, Carlos, who sleeps in Santi's old bed, can hear the ghost-child sighing in the darkness.

Outside Santa Lucia, the war between the Fascists and Republicans that began on July 17, 1936, still rages. Inside, the facility is run with a firm but distant hand by Dr. Casares (Federico Luppi) and the beautiful headmistress Carmen (Marisa Paredes), who has a prosthetic leg. There is intrigue inside the walls as well: sexual plotting and rumors about treasure hidden somewhere on the grounds.

Like the finer ghost stories, del Toro skillfully uses his haunting apparitions to signal the evils of the past that refuse to go away. His Carlos is an innocent, unaware of the orphanage's history until he hears its gravelike sigh. The horror in this film stays very close to the ground, allowing the human characters to create a realistic and well-nuanced drama of a dangerous life during wartime. It is like the embodiment of that William Faulkner line: "The past is never dead. It's not even past."

July 18

Once Upon a Time in America

YEAR RELEASED: 1984
DIRECTOR: Sergio Leone
WHO'S IN IT: Robert De Niro, James Woods, Elizabeth McGovern

"I like the stink of the streets."

After tearing the hell out of the spaghetti Western for so many years, there wasn't much else Sergio Leone could do afterward except take on the gangster film.

As dreamlike as his last great Western, *Once Upon a Time in the West* (1968), but surprisingly much less violent, this labyrinthine story follows a gang of Jewish gangsters from Brooklyn over the course of some five decades. The structure is elaborately tangled but fluidly so, jumping back and forth across time with ease. In 1932, David "Noodles" Aaronson (Robert De Niro) is released from jail and gets back in touch with the old Brooklyn gang just in time to see how they've prospered during Prohibition. His friend Max (James Woods) has done particularly well in bootlegging, and Noodles's childhood crush Deborah (Elizabeth McGovern) has grown up nicely. A bloody double-cross later, Max and Noodles start drifting apart.

Leone's fabulistic tone doesn't always help in understanding the plot but creates a mythic aura around it all, with the tenement canyons of New York replacing the soaring cliffs of Monument Valley.

There are claims that Leone turned down the chance to direct *The Godfather* so that he could do this long-gestating film, which would be his last; it was a smart choice.

Lost and Found

Once Upon a Time in America's running time was cut from 227 to 139 minutes and re-edited to run in chronological order for its American release, which ironically made it nearly incomprehensible. The 227-minute cut played at Cannes to wide praise.

July 19

Bad Lieutenant

YEAR RELEASED: 1992
DIRECTOR: Abel Ferrara
WHO'S IN IT: Harvey Keitel, Victor Argo, Paul Calderon

"Your forgiveness will leave blood in its wake."

The title is almost a joke, though it's hard to say that a film this brutally besotted with Catholic guilt would know to laugh. The bad lieutenant of the title (he is never named) is exactly that, a police officer so corrupted and fallen from grace that it's shocking Satan himself hasn't offered him a job. He's played by Harvey Keitel in the full flower of his early-1990s dark blooming. His anxiously crinkled face shows off his pursed-mouth fury, as though he himself can't believe what he's doing.

Keitel's Lieutenant ingests just about every known drug, sleeps with hookers, takes bribes, and gets himself murderously in debt to a Mafioso. There is occasionally some police work to do, and the script throws the Lieutenant a case designed to punch all his buttons. A nun is raped in an uptown church by junkies who desecrate the place afterward. It's an affront to the Lieutenant's vision of himself, where despite all the laws he's broken and drugs consumed, there remains a stubborn splinter of Catholicism, possibly the one thing holding him together.

Straddling the line between exploitative trash and gutter-art, Ferrara's film is very simply a tour of one man's self-created hell. Whether or not it's redemptive depends on how much of it you can stand to watch.

In Homage
One of the stranger remakes ever to come along was 2009's *Bad Lieutenant: Port of Call New Orleans*, directed by Werner Herzog. The only connection to the original appeared to be that it also featured a detective working on the dark side of sanity—in this case, Nicolas Cage.

Enter the Dragon

YEAR RELEASED: 1973
DIRECTOR: Robert Clouse
WHO'S IN IT: Bruce Lee, John Saxon, Jim Kelly

"Your style is unorthodox."

Bruce Lee's last film is the one that made him a star all around the world. In it, the wiry hero plays Lee, a Shaolin martial arts master recruited by an international spy agency to hunt down a renegade monk who now uses his skills for evil.

Lee keeps things simple. He's the rare action hero who actually seems humble. There is no gloating in his fighting, and very little in the way of clever comebacks. The fact that he has to go kick some guy's teeth out and figure out what to do with the nineteen other guys charging at him is nothing to be worried about—just another day.

Director John Clouse tries to give the film an exotic, James Bond feel, half-succeeding. Lee is joined by a couple of Americans, one played by John Saxon (he of a thousand straight-to-video flicks) and the other by African American karate champion Jim Kelly. The film moves swiftly from one fight scene to the next before dumping Lee into a compound filled with seemingly hundreds of opponents. These opponents break tradition with years of screen villains before and since, and don't wait to attack Lee one at a time, but rush him all at once. Needless to say, Lee dispatches them all with jaw-dropping ease. After this film, international audiences wouldn't embrace another marital arts star until Jackie Chan's mid-1990s ascent.

Production Notes
Bruce Lee died prematurely on July 20, 1973, just days before the premiere of *Enter the Dragon*. His son, martial arts star Brandon Lee, also died young (on the set of the film *The Crow*) just as his star was rising.

Rope

YEAR RELEASED: 1948
DIRECTOR: Alfred Hitchcock
WHO'S IN IT: James Stewart, John Dall, Farley Granger

"We killed for the sake of danger and the sake of killing."

Hitchcock's gimmicky one-take murder mystery is filmed almost entirely without edits, composed of nine single takes lasting up to ten minutes (the maximum amount of film that cameras then could hold). The end of each shot is obscured to create the illusion that it was all one solid take.

It's a neat stunt, but fortunately, the work itself is a solid and buttoned-up mystery. It's long thought to be based on the notorious 1924 case of Leopold and Loeb, the young, would-be Nietzschean supermen who committed what they thought was the perfect murder (Patrick Hamilton, the author of the original 1929 play, has denied the connection). In the film, the tension ratchets up ever so gradually until the claustrophobic apartment is almost foggy with anticipation.

James Stewart plays Rupert Cadell, the former schoolteacher of Brandon Shaw (John Dall) and Phillip Morgan (Farley Granger), the film's two arrogant socialite snots who strangled their friend David with a piece of rope to prove their apparent superiority. They stuff his body into a trunk and hold a dinner party around it. Cadell starts wondering why the two are so nervous.

Though some of the film feels stiffer than Hitchcock's wont, he gets particularly elegant work out of Granger, whose smug self-satisfaction he would make good use of again three years later in *Strangers on a Train*.

Courting Controversy

Though hints of a homosexual relationship between *Rope*'s young murderers were purposefully toned down, the film was described in the book *Hitchcock/Truffaut* as "Two young homosexuals strangle a college friend just for the thrill of it."

Rumble Fish

YEAR RELEASED: 1983
DIRECTOR: Francis Ford Coppola
WHO'S IN IT: Matt Dillon, Diane Lane, Mickey Rourke, Dennis Hopper

"Time is a funny thing. Time is a very peculiar item."

Rusty James (Matt Dillon) is a big king on a very small hill. It's a role he feels forced into because of the recent sudden absence of his older brother, Motorcycle Boy (Mickey Rourke). One day, Motorcycle Boy comes back in the midst of a rumble, the sort of thing he doesn't have patience for anymore. "Another glorious battle for the kingdom?" he asks. Lighter. Cigarette. Exhaustion. Rusty doesn't understand what's gotten into him. Once upon a time Motorcycle Boy ruled the roost; now all he cares about are his fighting fish (who show up as blotches of sharp color in a black-and-white film). The stage is set for disappointment and tragedy all around.

The more interesting of Francis Ford Coppola's S. E. Hinton duo, *Rumble Fish* holds up well compared to *The Outsiders*, if at least because it better understands the artificiality of Hinton's story. The first film was an angst-ridden, classic Hollywood Technicolor tearjerker, while the second had a chillier feel to it, closer to that of some lost German expressionist classic.

Dillon can do this kind of work in his sleep, as can Rourke and Dennis Hopper (as the patriarch of their supremely dysfunctional family). Meanwhile, Coppola's nephew Nicolas Cage snags a small role, and Tom Waits gets a nice soliloquy on the nature of time. The result might not be "Camus for kids," as the director once apparently called it, but then what is?

Production Notes
Although *Rumble Fish*'s industrial landscape is entirely different from the sunset-hued *The Outsiders*, both were shot in Tulsa, Oklahoma, birthplace of author S. E. Hinton.

The Long Goodbye

YEAR RELEASED: 1973
DIRECTOR: Robert Altman
WHO'S IN IT: Elliot Gould, Nina Van Pallandt, Mark Rydell, Sterling Hayden

"That's you, Marlowe. You'll never learn, you're a born loser."

Robert Altman's spry and quirky take on Raymond Chandler's biggest, most incomprehensible mystery is a detective story, but set twenty years after the book's 1953 publication, and kudos to Altman for not pretending America (and California, in particular) hadn't changed in the meantime.

This Philip Marlowe is played by Elliot Gould, doing his shambling comedic best. Gould's Marlowe may be quick with a laconic comeback like Bogart, but he's less of a stickler for professionalism. He has a sad look to him, but is still a contrast to the film's sun-baked post-hippie Southern California laziness—he wears a *tie* and *smokes*, for heaven's sake.

The plot starts simply, but the narrative strands soon pile up like a Los Angeles freeway interchange. Marlowe is asked by his buddy Terry Lennox (Jim Bouton) to drive him down to Tijuana. Afterward, Marlowe's questioned by the cops when Terry's wife is found murdered, and he's later threatened by a gangster. Meanwhile, Marlowe is hired by a rich woman (Nina Van Pallandt) to track down her alcoholic husband (Sterling Hayden, in his last great performance) who's disappeared. Somehow the two cases are connected. Along the way, Marlowe continually cracks wise, to hide his confusion more than anything else.

Altman and his cinematographer Vilmos Zsigmond concocted a sunny and hazy pastel look for this wry noir where, instead of dark and threatening shadows, evil blooms in broad daylight.

Production Notes

Screenwriter Leigh Brackett (who also helped adapt Chandler's *The Big Sleep* decades earlier) made substantial changes to Chandler's novel, and Altman threw in plenty of alterations himself, which didn't please some Chandler purists.

July 24

The Outlaw Josey Wales

YEAR RELEASED: 1976
DIRECTOR: Clint Eastwood
WHO'S IN IT: Clint Eastwood, Chief Dan George, Sondra Locke

"He's from Missouri, where they're all known to be killers of innocent men, women, and children."

You can tell that by the time he got around to making this jokey anti-Western in the mid-1970s, Clint Eastwood had had enough of his tight-lipped gunslinger persona. He plays that role again here, but this time Eastwood's character was at least partially there to be mocked.

Josey Wales (Eastwood) is a Missouri farmer whose family is killed in a raid by rampaging Unionist Jayhawkers. Devastated and looking for revenge, Wales joins up with a gang of pro-Confederate bushwhackers led by Fletcher (John Vernon) and after the same thing. When the war ends, Fletcher's men surrender, except Wales. After a double-cross, most of Fletcher's disarmed men are murdered, and he is forced to chase after Wales. On the run to Texas and a final showdown against his pursuers, Wales picks up a number of fellow travelers, including an old Cherokee man (Chief Dan George) and a young Navajo woman (Geraldine Kearns).

Given the screenplay's provenance, the film that resulted is not at all what would be expected. While there are numerous action scenes, the film leavens them with a casual, dry sense of humor, frequently at Eastwood's expense. This combination of wry humor and epic adventure (the latter reminiscent of *The Searchers*) makes this one of the most enjoyable Westerns to come out of Hollywood during a time when studios didn't quite know what to do with the old genres.

Production Notes

The Outlaw Josey Wales's first director was Philip Kaufman (*The Right Stuff*), who was eventually fired and replaced by Clint Eastwood. Some accounts say that Kaufman's loose and improvised style clashed with Eastwood's more efficient manner, while one story has it that they were simply both in love with Eastwood's costar Sondra Locke . . . and the actor won.

Red River

YEAR RELEASED: 1948
DIRECTOR: Howard Hawks, Arthur Rosson
WHO'S IN IT: John Wayne, Montgomery Cliff, Walter Brennan

"Get a shovel and my Bible. I'll read over him."

Fourteen years after rescuing a young boy survivor of the Indian massacre that begins the film, Matt Garth (Montgomery Clift) has become right-hand man on Thomas Dunson's (John Wayne) Texas ranch. Since the Civil War has left Texas economically devastated, they've got no choice but to herd all 10,000 head of cattle north in hopes that somebody will buy them. The last ranchers who tried this were slaughtered by Missouri border bandits, but Dunson is quick on the trigger ("I'm too good a gun for you to argue with"), as is Matt and new hire Cherry Valance (John Ireland), so the odds should be about even.

More a solid Western than Howard Hawks's later, jokier *Rio Bravo*, this cattle-drive saga also has a gloomier feel to it than much of Wayne's body of work. Dunson's mania about finishing the drive against all odds (Apaches, stampedes, harsh weather) takes on a Captain Ahab–like quality, predating Wayne's obsessive quest in *The Searchers* (1956). This is a Western set firmly in the iconic stance. Hawks often uses a series of tight close-ups, particularly in the famous sequence at the beginning of the drive, when Dunson bellows, "Take 'em to Missouri, Matt!" and all the cowboys yee-haw and flap their Stetsons. If anybody could make it to Missouri, it would be these guys.

In Homage

The iconic status of *Red River* is secured by Peter Bogdanovich's choice to make it the last film playing at the little Texas theater in his *The Last Picture Show* (1971).

Paths of Glory

YEAR RELEASED: 1957
DIRECTOR: Stanley Kubrick
WHO'S IN IT: Kirk Douglas, Adolphe Menjou

"I'm not afraid of dying tomorrow, only of being killed."

Stanley Kubrick's first epic is an ironically named and caustic World War I trench warfare drama based on a 1935 novel by Humphrey Cobb. Cobb's novel was itself based on a real incident from 1915 in which five French soldiers were executed for (alleged) mutiny. Pulp novelist Jim Thompson, who wrote Kubrick's previous film, *The Killing*, took a whack at the script, but his draft was canned in favor of one by Calder Willingham.

Somehow, Kubrick (born this day in 1928) was given the money for an expensive, elaborate war movie with a real downer of a plot, and Kirk Douglas came in to star. Playing Colonel Dax, Douglas is the stiff-jawed embodiment of courageous resolve in the face of upper-rank cowardice and ineffectualness. The centerpiece of the film is a suicidal assault by French forces on a densely defended German redoubt.

After the slaughter is over, the French generals cast about for somebody to blame. In their wisdom, they decide that some rank-and-file soldiers should be tried and executed, to serve as an example to the rest of the men. What results is a gripping, bleak portrait of unaccountable, blind cowardice in high places, highlighted by the film's contrasting of the squalid conditions of the soldiers' trenches and the exquisite luxury of the generals' villa.

Production Notes

The girl singing to soldiers at the end of *Paths of Glory* is Christiane Harlan, the niece of Veit Harlan, one of Josef Goebbels's favorite directors, most infamous for his anti-Semitic Nazi opus *Jew Süss*, banned in Germany. Stanley Kubrick married Christiane in 1958.

July 27

Dr. Strangelove, or: How I Learned to Stop Worrying and Love the Bomb

YEAR RELEASED: 1964
DIRECTOR: Stanley Kubrick
WHO'S IN IT: Peter Sellers, George C. Scott, Sterling Hayden

"Gentlemen, you can't fight in here, this is the War Room!"

Convinced that water fluoridation is a devious Commie conspiracy to "sap and impurify all of our precious bodily fluids," General Jack D. Ripper (Sterling Hayden, gloriously mad) sends his wing of nuclear-armed B-52 bombers to attack the Soviet Union. President Merkin Muffley (Peter Sellers, doing his best Adlai Stevenson) decides to help the Soviets shoot the bombers down to avoid full-on nuclear war, much to the annoyance of General "Buck" Turgidson (George C. Scott, viciously satirizing the overtestosteroned general he embodied years later in *Patton*). While Ripper's British attaché Captain Lionel Mandrake (Sellers again) tries to talk him into recalling his bombers, the crew of one B-52, thinking war has been declared, do their best to deliver their payload and thusly a nuclear apocalypse.

And it's a comedy.

Stanley Kubrick's greatest film started out as a straight, *Fail Safe*–esque techno-thriller, but the subject kept pushing it into satire. Thus Kubrick ended up with docudrama realism (the B-52's bomb safeguard mechanisms, the realist immediacy of the battle scenes as American troops try to fight their way onto Ripper's base) being set right next to full-on *MAD* magazine–type spoofery (the blatant phallic imagery, character names like Bat Guano). The combination is intoxicating and occasionally terrifying.

> **Lost and Found**
> *Dr. Strangelove* originally ended with the Russians and Americans having a massive custard pie fight in the War Room. The scene was filmed, but Kubrick's estate has yet to allow it to be seen.

The Palm Beach Story

YEAR RELEASED: 1942
DIRECTOR: Preston Sturges
WHO'S IN IT: Claudette Colbert, Joel McCrea, Mary Astor

*"Nothing is permanent in this world . . .
except for Roosevelt."*

This screwball comedy is bursting at the seams with punchlines and plotlines, to the point where you have to wonder what writer/director Preston Sturges left in his wastebasket. Released during the low, tense early days of World War II, the film doesn't have a care for anything but love, money, and good times.

Tom and Gerry (Joel McCrea and Claudette Colbert) seem to be one of those old Hollywood-style New York couples, with a posh apartment and generally wonderful life. But Gerry is restless on Park Avenue and frustrated by her inventor husband's increasing poverty. So with bracing speed, she hops a train to Palm Beach, hoping to meet up with some rich men. Potential relief shows up in the form of John D. Hackensacker III (Rudy Vallee), Bill Gates–rich and clueless—easy pickings for Gerry's huntress eyes and fresh-faced beauty.

The film alights in Florida, losing a little of its madcap energy (all those shotgun-wielding drunk millionaires on the train kept things popping) but gaining some dramatic energy when Tom shows up to fight for Gerry. However, he faces a potential distraction in Hackensacker's sister, who shouldn't have been a match for his wife. She *is* played, however, by the pert and whip-smart Mary Astor, so anything's possible.

While overshadowed by Struges's other 1942 comedy, *Sullivan's Travels*, this film is not just funnier but, with its constant digs at marriage, possibly more meaningful than that more overtly political film.

Auteur, Auteur

Between 1940 and 1946, Preston Sturges wrote and directed eight films, at least half of which are commonly counted among Hollywood's greatest comedies.

July 29

The Magnificent Ambersons

YEAR RELEASED: 1942
DIRECTOR: Orson Welles
WHO'S IN IT: Joseph Cotten, Dolores Costello, Agnes Moorehead

"The magnificence of the Ambersons began in 1873. Their splendor lasted throughout all the years that saw their midland town spread and darken into a city."

Set in an unnamed Midwestern city (assumed to be Indianapolis) during the late nineteenth century, Orson Welles's second film covers two generations of a family during this tumultuous time in American history. The willful Eugene Morgan (Joseph Cotten), a struggling inventor, courts Isabel Amberson (Dolores Costello) against the wishes of her stern father. She decides to marry instead the dull but more socially appropriate Wilbur Minafer. Their son, George (Tim Holt), is a self-obsessed brat. After Wilbur dies, Eugene, who has held a torch for Isabel all these years, starts his courtship anew. This infuriates the class-conscious George, who does everything he can to sabotage their love affair.

According to legend, Welles wrote the screenplay, based on Booth Tarkington's 1918 Pulitzer Prize–winning novel, in just nine days. Although a nostalgic look at an earlier era—one likely influenced by Welles's childhood in Kenosha, Wisconsin, as the son of a wealthy inventor—the film isn't fussy. It's a grand American epic created with the cocky nerviness that made Welles's Mercury Theatre such an innovative force. Welles again hired Gregg Toland as cinematographer, and the result, with its crisp deep-focus shots and dramatically expressionistic lighting, outdoes *Citizen Kane* for visual innovation. Unlike *Kane*, however, the film couldn't find an audience; it took home four Oscar nominations anyway.

Lost and Found

Convinced that *The Magnificent Ambersons* would be a disaster, RKO cut the film from 118 to 88 minutes, leaving great, inexplicable gaps in the story and destroying all the cut footage. That the mangled film which remains can still be considered a classic is even more testimony to Welles's talent.

July 30

Memento

$\mathcal{Q}$

YEAR RELEASED: 2000
DIRECTOR: Christopher Nolan
WHO'S IN IT: Guy Pearce, Carrie-Anne Moss, Joe Pantoliano

"It's amazing what a little brain damage can do to your credibility."

Memento opens with a Polaroid of a corpse in a dingy chamber, the blood drying slowly as the picture fades. The film then continues in reverse with Leonard (Guy Pearce), an insurance investigator whose wife was raped and murdered in an attack that left him with no short-term memory and a quest for vengeance as vivid as the clues he tattooed across his body. The man Leonard just shot was Teddy (Joe Pantoliano) a sneaky type who claims to be helping him find his wife's murderer—but then why has Leonard written "Do Not Believe His Lies" on the back of a Polaroid of Teddy?

This tricky, coiled film unspools backward from this quandary in neatly interlocking pieces. The brief interludes match the continually wiped-clean slate that is Leonard's mind. "Now, where was I?" is his refrain when his memory resets, whether it's in midchase or waking up next to a barmaid (Carrie-Anne Moss) who either wants to help or wishes him dead. The linking thread in all this is Leonard's "Remember Sammy Jenkis" tattoo, which remind him of a man with a case tragically similar to his. Leonard believes that with discipline and routine, he can train himself to complete his quest, unlike Sammy.

Not long after this film's surprise success, director Christopher Nolan was tapped to relaunch the *Batman* series with Christian Bale.

And the Winner Is . . .
Memento was nominated for two Oscars, for screenplay and editing, losing in the former category to Julian Fellowes for *Gosford Park* and in the latter to Pietro Scalia for *Black Hawk Down*.

The War Game

YEAR RELEASED: 1965
DIRECTOR: Peter Watkins
WHO'S IN IT: (commentators) Michael Aspel, Peter Graham

"Would the survivors envy the dead?"

To scare people, sometimes all you have to do is tell them the truth. At a mere forty-eight minutes, that's what Watkins's uniquely harrowing film does. It uses the accoutrements of stolid BBC film journalism (authoritatively moral voice-over, buttressing by facts and figures) to imagine the aftereffects of a "limited" nuclear attack on Brtiain. Watkins films in dramatic, you-are-there fashion, with jittery camera and sharp angles, making it easy to suspend disbelief at what you are seeing. Watkins creates the resulting mass terror and chaos with only the most basic special effects—white flashes, some prop guns, and makeup. Children scream as the bright blast sears their retinas. Refugees covered in burns and scar tissue stare blankly. Police try to stop cameras from filming them burning thousands of corpses. We see a bucket filled with the wedding rings of the dead (the inscriptions will be used for identification). The narrator reminds the viewer that everything they are seeing happened after Nagasaki or Dresden.

Science-fiction film has normally preferred to use nuclear war as an excuse for a big bang (think of the mushroom-clouds of *Terminator II*). But Watkins is after bigger game. He wants to shove this horror in the faces of citizens who don't know enough and the civil authorities who don't bother educating them. "This . . . is nuclear war," the narrator says, panning over the scorched faces of the dead.

Auteur, Auteur
Although the BBC refused to air *The War Game* until July 31, 1985, it gathered a fervent following after a limited theatrical release. The film won an Oscar for best documentary and was highly influential on Britain's nuclear disarmament campaign.

Do the Right Thing

YEAR RELEASED: 1989
DIRECTOR: Spike Lee
WHO'S IN IT: Spike Lee, Danny Aiello, Ossie Davis, Giancarlo Esposito, Bill Nunn

"Extra cheese is two dollars."

This film burns in your memory whether you like it or not, because of the utter completeness with which Spike Lee conjures up the time and place. It's a hot summer day in Brooklyn's Bed-Stuy neighborhood during the late 1980s. The temperature soars, animosities flare, and pointless arguments escalate; a riot is brewing.

It's a primarily African American neighborhood, and tension swirls around the few others still around. Mookie (Lee) is a deliveryman for the area's last pizzeria. His boss, Sal (Danny Aiello), keeps a display of photos showing Italian celebrities. Though he acts more color-blind than his overtly racist sons, Sal refuses a request to "put some brothers up on the wall." The whole neighborhood is a time bomb, and the photos in the pizzeria are the fuse. Misunderstandings escalate up and down the block, and the arrival of some thuggish cops doesn't help matters.

Lee's star cinematographer Ernest Dickerson overloads the saturated colors and jams his camera into cock-eyed angles, accentuating the sweltering heat and fraying nerves. One of the decade's finest cast of supporting characters comes in and out of frame, especially gentle giant Radio Raheem (Bill Nunn), whose "Love" and "Hate" rings are quoted from *Night of the Hunter*, and the block's elder statesman, Da Mayor (Ossie Davis). The film's violent conclusion is no catharsis—Lee suggests that nothing will change for the people on this block, unless it's for the worse.

Production Notes
In the notes that Spike Lee wrote while putting together his script idea for *Do the Right Thing*, he said, "It's been my observation that when the temperature rises beyond a certain point, people lose it."

Chasing Amy

YEAR RELEASED: 1997
DIRECTOR: Kevin Smith
WHO'S IN IT: Ben Affleck, Jason Lee, Joey Lauren Adams

"I always thought of them as Rosencrantz and Guildenstern meet Vladimir and Estragon."

Though its crude jokes would never be heard leaving Julia Roberts' lips, *Chasing Amy* is among the greatest romantic comedies ever made. Holden (Ben Affleck, before he was . . . *Ben Affleck*) and Banky (one-time skateboarder Jason Lee) are best friends and comic-book artists who get caught up in a hard-to-navigate romantic triangle. The vaguely more mature Holden gets a crush on lesbian comic artist Amy (Joey Lauren Adams), who ends up falling in love with Holden anyway. This throws both their worlds into turmoil, her lesbian friends seeing it as betrayal, as does the fantastically irritable and voluble Banky (who can't stand the thought of losing Holden). Then the other shoe drops.

Shot on half a shoestring, *Clerks* director Kevin Smith's third film is grainy and almost unfinished looking. The script is a raw outpouring of confessional dialogue, obscene jokes, and romantic yearning. Holden, Banky, and Amy talk themselves in circles, and then talk some more. Providing more dialogue are the drug-dealing duo Jay (Jason Mewes) and Silent Bob (Smith, delivering the poignant title story) whom Holden and Banky based their hit comic *Bluntman and Chronic* on. Smith clearly went all-in.

But between the talkiness and the geeky jokes comes a thoroughly hilarious and soul-searching exploration of love, jealousy, and insecurity.

Auteur, Auteur

In Kevin Smith's next film, *Jay and Silent Bob Strike Back* (2001), the duo find out there's going to be a *Bluntman and Chronic* movie and take a road trip to Hollywood to stop it from being made. Enjoyable enough, it's mostly an excuse for cameos by Carrie Fisher, Will Ferrell, Gus Van Sant, and Mark Hamill, and a lot more unprintable jokes.

Apocalypse Now

YEAR RELEASED: 1979
DIRECTOR: Francis Ford Coppola
WHO'S IN IT: Martin Sheen, Robert Duvall, Marlon Brando

"All I wanted was to get back into the jungle."

Coppola's film is part purple poetry and part sham, but all eye-searing spectacle. The near-perfect example of a film that shouldn't work and does, Coppola's monumental take on Joseph Conrad's *Heart of Darkness* transposes colonial Africa with the Vietnam War, yet keeps Western imperial attitudes intact. It's *sturm und drang* and overblown metaphors, but also a reminder of what a slightly mad director can do in the right circumstances, reality be damned.

Martin Sheen plays Captain Willard, one of those quietly murderous government agents who haunted American cinema during the 1970s. Long burnt-out, Willard is sent back into the jungle to track down Colonel Kurtz, a guerrilla fighter who went native, and "terminate his command." Willard undertakes a perilous river journey in a patrol boat whose crew is just about as gone with war-fever as he.

Coppola seeds the journey with kaleidoscopic vignettes—a bridge burning in the night, a mad airborne colonel who brings his men to battle in Wagner-blaring Hueys—that surpass anything he did afterward. In making points about the ugliness and hypocrisy of modern warfare, John Milius's script (with assistance from Michael Herr, who also helped Stanley Kubrick with *Full Metal Jacket*) ends up celebrating most of the excess that it was trying to critique. All the better for the audience.

Production Notes

One of the earliest versions of *Apocalypse Now* was to have been shot documentary-style in Northern California by George Lucas. Another idea would have sent the filmmakers with 16mm cameras to Vietnam itself . . . while the war was still being fought.

The African Queen

YEAR RELEASED: 1951
DIRECTOR: John Huston
WHO'S IN IT: Humphrey Bogart, Katharine Hepburn

"There's death a dozen times over down the river."

Set in "German East Africa" at the outset of World War I in 1914, John Huston's film of the C. S. Forester novel has Katharine Hepburn playing a prim British missionary stationed with her reverend brother in a remote village. After he dies from a blow delivered by a rampaging German soldier, a dazed Hepburn gratefully accepts a ride on the *African Queen*, a runty little ship piloted on a nearby river by Humphrey Bogart's Charlie Allnut, a Canadian jack-of-all-trades. Stuck deep in suddenly hostile territory, the two opposites make their precarious way downstream, daring rapids and trying to survive the smothering heat and dense insect clouds. When Hepburn comes up with a complicated revenge scheme to attack a German ship with a jury-rigged torpedo, Allnut seems just sun-dazed enough—and happy enough to have the attentions of a classy woman—to agree.

The story could charitably be described as contrived. But fortunately it doesn't matter much, as the film mostly just wants to watch these two negotiate their annoyances and (of course) quick-blooming love in a cramped, racketing space. Bogart was rarely this vulnerable onscreen, and his insecurities are immensely charming, while Hepburn's ramrod-stiff drawing-room manner makes you wish that there had been a Henry James adaptation she could have gotten in on.

Production Notes

During the filming of *The African Queen* (mostly on the Congo River) nearly everybody in the cast and crew became very ill. The exceptions were Humphrey Bogart and John Huston, who—it has been joked—were so continually drunk that nothing could have survived in their bloodstream.

Chinatown

$\mathcal{Q}$

YEAR RELEASED: 1974
DIRECTOR: Roman Polanski
WHO'S IN IT: Jack Nicholson, Faye Dunaway, John Huston

"You know what happens to nosy fellows?"

It is 1937, Los Angeles. The palm trees are everywhere, and oil rigs still dot the landscape, but big development is coming to the desert town. A big fish in what was then still a small pond, private dick Jake Gittes (Jack Nicholson, full of arrogant patter) is investigating the murder of the local water commissioner when he finds that it leads to a high-level conspiracy involving the theft of water rights. His first real clue about the size of his investigation comes when a henchman (played by the director, Roman Polanski) slices open Gittes's nose as a warning. Before it's over Gittes will have fallen in love with the dead commissioner's widow (Faye Dunaway) and gotten in far too deep with the wealthy and monstrously evil Noah Cross (director John Huston, giving a titanic performance).

Polanski's film, the most memorable of his Hollywood period, delivers on multiple levels. There is the thrill of watching a preindulgent Nicholson push Gittes from arrogant laziness to reluctant heroism. Robert Towne's historical background for his clever script (the possibly criminal deal that made Los Angeles into a city) provides resonance, and his bleak conclusion remains hard to watch. It swept up eleven Oscars nominations, and made large amounts of money. Everybody was happy except Gittes, who left an innocence he never knew he had on a dark street in Chinatown.

Auteur, Auteur

Robert Towne envisaged *Chinatown* as the first in a trilogy, both writing and directing the 1990 sequel, *The Two Jakes*. While beautifully done and certainly underrated, it was impossibly dense, and effectively killed any possibility of a third film.

August 6

Hiroshima Mon Amour

🌐 👤 🎭 ♥

YEAR RELEASED: 1959
DIRECTOR: Alan Resnais
WHO'S IN IT: Emmanuelle Riva, Eiji Okada

"I loved the taste of blood since I tasted yours."

Jean-Luc Godard described Alan Resnais's searing feature debut as "Faulkner plus Stravinksy," and that statement almost makes sense. The film has the lilting power of Stravinsky's music and the tortured sense of inescapable past that twisted through Faulkner's fiction like a malevolent vine.

Elle (Emmanuelle Riva, with the fire of a young Anne Bancroft) is a French actress filming in postwar Hiroshima, and having an affair with a Japanese man, Lui (Eiji Okada). She's passionate and flighty, loving and cold, and he's utterly enraptured; they're married to other people, approaching middle age, and doing something completely insane.

For the riveting first quarter-hour, we see them only as languorously caressing limbs, covered in some shiny film. They talk circles around Hiroshima, she insisting that she *knows*, having been to the museum, seen the re-enactment films, he retorting simply, "You saw nothing in Hiroshima" (Resnais shows the horrific newsreel footage, the burnt skin and deformed children). They cling to each other in fear of the past, her disgrace as mistress of a German soldier in occupied France, the loss of his family to the atomic bomb (which was detonated over the city on this day in 1945).

Marguerite Duras's script has an incandescent clarity to it, while Resnais's artful direction, informed by his past documentary work, is unflinchingly honest and wholly shorn of Western ideas of Asian exoticism. Screen lovers have rarely been this naked together, in every sense.

Courting Controversy

Today considered one of the decade's most unforgettable films, *Hiroshima Mon Amour* was turned down as the French selection for the Cannes Film Festival. It became a success, at least partially due to an ad campaign that emphasized the film's eroticism.

The Best Years of Our Lives

YEAR RELEASED: 1946
DIRECTOR: William Wyler
WHO'S IN IT: Myrna Loy, Fredric March, Dana Andrews, Harold Russell

"Last year it was 'Kill Japs!' and now it's 'Make Money!'"

Three World War II veterans hitch a flight home to Boone City, Iowa, on a bomber. They can't wait to get home, but once there, have no idea how to act.

Fred Derry (Dana Andrews, dashing, with a hint of pain) is a former bombardier and medal-heavy hero who now can't qualify for any job but soda jerk. Infantryman Al Stephenson (Fredric March) returns to his loving wife Milly (Myrna Loy, the picture of graciousness), beautiful children, and cushy bank job but can't get past the crushing bitterness. Homer Parish (Harold Russell), a sailor whose hands are now metal hooks, seems upbeat, but underneath assumes he's seen as a monster.

Released when the country was eager to forget the war, William Wyler's honest and moving film, helped by the rebelliously caustic humor of Robert Sherwood's script, plugged in to many veterans' sense of disillusionment. As his characters struggle to adjust, they lash out at the complacency and insensitivity of those around them. Gregg Toland shoots it cleaner and less expressionistic than his Orson Welles films. Many critics grumbled about its almost three-hour running time, and the public wasn't overly thrilled about its hopeful but downbeat mood. The Academy didn't care, however, as it picked up seven Oscars.

Production Notes

Several people involved with *The Best Years of Our Lives* were involved in the war effort: Harold Russell lost his hands while training paratroopers in 1944; William Wyler served in the U.S. Army Air Corps; and Myrna Loy worked as a Red Cross volunteer. The film itself was inspired by an August 7, 1944, *Time* article called "The Way Home."

August 8

Nashville

YEAR RELEASED: 1975
DIRECTOR: Robert Altman
WHO'S IN IT: Ned Beatty, Karen Black, Henry Gibson, Keith Carradine

"This is not Dallas, this is Nashville."

There is a weekend country and western music festival in Nashville, right on the cusp of the bicentennial. Flags will flap and politicians will cadge for votes. Of the thousands of people heading to town, this film tracks a screen-busting two dozen of them. There are womanizing singers, insincere political operatives, die-hard fans, and others (a BBC reporter, a gangly biker) who just seem lost.

Even more than the average Robert Altman film, *Nashville* (the high point of his Hollywood success) circles and dodges and nips at its story, teasing out plot strands from the confusing turmoil of voices like a cat tugging at yarn—playfully and fitfully. Altman brings authenticity to the story by having many actors (from Keith Carradine to Lily Tomlin and Karen Black) write and perform their own music. The Joan Tewkesbury script contains enough characters to justify giving short shrift to some, even if viewers are often left wondering what exactly is happening. It ends in sudden tragedy, a spasm of violence at once arbitrary and predictable.

This ensemble drama of uncommon ambition portrays an America coming to terms with Vietnam, riots, assassinations, Watergate, and all the rest. The result is a film always on the verge of spinning out of control but barely keeping the lid on with an optimism that may or may not be justified, just like the nation itself.

Auteur, Auteur

Robert Altman tried to one-up himself with *The Wedding* (1978), an oversized ensemble piece set at a large society wedding that was billed as featuring forty-eight major characters, twice as many as *Nashville*.

The Dirty Dozen

YEAR RELEASED: 1967
DIRECTOR: Robert Aldrich
WHO'S IN IT: Lee Marvin, Charles Bronson, Ernest Borgnine

"You've got one religious maniac, one malignant dwarf, two near-idiots . . . and the rest I don't even wanna think about!"

Robert Aldrich assembled the sort of cast that John Sturges might have put together a few years earlier for more heroic fare like *The Great Escape*—only he made them social malcontents, if not out and out psychotics. Lee Marvin (clearly just here for the paycheck, but still enjoying himself) plays Major Reisman, who's about to be busted for insubordination, only he's given one last chance. He's told to take a band of army convicts off death row, train them into something resembling a commando squad, and lead them deep into France to destroy a chateau full of high-ranking German officers. Reisman is as close as you'll find to a hero in this film, with a squad full of murderers, misfits, and one rapist (a highly disturbing Telly Savalas).

What Aldrich is banking on is that no matter how bad his protagonists are, they're going after Nazis, so nobody's going to worry about character flaws. Aldrich definitely enjoys the training part of the story more than the actual combat. He relishes the combative interplay of hard-bitten convicts given a devil's choice between certain death and very likely death. It makes for an unusual war film, to be sure, but in many ways a landmark one. After this, the good guys didn't always have to be so good. The result was box-office gold—and many, many dead Nazis.

Casting Call

Director John Cassavetes's sideline work as a threatening character actor in films like *Rosemary's Baby* (1967) and *The Dirty Dozen* helped finance his low-budget filmmaking career.

The Wizard of Oz

YEAR RELEASED: 1939
DIRECTOR: Victor Fleming
WHO'S IN IT: Judy Garland, Ray Bolger, Jack Haley, Bert Lahr

"Frightened? Child, you're talking to a man who's laughed in the face of death, sneered at doom, and chuckled at catastrophe. I was petrified."

A lovely and accidental work, the problem-plagued musical version of L. Frank Baum's curious 1900 fable looks as fresh now as the day it was filmed. Perhaps it has something to do with the eye-popping candy-store shades of its Technicolor scenes. That, or the menagerie of characters Kansas girl Dorothy Gale (Judy Garland) finds herself mixed up in once she's swept away to this mysterious land of Oz. Or maybe it's the songs by Harold Arlen and Yip Harburg, explosive with yearning and thrill.

There may be no explaining the appeal of this film, a hybrid thing, equal parts fantasy, musical, and vaudeville. This is one of those films many have grown up watching repeatedly at different ages, with varying reactions. Generally, one becomes more annoyed with Glinda the Good Witch and less frightened of the Wicked Witch as the years advance. But the Scarecrow (Ray Bolger), Tin Man (Jack Haley), and Cowardly Lion (Bert Lahr) remain the kind of companions you would want to have in a world like Oz. There are wonders to behold, but also houses dropping from the sky and winged monkeys on the prowl.

It's no place for children.

Courting Controversy

A persistent urban legend claims that in the background of one shot from *The Wizard of Oz* one can see a Munchkin actor swinging from a rope. Yet there has never been any evidence that any of the hundred-plus actors playing Munchkins took their lives on set.

The Last Seduction

YEAR RELEASED: 1994
DIRECTOR: John Dahl
WHO'S IN IT: Linda Fiorentino, Peter Berg, Bill Pullman

"Anyone check you for a heartbeat recently?"

No apologies. That's the secret of John Dahl's acerbic modern noir, in which a wife runs away from her husband with $700,000, leaving him to plead his case with a loan shark who "likes to play a little game with thumbs." There's no indication that she will feel any guilt about doing that to him, or what she *will* do to the next guy who gets stuck in her web.

The black widow of a wife, insurance executive Bridget (Linda Fiorentino, a steely and dangerous beauty), high-tails it out of New York to a small town while she works things out. Killing time in a bar, Bridget first rebuffs the advances of Mike (Peter Berg), then decides to keep him around for sex; the surprise of Fiorentino's no-nonsense sensuality is a bracing reminder of how backward thinking women's film roles still are.

The best parts of Steve Barancik's script detail the brusque Bridget adjusting to life in a quaint town under an assumed name. In no time, she's lied her way into a good job and is planning murder-for-hire schemes that she wants to sucker Mike into.

This was Dahl's second film in a row—before this came *Red Rock West* (1993)—to be first broadcast on television and only given a grudging theatrical release after word-of-mouth spread from limited screenings. Like its heroine, it's smart, quick-witted, not a little bit evil, and utterly unapologetic.

And the Winner Is . . .

Although Linda Fiorentino was thought a top candidate for a best actress Oscar, Academy rules prevented *The Last Seduction* from being nominated because it debuted on television before its theatrical release.

The Fog of War

YEAR RELEASED: 2003
DIRECTOR: Errol Morris
WHO'S IN IT: Robert McNamara

"There'll be no learning period with nuclear weapons. Make one mistake and you're going to destroy nations."

At the age of eighty-five, Robert McNamara did something nearly unprecedented for former high-ranking public officials—he sat down to talk about his mistakes.

A wunderkind air force analyst during World War II, McNamara helped plan the Japan firebombing strategy—one raid on Tokyo alone killed 100,000 people. Following a stint in private industry (he became president of Ford Motor Company), McNamara was chosen as Secretary of Defense by John F. Kennedy. After providing a bracing summation of the Cuban Missile Crisis (holding his fingers barely apart to show how close the world came to nuclear war), McNamara moves into the great tragedy of Vietnam. Although there's still a reluctance to apologize, he explains in dramatic detail how technocrats like himself pursued misguided strategies and ignored what the data was telling them. It's like watching Alan Greenspan admit to Congress that his entire economic philosophy has been flawed.

When McNamara first showed up to be interviewed by Errol Morris, it was only supposed to take an hour; he ended up talking for twenty. Even though the film is essentially one long interview (though some war footage is cleverly spliced in throughout, to the ominous strains of Philip Glass's score), Morris is skillful enough to make it feel more like a conversation and less a lecture. The result is one of the most crucial films ever made about American history.

Production Notes

For *The Fog of War*, Errol Morris invented the "Interrotron," a device that allowed an interviewee to speak directly to the interviewer while appearing to look right into the camera lens.

One, Two, Three

YEAR RELEASED: 1961
DIRECTOR: Billy Wilder
WHO'S IN IT: James Cagney, Horst Buchholz, Pamela Tiffin

"Some of the East German police were rude and suspicious. Others were suspicious and rude."

If you have to go out, it may as well be with a bang. But James Cagney is so perfectly polished in Billy Wilder's light-speed Cold War comedy, it makes you wish he hadn't taken the next two decades off.

Cagney plays C. R. McNamara, a Coca-Cola executive assigned to the firm's West Berlin office, where he agrees to look after the boss's flighty daughter, Scarlett Hazeltine (Pamela Tiffin), just before she announces that she's marrying an East German Communist (Horst Buchholz).

A celebration of verbal velocity, this is one of Wilder's funniest and most overlooked films, not to mention his last great one (a string of mediocrities like *Kiss Me, Stupid* and *The Fortune Cookie* would follow). Its screwball timing and razor-like political edge made a volatile and initially unpopular mix. (Being released just after the construction of the Berlin Wall, which began on this day in 1961, didn't help.)

Whatever the political ramifications, this is Cagney's show. He barrels through the picture, firing off one-liners without even appearing to aim. The rest of the cast scatters around him, trying their best to keep up with Wilder and I. A. L. Diamond's densely packed script, the first page of which read, "This piece must be played *molto furioso.*" Try and keep up.

Production Notes

Days before his scene at Berlin's Templehof Airport, Horst Buchholz was injured while racing his Porsche. Wilder had to build a replica of Templehof on a Hollywood sound stage and shoot the scene there once Buchholz had recuperated much later.

All About Eve

YEAR RELEASED: 1950
DIRECTOR: Joseph L. Mankiewicz
WHO'S IN IT: Bette Davis, Anne Baxter, George Sanders, Celeste Holm

"You have a point. An idiotic one, but a point."

Behind every great star is a scandalous crime. That is the message to be gleaned from Joseph L. Mankiewicz's deliciously fun backstage melodrama in which a sweet-seeming ingénue proves more than a match for the wily, cunning Bette Davis. At the film's start, Eve (Anne Baxter, deceptively adorable) is being feted by an enraptured theater community while fallen star Margo Channing (Bette Davis) and other casualties of Eve's ascent look on in petulant disgust. The exception is theater critic Addison DeWitt (George Sanders, cool and rough), who is a pile of happy cynicism in human form. The story unfolds in flashback.

Margo was once la grande dame of Broadway, then came star-struck Eve, wheedling her way into Margo's life as an all-around gofer. Of course, Eve wants to act as well, and it isn't long before she's finding ways of stealing the spotlight from Margo. While Margo spirals downward, Eve's star shoots upward, aided by a well-smitten Addison. Deals are cut and souls are sold; the price of fame isn't cheap.

Mankiewicz's film is funny, literate, and knowing, tracking the theater world's cycles of self-destructive narcissism with a biased eye. All the performances are fresh and energetic, particularly Sanders and Davis, who manages the fine trick of not overacting while portraying a chronic overactor.

And the Winner Is . . .

All About Eve received a record fourteen Oscar nominations (winning six), a number that wouldn't be broken until 1998 by James Cameron's *Titanic*.

Woodstock

YEAR RELEASED: 1970
DIRECTOR: Michael Wadleigh
WHO'S IN IT: The Who, Country Joe and the Fish, Joan Baez, Richie Havens, Joe Cocker

"We must be in heaven, man! There's always a little bit of heaven in a disaster area."

When the rains came, there wasn't any shelter. The bathroom situation left something to be desired. As the helpful public address system noted, the brown acid was best avoided. But if Michael Wadleigh's spacious and good-natured documentary on the three-day August 1969 concert in upstate New York is any indication, the festival was a sight to behold.

Camera crews prowled the site before the first notes were played and throughout, gauging reactions from blissed-out audience members and pleasantly surprised townsfolk. The miles of footage were stitched together by a crew that included a young Martin Scorsese, frequently using two- or three-part split screens to show the youth of America wandering in fields or bathing nude when not gawking at the performances. The music is a mixed bag, ranging from Sly and the Family Stone's proto-funk explosion to an unfortunate appearance by Sha Na Na.

The vibe captured by Wadleigh's cameras is as happy-go-lucky as the Maysleses' (directors of the Rolling Stones documentary *Gimme Shelter*) presentation of the Altamont concert riot a few months later was jangled and tense. There is a loop of self-congratulation, but it's mostly deserved. The immensity of what is recorded here is something unique in the realm of concert film. It's a postcard from a time when it seemed like this sort of thing could become the norm, and not the exception.

In Homage

Ang Lee's *Taking Woodstock* (2009) was a fictional story set at a small, family-run motel near the concert grounds. Though the film is about the turmoil caused by the concert, the bands themselves are only ever glimpsed from a distance.

Lawrence of Arabia

YEAR RELEASED: 1962
DIRECTOR: David Lean
WHO'S IN IT: Peter O'Toole, Omar Sharif, Alec Guinness

"The trick, William Potter, is not minding that it hurts."

An elemental epic of great, arcing vistas and burning moral choices, David Lean's film creates pure magic of the kind that makes you realize *this* is why we make and watch films. Praise is regularly hurled at Lean's mythic history of conquest like rice at a wedding. But the film not only stands up to its praise, it transcends it, rewarding viewing after delighted viewing.

Peter O'Toole plays T. E. Lawrence, a junior British officer with an interest in Arab language and culture who changes history after being sent to Prince Feisel (Alec Guinness), a Bedouin ally of the British against the ragged remains of the Ottoman Empire. With the force of a bright, blue-eyed oracle, Lawrence leads the demoralized tribes on a suicide mission against an Ottoman seaside fort.

After a stupendous victory, Lawrence becomes a warrior chieftain, decked out in the finest white robes, ceremonial dagger at his waist. He walks between two worlds, distrusted by his British commanders suspicious of his success but wholly prepared to sell him out once it comes time to revoke their promises to the Arab tribes, who trust him as a fearless and slightly mad leader. That Lawrence becomes a schizophrenic figure is no surprise. That O'Toole, who spent the rest of his career chasing a role as perfect as this, can embody this character's contradictory impulses so easily goes almost beyond acting.

In Homage

Steven Spielberg once said that after seeing *Lawrence of Arabia*, "I never wanted to do anything else with my life but make films."

August 17

Eddie Murphy: Delirious

 LOL!

YEAR RELEASED: 1983
DIRECTOR: Bruce Gowers
WHO'S IN IT: Eddie Murphy

"You don't have no ice cream. . . ."

The sensation of being in the presence of the funniest man in America runs through this concert film like an electric current. Already an international star because of *Saturday Night Live*, the twenty-two-year-old Murphy struts the stage of Washington, DC's Constitution Hall like he'd been doing this for decades. He is so confident that he (almost) pulls off the popsicle-shiny blood-orange costume misfire that even the early 1980s can't excuse.

Shot in a rough-and-ready style typical for cable-television events at the time, the film is all about the material, which is golden. A routine on children's insanity about ice-cream trucks turns into a song-and-dance number, which turns into an abrupt reminder of poverty. It's breathtakingly funny, the kind of perfectly honed story that later comics would endlessly mimic, sometimes without even knowing it. Your enjoyment of some other material—a riff on Mr. T as a gay man, for instance ("You lookin' mighty cute in them jeans, boy"), or some *Star Trek*–based gags—could depend entirely on your age and maturity. A couple jokes about AIDS will stop many cold (though one wonders how many other comics later scrubbed such material from their act once better information got out).

While Murphy's routine isn't as wall-to-wall funny as some of film's other greatest comedy concerts (Bill Cosby's *Himself*, Chris Rock's *Bring the Pain*, or Richard Pryor's *Live on the Sunset Strip*), his confidence and swagger provides an unbeatable record of a young comic in the glory of his fully developed talent, who may already have nowhere to go but down. *Best Defense* was only one year away.

Historically Speaking

Eddie Murphy's *Delirious* concert took place on August 17, 1983. At the end of the show, he mentions how much had changed since 1939, when African American contralto Marian Anderson wasn't allowed to perform on the very same stage because of her race.

229

Heathers

YEAR RELEASED: 1989
DIRECTOR: Michael Lehmann
WHO'S IN IT: Winona Ryder, Christian Slater

"Now that you're dead, what are you going to do with your life?"

When *Heathers* came out near the worn-out end of the 1980s, Hollywood teenagers were meant to be either happy idiots or mopey romantics. Then came Jason Dean (Christian Slater, doing a passable Jack Nicholson), riding in on a motorcycle, wearing a black trench coat, and pulling a gun on jocks who hassle him. Veronica Sawyer (Winona Ryder), a frustrated member of her high school's most powerful clique—all but her named Heather—is ripe for picking by J. D., whose hatred of high-school sadism plugs in to her need for a life change. His plans for revenge on the Heathers and their jock cohorts are more Columbine than prank, and soon Veronica discovers that "my teen angst has a body count."

Daniel Waters's sharp, quip-laden script viciously mocks everyone in its path. The three Heathers are quintessentially evil teen social dictators, but there are a few heroes in sight. Teachers and parents are limp and useless, while the putative antihero J. D. is satirized as a walking, talking teen rebel stereotype (check the initials). Even an awful but well-meaning antisuicide hit single is put in the crosshairs ("teenage suicide/don't do it!"). The spirit of Waters's fast-paced, irony-laden dialogue was mined in later films like *Mean Girls* (2004) and *Juno* (2007), which didn't match the original's black-hearted vision.

Lost and Found

The original ending of *Heathers* has become the stuff of legend: Veronica allows J. D.'s bomb to go off, killing everyone in the gymnasium. Next we join the dead students in heaven at prom, where all the cliques have reformed.

MASH

 LOL!

YEAR RELEASED: 1970
DIRECTOR: Robert Altman
WHO'S IN IT: Donald Sutherland, Elliot Gould, Sally Kellerman, Robert Duvall, Tom Skerritt

"That kind of informality is inconsistent with maximum efficiency in a military organization."

"Hawkeye" Pierce (Donald Sutherland) and "Trapper John" McIntyre (Elliott Gould) are doctors serving in a mobile army surgical hospital (a "MASH") during the Korean War. When not up to their elbows in the bloodied entrails of some nineteen-year-old draftee, they're raising hell: women, booze, what have you; it's either that or go mad.

This is a Robert Altman film that doesn't fit too easily into his body of work—perhaps because it made buckets of money and everybody has seen it. His signature moves are there: the organic flow of action, the sheets of interlinking dialogue, the casual disregard for dramatic arcs. But the script moves from one strong set piece to another, displaying a confidently vulgar humor that later comedies like *Stripes* (1981) would work so hard to attain.

Coming out when it did, everybody knew the film wasn't about Korea; it was about Vietnam. The hair was just too scruffy and the demeanor too lackadaisically Southern California and reflexively antiauthoritarian for it to be anything else. Though a couple parts have aged poorly (like the football game, with Fred Williamson in a role that cuts close to racial caricature), this bears viewing, if for nothing else than to wash off the stink that years of reruns of the mostly toothless sitcom version have left on the great American war comedy.

And the Winner Is . . .
MASH wasn't just a popular success, it was also nominated for five Oscars, winning for Ring Lardner, Jr.'s screenplay. The best picture winner that year was an entirely different kind of war film: *Patton*.

Star Wars: Episode V— The Empire Strikes Back

YEAR RELEASED: 1980
DIRECTOR: Irvin Kershner
WHO'S IN IT: Mark Hamill, Harrison Ford, Carrie Fisher, Billy Dee Williams

"Why, you, stuck-up, half-witted, scruffy-looking, Nerf herder!"

This sequel is one to be savored, not just for what it has but for what it *doesn't* have (Ewoks, and Jar Jar Binks, say). Though the first film in the *Star Wars* franchise (or fourth in the new, post–Jar Jar era) ended on a note of bliss (Death Star destroyed, all the rebels celebrating), the screen crawl at the start of this one reminds us that the war has a long way to go: "It is a dark time for the rebellion." The Rebel Alliance is on the run, and some have set up a base on the ice planet of Hoth. Luke Skywalker (Mark Hamill) is there, as are Han Solo (Harrison Ford), Princess Leia (Carrie Fisher), and the droids; it's the last time they'll all be together.

Once Darth Vader (the voice of James Earl Jones) lands his forces on Hoth—necessitating an epic battle, the best in the series, with ice-skimming fighters and armored personnel carriers the size of office buildings—the rebels will scatter across the galaxy to their various fates. While in most films such a dispersal of characters would be dramatic death, in this instance it allows the film to put each to the test, turning them into something more than action figures. Han and Leia's relationship deepens; the rare character with personality, Lando Calrissian (Billy Dee Williams) is introduced; as is Yoda, the dwarf Zen master and spiritual soul of the series. The script is livelier than expected, likely due to the input of Leigh Brackett, who delivered wit to a number of classic Howard Hawks films years before.

August 21

The Public Enemy

YEAR RELEASED: 1931
DIRECTOR: William A. Wellman
WHO'S IN IT: James Cagney, Jean Harlow

"You didn't get them medals for holding hands with them Germans."

Tom Powers is a hood, clean and simple. He is also a cautionary tale in a film that claims to be a message about how the slums breed crime and how it doesn't pay. Played by Jimmy Cagney as a jut-jawed, squint-eyed lout of the first order, Powers is the kind of guy who comes right out and demands what he wants. If you don't give it to him, well, he's got fists. If that fails, he's got a gun.

William Wellman's film is a cleanly structured gangster flick whose sociological interest (Wellman sets the scene with some great old newsreel footage) doesn't distract from its entertainment. Powers is a product of Chicago's Irish slums, doing business since childhood for a local boss called Putty Nose. In adulthood, he does well with bootlegging, living the high life of fine clothes and luscious broads who don't mind getting a grapefruit squished in their face when he's in a bad mood.

There's a moral here, laid out on the screen for one to read, literally. But Wellman understood that the people liked their rogues, and while these guys needed to suffer in the end for their crimes, it didn't mean that the audience couldn't enjoy vicarious thrills for an hour and a half.

Production Notes

William Wellman said in an interview that producer Darryl F. Zanuck allowed him to direct *The Public Enemy* because he promised to deliver "the most vicious picture ever made."

August 22

Dog Day Afternoon

YEAR RELEASED: 1975
DIRECTOR: Sidney Lumet
WHO'S IN IT: Al Pacino, John Cazale, Charles Durning, Chris Sarandon

"We're entertainment, right?"

A bank heist and hostage thriller that makes almost every other entry in either of those genres seem tired, Sidney Lumet's film takes the seeds of a real-life crime story and grows them into one of the decade's most affecting dramas.

Pacino holds center stage as Sonny Wortzik, one of history's least competent amateur bank robbers. Sonny and his friend Sal (a wonderfully dim John Cazale) rob a Brooklyn bank so the married Sonny can pay for his boyfriend's (Chris Sarandon) sex change operation. The problem is the bank doesn't really have any money for them to take. Sonny and Sal take hostages and try to figure out what to do. Sal is no help, and Sonny is a jangled heap of nerves, carrying on jittery phone conversations with his boyfriend and his wife (Susan Peretz) while the police and FBI hover outside. The cops seem just as confused, with a flustered Sergeant Moretti (Charles Durning) trying to keep the media carnival under control. Sonny's unpredictability makes Moretti's job that much harder, particularly once Sonny juices the crowd by chanting "Attica! Attica!" (referring to the 1971 upstate New York prison riot in which twenty-nine inmates and ten hostages died).

Pacino's wounded performance is the film's anchor, but Lumet's taut, empathetic direction brings it to masterpiece status. The stranger-than-fiction absurdities pile black comedy on top of bad decisions until the stunning, tragic finale takes your breath away.

Historically Speaking

The inspiration for Al Pacino's character in *Dog Day Afternoon* was named John Wojtowicz, who robbed a Brooklyn Chase Manhattan Bank on August 22, 1972. Some of Wojtowicz's proceeds from selling his story financed the sex-change operation of his boyfriend, Ernest Aron, who became Elizabeth D. Eden.

August 23

This Is Spinal Tap

YEAR RELEASED: 1984
DIRECTOR: Rob Reiner
WHO'S IN IT: Christopher Guest, Michael McKean, Harry Shearer

"It's such a fine line between stupid and clever."

The greatest trick that Rob Reiner and his cast of deadpan clowns pull off in this, perhaps the greatest mock-documentary (a "rockumentary" as Reiner, playing the self-important director, says) of all time, is making you forget that it's a joke.

Imagined as a tour following England's "loudest band," Spinal Tap, the film begins in laudatory style, with the band playing to large crowds. But trouble is brewing with their label and discord sparks between the mulleted band leaders, Nigel Tufnel (Christopher Guest) and David St. Hubbins (Michael McKean), childhood friends now at odds over David's astrology-obsessed wife.

As the tour continues and the crowds dwindle or disappear entirely, Spinal Tap confronts a crises that a real documentarian would kill to witness. The band soldiers on, dutifully blasting out numbers like "Hellhole" ("You know where you stand in a . . . Hellhole!") and "Stonehenge" ("Where the demons dwell and they do live well"). In between, they open up in one-on-one interviews where blissfully blithe ignorance delivered in mock-Cockney accents is the order of the day.

This Is Spinal Tap remains an eminently quotable comedy because of how deeply its cast submerge themselves in their roles. Time and again, Reiner's camera locks on to moments that make you care, even if just for a second, about these spandex-wearing lads from Squatney who just don't know why they keep losing drummers.

Lost and Found

Subsequent DVD releases of *This Is Spinal Tap* have included over an hour's worth of (mostly hilarious) deleted scenes.

Alphaville

🌐 👽 👤

YEAR RELEASED: 1965
DIRECTOR: Jean-Luc Godard
WHO'S IN IT: Eddie Constantine, Anna Karina

"You'll become something worse than dead. You'll become a legend."

In this fractured, self-satirizing sci-fi lark, Lemmy Caution (Eddie Constantine, tough as nails) is an intergalactic secret agent on a special mission from the Outerlands to the city of Alphaville. There, he's supposed to find renegade scientist Professor von Braun, aka Leonard Nosferatu (Howard Vernon), who is now running Alphaville by means of his Alpha 60 supercomputer. While conducting his investigation, Caution learns that the city's new computer-organized society runs along strictly scientific means now, and has no further need for art. He also meets the professor's model-beautiful daughter Natacha (Anna Karina) and promptly falls for her. This doesn't stop Caution from completing his mission; nothing will.

Although he later became a political intellectual, Godard's loony humor has rarely been on better display. A genre hodge-podge whose aims can be guessed at from one alternate title (*Dick Tracy on Mars*), the film has fun mixing high art with low. Even as Caution muscles his way around like a Mickey Spillane hero (trenchcoat, fedora, gun, and tough-guy glower), Alpha 60 spits out the kind of pseudo-philosophic aphorisms that would later characterize much of Godard's work ("Everything has been said, provided words do not change their meanings, and meanings their words"; "Sometimes reality is too complex for oral communication"). The resulting blend of genre adventure and arthouse depth is wonderfully unique.

Production Notes

Godard's microscopic budget resulted in sublimely low-tech fixes, such as Lemmy Caution driving a Ford Galaxy from one "planet" to the next and the city's self-destruction visualized by having some extras spin around in circles.

Time Bandits

YEAR RELEASED: 1981
DIRECTOR: Terry Gilliam
WHO'S IN IT: Craig Warnock, John Cleese, Sean Connery

"What sort of supreme being created such riffraff?"

It's not a typical kids' film, what with all the Monty Python–type gags, but kids seem to be the ones who enjoy this film the most. And why not? After all, the stars are thieving, roguish dwarves with the ability to travel through space and time. What kid wouldn't want that power?

In the year 2000, Kevin (Craig Warnock) is kidnapped by six hyperactive and not-too-nice dwarves, who are being chased by powerful figures known as the Supreme Being and Evil Genius. Kevin and the dwarves jump from one escapade to the next via time-traveling wormholes his kidnappers discovered on a map that they *may* have stolen. John Cleese pops by for a stint as Robin Hood, and there's a great knockdown battle between the Minotaur of Crete and a fierce warrior (Sean Connery). Ultimately they will have to come to some sort of reckoning with Supreme Being and Evil Genius, and do something about all that treasure the dwarves have stolen from different epochs.

All of this is, of course, just an excuse for ex-Pythons Terry Gilliam and cowriter Michael Palin to string together a series of history-based sketches not unlike the sort of thing they used to do on their TV show. There's a bleak element to the story— its vision of cold and distant godlike entities is far from reassuring—that children probably won't notice for all the dazzling effects and adventure on display.

Production Notes
Time Bandits was so unwanted in Hollywood that Terry Gilliam shot it without studio backing for a paltry $5 million.

August 26

The 39 Steps

🔍

YEAR RELEASED: 1935
DIRECTOR: Alfred Hitchcock
WHO'S IN IT: Robert Donat, Madeleine Carroll

"Beautiful, mysterious woman pursued by gunmen. Sounds like a spy story."

When Alfred Hitchcock got around to filming this John Buchan novel, it was already twenty years old, the product of an earlier war's mentality. Hitchcock produced it as England realized another great conflict was coming.

The scenario is a classic wrong-man-chase, which Hitchcock would resort to time and again over the years. Robert Donat plays Richard Hannay, an ordinary guy who tries to help a woman but ends up wrongly accused of her murder, once she's found knifed to death in his flat in London. He must then go on the run to prove his innocence. For a good part of the chase, Richard is paired with (at one point, literally handcuffed to) the beautiful and sassy Pamela (Madeleine Carroll), which makes the life-threatening risks he takes much more interesting.

Although the film's plot is breezy and smart, what stays with you after all the mystery has been cleared up in neatly British fashion is the landscape. Bernard Knowles's cinematography is wonderfully moody, particularly when the film reaches the Scottish highlands, with its stark lines and windswept moors.

The versatile novel was adapted many other times over the years for television and radio, including a comic live theater version (in which four actors frantically play 150 roles) that premiered in 2005.

Everyone's a Critic

John Buchan was originally upset that Hitchcock changed his novel so extensively. But after seeing the film, Buchan acknowledged that Hitchcock's take on the story actually improved on his.

Heat

YEAR RELEASED: 1995
DIRECTOR: Michael Mann
WHO'S IN IT: Al Pacino, Robert De Niro

"You sift through the detritus, you read the terrain, you search for signs of passing, for the scent of your prey, and then you hunt them down."

In Michael Mann's crime opus, two actors then at their peak—Al Pacino and Robert De Niro—each play the ultimate embodiment of his profession, one a detective and the other a thief. They spend the entire film circling each other but only meet once, for a few minutes in a coffee shop, where they talk shop and split off into the Los Angeles night.

Mann's film is structured around two great heists. The first one opens the film. A crack team in hockey masks led by Neil McCauley (De Niro) uses explosives and a big-rig to take down an armored car. The more that Detective Vincent Hanna (Pacino)—an obsessive bloodhound who seems to have last slept in the 1970s—learns about McCauley, the more he appreciates his skill. They later face each other in a daylight downtown bank robbery that turns into open street warfare, cops and robbers opening up on each other with automatic weapons in one of the most furiously choreographed shootouts in film history.

Around these heists and Hanna's chasing of McCauley, Mann wedges in another dozen or so vibrantly acted characters and a complex interplay of subplots, all captured with pristine widescreen cinematography. With its grandiose scope, the film's ambition to be the last word in modern American crime film is overwhelming. It has yet to be topped.

Production Notes

Michael Mann based Robert De Niro's character on real Chicago criminal Neil McCauley, who was shot dead in 1963 by a detective who he had had a cup of coffee with not long before.

Singin' in the Rain

YEAR RELEASED: 1952
DIRECTORS: Stanley Donen, Gene Kelly
WHO'S IN IT: Gene Kelly, Donald O'Connor, Debbie Reynolds, Jean Hagen

"She can't act, she can't sing, she can't dance. A triple threat."

This film is what people are talking about when they say they don't make 'em like they used to. Silent-film star Don Lockwood (Gene Kelly, optimistic as a sunrise) is making a film with the obnoxiously untalented star Lina Lamont (Jean Hagen) when *The Jazz Singer* messes up everything by making silent films instantly obsolete. A test screening of the hastily sound-dubbed film goes awry when the audience realizes that Lina has one of the most irritating voices ever heard.

Panic ensues until Don's buddy Cosmo Brown (Donald O'Connor) hits on an idea: why not hire that cute chorus girl Kathy Selden (Debbie Reynolds) to overdub Lina's voice? Good thing she can dance, too, because that allows Kathy, Cosmo, and Don to throw together some of the greatest dance sequences ever to grace an American movie screen.

The previous year, Kelly had blown away audiences with Vincente Minnelli's *An American in Paris*, a similarly exuberant musical that would otherwise have been his career highlight. This musical featured not just Kelly at the height of his dancing and choreographic prowess (he received a codirector's credit with Stanley Donen), but an even stronger story and lyrics from Adolph Green and Betty Comden. While everybody is familiar with clips of the title song (which though overplayed, is still a priceless snippet of pure happiness), the rest of this witty, sparkling musical is almost as good.

And the Winner Is . . .
Incredibly, *Singin' in the Rain* was only nominated for two Oscars, music score and supporting actress (Jean Hagen), yet won neither.

August 29

The Lady Eve

YEAR RELEASED: 1941
DIRECTOR: Preston Sturges
WHO'S IN IT: Barbara Stanwyck, Henry Fonda, Charles Coburn

"I need him like the axe needs the turkey."

Sometimes Preston Sturges just needed a story to get his actors going. In this case, it involves a rich kid, Charles Pike, with less common sense than the rare snakes he likes to study. At the beginning of the film, Charles (a particularly guileless Henry Fonda) boards an ocean liner after a long sojourn doing research in the Amazon. He's almost instantly in the crosshairs of Jean Harrington (Barbara Stanwyck), a card hustler who wants Charles's money and doesn't see why she shouldn't be able to get it. Her partner and father, "Colonel" Harry Harrington (Charles Coburn) agrees.

What follows is a one-sided battle of wits in which Jean runs circles around Charles, with Stanwyck's quick diction doing wonders with Sturges's knife-sharp dialogue. Charles can't do much but watch himself being taken advantage of. Granted, it's not all bad for him, what with the slow-moving ocean-liner luxury and all those strolls on deck with Jean, who has completely captivated him.

Stanwyck could take over a screen like few other actresses. This same year, she did similar duty in Howard Hawks's *Ball of Fire*, confounding a conclave of book-bound academics with her bracing, street-smart verbosity, and hot-to-trot looks. She's better in Sturges's film, but who wouldn't be, with lines like, "They say a moonlit deck is a woman's business office"?

And the Winner Is . . .

The Academy gave *The Lady Eve* just one nomination, oddly not to the filmmaker or any of the actors, but instead to Monckton Hoffe, the writer of the original story on which it was based.

241

August 30

Double Indemnity

🔍 👐

YEAR RELEASED: 1944
DIRECTOR: Billy Wilder
WHO'S IN IT: Fred MacMurray, Barbara Stanwyck

"I killed him for money—and for a woman. I didn't get the money and I didn't get the woman. Pretty, isn't it?"

Shot with a profusion of hard angles that mirror the tough dialogue, the film clicks together like train car couplings, no less enjoyable for the fact that it's all being told in flashback. Mild-seeming insurance salesman Walter Neff (Fred MacMurray) has a surprising dark side: he not only fell for a married woman, but helped kill her husband as well. Being an insurance guy helps you figure out how to do these things, it seems.

Neff plotted with his femme fatale, Phyllis Dietrichson (Barbara Stanwyck) for her hubby to buy the farm in a rare manner (falling from a train) that will force the insurance company to pay out on the double-indemnity clause. Of course, it doesn't work out that way, with Phyllis turning out to have a few cards up her sleeve, including an affair with her husband's daughter's boyfriend.

Billy Wilder's nasty piece of fun is almost a clinic in film noir—very likely the reason that Lawrence Kasdan would lift so much of it for *Body Heat*. Stanwyck's fatale is a slinky villainess with a sharp line of patter, while MacMurray—using the same predatory eye that he employed so effectively later in Wilder's *The Apartment*—plays the schlub who doesn't think he's a schlub.

Production Notes

Billy Wilder's writing partner, Charles Brackett, refused to work on *Double Indemnity*, thinking it immoral. The novel's author, James M. Cain, was unavailable. Raymond Chandler took the job, but though Cain believed they improved his story, Chandler and Wilder detested working together.

August 31

Days of Heaven

YEAR RELEASED: 1978
DIRECTOR: Terrence Malick
WHO'S IN IT: Richard Gere, Brooke Adams, Linda Manz, Sam Shepard

"Your sister keep you warm at night, does she?"

Terrence Malick's romantic second film opens with Bill (Richard Gere), a Chicago steel mill worker who kills his boss in a fight and then jumps town with his little sister Linda (Linda Manz) and girlfriend Abby (Brooke Adams). Hopping a train to Texas, they are hired to work the harvest on the sprawling wheat farm of a wealthy farmer (Sam Shepard). Bill tells everyone that Abby is his sister, which complicates things when the farmer falls in love with Abby and tries to marry her. She and Bill agree that she should do it, so that when the sickly farmer dies, they can scoop up his fortune. The vengeful ending coincides with an almost biblical plague of locusts.

Malick's story here is one not so much of people but of icons suspended against great scenic panoramas. The grand Ennio Morricone soundtrack and sumptuous cinematography create a waking dream of wide-open spaces, the rustling wheat fields in the distance, with the occasional person pensively staring, face lit by soft sunset glows. All the while, Manz narrates the film in a blankly dreamy manner that echoes Malick's *Badlands* (1973).

Violence lurks in the foreground, but it is not what you take away from the film. It's hard to pinpoint *what* you take away, but it's akin to the impressions of paintings that Malick evokes here (particularly Edward Hopper's *House by the Railroad*): beauty above all.

And the Winner Is . . .

Winning best director at Cannes, *Days of Heaven* was received less charitably at home, getting four Oscar nominations, but only winning for Nestor Almendros's cinematography. Malick took the next two decades off from filmmaking.

To Be or Not to Be

YEAR RELEASED: 1942
DIRECTOR: Ernst Lubitsch
WHO'S IN IT: Carole Lombard, Jack Benny

"What he did to Shakespeare we are now doing to Poland."

Coming to screens in 1942, not long before the war's turning point but far enough away that cautious optimism was still the watchword, Ernst Lubitsch's elegant little stage comedy has rarely been bested for making the Nazis appear not just evil, but *laughable*. Even decades later, Mel Brooks ran into trouble making the same point with *The Producers*.

Set in Nazi-occupied Poland (the Germans invaded on this day in 1939), Lubitsch's film begins as a sprightly piece about an ever-feuding couple, Joseph and Maria Tura, who are the star attractions of a theater company. Joseph (Jack Benny) is the buffoon, with Maria (Carole Lombard, coming off as the smartest person in every scene) managing the neat trick of two-timing him while still making him look like the schmuck. There's some fun to be had with stage pretensions, particularly the central joke in which Maria uses the start of Joseph's *Hamlet* soliloquy to sneak out for a liaison with a handsome pilot (Robert Stack).

Edwin Justus Mayer's script (from an idea by Melchior Lengyel, who also fostered *Ninotchka*) was accused of tastelessness at the time, and it's easy to see why. The Nazis are used mostly as the butts of jokes in Lubitsch's many intricately constructed screwball set-pieces, but as a whole, it's an impressively elegant takedown.

In Homage

For his 1983 remake, Mel Brooks cast himself in the Jack Benny role and his wife Anne Bancroft in the Carole Lombard position. It was a faithful adaptation but wholly unnecessary and—even less forgivable—just not that funny.

The Matrix

YEAR RELEASED: 1999
DIRECTOR: Larry Wachowski, Andy Wachowski
WHO'S IN IT: Keanu Reeves, Laurence Fishburne, Carrie-Anne Moss

"I imagine that right now you're feeling a bit like Alice, tumbling down the rabbit hole?"

Keanu Reeves plays Neo, a kung fu Christ figure in a sleek black trench coat who can hang in midair while bullets spin past harmlessly. Once a computer hacker who took the wrong pill, he was invited down the rabbit hole by a mysterious cat named Morpheus (a magisterial Laurence Fishburne, long overdue this kind of role).

Once in the *real* real world, Neo discovers the kind of thing that keeps paranoid schizophrenics up for days at a stretch. Earth was conquered years ago by aliens, who keep humans alive in massive vat-farms to generate electricity. The livestock people live in a computer simulation (the Matrix) that Morpheus and his band of rebels have discovered how to escape, but the rebels need some help in their war. That's where Neo comes in.

When the Wachowski brothers brought this film to light, it was the true birth of modern special effects. Their innovative "bullet-time" slow-motion in the suspended combat scenes and the seamless use of CGI in crafting the limitless immensity of the Matrix have been endlessly replicated since. Among the downsides are a cold cyberpunk cruelty and cribbing from too many sources to count (*Star Wars*, *Wizard of Oz*, pop philosophy, fortune cookies). The sequels are many times more pretentious and less fun than the original.

In Homage

Among the many books written about *The Matrix* trilogy are: *Philosophers Explore the Matrix*, *Jacking into the Matrix Franchise: Cultural Reception and Interpretation*, and *The Matrix and Philosophy: Welcome to the Desert of the Real*.

September 3

Kicking and Screaming

YEAR RELEASED: 1995
DIRECTOR: Noah Baumbach
WHO'S IN IT: Josh Hamilton, Chris Eigeman, Parker Posey, Olivia d'Abo

"I wish I was retiring after a lifetime of hard labor."

"What I used to be able to pass off as a bad summer could now potentially turn into a bad life." That's Max (Chris Eigeman), the resident grump of a gaggle of emotionally immobilized college grads. A philosophy major so overwhelmed with laziness that he'd rather leave a warning sign on a pile of broken glass than clean it up, Max is just the group's most vocal articulator of paralysis. Epic worrier Otis (Carlos Jacott) frets over finding a job (even the video store is asking for a second interview) while Skippy (Jason Wiles) has dealt with his postgraduate confusion by re-enrolling in school, to the annoyance of his girlfriend, Miami (Parker Posey). Max's roommate Grover (Josh Hamilton) is a so-far failed writer who spends his time dating college freshmen.

The heart of the fantastic debut, which is packed with caustic humor and the knowing cultural references common to a certain brainy brand of indie film, is a love story that plays in reverse. Grover has broken up with his girlfriend Jane (Olivia d'Abo) because, in essence, he was too paralyzed to follow her to Prague. Noah Baumbach's charming script interweaves Grover's current status with funny, touching scenes from his relationship with Jane. Their banter has a lightly ironic literacy to it; when Jane accuses him of acting like a child at times, Grover responds with winking sincerity, "but if I was a child, you'd find that endearing."

Auteur, Auteur

Noah Baumbach's father, novelist Jonathan Baumbach, appears briefly in *Kicking and Screaming* as a fiction seminar teacher, sighing with irritation.

246

The Legend of the Drunken Master

YEAR RELEASED: 1994
DIRECTOR: Chia-Liang Liu
WHO'S IN IT: Jackie Chan, Lung Ti, Felix Wong

"Drinking gives Herculean strength."

Set in nineteenth-century China, this follow-up to Jackie Chan's early classic *Drunken Master* (1978) pummels everything else the comedic action star has done into submission. This achievement would be impressive anyway, but given the fact that Chan was some sixteen years older when he made the furiously kinetic sequel, it's even more jaw-dropping.

Loyal but occasionally wayward son Wong Fei-hung (Chan) gets caught up in a conspiracy of foreigners trying to steal Chinese artifacts, which his "drunken boxing" fighting style would help stop. The problem is that Fei-hung's father believes fighting shames the family, leaving Fei-hung torn between loyalty to his family and his country.

As explicated in the first film, drunken boxing is a martial arts fighting style based on the idea that acting somewhat soused and lurching about makes one a better fighter. This gives Chan his version of Popeye's spinach: a few slugs of liquor and he's transformed into a grinning, unstoppable fighting machine.

Like most of Chan's best films, *Legend of the Drunken Master* marries astoundingly choreographed combat with a broad and family-friendly brand of physical comedy. Where it stands apart from the rest of Chan's work is in the joyful speed and furious intensity with which the film pulls it all off. This intensity is particularly notable in the unbelievably protracted, see-it-to-believe-it final battle scene, which stands today as possibly the greatest of its kind in film history.

In Production:

After numerous run-ins with Jackie Chan, director Chia-Liang Liu left *The Legend of the Drunken Master*. Chan took over directing, fixing the film with several months' worth of reshoots.

September 5

20,000 Leagues Under the Sea

👽 👪

YEAR RELEASED: 1954
DIRECTOR: Richard Fleischer
WHO'S IN IT: Kirk Douglas, James Mason, Peter Lorre, Paul Lukas

"This is an engine of destruction."

In the mid-nineteenth century, an underwater mystery is sinking ships around the world. An American frigate, the *Abraham Lincoln*, gives chase and is eventually sunk by its target. Three survivors of the *Lincoln*—American whaler Ned Land (a red-blooded and frequently bare-chested Kirk Douglas), French scientist Pierre Aronnax (Paul Lukas), and his assistant Conseil (Peter Lorre)—are taken captive by the underwater ship, which turns out to be a fantastic submarine piloted by the enigmatic Captain Nemo (James Mason, wearing that air of wearied gravitas better than ever). They are taken on a tour of the world's oceans, while Nemo reveals to them the secrets of his background and quest. The three are divided in their attitudes toward Nemo—Pierre is fascinated while Ned wants nothing more than to escape, and Conseil just looks worried about possibly drowning.

One of the few live-action Disney films not to trade solely in sentimentality, this adventurous underwater adaptation of Jules Verne's novel delved into more adult territory than was the studio's wont, particularly regarding Nemo's past (exploitation, slavery, and war-mongering). The expensive film was also remarkably advanced for the time in terms of special effects, many of which hold up well today, especially the limpid, gorgeous scenes of crewmen in heavy, clanking suits exploring the crystalline ocean waters. The film's centerpiece, a stormy battle with a giant squid, doesn't disappoint.

Production Notes

Perfectionist Walt Disney spent several hundred thousand dollars completely redoing *20,000 Leagues Under the Sea*'s giant squid battle scene, believing the entire film hinged on whether the audience bought into that battle. They did.

Naked Lunch

YEAR RELEASED: 1991
DIRECTOR: David Cronenberg
WHO'S IN IT: Peter Weller, Judy Davis

"Exterminate all rational thought."

The truly incredible thing about David Cronenberg's take on William S. Burroughs's famously unfilmmable novel is his decision to not really film it at all. Instead, he made a film *about* the book and how it came to be; it was a smart decision.

Peter Weller—with a properly dust-dry manner—plays the Burroughs stand-in, Bill Lee. He works as an exterminator (as Burroughs did) and hangs out with a couple of struggling beatnik writers modeled on Jack Kerouac and Allen Ginsberg. Lee tells his wife (Judy Davis) it's time for their William Tell routine, in which he places an apple on her head and aims to shoot it off. Only he shoots her in the forehead. (On September 6, 1951, the real William S. Burroughs shot and killed his wife Joan Vollmer in Mexico City.) Lee goes on the run to an open-air-market-filled fantasyland called Interzone, which looks suspiciously like Morocco, where the real Burroughs holed up. He starts to write, perhaps to escape. Reality deteriorates.

Cronenberg scrambles up episodes from the novel with incidents from Burroughs's life and creates a level-headed nightmare, where the deadpan Lee enters progressively deeper circles of hell, unable to purge the demons from his life. Cronenberg's decision to literalize some of the novel's more fantasy elements sometimes takes the film too far into comedy, but this remains a visionary, profoundly disturbing, and uneasily amusing piece of acidic literary cinema.

Courting Controversy

In 1993, new Twentieth Century Fox chairman Peter Chernin told the *Los Angeles Times* that *Naked Lunch* was a prime example of films he would *not* make: "While I admire it as a detailed, insightful look at drug addiction, I'm not sure about it as a moviegoing experience."

Suspiria

YEAR RELEASED: 1977
DIRECTOR: Dario Argento
WHO'S IN IT: Jessica Harper, Stefania Casini

"Do you know anything about witches?"

The single greatest reason you might be familiar with Dario Argento's name, this is an utterly unforgettable horror film that practically redefined the term. Somewhere between shock-rock opera and brutalist fever dream, the film unleashes everything it has on the women unlucky enough to be caught in its way—and then goes further.

Jessica Harper plays Suzy Bannion, an American student who goes to Germany to study ballet at a dance academy equipped with many long, blood-red corridors and strange happenings. Suzy becomes aware that the school is not what it seems, and not just because of the maggots that rain from the ceiling or the blind piano player mauled to death by his guide dog. The terrifying old ladies who run the place seem determined to drive their students mad. Could they be witches?

Argento, who is both the acknowledged grand master of Italian schlock cinema and also almost entirely unique within its tradition, didn't create a masterpiece by worrying about rationality. He set out to attack the audience with every weapon in his considerable arsenal, from the shocking stabs of violence to the nightmarishly coven-like academy building. What really plucks at the nerves, though, is the score, a devilishly shriek-laden assault on the senses by rock group Goblin. In the same way that director David Lynch can inject dread into the most mundane situations with little more than a slow zoom and a threatening low hum, Argento uses his demonic soundtrack to create a filmed asylum where escape seems impossible.

Auteur, Auteur

A director's director, Dario Argento's closest counterpart in American horror is probably George Romero, for whose *Dawn of the Dead* (1978) Argento not only composed the music but also did some editing work.

September 8

Menace II Society

YEAR RELEASED: 1993
DIRECTOR: Albert Hughes, Allen Hughes
WHO'S IN IT: Larenz Tate, Tyrin Turner

"My grandpops was always coming at us with that religion, and every time it would go in one ear and out the other."

Two years after John Singleton's *Boyz n the Hood* caused a furor, twin brothers and rap video directors Albert and Allen Hughes came out with a film also set in a poor, largely African American, gang-ridden LA neighborhood, but it couldn't have been more different. In place of *Boyz*'s mythic resonance, the Hughes brothers substituted a morality-free zone where casual violence was an everyday, numbing occurrence.

The film opens with two friends, Caine (Tyrin Turner) and O-Dog (Larenz Tate, evil but magnetic), going into a convenience store owned by a Korean couple. When the man tells O-Dog, "I feel sorry for your mother," he shoots both of them dead and takes the surveillance camera video tape. Though Caine hasn't quite sunk to the level of many of his friends in the neighborhood—he is actually managing to graduate from high school—he doesn't feel that he can give up his friendship with the sociopathic O-Dog, no matter that he was (in Caine's voice-over) "America's nightmare."

This bleak material is vibrantly brought to life by the Hughes brothers, using their music-video-training to deliver short, sharp shocks that are shy of glorification. Older African American directors like Bill Duke and Charles S. Dutton have small roles, passing the baton to new and frighteningly good talents.

Casting Call

The Hughes brothers tried to cast Tupac Shakur in *Menace II Society*, but a misunderstanding led to Shakur attacking Allen Hughes, leading to a short prison term for the rapper/actor.

Dark Star

 LOL!

YEAR RELEASED: 1974
DIRECTOR: John Carpenter
WHO'S IN IT: Brian Narelle, Cal Kuniholm, Dre Pahich, Dan O'Bannon

"Don't give me any of that intelligent life crap, just give me something I can blow up."

Shot for about five bucks while John Carpenter was attending USC, the film is a tongue-in-cheek homage to classic science fiction like *2001: A Space Odyssey*. The story is about four hippie-ish astronauts aboard the ship "Dark Star" whose multiyear mission involves finding "unstable" planets and blowing them up. A trailer for the film refers to them with mock heroic grandeur as "the twenty-first century planet smashers!"

They seem to have a good time, drifting around and destroying things. A haze of chemically altered dorm-room philosophizing hangs around the whole affair, but it's never tedious. Carpenter has an easygoing way with the film's humor. In one scene, an astronaut has to engage in a Platonic discourse with a grumpy bomb, giving the exchange a distinctly *Hitchhiker's Guide to the Galaxy* feel.

Dan O'Bannon wrote much of the film and also stars as one of the astronauts, Pinback, who is continually getting into fights with his pet space alien—who's really just a red beach ball. He would later resurrect some of the clichés used here in his groundbreaking screenplay for *Alien*. In that later, *much* more serious film, a group of astronauts are also on a long-term voyage with an alien presence aboard their ship, whose computer is also called "Mother."

Production Notes

Dark Star was John Carpenter's student thesis at USC, and it aroused some studio interest after festival screenings. Legend has it that Carpenter had to break in to a USC locker to retrieve the negative, as USC policy stated that the school owns all negatives of student films.

The Day the Earth Stood Still

YEAR RELEASED: 1951
DIRECTOR: Robert Wise
WHO'S IN IT: Michael Rennie, Patricia Neal

"We have come to visit you in peace and with goodwill."

At the start of this quiet classic, a flying saucer hovers past some familiar landmarks and lands on the Mall in Washington, DC. Curious strangers and the military start to gather around the shiny silver disk. Then an alien steps out; this is where the film departs from the usual Cold War scare-mongering. Klaatu (Michael Rennie) looks completely human, but is treated much as you would expect: a trigger-happy soldier shoots him in the arm. An indestructible robot named Gort then appears and has to be restrained from annihilating the humans. Klaatu later escapes from the hospital so he can observe what humans are like in their natural habitat, befriending the inhabitants of a boarding house.

Klaatu has a simple message: us aliens have been watching you humans, and we're getting worried. Your warlike attitudes have been your own problem, but pretty soon you're going to start exploring space, and that just won't fly. So, here's the deal: stop your nuclear arms race or for the good of the universe we'll have to exterminate you.

Notable for its calm and intelligent take on a hot-button topic, Robert Wise's film can seem at times like a morality lesson delivered by a humane, forward-thinking schoolteacher; but that's not a bad thing. Its powerful warning to live in peace or suffer the consequences couldn't present a starker or more ever-timely choice.

In Homage

Journalist Peter Beinart wrote in *Foreign Policy* magazine that President Ronald Reagan was "deeply affected" by *The Day the Earth Stood Still*, so much so that during his presidency, he "repeatedly invoked the prospect of an alien invasion as a reason for the United States and the Soviet Union to overcome their differences."

If . . .

YEAR RELEASED: 1968
DIRECTOR: Lindsay Anderson
WHO'S IN IT: Malcolm McDowell, David Wood

"When do we live? That's what I want to know."

The setting of this film is a British boarding school in all its bruising ugliness. The students crowd in the hallways, new "scums" being berated by the senior boys and everyone pelted with constant nagging to cut their hair, stand tall, show some spirit, and, damnit, follow the rules! Slinking through the scrum is Travis (Malcolm McDowell, for once perfectly married to a role), a malcontent with a slouch and a grin more insubordinate than any profane utterance. Given to preening nihilism and statements like "war is the last possible creative act," Travis has a plan for revenge.

A scandal when it first hit theaters, Lindsay Anderson's film was a frontal attack on the hallowed public school tradition that undergirded the British Empire. Before taking a turn for the surreal, it presents an ugly document of the system. Grimy housing, miserable food, layers of sadism, and sexual abuse—it's all presented as a factory for the production of savage, thoughtless servants of Queen and Country.

The film itself is beautifully put together, with Chris Menges (who later shot epics like *The Killing Fields*) behind the camera, and Stephen Frears (*Dangerous Liasions*) working as assistant to Anderson. It's a tricky amalgam of real-world satire and clownish surrealism, but once battle is waged on the school green, the whole thing comes together with the force of a dream. For a time, the image of McDowell wielding a machine gun on the school's roof became one of those indelible 1960s rebel icons.

In Homage
One of Lindsay Anderson's inspirations for *If . . .* was Jean Vigo's *Zéro de conduite* (made in 1933 but banned until 1945), about a boarding school where students violently revolt against their disciplinarian teachers.

Solaris

YEAR RELEASED: 1972
DIRECTOR: Andrei Tarkovsky
WHO'S IN IT: Donatas Banionis, Natalya Bondarchuk

"You love that which you can lose, yourself, a woman, a country."

After some mysterious events, including deaths, aboard a satellite orbiting the planet Solaris, psychologist Kris Kelvin (Donatas Banionis) arrives to investigate. What he discovers is that Solaris is not so much a planet as a organism with feelings that reacted to researchers' tests by creating live manifestations of the researchers' thoughts that now roam the station. Not long after his arrival, Kris receives his own visitor—a living image of his wife, Hari (Natalya Bondarchuk), who committed suicide on Earth. He isn't sure whether to be delighted or terrified, particularly when she starts asking him questions about herself that make it clear this creature is little more than his mental projection of her.

Physically manifested thoughts is a common-enough science-fiction film plot device—think *Forbidden Planet*, which came out only a few years before the 1961 Stanislaw Lem novel this film is based on. But the intensely psychological manner in which director Andrei Tarkovsky handles this theme (how well did Kris *really* know his wife?) is unprecedented in science-fiction cinema. The film proceeds glacially (Steven Soderbergh's excellent, underrated 2002 remake with George Clooney sped things up somewhat), but there's a sublime beauty here that shades into shocks of horror. This is particularly powerful in the scene where Kris shuts the door on "Hari" only to reopen it after she shrieks in banshee-like terror, unable to bear being away from him. After all, in this universe, he's the only human she knows.

Auteur, Auteur

Andrei Tarkovsky was annoyed at Stanley Kubrick's overly celebratory (he thought) handling of technology in *2001*, which partially inspired Tarkovsky to make *Solaris*.

Pee-Wee's Big Adventure

LOL! 👪

YEAR RELEASED: 1985
DIRECTOR: Tim Burton
WHO'S IN IT: Paul Reubens, Elizabeth Daily, Mark Holton

"Good morning, Mr. Breakfast!"

Rarely before was an act so centered on a character's laugh. In the case of Paul Reubens's Saturday-morning kids' show star, Pee-Wee Herman, that laugh is slightly unhinged, and barked at nearly any provocation: delight, fear, curiosity, or maybe it just being Tuesday.

In this film Pee-Wee is an unnaturally happy, well-rouged, ninety-eight-pound weakling in a bowtie and tight-fitting suit who lives in a toy-littered house where even breakfast is an adventure. Conflict arises when Pee-wee's most precious possession, his shiny red bike, is stolen. Suspicion centers on Pee-wee's spoiled rich grown-up child nemesis, Francis (Mark Holton). Clearly, a road trip across a backlot version of America (complete with bikers, hobos, truckers, and kitschy sideroad attractions) is called for.

Although you would never know it, this lighthearted film was Tim Burton's first. Long before becoming Hollywood's resident goth, Burton showcased his affinity for sunny cartoon wit dashed with surrealism. He stays out of Reubens's way, the right thing to do in a film that keeps the half-cracked gags coming. Among the touches that would later become Burton's trademarks are the lush and carnival-like Danny Elfman score.

A final chase scene through the Warner Bros. lot is self-referential without being obnoxious (Kevin Smith would liberally lift much of this years later for *Jay and Silent Bob Strike Back*), and it all ends with a smile and a hint of madness.

Production Notes

Before directing *Pee-wee's Big Adventure*, former Disney animator Tim Burton had only one credit to his name, a short comedy about a resurrected dog called *Frankenweenie* (1984).

Das Boot

🌐 💣

YEAR RELEASED: 1981
DIRECTOR: Wolfgang Petersen
WHO'S IN IT: Jürgen Prochnow, Herbert Grönemeyer

"Here in the middle of the sea, it's always another story."

The "Grey Wolves" of Nazi Germany's U-Boat fleet were an all-volunteer force. After watching Wolfgang Petersen's grueling rendition of one boat's combat tour, it's easy to understand why draftees couldn't be counted on (and why only one out of every four submariners survived the war). Just watching it is vicious enough.

A cold-eyed Jürgen Prochnow plays the veteran captain of U-96, which sets out from a French port in 1941, when the Allies were just starting to turn the tide in the Battle of the Atlantic. The officers are aware the odds are against them, making the best of their last night on land in the raving, drunken revel that opens the film.

Once U-96 (a real vessel commissioned this day in 1940) heads to sea, almost every moment is spent inside a narrow metal tube crammed with hissing equipment and fifty-odd increasingly filthy men. When the Allied destroyers come, all they can do is hide. Meanwhile, the depth charges blast, and Petersen's Steadicam whips down the narrow passages as though trying to find a way out. The hull creaks with reminders that it could rupture and drown them all at any moment. Later, at great depths, metal bolts come shooting out of the walls like bullets. It's not terribly shocking that one man has a psychotic break—it seems they *all* should.

Petersen continually pushes his characters and the audience to the brink, eschewing cheap heroics in favor of detailing the brutish facts of survival.

Lost and Found

A 1997 director's cut of *Das Boot* included additional footage that had been used in the German TV broadcast, running roughly three-and-a-half hours long. While this version could have stood a trim or two, the scope of Petersen's vision and his antiheroic stance is undeniably more completely realized.

City of God

🌐 👓

YEAR RELEASED: 2002
DIRECTORS: Fernando Meirelles, Kátia Lund
WHO'S IN IT: Alexandre Rodrigues, Leandro Firmino, Phellipe Haagensen

"People got used to living in Vietnam."

Meirelles and Lund's film is akin to a relentless siege on the heart and the mind, one filled with oversaturated colors, furious editing, brutal violence, and tragedy. This is the underground history of a nation, written in the bloody, searing language of the pulp novel.

Out of squalid poverty, government inaction, and a readily available supply of guns, Fernando Meirelles and Kátia Lund build a crime saga about gang warfare in the Brazilian *favelas* (slums) that alternates horror with pathos and historical sweep. With dashing camerawork and a fearless cast composed almost entirely of nonprofessionals, the filmmakers create an origin myth for the country's poor, showing how Brazil came to this sad place.

Rocket (Alexandre Rodrigues), the quietest of the kids we are introduced to, narrates as his flashbacks take us to the 1960s, when the future slum called "City of God" was just a brand-new collection of shacks in the dust. His preteen friends are a matched pair of future hoods: good-natured Benny and psychopathic killer L'il Dice, the spiritual cousin of O-Dog from *Menace II Society*.

Years later, Benny (Phellipe Haagensen) and L'il Dice, who has by this point changed his name to L'il Zé (Leandro Firmino) are adult gangsters, consolidating power in the *favela* by murder and intimidation. When a gang war erupts, it's a literal "war," with guns seemingly as easy to buy as candy. Those wielding weapons are often only ten years old, their eyes as dead as child soldiers in some African guerrilla band.

And the Winner Is . . .

City of God received four Oscar nominations: director, adapted screenplay, cinematography, and editing, but did not win any.

258

The Big Sleep

YEAR RELEASED: 1946
DIRECTOR: Howard Hawks
WHO'S IN IT: Humphrey Bogart, Lauren Bacall, Charles Waldron, Martha Vickers

"I don't mind if you don't like my manners; I don't like them myself. They are pretty bad. I grieve over them on long winter evenings."

Humphrey Bogart's smart-alecky Philip Marlowe is perhaps his best creation. Even the Sam Spade (similarly chivalrous and sarcastic) he did for John Huston in *The Maltese Falcon* a few years earlier couldn't compare. Here, within minutes, he's trading barbs with the two spoiled daughters of the wealthy General Sternwood (Charles Waldron), who hires Marlowe to figure out who's blackmailing him. The younger daughter, Carmen (Martha Vickers), is a thumb-sucking daddy's girl with a taste for gambling, drugs, and bad guys. The older one, Vivian (Lauren Bacall), is a tall drink of whiskey who goes round and round with Marlowe before falling in love with him.

Soon after Marlowe's on the case, William Faulkner's convoluted screenplay stops making sense. Fortunately, nobody will care too much, as cowriters Leigh Brackett and Jules Furthman studded the film with a raft of witticisms for Marlowe to deploy against the cons and thugs that stand in his way ("Such a lot of guns around town and so few brains"). The smoky rapport between Bacall and Bogart—particularly a chat about gambling that turns into a hilariously filthy series of double entendres—has few parallels in cinema. When Vivian sighs in frustration, "I guess I'm in love with you," it's more romantic than a thousand flower bouquets.

Production Notes
One story has a baffled Howard Hawks asking William Faulkner to explain the screenplay to him. Faulkner couldn't help, saying he took everything from Raymond Chandler's novel. Chandler himself demurred as well, joking that he was drunk at the time.

Lord of the Flies

YEAR RELEASED: 1963
DIRECTOR: Peter Brook
WHO'S IN IT: James Aubrey, Tom Chapin, Hugh Edwards

"After all, we're not savages, we're English."

William Golding's 1954 novel about English schoolboys stuck on a desert island during some unspecified war gets a stark rendering here from Peter Brook, who presents it cold and without adornment.

The stripped-down credits show English children at school and playing cricket; civilized. These scenes are then intercut with shots of missile launchers, airplanes, a map of the Pacific, a plane going down in flames. Then we're on the island, in the brush, scrabbling about with Ralph (James Aubrey) and "Piggy" (Hugh Edwards) as they try to find the other survivors. Ralph is voted chief by the young boys, but a rival quickly makes himself apparent. Jack (Tom Chapin) appears at the head of a column of black-cloaked choir singers, who soon become his stick-wielding bodyguards.

Golding's drama was about the paper-thin line that separates even these youthful best-and-brightest types from debased savagery, and Brook illuminates that theme with a white-hot clarity. His youthful cast hurls themselves into the act with abandon, playing at being boys playing at war while the world beyond the horizon is busy annihilating itself. We all know the doom that awaits the boys, who try to maintain a semblance of reason amidst the slide into idolatry and sacrifice, but that doesn't make the film's denouement any less harrowing.

Auteur, Auteur

Theater impressario Peter Brook had commercial success with *Lord of the Flies*, but his other films had more limited appeal. A well-known perfectionist, he once said, "I haven't yet made a film I liked."

Waiting for Guffman

YEAR RELEASED: 1996
DIRECTOR: Christopher Guest
WHO'S IN IT: Christopher Guest, Eugene Levy, Catherine O'Hara, Fred Willard

"We're bicoastal if you consider the Mississippi River one of the coasts."

Blaine, Missouri (*Missour-ah* as the locals would have it), is preparing to celebrate the 150th anniversary of the small town's founding. For the big event, Corky St. Clair (director Christopher Guest), previously best known for a live musical adaptation of *Backdraft* that burned down a theater, is putting on a historical revue called "Red, White, and Blaine" that will explain how Blaine came to be known as "The Stool Capital of the World." Guest's goof on theater troupes and impossible dreams follows Corky putting the show together and dreaming of Broadway after he hears that a New York theater bigwig, Mr. Guffman, will be coming to Blaine to see his show.

Over a decade after delivering the keynote performance in Rob Reiner's fake documentary *This Is Spinal Tap*, Guest took the director's reins and further honed that film's brand of subtle satire. He plays the lead, delivering in camp falsetto the portrait of a long-striving dancer/singer/choreographer who remains oblivious not only to his lack of talent, but also to how poorly he hides his sexual orientation. Corky's cast—ranging from Fred Willard's blowhard travel agent to Eugene Levy's relentlessly corny dentist—gets just as wrapped up in his wild fantasies as he does. The revue itself is something to behold, performing the neat trick of being embarrassing to watch yet infectious, much like the film itself.

Auteur, Auteur

Christopher Guest reunited many *Waiting for Guffman* players for a string of similar comedies like *Best in Show* (2000) and *A Mighty Wind* (2003).

A Woman Under the Influence

YEAR RELEASED: 1974
DIRECTOR: John Cassavetes
WHO'S IN IT: Gena Rowlands, Peter Falk

"Mabel's not crazy, she's unusual."

In this sprawling John Cassavetes psychodrama—his best-known film—family is a big and friendly thing; it's also a prison. The Longhettis, Mabel (Gena Rowlands) and Nick (Peter Falk), have three children and little idea of how to live together in peace.

At first it seems clear that Mabel is the issue. A tight bundle of nerves and tics (ingeniously related by Cassavetes's wife, Rowlands), she can't control her swings between manic euphoria and cracked desperation. But the more we see of Nick and the psychotic anger he hides under a man's man bravado, it's apparent that he's almost as big a problem—only he's the man, so his rages get shrugged off. The episodes mount, and Mabel gets backed into a corner and is finally committed to an institution.

Cassavetes's camera wanders in and around the drama, as Nick and Mabel rage at each other, usually in the presence of too many other people. His habit of pulling the characters' most naked moments out for public display makes it tough to watch at times. The pummeling insistence of the performances has a lot of early Scorsese in it, without the focus on violence. While Cassavetes's gruff, low-budget style strongly influenced indie filmmakers of later decades, few would manage to rival the impressive ambition and emotional honesty of this troubling family affair, where parties are more like forced marches to oblivion than events to enjoy.

And the Winner Is . . .
A Woman Under the Influence was nominated for two Oscars (actress and director), and three Golden Globes, winning only the Golden Globe for Gena Rowlands.

12 Angry Men

YEAR RELEASED: 1957
DIRECTOR: Sidney Lumet
WHO'S IN IT: Henry Fonda, Martin Balsam, Lee J. Cobb, Jack Klugman, E. G. Marshall, Jack Warden

"Baltimore? That's like being hit in the head with a crowbar once a day."

Sidney Lumet's first feature film, made after several years working in television, was nominated for three Oscars, and is just as enthralling today as it was then. In a stifling-hot jury room that screams of institutional neglect, a dozen men identified only by number gather to reach a verdict in the trial they've just witnessed. A Hispanic teenager is charged with murdering his father, and the evidence is stacked against him. A guilty verdict means the death sentence. Just after the bailiff has shut them inside, the jurors are ready to find the kid guilty and call it a day. Except one.

As the personification of liberal thoughtfulness, Juror number 8 (Henry Fonda) acts like a steady drip of water, finding little cracks in the case and inserting reasonable doubt. The tensions are ratcheted upward, exacerbated by Lumet's claustrophobic direction; this is the *Das Boot* of trial films.

The barbs become sharper as prejudices are revealed—ranging from one man's outright racism to another's impatience to cut out early for a baseball game—and the tide begins to turn in number 8's favor. (A particularly deft exchange has one juror saying that the defendant "don't even speak good English," to which an immigrant juror replies, "He *doesn't* speak good English.")

In Homage

Reginald Rose's 1954 teleplay became a feature film three years later, a William Friedkin–directed teleplay in 1997, a Broadway play in 2004, and in 2007 a Russian-language version set against the Chechen War.

September 21

Lost in Translation

YEAR RELEASED: 2003
DIRECTOR: Sofia Coppola
WHO'S IN IT: Scarlett Johansson, Bill Murray

"For relaxing times, make it Suntory time."

Charlotte (Scarlett Johansson) is a young woman recently married to a photographer who never looks at her as carefully as he does his camera. Having tagged along with him to Tokyo for his work, she is left to her own devices, hanging around the hotel, visiting tourist sites, and taking photos of her own.

In the same hotel is Bob Harris (Bill Murray), a movie star on the downward slope. He's in Japan to accept an ungodly amount of money for making commercials for Suntory whiskey. After the long and grating shoots where you can feel the self-loathing wafting off of Bob, he kills time in the hotel bar, unable to sleep because of jet lag. Charlotte and Bob strike up a surprising friendship, exploring Tokyo and talking with the eagerness of lonely teenagers. Their relationship dances between flirtation and friendship, each of them needing something from the other but not quite sure what it is.

Sofia Coppola's gracefulness as a director extends beyond the gauzy beauty of the film's look and her keen feel for music (note the usage of Jesus and Mary Chain's dizzily romantic "Just Like Honey"). She handles her actors with a rare delicacy, catching Murray in rare moments of bared-soul gaiety and weakness. Johansson, who tends to look lost when not directed by Woody Allen, blossoms under Coppola's direction, that characteristic quietude marking her as a lost and questing soul. Together, the three make wonderful, sad music.

> **And the Winner Is . . .**
> *Lost in Translation* was nominated for four Oscars, winning for best original screenplay.

Persepolis

YEAR RELEASED: 2007
DIRECTORS: Vincent Paronnaud, Marjane Satrapi
WHO'S IN IT: (voices of) Chiara Mastroianni, Catherine Deneuve

"I've been told, 'If you go back, I don't know what will happen.'"

A piece of animated art perfection that astounds with wry humor and world-weary insight, this black-and-white adaptation of Marjane Satrapi's prize-winning graphic autobiography shows that while you can't go home again, it doesn't mean you should ever stop trying.

The film, which Satrapi codirected with Vincent Paronnaud, starts with the author sitting in an airport and smoking agitatedly. She's supposed to fly home to Iran, but something is keeping her from it. When the story flashes back to her childhood, the reason for her fear becomes clear. Satrapi was a scrappy little tomboy in late-1970s Tehran, whose music tastes ran to Iron Maiden, when about the only music that could be bought from black-market vendors was "Jackson Michael" cassettes.

Her rebellious streak doesn't jibe well with the new mood in Iran following the overthrow of the Shah. Satrapi's story delineates the downward spiral from the revolution's giddy freedom to autocratic theocracy, leading to her being castigated for not wearing a veil. With the eruption of the Iran-Iraq war on September 22, 1980—rendered here in particularly nightmarish fashion—the mood sours further, and Satrapi's parents send her to Europe for schooling and safekeeping.

Paronnaud and Satrapi's exquisite artistry astounds throughout this film, with its finely etched shadings of comedic exaggerations and stark images of war from a child's viewpoint. Along with *Akira* (1988), this is one of the strongest arguments for the notion that the best medium to adapt graphic novels into films is animation, not live action (see *Watchmen*, *Hellboy*, and too many other misadventures to count).

Courting Controversy

The Iranian government was displeased with the release of *Persepolis*, decrying what it thought were "unrealistic" portrayals of the revolution.

September 23

The Conversation

YEAR RELEASED: 1974
DIRECTOR: Francis Ford Coppola
WHO'S IN IT: Gene Hackman, John Cazale

"We'll be listening to you."

An unnerving masterpiece of a film, the likes of which you wish Francis Ford Coppola still had the ability to make today, this is a taut spider-web story about a repressed surveillance expert who gets far more involved in the world around him than he ever wanted to be.

Harry Caul (Gene Hackman, brooding behind a repressive pair of glasses and mustache) is the classic invisible man. He's legendary at his job, bugging and watching people, but not so good at human interaction. On assignment for a powerful executive (Robert Duvall), Caul spies on the executive's wife strolling with another man in San Francisco's Union Square. It's a tricky situation because of one line of dialogue that he goes back to repeatedly. Is it "he'd *kill* us if he had a chance" or is it "he'd kill *us* if he had the chance"? Caul's minutiae-trained mind digs deeper into the evidence, separating circumstance from conspiracy, reality from paranoia. When he believes his own apartment is bugged, he tears it to shreds in a calculated frenzy.

Coppola's cerebral thriller, finished just as he was getting started on *The Godfather: Part II*, is his last work where everything fits together perfectly. His script is as spare and tight as Dean Tavoularis's cool-toned camerawork. While the paranoid sensibility was particularly relevant to its Watergate time frame, the view of omnipresent surveillance seems more relevant with each passing day.

In Homage

Heavily influenced by Michelangelo Antonioni's *Blow Up* (1966), *The Conversation* itself helped shape Brian De Palma's *Blow Out* (1981), in which John Travolta played a surveillance expert who is sucked into a plot involving a political assassination.

Women on the Verge of a Nervous Breakdown

 LOL!

YEAR RELEASED: 1988
DIRECTOR: Pedro Almodóvar
WHO'S IN IT: Carmen Maura, Antonio Banderas, Rossy de Palma, Fernando Guillén

"The mambo goes best with this decor."

This plot shows what happens when actors date each other. Iván (Fernando Guillén), a veteran playboy soap opera star with a courtly, graying, untrustworthy demeanor, has announced he's breaking up with TV actress Pepa (Carmen Maura, a force to be reckoned with), leaving her a wreck.

Pepa tries to track him down, her need for closure descending into nervous collapse. Adding to Pepa's deteriorating mental state are the people who keep barging in to her penthouse: a couple of prospective renters (Rossy de Palma and a very young-looking Antonio Banderas), a friend who just found out that her new boyfriend is a Shiite terrorist, and some cops looking to investigate said terrorist. Adding some fun to the mix is a pitcher of gazpacho spiked with sedatives and Iván's gun-wielding ex.

The film's escalating comic chaos comes off like an underground cabaret take on *I Love Lucy*, with one mistake or misunderstanding begetting another. What keeps writer/director Pedro Almodóvar's precisely choreographed and vividly photographed (all those blazing reds) film from degenerating into camp overkill is the dignity he affords each of his performers, particularly the women. They might all be coming unglued, but that doesn't mean they won't be immaculately dressed or presented as women worthy of respect.

Although Spain's enfant terrible had been writing and directing since the mid-1970s, this film was Almodóvar's ticket to international success.

In Homage

A live stage musical of *Women on the Verge of a Nervous Breakdown* opened on Broadway in the fall of 2010.

Mildred Pierce

YEAR RELEASED: 1945
DIRECTOR: Michael Curtiz
WHO'S IN IT: Joan Crawford, Jack Carson, Zachary Scott, Eve Arden, Ann Blyth

"Veda's convinced me that alligators have the right idea: they eat their young."

It's hard to imagine what Michael Curtiz's adaptation of James M. Cain's bestselling potboiler *Mildred Pierce* would have been like if his first choice, Bette Davis, had accepted the part. By going with Joan Crawford (whom many considered washed up at this point), he not only saved her career, but he likely saved the film as well.

The film opens with Pierce's playboy husband Monte Beragon (Zachary Scott) being shot in his beach house. He collapses, saying only, "Mildred"; later, she tells the police her story. A working-class woman with two daughters, Pierce had divorced her first husband and opened a business with the help of old friend Wally (Jack Carson), a restaurant chain that makes her rich. But no amount of money could satiate the vicious snobbery of her older daughter Veda (Ann Blyth). Mildred's relationship with Monte, who has more charm and breeding than money, bleeds her dry almost as much as Veda does. Then the creditors come calling.

Curtiz handles this intoxicating noir with aplomb, coaxing vivid performances from everybody onscreen. The brilliant Eve Arden (playing Mildred's restaurant manager) gets most of the script's best sarcastic jabs, while Blyth plays the role of the viciously ungrateful teenager to the hilt, and Carson just gads about cracking wise. Ernest Haller's cinematography is elegantly dramatic, particularly in his frequent close-ups of Crawford, who was never more regal or more human.

And the Winner Is . . .

Mildred Pierce was nominated for six Oscars, but only Joan Crawford won. Supposedly Crawford feigned an illness and summoned the press to her bedside, where she accepted the award.

West Side Story

YEAR RELEASED: 1961
DIRECTOR: Jerome Robbins, Robert Wise
WHO'S IN IT: Natalie Wood, Richard Beymer, George Chakiris, Rita Moreno

"We ain't no hoodlums, we're just misunderstood."

The 1957 musical *West Side Story* was a rare theatrical combination, with witty and tender lyrics from Stephen Sondheim, thrilling Jerome Robbins choreography, and a Leonard Bernstein score that alternated pulse-racing jazz riffs with pretty, soaring melodies. Much as Orson Welles updated *Julius Caesar* as a fascist allegory in 1937, Sondheim et al brought *Romeo and Juliet* into the postwar era, turning those battling Veronan clans into Manhattan street gangs.

The white gang, the Jets, is antsy about incursions by the Puerto Rican gang, the Sharks. The Jets leader wants a rumble to settle things. But then his best friend and ex-Jet Tony (Richard Beymer) falls for Maria (Natalie Wood), the sister of the Sharks' leader, Bernardo (George Chakiris). Neither side approves, and blood will be spilled no matter what Tony and Maria do.

Everything that works onstage clicks together with perfect symmetry in a film version that waters down none of the tragedy, violence, or angry racial commentary. While Natalie Wood is nobody's idea of a Puerto Rican girl, she shines with all the bright optimism the role requires. Blowing everyone out of the water, though, is Rita Moreno as Bernardo's girlfriend: the verve and pop that she brings to the electric rooftop staging of "America" is one of the finest moments in film musicals.

Production Notes

West Side Story opened on Broadway on September 26, 1957. The show's choreographer, Jerome Robbins, was codirector on the *West Side Story* film before his delays and budget overruns led to his firing. The scenes he directed (the jazzy opening ballet, "Cool") are strikingly innovative, however, and definitely the film's highlights.

Five Easy Pieces

YEAR RELEASED: 1970
DIRECTOR: Bob Rafelson
WHO'S IN IT: Jack Nicholson, Karen Black

"All you have to do is hold the chicken, bring me the toast, give me a check for the chicken salad sandwich, and you haven't broken any rules."

Bob Rafelson's film of wearied boredom remains most famous for a rage-filled scene in which Jack Nicholson tries to order toast. You could say it expresses his frustration at a nonsensical rule, or that it shows a jerk used to heaping abuse on others. Both answers would be correct.

A live-wire Nicholson plays Robert Dupea, a disgruntled oil-field worker who shows his true colors during an epic traffic jam, during which he impatiently climbs onto the back of a truck carrying a piano and starts to play. Beautifully.

Robert hails from a wealthy artistic family, and to flee that world he purposefully burrowed himself deep into one of rattletrap houses, country music, and limited prospects. But he's not happy there either, and lashes out with an irritable snobbery. When Robert takes a road trip home to visit his sick father, it becomes clear that there isn't a spot on this earth where he would be comfortable, or a person he would be happy with.

Add some younger actors and a few modernized updatings, and this story could be any number of small-scale films from the 1990s and 2000s about rootless men adrift in blue-collar, highway America. It's a looping kind of story that comes into very sharp focus in a number of finely etched scenes, particularly one where a suddenly vulnerable Robert unburdens himself to his silent father.

Production Notes

The screenwriter of *Five Easy Pieces*, Carole Eastman, based the character of Robert Dupea on both her brother and her friend, Jack Nicholson.

Sliding Doors

YEAR RELEASED: 1998
DIRECTOR: Peter Howitt
WHO'S IN IT: Gwyneth Paltrow, John Hannah

"Never make a joke about a woman's hair, clothes, or menstrual cycles—page one."

This is one romantic comedy that there's no need to feel embarrassed about liking. Helen (Gwyneth Paltrow) is a high-functioning London PR flack who gets the sack one morning. Then she misses her train—or doesn't, resulting in radically different outcomes for her life. Peter Howitt's film takes the moment of a train's door shutting to split Helen's life into two universes, and it flips back and forth between them before (possibly) reuniting at the end.

In the world where Helen catches her train, she finds her boyfriend in the sack with his bossy American ex-girlfriend. A single Helen then starts her own business and starts seeing a man from the train, James (John Hannah). In Helen's other, much less promising universe, she misses the tryst, takes a job as a waitress and finds out far too late about her boyfriend's affair.

Writer/director Howitt presents his story with a brightness and intellect that puts any cares about lacking originality to the side. Rarely an engaging lead, Paltrow holds the stage with ease, particularly in her scenes with Hannah. For his part, Hannah is almost unnervingly charming; the ease of his rapport with Paltrow is the stuff of magic.

In Homage

Many critics have pointed out that *Sliding Doors* bears similarities to the 1981 Krzysztof Kieslowski film *Blind Chance*. In that film, banned for years by the Polish government because of its political content, three different outcomes are shown for a medical student after he runs to catch a train.

Brief Encounter

YEAR RELEASED: 1946
DIRECTOR: David Lean
WHO'S IN IT: Trevor Howard, Celia Johnson

"It's awfully easy to lie when you know you're trusted implicitly."

A workaday little tearoom at the Milford Junction train station becomes the improbable setting for one of the cinema's greatest, most tear-sodden romances in this David Lean adaptation of the Noel Coward play. Laura Jesson (Celia Johnson) is a happily married housewife who takes the train in every Thursday to shop. Dr. Alec Harvey (Trevor Howard) comes into town on the same day to work at a hospital. A chance encounter turns into lunch turns into going to a film turns into marvelous conversation turns into furtive lies turns into passionate kisses and the knowledge that "this" (whatever it is) cannot continue.

Lean shoots this tragic romance like a crime noir to drive home its permeating sense of guilt and furtiveness. The two leads are trusted to carry the burden in a film shot largely in close-up, showing Johnson's wide eyes seeking relief from the torment of this love. The story comes from her perspective and is told via an ardently delivered internal monologue, spoken imaginatively to her utterly decent and completely clueless husband. She aches with guilt at her escalating lies but can't stand continuing a romance delineated by the clanging of bells announcing the next train's departure. The hopelessly doomed manner in which the two rush toward the affair has a Graham Greene feel, full of regret but wholly inescapable. It's beautiful and achingly sad.

Auteur, Auteur
In just a few years, David Lean collaborated on four films—*In Which We Serve* (1942), *This Happy Breed* (1944), *Blithe Spirit* (1945), and *Brief Encounter*—with Noel Coward.

Point Blank

YEAR RELEASED: 1967
DIRECTOR: John Boorman
WHO'S IN IT: Lee Marvin, Angie Dickinson, John Vernon, Sharon Acker

"Why do you run around doing things like this?"

In this crime flick, which critics have always appreciated more than audiences, John Boorman's cold-hearted meditation on revenge still retains a hard perfection no matter how many films have drawn from the same well.

Based on a pulp novel by Richard Stark (a pen name for Donald Westlake), the film is about what happens when criminals turn on each other. Walker (Lee Marvin, without a drop of blood in those toughened veins) and Mal Reese (John Vernon) meet at the emptied Alcatraz prison to divvy up some loot. Walker gets a bullet and falls into the bay, while Mal runs off with his wife (Sharon Acker). Only Walker doesn't die. Instead he starts hunting for clues about getting his $93,000 back. To do so, he systematically dismantles the crime syndicate standing between it and him, with assistance from Angie Dickinson along the way.

It doesn't do justice to Walker's intentions to call him obsessed. He is too methodical, too organized, for that word to apply. There is little satisfaction in his chase of the $93,000, only a monk-like devotion to his job. Boorman sends Walker through a maze-like series of encounters, shot to emphasize the harsh angles and flat panes of color of Southern California's architecture. It's almost as though Walker never left the prison.

In Homage

In Brian Helgeland's unnecessary 1999 remake of Stark's novel, *Payback*, Mel Gibson turned the Lee Marvin role into another of his revenge-obsessed near-psychopaths. The violence is much more extreme and the point hard to decipher.

Eight Men Out

YEAR RELEASED: 1988
DIRECTOR: John Sayles
WHO'S IN IT: John Cusack, Don Harvey, John Mahoney

"Sports writers of the world unite! You have nothing to lose but your bar privileges."

Close to the end of the Reagan era and fresh off *Matewan* (1987), a drama about coal miners on strike, indie stalwart John Sayles turned his pro-labor sentiments in an unexpected direction: baseball.

In 1919, despite beating the pants off nearly every other team, the Chicago White Sox are a downcast and underpaid lot, sitting ducks when a gambling syndicate headed up by Arnold Rothstein (Michael Lerner) pitches them an idea to throw the World Series, which began on October 1. The men who would soon go down in history as "The Black Sox" see no reason *not* to do it. Of course, when the scandal is unveiled, they'll be the ones to suffer, not Rothstein.

Sayles, who based his wide-ranging screenplay on Eliot Asinof's 1963 book, goes here for a deceptively upbeat tone, with perky period and sunny cinematography by Robert Richardson. But this is no nostalgic journey to a bygone, innocent age. Sayles employs a jam-packed cast of vivid characters, including D. B. Sweeney as the tragic "Shoeless Joe" Jackson, and John Cusack as Buck Weaver, who's unsure about the scheme but gets swept up in it anyway. Meanwhile, Sayles (a good character actor in his own right) and the wonderfully hammy Studs Terkel play sports writers who serve as a knowing chorus watching the steamroller that's about to run these guys over. As Terkel shrugs at the end, "it's Chicago."

Auteur, Auteur

Eliot Asinof told *GQ* in 1988 that he was pleased that John Sayles "didn't try to steal the book—he's the first person who ever paid me in full."

October 2

Duck Soup

LOL! 👫

YEAR RELEASED: 1933
DIRECTOR: Leo McCarey
WHO'S IN IT: Groucho Marx, Harpo Marx, Chico Marx, Margaret Dumont

"I wonder whatever became of me? I should have been back here a long time ago."

In the kingdom of Freedonia, the indebted rulers are begging the wealthy Mrs. Gloria Teasdale (Marx brothers' regular foil, Margaret Dumont) for another loan. She agrees, but only if the brilliant Rufus T. Firefly (Groucho Marx) is made president. Meanwhile, the neighboring state of Sylvania sends a pair of bumbling spies, Pinky (Harpo Marx, silent as ever) and Chicolini (Chico Marx, playing his Italian shtick to the hilt), to spy on the new Freedonian leader. War erupts after Firefly believes he has been insulted by the Sylvanian ambassador, and he turns out to be a less than perfect wartime president.

Anarchy has rarely reigned more beautifully, with Groucho running verbal rings around the swells, and Harpo and Chico reducing everyone to stuttering fury (Harpo's pockets supplying an endless arsenal of mayhem tools, from blowtorch to scissors). It's a tossed-together, Broadway revue-style amalgam of slapstick skits, bandied repartee, and nonsense song that also manages to be a snappy little satire on patriotism and war-mongering. In the midst of all this, the Marxes put together one extended gag—a scene involving a fake mirror and the three of them dressed exactly alike—that still stands as one of the funniest and expertly executed in film history.

Production Notes

Duck Soup director Leo McCarey was pushed into making the film by his studio contract. He later said, "The most surprising thing about this film was that I succeeded in not going crazy, for I really did not want to work with [the Marx brothers]: they were completely mad."

Children of Men

YEAR RELEASED: 2006
DIRECTOR: Alfonso Cuarón
WHO'S IN IT: Clive Owen, Chiwetel Ejiofor, Michael Caine

"Very odd, what happens in a world without children's voices."

A line of graffiti says it all. Early in Alfonso Cuarón's liberal adaptation of P. D. James' futuristic novel he pans past a wall with this message: "Will the last person to die please turn out the lights?"

It's the year 2027 and the human race can see the end of itself. For reasons unknown, no woman has been able to bear a child for years. Theo Faron (Clive Owen) is a British government bureaucrat pulled into a scheme by his ex-girlfriend Julian Taylor (Julianne Moore) to get papers for an immigrant girl. When Faron meets the girl, Kee (Claire-Hope Ashitey), he's surprised to see that she's pregnant. For mysterious reasons, he must help get Kee through a falling-to-chaos Britain to rendezvous with some group called the Human Project.

Cuarón's emphatic take on this chase-heavy story whips all the dystopian gloom into a furor. Multiple times, Cuarón films long action sequences in a single fluid take, eerily replicating the sensation of actually being there as it unfolds. This is taken to an entirely different level at the end, where Faron dashes through a lengthy battle set inside a fundamentalist-packed refugee camp, camera doggedly following him through the astoundingly choreographed mayhem.

Even with all the despair and paranoia—the omnipresent security apparatus only barely more advanced than our own—Cuarón finds a rare poignancy, crafting a smart science-fiction film that put all the special-effects bonanzas of the 2000s to shame.

Production Notes

For one unbelievably tricky four-minute shot, director Alfonso Cuarón built a revolutionary camera rig of almost unprecedented complexity that was able to travel in and out of a moving car while it was speeding through a highly choreographed action scene.

Planet of the Apes

YEAR RELEASED: 1968
DIRECTOR: Franklin J. Schaffner
WHO'S IN IT: Charlton Heston, Roddy McDowell, Kim Hunter

"If this is the best they've got around here, in six months we'll be running this planet."

A quartet of astronauts on a six-month space voyage are readying for their final approach to Earth, which they expect to have aged hundreds of years in their absence. But when they crash-land in a desert lake, they realize things have gone wrong. When they encounter a tribe of mute humans being rounded up with nets by horse-riding, rifle-wielding, jackbooted apes, they realize things have *really* gone wrong.

Charlton Heston takes center stage here as the cynical George Taylor, who survives the hunt and is tossed into a cage where other humans are penned up for research. When a pair of chimpanzee doctors, Zira (Kim Hunter) and Cornelius (Roddy McDowell), realize that Taylor can speak, they make the case to their superiors that he be treated as a special case, not just an animal.

While Franklin J. Schaffner's film is not one for subtlety (Heston spends most of the film speaking through gritted teeth, and the action scenes are bluntly handled), Michael Wilson and Rod Serling's idea-laden script more than compensates. There are playful digs at human society, with references to racism (a quota on chimpanzees) and religious censorship (a conclave of religious and scientific ape leaders refuse to admit that Taylor has feelings and a conscious; it's an alien *Inherit the Wind*). The twist ending and Heston's hyperbolic bellowing may long have become the stuff of parody, but it still makes a sharp point.

In Homage

Planet of the Apes spawned four sequels, two TV series, and a 2001 Tim Burton remake; none add much to the original.

Monty Python and the Holy Grail

YEAR RELEASED: 1975
DIRECTOR: Terry Gilliam, Terry Jones
WHO'S IN IT: Graham Chapman, Eric Idle, John Cleese, Michael Palin

"Strange women lying in ponds distributing swords is no basis for a system of government."

This film is gut-bustingly funny or painfully tedious, depending on your point of view—and maturity level. A mock epic with plenty of songs and bloodshed, the film mocks the seriousness of British historical television while poking fun at everything from witch-burnings to Camelot and the Round Table. The thin plot follows the quest of a clueless King Arthur (Graham Chapman) as he rounds up knights to assist him in his quest for the Holy Grail. Joining them are Sir Galahad the Pure (Michael Palin), Sir Lancelot the Brave (John Cleese), and Sir Robin-the-Not-Quite-So-Brave-as-Sir-Lancelot (Eric Idle). They encounter dangers, from a Black Knight (Cleese again) who steadily gets all his limbs whacked off, to a deceptively cute white bunny ("that rabbit's got a vicious streak a mile wide! It's a killer!").

By all accounts, the filming was a trainwreck. Many in the troupe drank liver-annihilating amounts of alcohol, which only exacerbated the production problems that kept cropping up. This definitely led to the film's half-finished quality, with skits abruptly shutting down and transitions that barely deserve the name. But the film's ragged nature only enhances the surreal quality of the comedy, which is much sharper than the sometimes more labored jokes of later Python films like *Life of Brian* (1979) and *The Meaning of Life* (1983).

In Homage

In 2005, Eric Idle turned *Monty Python and the Holy Grail* into a Broadway musical called *Spamalot!* It was directed by Mike Nichols and starred Tim Curry, Hank Azaria, and David Hyde Pierce.

The Jazz Singer

YEAR RELEASED: 1927
DIRECTOR: Alan Crosland
WHO'S IN IT: Al Jolson, May McAvoy, Warner Oland

"Wait a minute, I tell ya! You ain't heard nothin'!"

The nerve of this kid! Little Jakie Rabinowitz is the only son of the great Cantor Rabinowitz, and the men in his family have been cantors going back five generations. But Jakie doesn't want to sing in his Lower East Side synagogue; he'd rather belt out jazz numbers in a beer hall. Once word gets back to his father, little Jakie is out, disowned. Meanwhile, his mother Sara (Eugenie Besserer) pines grandly.

Years later, little Jakie is all grown up (played by Al Jolson, himself a cantor's son, with a winking lightness), calling himself Jack Robin, singing jazz numbers. Things come to a head on Jack's opening night in a big Broadway show, when he must choose between going onstage or going to sing at the temple on Yom Kippur in order to lift the spirits of his deathly ill father.

An eight-cylinder immigrant family melodrama bubbling over with rebellious children, furious fathers, and mournful mothers, this film isn't just notable for being the first feature-length film with audible dialogue. It's also a rare attempt by early Hollywood to depict an ethnic minority in a dignified manner—but for that cringe-worthy climactic scene when Jack performs in blackface.

Alfred A. Cohn's Oscar-nominated screenplay was adapted from Samuel Raphaelson's play, which he was supposedly inspired to write after seeing Jolson—himself the son of a cantor—perform.

Production Notes
The Jazz Singer—which premiered in New York on October 6, 1927, to coincide with the eve of Yom Kippur—was actually not the first non-silent feature film. The 1926 Warner Bros. film *Don Juan* featured some musical accompaniment and sound effects.

October 7

The Terminator

YEAR RELEASED: 1984
DIRECTOR: James Cameron
WHO'S IN IT: Arnold Schwarzenegger, Michael Biehn, Linda Hamilton

"There was a nuclear war. A few years from now, all this, this whole place, everything, it's gone. Just gone."

Sarah Connor (Linda Hamilton, director James Cameron's one-time wife) is a single female Los Angeleno with an annoying, Walkman-obsessed roommate, a lousy waitress job, *and* a T-800 killing machine (Arnold Schwarzenegger) that's transported from the future and is stalking around the city killing every woman who shares her name. As another traveler from the future, Kyle Reese (Michael Biehn), explains to her, she's going to give birth to a son, John Connor, who will later lead the human resistance against the malevolent artificial intelligence that has taken over the world. Oh, and there's a nuclear war coming. And that T-800? *Really* hard to kill. But Reese has a shotgun and knows how to make plastic explosives from household items, so they have a shot.

The time paradox loops in Gale Anne Hurd's tight script resonated beyond the original film, spawning several sequels and a TV series. By introducing the possibility that Reese and Connor's fighting off the seemingly unstoppable T-800 (multiple shootouts, big-rig chase scenes, and a fiery climax at a factory) is a foregone conclusion, the film destabilizes the very notion of action film drama. Cameron's in-joke-laden sequel *Terminator II: Judgment Day* (1991) upped the special effects ante but lacked the scrappy punk integrity of the original.

Courting Controversy

Author Harlan Ellison (*A Boy and His Dog*) sued James Cameron, claiming that *The Terminator* too closely resembled some of his works. A credit acknowledging Ellison was included in subsequent releases of the film.

Alien

YEAR RELEASED: 1979
DIRECTOR: Ridley Scott
WHO'S IN IT: Sigourney Weaver, Tom Skerritt, John Hurt

"I admire its purity."

Dan O'Bannon's screenplay is a monster movie not unlike Howard Hawks's *The Thing from Another Planet* (1951), only tricked out with a more unsettling sense of threat and perversity. On board the deep-space freighter *Nostromo*, the crew is awakened from hypersleep after the ship detects a distress signal from a nearby planet. Three crewmen investigate, discovering a massive derelict alien craft and thousands of strange egglike pods. Kane (John Hurt) is attacked by a creature from one of the pods that latches onto his face. The three are admitted back to the ship by Ripley (Sigourney Weaver) in violation of quarantine rules, and the face-hugger is removed. Kane seems all right until he convulses and a screeching creature bursts out of his chest cavity in a bloody spew. Now it's a battle for survival in an enclosed space.

Where the sequels use the acid-bleeding, fast-breeding, parasitic aliens as an excuse to play haunted house in space with guns, director Ridley Scott aimed for persistent, unspecified dread. The script played with notions of impregnation and disease, while the futuristic industrial squalor design scheme borrowed as much from David Lynch (*Eraserhead*) as it did from Stanley Kubrick (imagine *2001* with half the lightbulbs knocked out). Like the alien seeds, the film's horror doesn't hit you all at once but hangs around to be birthed later.

Auteur, Auteur

After his first film, *The Duellists* (1977)—set during the Napoleonic Wars—Ridley Scott planned to do another period piece, *Tristan and Isolde*. Then he saw *Star Wars*. Not long after, Scott received the script for *Alien* and made that his next project.

Che

YEAR RELEASED: 2008
DIRECTOR: Steven Soderbergh
WHO'S IN IT: Benicio Del Toro, Demián Bichir, Rodrigo Santoro

"Shoot me, you coward. You are only killing a man."

Before Steven Soderbergh started work on his biopic of Ernesto "Che" Guevara, the Argentine medical student who helped lead the Cuban Revolution, he couldn't understand why there were so few films about him. Then he started researching and realized Che's life had too much to pack into one film. So Soderbergh made *two* films.

Part one, *The Argentine*, shows the revolutionary Che in 1959, not an abstracted T-shirt icon but an asthmatic man rallying his poorly equipped rebels in the Cuban forest. A passionately engaged Benicio Del Toro dynamically refuses to play Che as an icon, and Soderbergh—who shoots him at a distance, not close up and worshipful—does the same. Soderbergh wants to show how Che and Fidel Castro's lightly armed squads defeated Batista's army, the brilliant strategic insights that led from victory to victory.

Part two, *The Guerrilla*, is a tougher slog. It's 1967 and a restless Che has been dispatched with a tiny band from Cuba to Bolivia, where he is supposed to plant the seeds of revolution. Just as everything went right in the first film's campaign, everything goes wrong here, with nonexistent peasant support and a dedicated, well-trained American-backed army hunting them down. Hence Che's death on this day in 1967.

Together, the two films—initially released in a roadshow edition, with an intermission, that ran nearly five hours—present one of history's great war films, exactingly recorded and rigorously researched. By not engaging with the T-shirt Che, Soderbergh and Del Toro emerge on the side of history with a film that, even more than the *Battle of Algiers* (1966), could be used as a text by future revolutionaries.

Reds

YEAR RELEASED: 1981
DIRECTOR: Warren Beatty
WHO'S IN IT: Warren Beatty, Diane Keaton

"Voting is the opium of the masses in this country. Every four years you deaden the pain."

Warren Beatty assembled a cast of thousands for his oversized political history film (five years in the making) about John Reed, the American journalist who memorably covered the Russian Revolution that began on this day in 1917.

Producer and director Beatty plays the charming, moody Reed, whom we meet in the political ferment of New York just before the World War I, romancing smitten bourgeoisie Louise Bryant (Diane Keaton, in a welcome break from romantic comedies). She's a writer as well, and the film follows their involvement in the turmoil of movements (labor, feminist) bubbling through the city. Eventually they heed the drumbeat of the 1917 October Revolution.

Although Beatty produced an epic of epic length (three and a half hours), it was an intimate epic. Some scenes aim for Great Historical Drama—that journey across the snows of Russia, say—and Vittorio Storaro's cinematography and Stephen Sondheim's music provide a stamp of importance. But Beatty's heavily researched script really wants to tell the stories of those who populated America's last great radical and artistic movement. Thus there's Jack Nicholson as Eugene O'Neill, Maureen Stapleton as anarchist Emma Goldman, and many others, all casually superb.

This was the last major Hollywood film to be released with an intermission, and was considered such a quality, nonpartisan piece of artistry that Ronald Reagan arranged a screening at the White House.

Production Notes

To give them background information on *Reds*, Warren Beatty lectured extras in one scene about John Reed's labor activist legacy. The extras then went on strike for higher pay and won.

Out of Sight

YEAR RELEASED: 1998
DIRECTOR: Steven Soderbergh
WHO'S IN IT: George Clooney, Jennifer Lopez, Ving Rhames

"No more timeouts."

When Steven Soderbergh came out with this Scott Frank–scripted adaptation of the Elmore Leonard novel, it seemed as though he had simply decided to smartly go Hollywood. It's not as though he hadn't been busy, but his acclaimed, idiosyncratic works like *Sex, Lies, and Videotape* (1989) and *Schizopolis* (1996) weren't setting the world on fire. For his part, George Clooney had yet to convince anybody that he could translate his television fame into film stardom.

Clooney plays Jack Foley, a Florida bank robber sent back to prison after almost pulling off a clever heist (with no gun, just some flirty talk). He gloms on to a jail break, tunneling out right in front of federal marshal Karen Sisco (Jennifer Lopez, in maybe her last credible performance). Foley and his ride, Buddy (Ving Rhames), take her hostage, Foley hiding in the trunk with her (a taut, flirtatious scene that reverberates throughout the film). They separate and Sisco gives chase, ending up in snowy Detroit, where Foley, Buddy, and some unwelcome psychopaths (including a casually terrifying Don Cheadle) team up to pull a big job that has disaster written all over it.

Steering his large, talented cast through one of Leonard's typically busy plots with aplomb, Soderbergh lets the smart, crisp dialogue drive the plot. He jazzes up the proceedings with some New Wave–ish tricks (freeze frames in particular) and a mellow, loungey score that indicates none of this should be taken too seriously. Although a modest box-office success, the film's pulp crime professionalism was a hit with critics. Soderbergh became a Hollywood A-lister, and George Clooney a movie star.

October 12

Sid and Nancy

YEAR RELEASED: 1986
DIRECTOR: Alex Cox
WHO'S IN IT: Gary Oldman, Chloe Webb

"Boring, Sidney. Boring, boring!"

Like so many stories about music and drugs, this one starts out a gas and ends a bummer. The main characters could charitably be described as idiots and the screenplay glances only occasionally at the historical record before ricocheting off into some other universe. But the cultural memory of Sid Vicious and Nancy Spungen's flameout was created by this anxious, ambitious work, which took the punk movement more seriously than any other fictional film had.

Gary Oldman bursts out of the screen as Sid, the none-too-bright and hardly talented bassist for the Sex Pistols, the gimmicky but electrifying leaders of the late-1970s British punk scene. After some all-too-brief scenes where we see Sid running around London with friend Johnny Rotten (Andrew Schofield), the band's green-haired, snarling singer, he meets up with Nancy (Chloe Webb). A whiney American drug addict and groupie, Nancy latches on to Sid and it's all downhill.

From depicting the London punk scene in its spit and fury, the film downshifts into junkie gloom once Sid decamps for New York's Chelsea Hotel with Nancy in tow. The film's relentlessly downbeat later sections provide *Repo Man* director Alex Cox with many opportunities for poignant, impressionistic moments: the two kissing in an alleyway while trash cans fall around them in slow-motion, a dreamlike performance of "My Way."

Historically Speaking

Many people have questioned the historical accuracy of *Sid and Nancy*, none more so than Johnny Rotten (now John Lydon). When asked if the film got anything right in its portrayal of his friend Sid Vicious, he once replied, "Maybe the name Sid."

October 13

The Wages of Fear

YEAR RELEASED: 1953
DIRECTOR: Henri-Georges Clouzot
WHO'S IN IT: Yves Montand, Charles Vanel, Peter Van Eyck

"When someone else is driving, I'm scared."

In the dusty and remote South American town of Las Piedras, a couple of down-on-their-luck Frenchmen, Mario (Yves Montand) and Jo (Charles Vanel), are restless for work. When an opportunity comes for money and escape, they round up a couple of lazy buddies and jump at it. Unfortunately the job involves driving two trucks packed full of nitroglycerin hundreds of miles over rutted roads to an American-owned oil field. But, money is money, and Las Piedras isn't looking any friendlier. Off they go, white knuckles on the steering wheel and blood-rimmed eyes peeled wide for every potentially killer bump in the road.

An exercise in cinematic tension, *The Wages of Fear* pushes its pulpy scenario to the edge of credibility without crossing over. Director Henri-Georges Clouzot goes all in on a story where nearly every second threatens to be climaxed by an earth-rending explosion, and keeps that tripwire fear humming throughout.

The film's mood is so cynical that it verges on existentialist, with scoundrels and scammers as protagonists, stylishly decadent European wasters (Montand's man-on-the-make is particularly alluring) looking for the big score in a Third-World backwater, where they assume everything is for sale. Clouzot's critique of their self-destructive, suicidal attitudes is wincingly visualized in the legendary scene where they must drive through a deep pool of oil that tars them, black as sin.

Auteur, Auteur

William Friedkin remade *Wages of Fear* in 1977 as the big-budget bust *Sorcerer*. Critics were hostile, and audiences stayed away. Friedkin's career (his previous two films, *The Exorcist* and *The French Connection*, were hugely successful) took years to recover.

The Night of the Hunter

YEAR RELEASED: 1955
DIRECTOR: Charles Laughton
WHO'S IN IT: Robert Mitchum, Lillian Gish, Shelley Winters

"Help me to get clean."

In Charles Laughton's single film as a director, Robert Mitchum plays the mad "Reverend" Harry Powell, who's got a switchblade, the Good Book, and the words *love* and *hate* tattooed on his fingers; he'll tell you why they're there if you're curious.

The story is fairy-tale, but the kind that children like, with adults as brutal as they are useless and young people like themselves in mortal danger. Powell, in jail for car theft, hears a man on his way to execution tell about a stolen cache of $10,000 he hid at his widow's place. Once Powell is out, he goes looking for the money, thinking it's all by the grace of God (whom he frequently converses with, out loud) that he knows about it. He marries the widow (Shelley Winters), and when that doesn't bring him any closer to the money, he brings out that switchblade and turns to her two children.

Laughton's intent was to make an epically Gothic film of the imagined South, where the religion that stalks the nightmare fields isn't exactly a reassuring creed, and there's a hint of madness in the air. Though he certainly succeeded, this stunningly photographed film was far from appreciated. The film died a quick death upon release, showing that genius can take a while to work its way into the system.

In Homage

Among the films that have referenced Robert Mitchum's *love* and *hate* tattoos from *The Night of the Hunter* are *The Rocky Horror Picture Show* (1975), *The Blues Brothers* (1980), and *Do the Right Thing* (1989).

October 15

Salvador

YEAR RELEASED: 1986
DIRECTOR: Oliver Stone
WHO'S IN IT: James Woods, Jim Belushi

"Is that why you're here, Colonel? Some kind of post-Vietnam experience like you need a rerun or something?"

Salvador is a blustering and impatient film with all the braggadocio of a barroom brawler who wants to take on all comers, but that lends it an unusual strength, a gutter brand of integrity. With his patented terrier-like intensity, James Woods plays bottom-dwelling journalist Richard Boyle who talks his even sleazier friend, Dr. Rock (Jim Belushi) into heading down to El Salvador in search of cheap drugs, cheaper women, and maybe a story. After a *Fear and Loathing in Las Vegas*–like ride south of the border, Boyle hits on a story. The country's American-backed military junta is turning the countryside into a war zone, with mass graves, assassinations, and disappearances in the night. At the sight of so much brutality, Boyle's jaded eyes are opened, and he leaps onto the story like it's a lifeline.

Oliver Stone's film, which he also cowrote, is impassioned propaganda of the highest order. Boyle serves as his witness to the many atrocities committed in El Salvador in the name of fighting Communism, particularly the assassination of Archbishop Romero and the killing of the American Maryknoll sisters. In a memorable scene at the U.S. Embassy, Boyle becomes a mouthpiece for sanity in the midst of horror. By making his angel a tarnished one, Stone hopes that he'll be believed when bearing the bad news.

And the Winner Is . . .

Salvador was nominated for two Oscars (actor, James Woods, and screenplay). Oliver Stone ran against himself in the latter category, where *Platoon*, his much bigger hit, was also nominated.

The Bridge on the River Kwai

YEAR RELEASED: 1957
DIRECTOR: David Lean
WHO'S IN IT: Alec Guinness, William Holden, Sessue Hayakawa, Jack Hawkins

"Be happy in your work."

It is 1943, in a Japanese POW camp in Burma. The few prisoners left are either digging graves or finding a quiet, shady place to rot away when a new batch comes marching into camp, led by Colonel Nicholson (Alec Guinness), ramrod-stiff and barely breaking a sweat in the jungle steambath. After the camp commander, Colonel Saito (Japanese silent-film icon Sessue Hayakawa), tells the British prisoners that they'll help build a nearby bridge, Nicholson reminds him that the Geneva Convention says his officers won't do manual labor. One standoff later, Nicholson is helping Saito build his bridge, taking a strange pleasure in the work. Meanwhile, a well-past-cynical American, Shears (William Holden, the voice of humanist reason), escapes the camp, only to get sent back to blow up Nicholson's precious bridge.

Unlike most commonly referenced antiwar films, which celebrate the same violence they're supposedly excoriating, Lean's sweaty and slightly mad jungle masterwork is thoroughly disgusted with the entire endeavor. Even such a grand cause as World War II seems here just another excuse for petty-minded men to arbitrarily wield the power of life and death.

It doesn't have quite the size and sweep of Lean's *Lawrence of Arabia* (but then, what does?), though it evocatively captures the horizon-stretching dark mysteries of the Burmese jungle. What the two films share—besides highly confrontational drama and great work from Guinness and Jack Hawkins (here playing a jolly-good-show commando)—is a belief that war is never simple, but always a muddle.

And the Winner Is . . .

The Bridge on the River Kwai received eight Oscar nominations and won in all but one category. Sesseue Hayakawa lost best supporting actor to Red Buttons, for *Sayonara*.

October 17

Mr. Smith Goes to Washington

YEAR RELEASED: 1939
DIRECTOR: Frank Capra
WHO'S IN IT: James Stewart, Jean Arthur, Claude Rains

"This is no place for you, You're halfway decent."

Frank Capra's flag-waving salute to America and democracy begins with a senator dying unexpectedly, pushing the political machine in his unnamed Western state to choose a new one fast, because there's a lot of dirty money at stake in a pending bill about a new dam project. They choose a fresh-faced young leader, Jefferson Smith (James Stewart), figuring he'll serve out a few months and vote the way the senior senator, once-idealistic but now thoroughly corrupted Joseph Paine (Claude Rains), tells him to.

Initially, things go as planned. Jefferson is so wide-eyed about just being in Washington that he barely notices anything. His sarcastic secretary, Clarissa Saunders (a hard-boiled Jean Arthur) shows the kid the ropes when he wants to sponsor a bill for a boys' camp—which happens to be on land the machine needs for their dam. The machine tries to buy off Smith, leading to his epic, hoarse-voiced filibuster.

Sidney Buchman's screenplay has some tough messages about corruption that survive the Capra kitsch. Though more sentimental than even *It's a Wonderful Life*, Capra's film delivers plenty to enjoy. Saunders's cynical back-and-forth with reporter Diz Moore (Thomas Mitchell) and some sequences following the media's fight to slander Smith have particular resonance today. In Rains's imperial take on a fallen icon, he embodies all the crushed hopes of every reformer chewed up by the system.

And the Winner Is . . .

Mr. Smith Goes to Washington was nominated for eleven Oscars but only took home one award, for original story. *Gone with the Wind* swept, with nine wins.

Six Degrees of Separation

YEAR RELEASED: 1993
DIRECTOR: Fred Schepisi
WHO'S IN IT: Stockard Channing, Donald Sutherland, Will Smith

"Have we become these human jukeboxes?"

Flan (Donald Sutherland) and Louisa Kittredge (a simply stunning Stockard Channing) have the life. He buys and sells fine art, while she does the *New York Times* crossword in their gorgeous Manhattan apartment.

Then one night, the doorman brings in Paul (Will Smith, in a daring performance), a young African American man bleeding from a mugger's knife wound. He explains that he's a friend of their children at Harvard and needs help. Initially skeptical, the Kittredges are won over; Paul's dropping of the right names wears away their shock at allowing a young man with his skin color into their refined apartment. Don't worry, his manner says, I'm one of *you*, not one of *them*. Paul's father is Sidney Poitier, after all, and he attended the finest schools.

Only he isn't, and he didn't. Things get upended when the Kittredges find Paul in their son's bedroom with a male hustler. Kicking him out, they find their kids have never heard of him. How and why Paul transformed himself into such a desirable visitor is unraveled slowly and with skill. Even more fascinating is the evolution of Louisa, whose comforting world of recycled wit is utterly uprooted. Her final, tearful soliloquy, refusing to turn Paul into just another story to dine out on, is among the most emotionally devastating yet ultimately uplifting scenes ever filmed.

Production Notes

For his 1990 Tony-winning play *Six Degrees of Separation*, John Guare based the character of Paul on real-life scammer David Hampton, who pretended to be Sidney Poitier's son to gain entry into many New Yorkers' homes. Hampton was arrested on this day in 1983.

Imitation of Life

YEAR RELEASED: 1959
DIRECTOR: Douglas Sirk
WHO'S IN IT: Lana Turner, Juanita Moore, Sandra Dee, Susan Kohner

"She can't help her color, but I can."

On the crowded beach at Coney Island in 1947, widow and would-be actress Lora Meredith (Lana Turner) finds her daughter Susi playing with another girl, Sarah Jane. Lora is shocked to discover that the African American woman she thought was Sarah Jane's nanny, Annie Johnson (Juanita Moore, dignified without being saintly), is her mother: "Sarah Jane favors her dad; he was almost white." Finding out that the Johnsons are homeless, Lora invites them back to her cold-water flat. For free room and board, the industrious Annie watches the kids so Lora can go on auditions.

Years later, Lora is a Broadway star. The four have moved to a big house, Annie has a salary, and the girls are grown up. Susi (Sandra Dee, a summer's worth of sunshine) is still blindingly happy, but Sarah Jane (Susan Kohner) is resentful and rebellious. With Lora's career taking over more of her life and Sarah Jane secretly passing as white (she's embarrassed by everything Annie represents), the two women increasingly seem like performers in their own lives.

Douglas Sirk's highly stylized remake of this 1934 melodrama goes for the heartstrings with its story of women forced into fakery for survival, and it rarely misses its mark. Sirk seeds the film with race and class critiques, as with the beating Sarah Jane gets from her boyfriend when he discovers her secret. Kohner and Moore deservedly won Oscars for their portrayal of a mother and daughter torn apart by racism.

Auteur, Auteur

Although *Imitation of Life* was one of the highest-grossing films of 1959, it would be Douglas Sirk's last completed feature.

The Harder They Come

YEAR RELEASED: 1973
DIRECTOR: Perry Henzell
WHO'S IN IT: Jimmy Cliff, Carl Bradshaw, Basil Keane

"The hero can't die until the last reel."

Ivan (reggae star Jimmy Cliff) arrives in the bustle and turmoil of Kingston, Jamaica. Tagged instantly as a "country boy," barely five minutes later all his possessions are stolen. Another urban refugee, Ivan prowls the city looking for work, but there's little to be had. Like many other aspirants, he tracks down the city's biggest record producer and pitches himself as the next great star. After a run-in with the police, the raw country boy turns big-city hustler, cutting a hugely popular single (the infectious title track) just before becoming the target of a massive police manhunt.

Perry Henzell's rough-hewn film can be read as little more than a Caribbean exploitation flick, with stock characters and stiff dialogue revolving around a wish fulfillment fantasy. This film is also, however, a document of its time and place, showcasing the ragged underside of Kingston society, with its falling-down shacks, trash heaps, routine violence, and crowded gospel churches. The soundtrack is golden, with Cliff's catchy single in heavy rotation next to ska and reggae classics like "Pressure Drop" and "Johnny Too Bad." Also, while the concluding police dragnet is full of B-grade action film clichés, it hints that we're just watching Ivan's fantasy, that he is in fact still sleeping in that wrecked car on the Kingston streets, dreaming of the big time.

In Homage

The Harder They Come is widely seen as the film that introduced American audiences to reggae. Ironically, Jimmy Cliff wasn't able to capitalize on the film's success as much as Jamaica's next reggae superstar, Bob Marley.

October 21

The 400 Blows

YEAR RELEASED: 1959
DIRECTOR: François Truffaut
WHO'S IN IT: Jean-Pierre Léaud, Claire Maurier, Albert Rémy

"If he came home, he would only run away again."

François Truffaut's feature writing/directing debut remains his greatest masterpiece. When we first see young Antoine Doinel (Jean-Pierre Léaud), he is in a classroom being handed a pinup calendar by another boy. Antoine hangs on to it for a moment, and so gets sent into the corner. Antoine's mother (Claire Maurier) and stepfather (Albert Rémy) don't care for him much more than his angry teacher does. Antoine is no rebel; he's simply one of those kids who acts up, and so gets caught in a spiral where everything he does wrong is considered further proof of his essential worthlessness. So when Antoine gets in actual trouble (he steals a typewriter but gets caught trying to return it), his parents are all too happy to jettison him from their lives. Antoine is then processed by the police and put into an isolated home with other delinquents.

Heavily autobiographical, the film is a deeply sympathetic portrayal of adolescence on the loose. While there are starkly Dickensian moments here, Truffaut leavens them with his trademark fun and wonder. Nowhere is this more apparent than in a scene at a children's puppet show; the sea of wide-eyed, upturned faces is one of French cinema's most resonant images. The wonderfully misty cinematography is by Henri Decaë, who later shot some of Jean-Pierre Melville's existentialist crime films like *Le Samourai*.

And the Winner Is . . .

In an impressive coup for a first-time feature, *The 400 Blows* was given the 1959 Cannes Film Festival Grand Prize for direction, the New York Film Critics Award for direction, and many other prizes.

Repulsion

YEAR RELEASED: 1965
DIRECTOR: Roman Polanski
WHO'S IN IT: Catherine Deneuve, Ian Hendry, John Fraser, Yvonne Furneaux

"I must get this crack mended."

Roman Polanski's psychological horror film starts with a close-up on a human eye, twitching. The eye belongs to Carole (Catherine Deneuve, trembling in nervous frigidity), a Belgian woman living in a London apartment with her sister Helen (Yvonne Furneaux). Carole has a boyfriend, Colin (John Fraser), but the idea of intimacy repulses her. Even worse for Carole are the sounds Helen and her boyfriend, Michael (Ian Hendry), make at night. Carole cleans herself in a manner that suggests deeper issues.

When Helen and Michael take off for a vacation in Italy, leaving Carole alone in the apartment, instead of her tension lessening, it increases. Deprived of external targets to focus on, Carole's terror of physicality (which could be an extreme form of germophobia, or a kind of neurotically terrified perpetual virginity) turns inward. Soon, her churning nightmarish worries begin to physically manifest themselves in the apartment. Swinging a wardrobe door shut, she catches sight of an imaginary, threatening man. Hands reach out of the walls to grab her. As Carole's mind deteriorates, cracks appear throughout the apartment and soon the walls are literally crumbling. When real people attempt to enter Carole's interior world, a violent defense seems to her the only rational recourse.

Though he would return to thrillers later in his career (*The Ninth Gate*), Polanski never again matched the mix of stark, avant-garde visuals and gut-level horrifying imagery that makes *Repulsion* such a waking nightmare.

Auteur, Auteur

Speaking about *Repulsion*, Polanski said, "What interested me in making it is the study of a girl's disintegration; withdrawal turning to violence."

The Blair Witch Project

YEAR RELEASED: 1999
DIRECTOR: Daniel Myrick, Eduardo Sánchez
WHO'S IN IT: Heather Donahue, Joshua Leonard, Michael C. Williams

"There's people out here messing with us."

Three young film students—Michael, Joshua, and Heather—drive out into the Maryland woods to make a film about a legend that they've come across called "The Blair Witch." They interview some townspeople about it, garnering scraps of exposition here and there about a suspected witch banished from a nearby village in the 1800s who was believed to haunt the area, periodically stealing and murdering children.

After one especially batty old lady tells them about seeing the Blair Witch in the woods, the three decide to head out there and get some more footage. They park their car and march into the wilderness. At night one of the men thinks he hears cackling. Not long after, they're irretrievably lost.

The effectiveness of Daniel Myrick and Eduardo Sánchez's homespun ghost story hinges almost entirely on the power of suggestion. There are whispers in the night and mysterious piles of rocks, which by themselves don't mean much, but along with the wobbly photography and increasingly panicked dialogue, they help create an air of campfire ghost-story menace. After a time, the daylight scenes become almost more frightening, as starvation becomes a serious proposition. "This is America!" Heather exclaims with disbelief when faced with the idea that they could be permanently lost. "We've exhausted all our natural resources!"

Production Notes

The pre-release hype for *The Blair Witch Project*—complete with a website that appeared to tell the true story of three missing students— was so fervently followed and skillfully crafted that many people believed the movie was based on truth.

A Fish Called Wanda

YEAR RELEASED: 1988
DIRECTOR: Charles Crichton
WHO'S IN IT: John Cleese, Jamie Lee Curtis, Kevin Kline, Michael Palin

"The central message of Buddhism is not 'every man for himself.'"

John Cleese's one great post–Monty Python film creation was this comedic buffet, which he also wrote. He inhabits a graying corpse of an English lawyer, Archie Leach (Cary Grant's real name). Leach's life gets a jolt when he defends Georges Thomason (Tom Georgeson), the head of a ring of double-crossing jewel thieves. George's lover Wanda (Jamie Lee Curtis, whose fresh beauty and cherry-bomb laugh was never better utilized) is also sleeping with Geoege's weapons guy, Otto (Kevin Kline), while trying to seduce Archie, thinking that will help her get to the $20 million in jewels. Wanda wraps every man in the film around her finger with such ease you almost feel pity for the clods, except Otto, the Nietzsche-spouting ugly American who objects when Wanda calls him stupid, saying, "Apes don't read philosophy." "Yes, they do," she snaps, "they just don't understand it!"

Director Charles Crichton handles the film with a crisp efficiency, harkening back to his days as director of some of England's better postwar "Ealing comedies" (named for the studio that produced them) like *The Lavender Hill Mob* (1951). His soberness balances out the script's more Python-esque loopiness, like the extended stuttering gag between Cleese and Palin, or the pop-intellectual jokes at Otto's expense. Few filmmakers have ever made the death of so many cute little dogs and fish so funny.

In Homage

After *A Fish Called Wanda* became a hit, there was a great push to make a sequel. The result was *Fierce Creatures* (1997), a comedy about a failing zoo that reunited the entire cast but was widely considered an abject failure.

Henry V

YEAR RELEASED: 1944
DIRECTOR: Laurence Olivier
WHO'S IN IT: Laurence Olivier, Robert Newton, Leslie Banks

"We few, we happy few, we band of brothers!"

For the first half-hour of Laurence Olivier's rollicking take on Shakespeare's jingoistic history play, he fascinatingly shoots the play *as a play*. We're in the Globe Theatre, seeing the production as the audience would, with flubbed lines, missed cues, boos and hisses when the French are mentioned, broad hilarity when the actors mug for a laugh, and brief pauses for rain (the Globe being roofless).

Once Olivier's film leaves the Globe, it loses some adventurousness but gains the advantage of clarity. Onstage, the language had come fast and thick, rushed for an impatient crowd. Onscreen, the plot coheres: Henry V, king of England, is entangled in a land rights dispute with the king of France that leads to war. At the field of Agincourt, a tired, dirty, and outnumbered English force meets a vastly superior French army, yet defeats them handily. The gaudily arrayed French knights go down in heaps under the arrow storms of the plain-dressed English yeomen.

The battle scenes were shot in Ireland, which was neutral during World War II. While Olivier's intent is clearly propagandistic in playing up Henry's rouse-the-troops speeches, he doesn't neglect the bawdy comedy and displays it all with bright heraldic colors. He's broad in intent, just like the Bard—credited here as "Will Shakespeare."

Historically Speaking

The full title that appears onscreen at the start of *Henry V* is *The Chronicle History of King Henry the Fift with His Battell Fought at Agincourt in France*, which was how it appeared in the play's 1600 folio edition.

Brazil

YEAR RELEASED: 1985
DIRECTOR: Terry Gilliam
WHO'S IN IT: Jonathan Pryce, Robert De Niro, Katherine Helmond, Bob Hoskins, Michael Palin

"This is your receipt for your husband, and this is my receipt for your receipt."

The world of Terry Gilliam's masterpiece is a dystopian one familiar to readers of *1984* (George Orwell's estate could well be due royalties). Yet, the film is marinated in a Monty Python–esque humor that, instead of alleviating the story's gloom, only seems to make it even blacker.

Jonathan Pryce plays Sam Lowry, a civil servant who discovers that a bug falling into a teletype machine has resulted in Harry Buttle, family man, being arrested instead of Harry Tuttle, enemy of the state. This is Sam's moment of awakening, and he begins to dream of battling the system. He ties into a network of resisters led by renegade sanitation engineer Tuttle (Robert De Niro).

Viewers can easily predict that Sam's dreams are only wishful thinking. Not so obvious is the all-enveloping darkness that Gilliam's comic fantasia (grand, with Fritz Langian sets and surreal skits) contains. Helped by cowriter Tom Stoppard, Gilliam delivers an intelligently wrought, mazelike scenario where dreams seem less an escape than a path to danger. This world is different from Orwell's in that its bureaucracy is wholly inefficient, and thus more terrifyingly real. These torturers and stormtroopers are just regular civil servants, working toward a pension. That they can go about crushing lives as easily as a clerk stamping forms brings a stark realism to what would otherwise have been an exercise in goofy dystopia.

Courting Controversy

The bleakness of *Brazil* made its distributor, Universal, nervous enough to insert a happier ending. Terry Gilliam screened his version to Los Angeles critics, who helped pressure Universal to release Gilliam's cut.

Aguirre: The Wrath of God

YEAR RELEASED: 1972
DIRECTOR: Werner Herzog
WHO'S IN IT: Klaus Kinski, Cecilia Rivera

"Things are not turning out as we had expected."

This very loosely historical film opens in 1560, with armored Spaniards and hundreds of enslaved Incans snaking down a treacherous Andean path toward the green hell that will consume them in their search for the fabled El Dorado. The expedition's leader, Gonzalo Pizarro (half-brother of the more famous explorer Francisco) sends a group rafting down a turbulent river to see if anybody knows where this giant city of gold is. *That* group, lead by a feckless nobleman and his half-mad lieutenant, Aguirre (Klaus Kinski, face creased by darkness and with the blazing eyes of a prophet), goes from troubled to insane in days.

Francis Ford Coppola was accused of copping Werner Herzog's imagery for *Apocalypse Now*. There is some connection in both film's hallucinatory and threatening river-drifting, but true or not, Herzog was after something different. He isn't as impressed with madness and power as Coppola. The expedition's laughable attempts at glory-seeking become more comic than tragic. The film eventually turns farcical, with a talking severed head, and a man who has just been shot by an unseen Indian saying, "long arrows are in fashion" before dying. Herzog's curious odyssey is never anything less than arresting. His daredevil filmmaking style is complemented by a refusal to heroicize the suffering. This is the New World's revenge.

Casting Call

Klaus Kinski lept into snarling character on the *Aguirre* set, shooting at extras with a rifle and having to be physically threatened in order to keep him on location. In 1999, Werner Herzog made a documentary about their troubled collaboration titled *My Best Fiend*.

October 28

The Yards

YEAR RELEASED: 2000
DIRECTOR: James Gray
WHO'S IN IT: Mark Wahlberg, Joaquin Phoenix, Charlize Theron

"If it's on a train or a subway, we make it or we fix it."

The Yards starts on the subway, with ex-con Leo (Mark Wahlberg) looking like someone who hasn't seen the sun or a smile in a lifetime. Back at his mother's apartment on a scruffy sidestreet in Queens, a cozy, suffocating nest of people await: Leo's mother, nearly dead from sorrow; his friend Willie (Joaquin Phoenix); and Leo's cousin, Erica (Charlize Theron), now engaged to Willie. They weave a net that could put Leo right back inside.

James Gray's carefully crafted film is dense with familiar themes (good kid gets sidetracked by misplaced loyalties), but is given a special resonance by this wildly gifted director. Gray throws some curveballs in making Willie not the deeply loyal childhood buddy, but a perversely greedy thug. Those shared looks between Erica and Leo don't seem entirely innocent, either.

Bringing a somber weight to the story are a trio of greats—James Caan and Faye Dunaway as Erica's parents, and Ellen Burstyn as Leo's mother. The film's look, with its rich chocolate-brown and black shadows, the sense that everything is lit by candlelight, and its examination of the tight bonds of familial and municipal corruption, brings to mind *The Godfather: Part II.*

The film ends on the subway as well. All is not quite well with the universe—Leo is circling the tenements and train tracks of the neighborhood he seems condemned to inhabit.

Auteur, Auteur

Director and cowriter James Gray was reportedly the model for the compulsive, megalomaniacal director Billy Walsh on the HBO series *Entourage*, executive produced by and loosely based on the experiences of *The Yards* star Mark Wahlberg.

American Graffiti

YEAR RELEASED: 1973
DIRECTOR: George Lucas
WHO'S IN IT: Richard Dreyfuss, Ron Howard, Cindy Williams

"Tonight, things are going to be different."

The film that launched the 1950s retro malt-shop craze is, ironically enough, not even set in that decade. It's the early 1960s. As the sun sets in a riot of rich purple hues behind a small California town's drive-in and Bill Haley and the Comets blast on the soundtrack, the local youth gather for a last night of cruising around. A trio of friends have been killing time since graduation, but tomorrow summer ends, and adult life begins; none are eager for dawn.

Steve (Ron Howard) is trying to convince his girlfriend, Laurie (Cindy Williams), that they should see other people in college. Curt (Richard Dreyfuss) just won a scholarship but is conflicted about leaving town. Prototypical nerd Terry (Charles Martin Smith, some fine acting going on behind those coke-bottle glasses) just wants to have one fun night. John (Paul Le Mat), the reigning hot-rodder, knows he'll be stuck in the town; in the meantime, he'll cruise around. There is little story, just one last night looking for fun or purpose.

While there's nostalgia in Lucas's bright vision, this is hardly a rose-tinted-glasses film. Each of these characters is lost and searching for something, though they don't know what. In the darkness on the edge of town, Vietnam looms.

Lucas's second film after *THX 1138* was a smash hit and gave him the studio clout to film *Star Wars* (whose Harrison Ford has a small role here as an arrogant hot-rodder).

In Homage

In Rob Reiner's *Stand By Me* (1986), Dreyfuss would (briefly) play a kind of latter-day Curt, a writer looking back on his childhood in a film laden with golden-oldies hits.

When We Were Kings

YEAR RELEASED: 1996
DIRECTOR: Leon Gast
WHO'S IN IT: Muhammad Ali, George Foreman, Don King

"Last night I cut the light off in my bedroom, hit the switch, and was in the bed before the room was dark."

In August 1974, boxing champs were still famous celebrities, and it had no more famous celebrity, then or now, than Muhammad Ali. That month, Ali flew to Zaire for the biggest, most hyped boxing match of all time, and it seemed like the whole world went along to watch him fight heavyweight champion George Foreman. "The Rumble in the Jungle," which took place on October 30, 1974, was the brainchild of promoter Don King, who ensured it was ethically compromised from the start.

Shown at the height of his self-promoting prowess, all buffoonery and poetry, Ali is endlessly engaging, and he knows it. In almost comic contrast is Foreman; long before his reinvention as a grill salesman, he is sullen and borderline frightening. Leon Gast interviews boxing aficionados like George Plimpton and Norman Mailer, the latter of whom is particularly articulate in discussing the finer points of Ali's artful combat.

Not just a snapshot of a time when boxing was the sport of kings, Gast's wildly entertaining film is also a portrait of an important time in African American consciousness. Ali's journey to Africa is a kind of awakening; you can see the wonder and emotion in his awed face. When the crowd chants for him, "Ali, Bomaye!" ("Ali, kill him!"), it's as though he had found a new home.

And the Winner Is . . .

Muhammad Ali and George Foreman joined Leon Gast onstage when the film won the best documentary Oscar. Foreman told the press he'd seen the film several times, and said, "I keep thinking the ending will change."

October 31

Donnie Darko

YEAR RELEASED: 2001
DIRECTOR: Richard Kelly
WHO'S IN IT: Jake Gyllenhaal, James Duval, Jena Malone, Maggie Gyllenhaal

"Why are you wearing that stupid man suit? Take it off."

What would you do if you walked downstairs in the middle of the night and a creepy, man-sized rabbit named Frank told you that the world was going to end? In 28 days, 6 hours, 42 minutes, and 12 seconds, to be exact—on October 31, 1988. If you were teenager Donnie Darko (Jake Gyllenhaal, emotive and affecting), you might be partially relieved because while you were talking to the rabbit, a jet engine from an airplane crashed into your bedroom.

The world that writer/director Richard Kelly concocts in this 1988-set film is like something from the television show *Lost*, where seemingly random and surreal events point toward mysterious linkages and dark purposes underpinning reality. Donnie has been seeing a therapist, but Kelly doesn't write off everything as Donnie's mental problems; there is *something* going on here. The teachings of a creepy self-help guru (Patrick Swayze, disarmingly effective) start infiltrating Donnie's school. And there's the matter of that jet engine: nobody knows where it came from.

For any filmmaker, this would be an auspicious debut. For a newcomer like the almost overtalented Kelly, it's something else entirely. Kelly wrangles a densely woven screenplay like a seasoned veteran, but also shoots the whole thing beautifully and uses period music (Joy Division, Echo & the Bunnymen) to maximum effect. The film is maybe a bit like Frank: big, frightening, and otherworldly, but difficult to ignore.

> **In Homage**
> As happens sometimes with cult films, in 2009 a straight-to-video sequel to *Donnie Darko* was released, *S. Darko*, but it was not associated with any of the creators of the original.

November 1

The Battle of Algiers

🌐 💣

YEAR RELEASED: 1967
DIRECTOR: Gillo Pontecorvo
WHO'S IN IT: Brahim Haggiag, Jean Martin, Saadi Yacef

"The law's often inconvenient, Colonel."

Though the opening titles state that no newsreel footage was used in this film about the 1950s Algerian insurgency (which began on November 1, 1954), it's still hard to shake the feeling that you're watching the real thing.

Gillo Pontecorvo's nervewracking war film starts with insurgent leader Ali La Pointe (Brahim Haggiag) hopelessly cornered by his French nemesis, Colonel Mathieu (Jean Martin), and reflecting on his rise from crook to revolutionary inspiration.

Pontecorvo based his film on the book by Saadi Yacef, a veteran of this conflict who also plays a role in the film. He tells his story with precision and technical accuracy, tracking the increasing one-upmanship of the urban fighting. What will surprise few watching this today is the brutality of the insurgents' tactics. Still shocking, however, is how quickly the French forces lower their standards to that of the insurgents, torturing and bombing with a savagery that looks likely to bring more Algerians to the cause in the long run.

While the film's grainy documentary feel affects nonpartisanship, it's not hard to figure out which side Pontecorvo is on (Pauline Kael called it "probably the only film that has ever made middle-class audiences believe in the necessity of bombing innocent people"). Pontecorvo doesn't forget to show the French side, particularly in his sympathetic portrayal of Colonel Mathieu, who pointedly tells journalists, "If you want France to stay [in Algeria], you must accept the consequences."

Courting Controversy

Gillo Pontecorvo's re-creation of modern urban guerrilla warfare was considered so true to life that after the invasion of Iraq, Pentagon officials screened it as research.

The Sweet Smell of Success

YEAR RELEASED: 1957
DIRECTOR: Alexander Mackendrick
WHO'S IN IT: Burt Lancaster, Tony Curtis, Susan Harrison

"You're dead, son. Get yourself buried."

Rarely has as viciously minded a film as this wrung so many smiles out of viewers. As sleazy a piece of work as ever wormed around New York City, Sidney (Tony Curtis, never better) is a press agent always hustling columnist J. J. Hunsecker (Burt Lancaster, finding that playing the villain agreed with him mighty well). Hunsecker is a Walter Winchell type who makes and breaks careers with the snap of his fingers. Then, a stroke of luck: Hunsecker's sister Susan (Susan Harrison) has fallen in with a jazz musician, a development that the alternately lustful and prudish gossiper isn't pleased by. So Hunsecker, whose protectiveness has an ugly tint, brings Sidney on to keep an eye on Susan. Sidney's devotion to duty turns disastrous, dragging down the hypocritical house of cards that Hunsecker has built.

A sour-souled film that nevertheless contains a multitude of treats, Alexander Mackendrick's comedic and sharp-witted tour of status-seekers' hell is an exercise in fine acting and writing. ("I'd hate to take a bite out of you. You're a cookie full of arsenic.")

The engine driving it all, besides the actor-friendly direction from Mackendrick and yet another great jazzy Elmer Bernstein score, is Ernest Lehman's tangy screenplay, given plenty of help by playwright Clifford Odets.

Production Notes

According to Tony Curtis, some of the best lines in *The Sweet Smell of Success* were actually created on set, with a frantically working Clifford Odets once calling Curits over to show him a fresh line: "The cat's in the bag and the bag is in the river."

Once Upon a Time in the West

YEAR RELEASED: 1968
DIRECTOR: Sergio Leone
WHO'S IN IT: Charles Bronson, Henry Fonda, Jason Robards, Claudia Cardinale

"I got a feeling that when he stops whittling, something's gonna happen."

Three men, unsavory types, linger at a lonely train station. A fly buzzes. Sweat accumulates. Water drips onto one man's wide-brimmed hat. He takes the hat off, drinks the water, puts it back on. The train pulls up, departs, leaving Charles Bronson, a crinkle in his eye and harmonica in his hand. He rides off, three bodies in his wake.

This opening is as precisely calibrated and witty as the remainder of the film is sprawling and dreamlike. This isn't a criticism, just an acknowledgement that those looking for another of Leone's spaghetti Westerns may leave disappointed. There are iconic roles aplenty, from Bronson's quizzical gunman to Jason Robards's cackling drunk of a chorus and Henry Fonda's burnt-dry villain.

The story, an amalgam of violent flashbacks and vengeful impulses, flies all over the place, as one would expect from a Western concocted by Leone and fellow Italian fantasists Bernardo Bertolucci and Dario Argento. After all, this is a trio of filmmakers dedicated to the dream of cinema and little else. Why else would they drop their characters into a stretch of desert barely able to support cactus, let alone human beings? Because that's where Westerns should be set, that's why.

Lost and Found

The studio edited about twenty minutes from *Once Upon a Time in the West* for its American release, but several other cuts over the years have restored most of that footage. The 165-minute 2003 release is as close to Sergio Leone's original as can be found.

Psycho

YEAR RELEASED: 1960
DIRECTOR: Alfred Hitchcock
WHO'S IN IT: Anthony Perkins, Janet Leigh, John Gavin, Martin Balsam

"A boy's best friend is his mother."

Given $40,000 by her boss to deposit at the bank, Marion Crane (a flighty Janet Leigh) hits the road with the cash and checks into the Bates Motel. The clerk, Norman Bates (Anthony Perkins) talks about his sick mother in the big creepy house on the hill above the motel. That night, after Marion's decided to give the money back, she's brutally murdered in her shower by an unseen, knife-wielding assailant. Norman is helpful with those who come looking for Marion but doesn't like the questions about his mother.

Hitchcock's arguably most disturbing film gets pigeon-holed as horror. It's easy to see why, as the centerpiece is the single most famous death scene in all of cinema (its slashing editing is as well studied as the Rosebud sequence in *Citizen Kane*). But there's little of the nervous-laugh tension-and-release that horror films specialize in. It starts as pedestrian crime story, with those scenes of Marion in flight offering little but Bernard Hermann's score—his blackboard-scraping violins provide all necessary exposition. But Norman—Oedipal, skinny, and needy—makes the film something else entirely. Hitchcock doesn't just play Freudian tricks with Norman; he leverages in some metaphorical games, particularly the avian obsession. Notably, Hitchcock's next film would be his only other major film to be classified as horror: *The Birds* (1963).

In Homage

In 1998, Gus Van Sant released his shot-for-shot re-creation of Hitchcock's *Psycho*, with the only differences being it was shot in color and with different actors. Vince Vaughn was credibly cast as Norman Bates, while Anne Heche made a poor substitute for Janet Leigh.

To Kill a Mockingbird

YEAR RELEASED: 1962
DIRECTOR: Robert Mulligan
WHO'S IN IT: Gregory Peck, Mary Badham, Brock Peters, Robert Duvall

"Jean Louise, stand up. Your father's passing."

Robert Mulligan's striking film, faithfully adapted by Southern playwright Horton Foote from Harper Lee's powerful, Pulitzer Prize–winning novel, stands today as the final word in American civic heroism.

Set in the small Alabama town of Maycomb during a hot summer in 1932, the story is told through the eyes of Scout (Mary Badham), a six-year-old tomboy whose sing-song narration and lilting descriptions give a fairy-tale frosting to the events that open her eyes to the ways of her world.

An African American man, Tom Robinson (an unemotional Brock Peters), is accused of raping a white woman, and the town is ready for a lynching. Scout's father, Atticus Finch (Gregory Peck), with the stoic calm of antiquity that his name would suggest, takes the case, much to the chagrin of many local whites, who are baying for blood. The resulting trial shows Atticus dismantling piece by piece the flimsy threads of the case against Tom, which quickly seems to be nothing more than lies held together by bone-bred prejudice.

Mulligan does the smartest thing possible with Lee's allegorical classic: he stays out of the story's way. Casting is dead-on right across the board, with Peck's statuesque heroism never better utilized and a young Robert Duvall making a notable feature debut as the mysterious Boo Radley.

Production Notes

Harper Lee never wrote another novel after *To Kill a Mockingbird*. Also, though her work as Scout was widely acclaimed, Mary Badham (the younger sister of director John Badham) took less than a half-dozen television and film jobs over the next four decades.

Yi Yi: A One and a Two

YEAR RELEASED: 2000
DIRECTOR: Edward Yang
WHO'S IN IT: Wu Nianzhen, Issey Ogata, Elaine Jin, Ke Suyun

"Taiwan has the best copycats."

Writer/director Edward Yang's near-three-hour multigenerational opus is a quiet epic. Three generations of a family are followed in the wake of their grandmother's slipping into a coma, each dealing with their own crises, and mostly ignorant of everyone else's. And because the doctor suggested talking to their grandmother to keep her brain active, they all begin using her as unwilling confessor.

The father, Nj Jian (Wu Nianzhen), runs into Sherry (Ke Suyun), his high-school girlfriend and first love, and starts wondering whether he didn't make the wrong choice. His wife, Min-Min (Elaine Jin) doesn't know what she is doing with her life. Their children nurse their own private psychodramas.

Swirling around these points of conflict are a plethora of larger family subplots, ranging from business schemes to weddings to marital jealousies. Yang weaves it all together with a style so transparent and clean it can barely even be called a style. The look is bright and straightforward, with invisible undercurrents, much like the middle-class professional Taipei world it's set in. Yang's mood is simultaneously contemplative and light, with humorous notes (a childish prank, an interfamilial brawl that turns operatic) balancing out the darker material. Like the best character-focused Asian directors, Yang doesn't lose track of each character's needs against the backdrop of plot. It's a grand and sweetly formed family drama, echoing with sadness and beauty.

Auteur, Auteur

Over the course of his career, Edward Yang helped lead a renaissance in Taiwanese cinema. His last film and greatest success, *Yi Yi*, won best director at the Cannes Film Festival.

Ran

YEAR RELEASED: 1985
DIRECTOR: Akira Kurosawa
WHO'S IN IT: Tatsuya Nakadai, Akira Terao, Jinpachi Nezu

"One arrow is easily broken, but not three together."

Aging Lord Hidetora (Tatsuya Nakadai) prepares to step down from decades of rule over his painfully won domain in fifteenth-century Japan, announcing that he will divide his kingdom equally between his three sons. Hidetora has barely renounced power, however, before the struggle for dominance begins. By the time it is over, the once-indomitable warlord will be wandering in the wilderness, mad, howling, and utterly forsaken.

Akira Kurosawa was seventy-five when he adapted *King Lear*, but his prowess hadn't dulled at all since transposing Shakespeare's *Macbeth* into a haunted Japanese forest in 1957's *Throne of Blood*. Kurosawa's *Lear* keeps close to the Bard's intent, painting a world where those who tell the truth, like Hidetora's Fool or the one son who stays true, are punished for it.

Although the story is foretold, the savagery with which Hidetora's heirs turn on him is still shocking. In no time, the two sons who once flattered their father in self-serving fashion have marshaled their armies against his small remaining retinue. The bleakly poetic images of the ensuing bloodshed—color-coordinated columns of soldiers streaming into battle, carelessly piled corpses, a stunned Hidetora helplessly flinging a broken sword at his attackers—are presented mostly in silence. When the sound comes, it's shattering, like the crashing of storm-tossed waves on a rocky shore. The film only builds from that point on, with Kurosawa (who storyboarded the whole thing in watercolors) unleashing one dreamlike image after another; it's a terrible beauty.

And the Winner Is . . .

Ran was nominated for four Oscars, an unusual feat for a foreign film during the 1980s and unheard of at the time for an Asian film.

Casablanca

YEAR RELEASED: 1942
DIRECTOR: Michael Curtiz
WHO'S IN IT: Humphrey Bogart, Ingrid Bergman

"Oh, he's just like any other man, only more so."

In Michael Curtiz's casually proficient take on a play called *Everybody Comes to Rick's*, Humphrey Bogart plays the grumpy owner of a café in the North African city where all manner of folks come together to escape the gathering clouds of war. It's a time of refugees and shifting loyalties, and Rick slouches in the middle of it, white jacket on and cigarette smoldering, daring all these idealists and collaborators to make him give a damn. Bogart's performance is like a dry run for what he would do for Howard Hawks three years later in *To Have and Have Not*, and what most every other leading man would *try* to do forever after: portray the cynic with a snappy line of patter who finally makes the moral choice, but on *his* terms.

This film may not deserve the adulation forced upon it by all those years of repeat screenings and "classic film" tributes (consider its enshrinement in *When Harry Met Sally*), but that doesn't mean it *isn't* a classic film. All you have to do is witness Ingrid Bergman's hopelessly tragic dilemma as the woman with the impossible choice, the well-tooled dialogue, a supporting cast thick with greatness (Sydney Greenstreet, Peter Lorre, and *Cabinet of Dr. Caligari*'s Conrad Veidt), and the café itself, that zone of intoxicatingly languorous danger.

Never mind the clips of "here's looking at you, kid" that everyone has seen uncounted times—this film can stand a little overpraising.

And the Winner Is . . .
Casablanca was nominated for eight Oscars, winning three (director, picture, and screenwriting).

The Usual Suspects

YEAR RELEASED: 1995
DIRECTOR: Bryan Singer
WHO'S IN IT: Gabriel Byrne, Benicio Del Toro, Kevin Spacey, Stephen Baldwin, Kevin Pollack, Chazz Palminteri

"The greatest trick the Devil ever pulled was convincing the world he didn't exist."

By creating one of cinema's most indelible, though unseen, criminals, Byran Singer returns fear to the realm of imagination. A ship blows up in San Diego harbor and the police find a couple of survivors among the bodies. One is a badly burned Hungarian terrified of what one Keyser Soze is going to do to him. The other, Verbal Kint (Kevin Spacey), fills them in on what happened. The usual suspects of the title are a crew of thieves and malcontents who start pulling heists after being thrown into jail together. They run afoul of Soze—a mythic gangster whose legend is in inverse proportion to the number of people who've actually seen him—and are forced into his servitude.

The crew is a stew of tough-talking types, from the half-mad assassin (Stephen Baldwin) to the dark-eyed mastermind (Gabriel Byrne) to the curious mumbler (Benicio Del Toro). While none quite believe in Soze's legend, none will dismiss it, either. Once his name is invoked, they all clam up like children terrified at the mention of the boogeyman.

Singer's film followed the post–*Reservoir Dogs* vogue for multicharacter, plot-heavy crime sagas with a fluid sense of time and a hint of irony. Unlike nearly all the imitators, though, this one (thanks to Christopher McQuarrie's twist-tied screenplay) stood tall on its own merits. It's a dark-souled crime saga that might live in a comic-book universe but it's at least a thoroughly developed one.

Scarface

YEAR RELEASED: 1932
DIRECTOR: Howard Hawks
WHO'S IN IT: Paul Muni, Ann Dvorak

"They'll be shooting each other like rabbits!"

Ben Hecht's screenplay for this Prohibition-era Howard Hawks gangster classic was clearly based on the exploits of Al Capone—Hecht picked up material working as a Chicago newspaperman during the town's gang wars. Despite the connections, he called his unstoppable one-man Italian immigrant crime wave Tony Camonte (Paul Muni). Given all the parallels to Capone, the name change was a fig leaf, but that's what screenwriters do when real gangsters show up at your door and start making demands, as apparently happened to Hecht.

Muni plays Camonte as a casually brutal animal, all clownish eye-waggling and violent moods, layered with an "Italian" accent as entertaining but inauthentic as the Cuban accent Al Pacino used in Brian De Palma's inferior 1983 remake. (Where Pacino was an Italian-American playing Cuban, Muni was born Muni Weisenfreund in Ukraine and got his start in the Yiddish theater.) It's an exaggerated portrayal that meshes perfectly with Hawks's over-the-top treatment of the story. He packs the screen with visual gags—the "X" motif that Hawks works into every shot where a rival of Camonte's has been killed—and nearly constant barrages of gunfire. A deathly-looking Boris Karloff shows up as one of Camonte's beleaguered enemies, and his is not even the most outrageous performance on display.

Courting Controversy

Hollywood's morals censor Will Hays was so offended by *Scarface*'s violence that he inserted a cringe-worthy scene where a newspaper editor pushes citizens to agitate for laws to deport foreign-born gangsters, causing a stereotypically "ethnic" man to say, "That's-a true. They bring nothing but disgrace to my people."

Patton

YEAR RELEASED: 1970
DIRECTOR: Franklin J. Schaffner
WHO'S IN IT: George C. Scott, Karl Malden

"No bastard ever won a war by dying for his country. He won it by making the other poor dumb bastard die for his country."

George C. Scott steps into General George S. Patton's gleaming boots and starched uniform as though he had been practicing for the role all his life. The opening sequence sets the tone, with director Franklin J. Schaffner shooting Scott in front of a screen-spanning American flag, lecturing unseen troops with bloody-fanged relish: follow me through hell to glory and honor. Afterward, Patton appears in Tunisia, 1943, taking over after a devastating American defeat. Not long after, the spit-and-polish general has turned the tide on the Germans and their most brilliant general, whose text Patton has studied. A victorious scene has Patton looking through binoculars at fleeing German soldiers, bellowing, "Rommel, you magnificent bastard, *I read your book!*"

From Africa to Italy to England, France, and Germany itself, the film follows Patton's rise, fall, and rise as his lust for glory competes with strategic impulse time and again. His genius is never questioned, though his sanity certainly is (he believed in reincarnation, pausing at the site of the battle of Carthage, *c.*149 B.C., and speaking about it as though he had been present). While the end result is a conflicted one—is he genius or madman, and does it matter?—Scott's dominating performance, all braggadocio and winking humor, sweeps all such considerations to the side.

Historically Speaking

Surprisingly for a Hollywood epic, *Patton* keeps close to the historical record on most matters. One exception is that the real General Patton (born this day in 1885) had a high and squeaky voice, a far cry from George C. Scott's deep growl.

Rear Window

🔍

YEAR RELEASED: 1954
DIRECTOR: Alfred Hitchcock
WHO'S IN IT: James Stewart, Grace Kelly, Thelma Ritter, Raymond Burr

"We've become a race of Peeping Toms. What people ought to do is get outside their own house and look in for a change."

L. B. Jeffries (a clever and smart-alecky James Stewart) is a photographer, so his job is to look. Problem is, he got a little too close to the action on the last assignment and now he's holed up in his New York apartment during a summer heat wave with a broken leg in a giant, ungainly cast.

That still leaves him with a lot of time to kill between visits from his crusty masseuse (a wisecracking Thelma Ritter) and goddess of a girlfriend, Lisa Fremont (Grace Kelly). So he watches people out the window with his telephoto lens—particularly the Thorwalds across the courtyard. One night Jeffries sees something, and after that, Mrs. Thorwald is nowhere to be seen; Jeffries suspects Mr. Thorwald (Raymond Burr) of murder. Everyone but Lisa thinks he's gone nuts. They start sleuthing together, Lisa willing to handle the legwork that is denied him.

Not as lighthearted as Hitchcock's more frivolous entertainments or serious as his darker psychodramas, this film has it all: thrills, romance, snappy humor, and a subtext about voyeurism that doesn't weigh down the narrative. Though the film doesn't once leave Jeffries's line of sight, it never feels claustrophobic; the teeming city outside his window, full of danger and possibilities, is all the world he seems to need. It's certainly all that we require.

Casting Call

As an inside joke, for *Rear Window*, Hitchcock (who clashed with producer David O. Selznick) apparently had Raymond Burr utilize many of Selznick's mannerisms to play a suspected murderer, and even dressed Burr like Selznik.

Fantasia

YEAR RELEASED: 1940
DIRECTOR: Various
WHO'S IN IT: None

"It's funny how wrong an artist can be about his own work."

Walt Disney's feature-length compilation of animated segments set to different classical compositions failed at the box office. Its music choices were derided as bourgeois, and the animation called cutesy and annoying. This may be true, but who cares when the dinosaurs were so cool?

After an annoyingly educational bit with Bach's *Tocata and Fugue in D Minor*, the film moves into its first crowd-pleaser: a beautiful take on Tchaikovsky's *Nutcracker Suite*, complete with dancing sugar plum fairies. After that comes Paul Dukas's *The Sorcerer's Apprentice*, the film's most famous piece, and with Mickey Mouse as the hapless apprentice comically trying to stem the watery tide his magical conjurings brought about. It's the only segment with a recognizable Disney character. Of the remaining pieces, two hit home particularly well for the kids the film is aimed at (a point many critics have tended to forget): Stravinsky's thunderous *The Rite of Spring* (a literal depiction of Earth's history, complete with raging dinosaurs) and Mussorgsky's bombastic *Night on Bald Mountain* (witches and devils, oh my!).

The film premiered on November 13, 1940, and played around the country in a roadshow edition at theaters with specially made audio equipment (Fantasound!). Disney's habit of frequent theatrical rereleases garnered the film a growing cult following—particularly with a trippy 1960s poster campaign that almost begged hippies to come see it under chemical modification; many apparently obliged.

Auteur, Auteur

Some of the pieces that Walt Disney wanted in a *Fantasia* sequel were Holst's *The Planets*, Brahms's *First Symphony*, and Gershwin's *Rhapsody in Blue*; only the Gershwin made the cut when *Fantasia 2000* finally appeared in 1999.

Raging Bull

YEAR RELEASED: 1980
DIRECTOR: Martin Scorsese
WHO'S IN IT: Robert De Niro, Cathy Moriarty, Joe Pesci

"I heard things."

Jake La Motta: a nice guy, until you get to know him. In real life, La Motta (Robert De Niro) was a boxer best known for being able to take near-insane amounts of punishment. Like many professional fighters, La Motta's personal life was a shambles. His ability to dish out and take punishment worked just fine in the ring, but when it came to dealing with his deadbeat brother Joey (Joe Pesci) and his blond trophy wife Vickie (Cathy Moriarty), whom he constantly accuses of having affairs, it was destructive. Expect much shouted dialogue of an unprintable nature.

Martin Scorsese was in a bad place when De Niro came to him with the La Motta project, in the hospital after a partly drug-related breakdown. What the two of them came up with, though, was something worth getting out of bed for. The film they crafted was not only the story of a boxer's rise to professional glory and slide to lowlife disgrace (later scenes showing a wasted and fattened La Motta sleazing around in a nightclub are almost unbearable), it was also an ode to pain and endurance. Michael Chapman's black-and-white cinematography swings from capturing the savage beauty of the boxing ring's deadly geometry to the rough-cut tawdriness of La Motta's slash-and-burn home life. Scorsese's brutally guilt-ridden viewpoint was never so ardently Catholic, and De Niro's pain never bloodier—in every sense.

Auteur, Auteur
Raging Bull was a complete success for Martin Scorsese, scooping up seven Oscar nominations and two wins.

Empire of the Sun

YEAR RELEASED: 1987
DIRECTOR: Steven Spielberg
WHO'S IN IT: Christian Bale, John Malkovich, Miranda Richardson

"I can't remember what my parents look like."

Jim Graham (Christian Bale, in an astoundingly assured film debut) is a young British boy living in Shanghai in 1941. Jim's a strange, dreamy lad, so when the Japanese invade and Jim is hurled into a crowd of Chinese refugees, he doesn't quite understand what's happening. In one devastating scene, Jim reaches for a toy plane he dropped and loses his mother's hand—he will spend the rest of the war on his own.

Years of imprisonment strip away Jim's civilized veneer until at war's end he's half-mad. In between, Spielberg unleashes the full range of his visual skills on the screen, with dreamy images of war as seen through the eyes of a shell-shocked child: kamikaze pilots flying into the rising sun, the atom bomb at Hiroshima witnessed as a distant flash and scudding of clouds.

Steven Spielberg's adaptation of J. G. Ballard's autobiographical novel was his first real bid for cinematic seriousness. Accused of being nothing more than a manufacturer of popcorn sentimentality, here Spielberg throws everything he has at the screen. It doesn't all work, but the things that do steal your breath away.

Critics weren't sure about the film, neither were audiences. Spielberg took the hint and did another *Indiana Jones* film; it would be years before he returned from the world of dinosaurs and treasure hunters.

Production Notes

David Lean was to film J. G. Ballard's book, with Steven Spielberg producing. But Lean became so engrossed in adapting Joseph Conrad's *Nostromo* that he passed the reins to Spielberg. Lean died from cancer in 1991, months before filming of *Nostromo* was to begin.

The Sound of Music

YEAR RELEASED: 1965
DIRECTOR: Robert Wise
WHO'S IN IT: Julie Andrews, Christopher Plummer

"You brought music back into the house."

In 1930s Austria, the young Maria (an astoundingly fresh-faced Julie Andrews) isn't making out so well at her convent. A wealthy man nearby, Captain von Trapp (Christopher Plummer), needs a governess for his seven children; Maria will do. At the house, Maria quickly earns the trust of the children with her fun attitude and propensity for leading them all in catchy harmonies. But she arouses the hatred of the captain, who now hates music for the same reason he ignores his children— they only stir up memories of his dead wife. But Maria persists, and soon the captain not only acquiesces to bringing music back into the house, but starts falling in love with Maria, to the chagrin of his icy baroness fiancée (Eleanor Parker). Not long after, Austria invites the Nazis in, and once swastikas start flying, the von Trapps make plans for escape.

The Sound of Music began as a 1959 Rodgers and Hammerstein musical, inspired by the real Maria's book, *The Story of the Trapp Family Singers*. The diversely talented Robert Wise directed the film, while Ernest Lehman, who had adapted *West Side Story* for Wise in 1961, wrote the screenplay. The result was a some-times over-large production that (understandably) lavishes time and attention on the beautiful Salzburg settings at the expense of realistic interactions between the characters. But while the story can be almost unbearably saccharine onstage, Wise's film version is smart enough to leave the heavy lifting in Andrews and Plummer's capable hands.

Historically Speaking

The musical of *The Sound of Music* opened on November 16, 1959, at the Lunt-Fontanne Theatre in New York. It ran until January 1963 and won six Tony Awards.

The War of the Roses

 LOL!

YEAR RELEASED: 1989
DIRECTOR: Danny DeVito
WHO'S IN IT: Michael Douglas, Kathleen Turner, Danny DeVito

"When I watch you eat, when I see you asleep, when I look at you lately, I just want to smash your face in."

It's not that Oliver (Michael Douglas) and Barbara Rose (Kathleen Turner) *hate* each other so much as they would really just like the other one to stop breathing entirely.

The relationship started in passion but settled into a marriage where the disappointments stacked up. By the time their children are off to college, Barbara wants out. That would be bad enough for Oliver, but the fact that she wants the house is just too much for him to take. So the battle begins.

As a filmmaker, Danny DeVito has made a specialty out of a particularly severe brand of black comedy that frequently delves into the realm of fantasy. He presents this story as a cautionary tale, told by a divorce lawyer (DeVito) to a client: "I get paid $450 an hour to talk to people, so when I offer to tell you something for free, I advise you to listen carefully." The forthcoming story is a nasty one, with his perfectly matched leads (this was their third pairing in the 1980s) engaging in warfare that resembles a Looney Tunes cartoon for dysfunctional yuppies. There are many moments in which the film could have pulled back and found some sentimental solace; DeVito passes those moments by with an evil chuckle.

It's as viciously entertaining as anything since *Who's Afraid of Virginia Woolf?*

And the Winner Is . . .

The War of the Roses was nominated for three Golden Globes, for both lead performances and best comedy/musical—but did not win any.

Kids

YEAR RELEASED: 1995
DIRECTOR: Larry Clark
WHO'S IN IT: Leo Fitzpatrick, Justin Pierce, Chloë Sevigny, Rosario Dawson

"What happened?"

The opening of cult photographer Larry Clark's controversial debut is squirm-worthy, with Telly (Leo Fitzpatrick) making out with a younger, barely adolescent girl and talking her into sex. Clark shoots it close; every smack of their lips is jarring. After Telly's success, he meets up with his sidekick, Caspar (Justin Pierce), a kid who looks and acts like he's been sniffing glue since kindergarten. After describing his conquest in grotesque detail, Telly announces he's on a quest to deflower another young virgin that day, and he's already got her staked out.

While Telly cruises the city looking for his new girl, one of his previous victims, Jennie (Chloë Sevigny), finds out she's HIV positive. Jennie frantically looks for Telly while he hunts down his latest virgin.

The screenplay by Harmony Korine (a skateboarder whom Clark met on the street) uses these two journeys to take viewers through all the kids' different hang-outs: crash pads, Washington Square Park, a drug-fueled rave, an uptown apartment where the parents are missing. The forty-ounce beers flow and joints are passed, fights ignite for no reason, and everybody seems to be on the prowl in a fog of hostility, boredom, and predatory lust.

Clark's camera repeatedly shifts into voyeurism, but his vivid atmosphere that crosses hallucinatory dreaminess with a docudrama immediacy (it has been years since any film treated HIV this bluntly and seriously) still demands respect, and even shock.

Courting Controversy

The furor around *Kids*'s explicit nature pressured Miramax Films—by then part of the Disney corporation—into setting up an independent company, Shining Excalibur Films, solely to distribute the film.

Taxi Driver

YEAR RELEASED: 1976
DIRECTOR: Martin Scorsese
WHO'S IN IT: Robert De Niro, Cybill Shepherd, Jodie Foster, Harvey Keitel

"Someday a real rain will come and wash all this scum off the streets."

A little over a decade before *When Harry Met Sally* (1989) signaled that it was safe to return to New York, this scorching Martin Scorsese tract of urban angst did its best to ensure that everybody who didn't live there would stay the hell away.

Travis Bickle (Robert De Niro, back in his *Mean Streets* playfully psychotic mode) is the taxi driver haunting the streets of Manhattan. A perpetual liar who sends his parents fanciful cards about working for the Secret Service, Travis works the night shift, where he sees every manner of perverse decay, falling further into his interior world of invented grandiosity.

His attraction to political campaign volunteer Betsy (Cybill Shepherd) goes nowhere after a clueless Travis takes her to a porn film on their first date. An obsession with the senator Betsy worked for, and his efforts to save twelve-year-old prostitute Iris (thirteen-year-old Jodie Foster) from her pimp (Harvey Keitel) intersects fatefully with his increasing fixation on guns.

Initially controversial because of its over-the-top violence and the disturbing inclusion of Iris, Scorsese's searing diary of a murderous lunatic now seems a particularly apt reflection of its time. The sensation of a society inexorably collapsing on itself wasn't art; it was the sort of thing that people saw on the news every night.

Production Notes

Paul Schrader's script for *Taxi Driver* came from a variety of sources: his own experiences living rough in New York, his love of guns, Jean-Paul Sartre's novel *Nausea*, and the diaries of Arthur Bremer, who tried to assassinate Governor George Wallace.

November 20

Blade Runner

YEAR RELEASED: 1982
DIRECTOR: Ridley Scott
WHO'S IN IT: Harrison Ford, Rutger Hauer, Sean Young

"Have you ever retired a human by mistake?"

Adapted liberally from Philip K. Dick's novel *Do Androids Dream of Electric Sheep?* Ridley Scott's second foray into gloomy science fiction (after *Alien*) was not just a template for the progression of science-fiction futurism but his most enduring film.

Rick Deckard (Harrison Ford, credibly world-weary) is a retired "blade runner" in a near-future Los Angeles where it's always raining and the human race just seems worn out. Deckard's old job was hunting down "replicants," androids who can pass for human. He's put back to work after a band of replicants go on a killing spree. Deckard finds out they're advanced models, implanted with memories that provide the illusion of human emotions and empathy. But to retain control, their makers implanted the new-model replicants with an expiration date, which seems to be driving their frantic, murderous quest.

The film does have weaknesses—art direction for its own sake, and a stiff narration, the latter of which was removed in later director's cuts. Yet Scott's vision of a chaotic future, where the streets all look like Chinatown at rush hour and cars fly like night birds through the strobelit haze, is something that you sink right into. The replicants' childlike need to understand their true nature is as primal a story as can be imagined. In a world where the humans seem hard-pressed to bother living, these machines are *demanding* more life.

Production Notes

Screenwriter Hampton Fancher got the title for *Blade Runner* not from the original source novel (a wordier but much more apt title) but from a wholly unrelated, futuristic work by William S. Burroughs.

Kiss Me Deadly

YEAR RELEASED: 1955
DIRECTOR: Robert Aldrich
WHO'S IN IT: Ralph Meeker, Albert Dekker, Maxine Cooper

"How civilized this earth used to be."

If Robert Aldrich's phenomenally nihilistic, hugely enjoyable take on Mickey Spillane's knuckle-headed private-dick novel required a label, Man vs. World might work fine.

Ralph Meeker plays Mike Hammer, always looking for a nail. One night on a dark road, Mike almost runs over a terrified and barefoot blond. Some thugs cut them off, kidnap her, and send Mike to the hospital. When he comes out, Mike looks into the mysterious blond's past, and discovers shady dealings, complete with low-life bookies and dirty secrets to be unveiled. Mike thinks there's money to be made; also, some vengeance would be nice. So he goes stalking around Los Angeles' seedy side (a lot of great period detail captured by Aldrich), looking for information and spoiling for a fight. He gets both, in spades.

Aldrich made nasty movies about nasty people—this was rarely more the case than here. Not only is Mike a thickheaded, out-for-himself kind of guy (his private detective business is more sleazy divorce work than puzzling whodunnits), but just about everyone he comes across is as bad or worse. Moral turpitude aside, this makes for a riveting experience, particularly once a mysterious case with secret, glowing contents shows up. What's inside could be very dangerous for the human race, and Mike is the absolute *wrong* guy to possess it.

In Homage

The device of the curious case with the glowing material inside, around which *Kiss Me Deadly*'s action revolves, has been appropriated for at least two other films: *Repo Man* (1984) and *Pulp Fiction* (1994).

JFK

YEAR RELEASED: 1991
DIRECTOR: Oliver Stone
WHO'S IN IT: Kevin Costner, Gary Oldman, Donald Sutherland, Joe Pesci, Tommy Lee Jones

"You are so naive."

Oliver Stone's take on JFK assassination theorizing is based in part on New Orleans District Attorney Jim Garrison's *On the Trail of the Assassins*. Fittingly, Stone makes Garrison (Kevin Costner, appealingly all-American) the star investigator of this dense mystery that links New Orleans characters like businessman Clay Shaw (Tommy Lee Jones, exquisitely camp) and ex-seminarian David Ferrie (Joe Pesci, dialed up to 11) to a shady network of anti-Castro Cubans, Mafiosi, and right-wing extremists associated with Lee Harvey Oswald (an uncanny Gary Oldman). After meeting in Washington with the mysterious X (Donald Sutherland), Garrison becomes convinced that the November 22, 1963, assassination was a coup by pro-war elements terrified Kennedy would have pulled out of Vietnam.

As a mystery, Stone's film is intoxicating brilliance. He weaves together bright scraps of paranoid insinuation, delivering a dizzying blend of styles (from grainy black-and-white to oversaturated color) chopped together with dreamlike logic. Pieces of historical truth are scattered in, just closely enough for suggestion to fill in the rest. Having nearly every working actor in Hollywood show up for Stone's conspiracy carnival helped sell what was admittedly a wild piece of conjecture.

The X-Files premiered three years later; it and all its imitators may not have been possible without this work of curious genius, which mainstreamed antiestablishment paranoia.

Historically Speaking

To say that *JFK* departs from the historical record is to be generous. Fittingly, the film's most informative character, X, is a largely fictional creation. His dialogue is based on statements from former U.S. Air Force colonel L. Fletcher Prouty, who has been called an all-purpose conspiracy expert.

Bride of Frankenstein

YEAR RELEASED: 1935
DIRECTOR: James Whale
WHO'S IN IT: Boris Karloff, Colin Clive, Ernest Thesiger, Elsa Lanchester

"To a new world of gods and monsters!"

Decades before *Jurassic Park*, Hollywood loved giving B-list pictures the A-list treatment. James Whale's shameless, and shamelessly fun, sequel to his 1931 hit *Frankenstein* is a case in point. It's a monster movie that shouldn't exist in the first place (the monster died in the last movie, a problem the studio supposedly handled by cutting the final death scene from all the prints they could find) but is treated with all the production values of an Oscar-grubbing prestige piece. Who cares that the actors in the German village have Irish and English accents?

Whale's playful tone is apparent in a too-cute prologue, in which Mary Wollstonecraft Shelley (Elsa Lanchester) is chatting about her novel in a drawing room with Lord Byron (Gavin Gordon) and Percy Bysshe Shelley (Douglas Walton). Both Henry Frankenstein (Colin Clive) and the monster (Boris Karloff) survived the last film's torch-wielding mob. The burnt monster wanders the countryside, making friends with those who don't scream at his approach, and invariably killing those who do.

That Whale wasn't taking things too seriously is apparent in his treatment of the monster, who gets some basic ESL training ("Drink! Good!") and develops a few new vices in addition to homicide (cigars, in particular). Also enjoying his evil endeavors is one Dr. Pretorius (Ernest Thesiger, playing the villain so camp he makes the actors playing Byron and Shelley look butch in comparison).

No matter how loony the plot or low the comedy, though, Whale makes it look fantastic. John J. Mescall's cinematography is masterfully sharp and expressionistic, while the soaring interiors are lavishly deluxe. Hollywood Pop Gothic at its best.

A Hard Day's Night

YEAR RELEASED: 1964
DIRECTOR: Richard Lester
WHO'S IN IT: John Lennon, Paul McCartney, George Harrison, Ringo Starr

"Stop being taller than me."

After the opening sequence, where we hear the title song as the four Beatles try to escape their fans, Richard Lester's film settles into a goofier rhythm that's hard to put a label on. The band is on its way to a television studio where they're going to perform live, but little obstacles keep cropping up, most particularly the Liverpudlian scamps' penchant for wordplay and tweaking their managers' patience.

Considering that they were still pretty fresh to music stardom, the Beatles put in a worthy showing as the prank-prone ringleaders of Lester's slapstick circus. In between some genial mockery and gags, the film cuts back to the crisply executed music numbers, which were, of course, the whole reason this opportunistic film was cranked out to begin with.

Lester's first feature film established the jocular, jazzy, post–New Wave visual style (a lot of crash zooms, quick editing, and off-kilter camera angles) that would be his trademark throughout the 1960s. It also showed his penchant for overlapping, deadpan comic skits that whip by almost before you have a chance to catch what's happening. It's a style that culminates in his nearly unintelligible 1967 satire *How I Won the War*, which featured an angelically benign John Lennon—only three years older but with a world's worth of extra weight on his shoulders.

Auteur, Auteur

Before shooting *A Hard Day's Night*, Richard Lester had worked as everything from morning disc jockey to puppeteer on Ed Sullivan's *Toast of the Town*. He was also a musician and composer who had toured Europe, earning money by playing in bars and cafés.

Home for the Holidays

YEAR RELEASED: 1995
DIRECTOR: Jodie Foster
WHO'S IN IT: Holly Hunter, Robert Downey, Jr., Anne Bancroft, Charles Durning

"That was absurd, let's eat dead bird."

Thanksgiving: the time of year when a family's far-flung offspring come winging home. As Claudia Larson (Holly Hunter), the put-upon protagonist of Jodie Foster's blithe family comedy, puts it: "We don't have to like each other . . . we're family."

The absurdities start early. Just before getting on a plane to fly home, single mom Claudia is fired from her museum job and then, for no apparent reason, makes out with her now ex-boss. At the airport, her daughter, Kit (Clare Danes), informs her that she's decided to lose her virginity over the holiday weekend. Without Kit for distraction, Claudia has no shield to ward off her parents (Anne Bancroft and Charles Durning, a phenomenal pair) and their fretful, exhausting prattle.

As the family trickles in for the feast, the tension and humor mount. Claudia's perfectionist sister Joanne (Cynthia Stevenson) arrives in a flurry of worry, exacerbated by being picked at by their brother Tommy (Robert Downey, Jr., stealing the show without even trying), a class clown whose homosexuality Joanne *really* doesn't approve of.

Plenty of comedies have succeeded in showcasing family dysfunction in close quarters; years' worth of sitcoms have depended on it for material. But Foster's film goes for a warmer, sadder, truer kind of comedy, where family becomes as claustrophobic and infuriating as it is reassuring and necessary.

Production Notes
Home for the Holidays screenwriter W. D. Richter is better known for writing films like John Carpenter's martial arts adventure *Big Trouble in Little China* (1986) and directing the cult sci-fi comedy *The Adventures of Buckaroo Banzai* (1984).

Invasion of the Body Snatchers

YEAR RELEASED: 1956
DIRECTOR: Don Siegel
WHO'S IN IT: Kevin McCarthy, Dana Wynter

"You're next!"

Anticommunist propaganda or anticonformist screed; the fears undergirding this postwar sci-fi classic are so universal that whatever you think its meaning is, you're probably right. In the small town of Santa Mira, a number of people tell Dr. Miles Bennell (Kevin McCarthy) that their family members are acting odd, not like themselves. Miles is then alerted to something his friends have found: a clone that looks just like a human, only blanker. He eventually puts two and two together: strange alien pods have been seeded all over the town, and once a human goes to sleep, his mind is taken over by the pods. The human then awakens as a pod person, part of an invisible network of like-minded clones.

The horror of Don Siegel's film is twofold: first, being triggered by sleep, the pod takeover is inescapable; and two, the end result may not even be that noticeable. It's likely no mistake that the next most memorable usage of this plot device came with *Nightmare on Elm Street*. That horror franchise about teenagers thrown into mortal danger when they fall asleep was launched in 1984, another time of fervent flag-waving and social conformity.

A crackerjack script and an efficient style keeps this a short, tightly wound piece of work, like most of Siegel's films. It didn't win any awards, since this was back before the Oscars paid attention to films with aliens.

Casting Call
Director Sam Peckinpah (*The Wild Bunch*) first worked as an assistant for Don Siegel, even doing some uncredited script work on *Invasion of the Body Snatchers*, in which he also has a cameo as a meter reader.

The Hurt Locker

YEAR RELEASED: 2009
DIRECTOR: Kathryn Bigelow
WHO'S IN IT: Jeremy Renner, Anthony Mackie, Brian Geraghty

"Everyone's scared about something, you know?"

Nobody in their right mind would ever argue that war is fun, but it would take a willing suspension of disbelief to claim that it's never exciting. To this point, Kathryn Bigelow's incendiary Iraq War film starts with a quotation that tells you everything you need to know about her main character: "War is a drug."

William James (Jeremy Renner) is the newest member of an EOD (explosive ordnance disposal) team, and he enjoys his job a little too much. This stands in stark contrast to team members JT Sanborn (Anthony Mackie), a by-the-book guy, and Owen Eldridge (Brian Geraghty), who is less high-strung and just trying to get along.

James's job is to stalk out to wherever the bomb is in a bulbous, astronaut-like suit of armor and disarm it while Sanborn and Eldridge cover him. Personalities clash like rams competing for dominance, with James dragging them closer to the edge to get his fix. Even if they survive the war, it may ruin them for anything else in their lives, for where else can they get that drug?

Working on a negligible budget with no stars (though Ralph Fiennes and Guy Pearce make brief, unbilled appearances), Bigelow shows her knack, honed over years of potent genre pictures, for building tension until it snaps and crackles. The punchy screenplay is by former embedded journalist Mark Boal, who cowrote *In the Valley of Elah* (2007), another great Iraq War film which nobody wanted to see.

And the Winner Is . . .

The Hurt Locker was nominated for nine Oscars, winning six, including for best director, making Kathryn Bigelow the first woman to win that award.

November 28

The Thin Blue Line

YEAR RELEASED: 1988
DIRECTOR: Errol Morris
WHO'S IN IT: Randall Adams, David Harris

"Criminals always lie."

Through a mix of interviews and cleverly shot re-creations, documentary filmmaker Errol Morris tells the story of death row inmate Randall Adams. On November 28, 1976, Dallas police officer Robert W. Wood was shot dead during a routine traffic stop. His partner was sitting in the car at the time and was too late to respond; Morris repeatedly returns to a slow-motion image of her throwing her milkshake out the cruiser window when she heard the shot. It's the kind of rhythm that pulses throughout the film. Minimalist composer Philip Glass's eerie score also brings an insistent quality to the overwhelming evidence he ultimately presents.

The case against Adams was built almost entirely on the testimony of teen-aged drifter David Harris, who said he was in the car with Adams when they were pulled over and that Adams had shot Wood. Morris—who later stated that the reason he made the film was to get Adams off death row—steadily builds the case against Harris like a prosecutor, leading to the inescapable conclusion that Harris was the culprit.

Morris's popular, gripping film did several things. First, it assured him of a steady career afterward. Second, it established the visual and editing template for the entire subgenre of true-crime shows that populate broadcast television. Third and most important, in March 1989, Randall Adams was freed from jail.

And the Winner Is . . .
Although the film surprisingly didn't receive an Oscar nomination, a 1988 *Washington Post* survey of 250 critics voted *The Thin Blue Line* the best film of the year.

Shock Corridor

YEAR RELEASED: 1963
DIRECTOR: Sam Fuller
WHO'S IN IT: Peter Breck, Constance Towers

"What a tragedy. An insane mute will win the Pulitzer Prize."

Subtle as a kick to the head, writer/director Sam Fuller's mental institution mystery is a combustible mix of tabloid journalism and histrionic melodrama. Johnny Barrett (Peter Breck) is an ambitious reporter, desperate to win a Pulitzer. To solve a murder in a mental institution, he fakes insanity and gets committed.

Once inside, the reporter tries to keep on track, interviewing the three patients who witnessed the murder. Their being insane not only makes Johnny's job harder, but also seems to be rubbing off on him. Each of the three is a Freudian microcosm of sublimated guilt or shame: a Korean War vet pretending to be a Confederate general because he's guilty over siding with the North Koreans; a regretful nuclear scientist hiding in childhood behavior; and—in the film's most powerful, indelible creation—an African American man so traumatized by racism that he's taken on the persona of a KKK member.

No doubt this is all laughable by modern psychotherapeutic standards, but Fuller uses the kaleidoscopic world of the asylum—memorably shot by the great Stanley Cortez of *The Night of the Hunter* (1955)—to cast a withering glance at America's dark soul. The result might be ridiculous, but like the best tabloid journalism, there's some disquieting truths underneath it all.

Auteur, Auteur

Former journalist and World War II veteran Sam Fuller made *Shock Corridor* at the height of his pulp filmmaking career. Though limited to a tiny budget ($222,000), Fuller was given the rarest of gifts for a B-film director: final cut.

The Treasure of the Sierra Madre

YEAR RELEASED: 1948
DIRECTOR: John Huston
WHO'S IN IT: Humphrey Bogart, Walter Huston, Tim Holt, Alfonso Bedoya

"Nobody puts one over on Fred C. Dobbs."

B. Traven's 1927 novel was the source for John Huston's gritty examination of greed and morality in the lawless mountains of post-revolutionary Mexico. The literary-minded Huston wrote the script, apparently with the blessing of Traven himself.

Humphrey Bogart plays Fred Dobbs, one of three men looking for gold south of the border. Along for the ride are Howard (Huston's father, Walter) and Curtin (Tim Holt). They scrabble along in the wilderness, looking for riches. Once they actually come across gold, the bonds between this trio of treasure seekers will fray quicker than even they can comprehend. Even though we all know that this will happen, the quick savagery with which the men turn on each other still manages to surprise.

Huston and Bogart had more fun in their other 1948 film, the storm-tossed gangster flick *Key Largo*. But that one was a little too easy for this team; with *Sierra Madre* (on-location shooting, weightier issues of trust and greed) they actually had to stretch. This is true of Bogart in particular; his Dobbs—all stubbled snarl and bug-eyes, with dollars on his frantically deceptive brain—is just about as vicious a piece of work as he ever concocted.

Everyone's a Critic

Although *The Treasure of the Sierra Madre* received four Oscar nominations, it wasn't well received by the moviegoing public, perhaps because the basic unpleasantness of Humphrey Bogart's Fred Dobbs was so far removed from the actor's reluctantly romantic heroes.

Match Point

YEAR RELEASED: 2005
DIRECTOR: Woody Allen
WHO'S IN IT: Jonathan Rhys Meyers, Matthew Goode, Emily Mortimer, Scarlett Johansson

"People are afraid to face how great a part of life is dependent on luck."

There is not a joke to be had in this steely work of criminal amorality, which is fine, because it's also the most vibrant film Woody Allen had produced in years. The story is set in London's monied upper crust of London, which a couple of lower-class operators wheedle into and cause mayhem. Jonathan Rhys Meyers (so affectless he almost disappears) plays tennis pro Chris Wilton, who befriends the wealthy Tom Hewett (Matthew Goode). Seeing his chance, Chris burrows closer to the nexus of money, first affecting shared tastes and then making a play for Tom's demure sister Chloe (Emily Mortimer). After Chris marries Chloe and her father sets him up with a great job, he seems to have it made. But then there's Tom's sultry American fiancée Nola Rice (Scarlett Johansson), who has eyes for Chris as well.

Although Allen's previous ventures into serious drama often seem strained by their seriousness, like *Crimes and Misdemeanors* (1989), in this film he displays perfect control of his story's mood and pacing. Each element in this intricately plotted film slots into place with ease. The musings on luck, class, and morality enhance rather than detract from the swiftly mounting tension. The conclusion is so well crafted and chilling that it makes you wonder whether Allen should have been doing crime films all along.

Auteur, Auteur

Having left New York to make a film for the first time in years, after *Match Point*, Woody Allen made two more films in London, with increasingly diminished results: *Scoop* (2006) and *Cassandra's Dream* (2007).

Kill Bill: Vol. 1

YEAR RELEASED: 2003
DIRECTOR: Quentin Tarantino
WHO'S IN IT: Uma Thurman, Lucy Liu, Vivica A. Fox

"I've allowed you to keep your wicked life for two reasons."

By the time he got around to making the *Kill Bill* duology, Quentin Tarantino had been going on about his love of genre and exploitation films long enough that it seemed well overdue for him to just go ahead and make one or two himself.

The tale of a woman who has dedicated herself to revenge, part 1 whips through genres with breathless speed and gleeful abandon. The Bride (Uma Thurman) was once a member of the Deadly Viper Assassination Squad. But when the Bride decided to go straight and get married, the other vipers and their boss, Bill (David Carradine), massacre everyone at the wedding, leaving her for dead. Waking up in a hospital four years later, the Bride tracks down the vipers to exact revenge.

There are heavy servings of tongue-in-cheek humor throughout. Tarantino puts a *Star Trek* quotation up on the screen with mock grandeur ("'Revenge is a dish best served cold' —Old Klingon proverb") and much of the Bride's over-heated dialogue falls *just* shy of self-parody. But Tarantino's devotion to all those bottom-rung drive-in flicks that inspired it is unwaveringly respectful, an approach that—along with Robert Richardson's richly colored cinematography—makes this film such a blast. If only the same could be said about the self-indulgent follow-up.

Production Notes

When Quentin Tarantino ran into Uma Thurman at a Miramax party, she reminded him of an idea he'd come up with in a conversation they'd had on the set of *Pulp Fiction* (in which Thurman's character revealed she had once been in a pilot for a TV show about a Deadly Viper Assassination Squad–like group called Fox Force 5) for a film about a female assassin—this became the genesis for *Kill Bill*.

Breathless

🌐 👤 ❤️ 🔍

YEAR RELEASED: 1960
DIRECTOR: Jean-Luc Godard
WHO'S IN IT: Jean-Paul Belmondo, Jean Seberg

"Shall we steal a Cadillac?"

Years before recklessly homicidal killer youths on the run would scorch a path that lead straight from *Bonnie and Clyde* to *Natural Born Killers*, Jean-Luc Godard set loose a pair of beautiful young lovers who still stand tall against those who followed. Michel (Jean-Paul Belmondo) is your prototypical couldn't-care tough guy. Movie-obsessed—as all good protagonists in films by French New Wave directors must be—Michel patterns himself after the great silver-screen tough guys. We see him admiring a Humphrey Bogart film poster, and ever after, he's cocking his hat, hiding behind sunglasses and cigarettes, and running his thumb over his lips in imitation of Bogie.

Given this armor of detached cool, it isn't surprising when Michel, during a routine traffic stop, guns a policeman down with no more thought than he would give to lighting a match. Later on, he checks in with Patricia (Jean Seberg), a pert American girl who doesn't seem to mind so much that he's a murderer. Although Michel is wanted by the police, he continues to hang around Paris, making vague plans to pick up some money he is owed and escape; the closing net of the law seems as inevitable as the end of those gangster films he loves.

In this, his first film, Godard made an impact few other filmmakers could equal. The jerky look and rough interplay of jump-cuts, as well as the story's casual amorality, announced the start of the so-called French New Wave. Legions of film directors tried to imitate Godard's style but were usually about as effective as Michel channeling Bogie.

Wings of Desire

YEAR RELEASED: 1987
DIRECTOR: Wim Wenders
WHO'S IN IT: Bruno Ganz, Otto Sander, Solveig Dommartin, Peter Falk

"To say 'ooh!' and 'ah!' . . . instead of always 'ja' and 'amen'."

In German director Wim Wenders's sumptuously imagined fantasy, angels watch the inhabitants of Berlin with silent patience. Then, one of them, Damiel (Bruno Ganz) decides to find out what it's like to be human after falling in love with a trapeze artist (Solveig Dommartin). It must have been the wings she was wearing.

Wenders's angels are always there, not necessarily to intervene in human affairs, but to provide invisible comfort to everyone they come across, from a mournful old writer to Peter Falk (playing himself, in an unusually playful note from the normally dour Wenders). We see the angels lingering around the city with their slicked-back hair and dour trenchcoats, listening to human's cascades of worry, which run as a murmuring interior soundtrack. One angel leans in to touch a despairing person, who then straightens up, feeling just a bit better with no idea why.

It's not always the easiest fantasy to swallow, and there are times (particularly the concluding monologue by Dommartin) when the film lurches into self-importance. But the romantic beauty of Wenders's central vision, captured in luminous black-and-white by Henri Alekan, makes it almost impossible *not* to buy into.

In Homage

In 1996, there came the inevitable remake, with Nicolas Cage as the angel and Meg Ryan as his human love. *City of Angels* proved surprisingly faithful to the original's spirit (if not the look, with color cinematography and a Los Angeles setting).

December 5

Laura

🔍

YEAR RELEASED: 1944
DIRECTOR: Otto Preminger
WHO'S IN IT: Gene Tierney, Dana Andrews, Clifton Webb, Vincent Price

"I can afford a blemish on my character, but not on my clothes."

The girl of the film's title is dead before it even gets started. Laura Hunt (Gene Tierney, impossibly beautiful) was a gorgeous, successful young advertising professional engaged to marry flighty socialite Shelby Carpenter (Vincent Price, looking strangely human). Unfortunately, Laura opened her door one night to a load of buckshot at point-blank range.

We begin with detective Mark McPherson (Dana Andrews, fedora cocked as rakishly as his cigarette) interviewing Laura's acquaintances, all of whom seem suspicious to McPherson. Of particular interest is the silky-mannered gossip columnist Waldo Lydecker (Clifton Webb), who not only gave Laura her start in the business, but took a too-active interest in the men she dated, a group he was frustratingly not a member of.

Otto Preminger's mystery has the clipped, sarcastic dialogue of a noir, but the repressed emotions and fancy interiors of the English drawing-room mystery. There is also a heavy layering of gothic romance (think Hitchcock's *Rebecca*) in how McPherson becomes obsessed with Laura's memory. It's this surprising fixation by a supposedly hard-nosed cop that is the most remembered, and most copied, element of the film. The glossy, luminous black-and-white cinematography is by Joseph LaShelle (he won an Oscar for it) and the sentimental, hard-to-forget music theme is by David Raskin.

Production Notes

After a poor early screening of *Laura*, studio chief Daryl Zanuck reportedly called for a new ending with narration saying the whole story was a figment of Lydecker's imagination. The studio only changed it back after gossip columnist Walter Winchell said he loved everything about the film except for its new ending.

December 6

Gimme Shelter

YEAR RELEASED: 1970
DIRECTOR: Albert Maysles, David Maysles, Charlotte Zwerin
WHO'S IN IT: Mick Jagger, Charlie Watts, Keith Richards, Mick Taylor, Bill Wyman

"Oh dear, what a shame."

On December 6, 1969, Albert and David Maysles and Charlotte Zwerin followed a short Rolling Stones tour to Altamont Speedway in Northern California, where they headlined a free concert. Around 300,000 people showed up, and the resulting chaos—given the crowds, the lack of planning, and the Hell's Angels working "security"—was a foregone conclusion. Still, nobody expected a man to get knifed to death in front of Mick Jagger.

What should have been a musical celebration turns into a postmortem. Early on, the filmmakers show their footage to Jagger and drummer Charlie Watts, neither of whom seem to comprehend what happened; everything we see after that is buildup to the frenzy of Altamont. The generous segments of early concert footage were mostly shot in Madison Square Garden, where we witness Jagger prancing and prowling as he's done for decades. The songs themselves ("Jumpin' Jack Flash," "Wild Horses") have a raw abandon that the band hasn't delivered for some time.

Altamont itself is a chaotic affair, with the Angels clearing the band's way to the stage by simply riding their bikes through it. When the moment comes, it's lost in the chaos of the crowd, only revealed later by a slow-motion replay for Jagger, whose blank face reveals little. It was just four months after Woodstock, and cliché or not, the 1960s were officially over.

> ### Everyone's a Critic
> Of *Gimme Shelter*, *Variety* wrote: "By promising and delivering footage of a murder and by framing and structuring the film to build suspense around the event, the filmmakers have played their trump [card] in a manner many may find inexcusably callous."

Down by Law

YEAR RELEASED: 1986
DIRECTOR: Jim Jarmusch
WHO'S IN IT: Tom Waits, John Lurie, Robert Benigni, Nicoletta Braschi

"It is a sad and beautiful world."

Down by Law is in black-and-white, same as Jim Jarmusch's indie hit *Stranger Than Paradise* (1984). The two films also share a downbeat humor personified by underground musician John Lurie, who starred in both films. *Down by Law* is sharper and more focused, its sensational New Orleans and Louisiana bayou settings captured this time by the wide-angled lens of Robby Muller, who had made the American West look like a neighbor to paradise in *Paris, Texas* (1984). Even the squalor has a certain artistry.

Amidst the squalor, three men in are in a Louisiana prison cell. Zack (Tom Waits, dry and mordant) is an out-of-work disc jockey. Jack (Lurie, glum) is a pimp, and not a terribly good one. Both have been framed, but they don't seem capable of making anybody else realize that. Sharing their cell is excitable Italian tourist Roberto (Roberto Benigni, as over-the-top as ever), who is actually in for killing somebody. They escape through the swampland, coming across a house inhabited by the beautiful Nicoletta (Nicoletta Braschi, Benigni's wife).

Where Jarmusch's later films could drift off into pure pose, this alluring hipster jailbreak comedy has more heart than expected. Like in *Stranger*, when contact with a wide-eyed foreigner provides grist for revelation, Zack's and Jack's cool attitudes are constantly being challenged by Roberto's effusive eruptions of garbled but enthusiastic English. Through his eyes they, and we, see the world anew.

Production Notes

The excellent soundtrack for *Down by Law* features songs by Tom Waits ("Jockey Full of Bourbon," "Tango Till They're Sore") and original music by his costar John Lurie.

The Butcher Boy

 LOL!

YEAR RELEASED: 1997
DIRECTOR: Neil Jordan
WHO'S IN IT: Eamonn Owens, Fiona Shaw, Stephen Rea

"The Francie Brady 'Not a Bad Bastard' award goes to . . . by God, I think it's Francie Brady!"

The most terrifying child ever to appear on a movie screen can be found in Neil Jordan's horrific and frighteningly funny comedy of madness and apocalyptic nightmares. The freckle-faced, cherubic lad, Francis Brady (Eamonn Owens), lives in a small, conservative Irish town in the early 1960s. Da Brady (Stephan Rea) is a hollering drunk of a musician who beats on Francis when he's in the mood, while poor, daft Ma Brady spends her time in fantasyland, baking cakes and talking nonsense.

Nothing seems to bother Francis, delivering a near-constant narration that plays his hilariously manic optimism off Elliot Goldenthal's chipper, off-key musical score. It's no shock that Francis turns out to have more than a few screws loose, which becomes apparent once his home life deteriorates even further.

After Ma is sent off to an asylum, and Francis spends time at a boarding school, his imaginary life becomes a fevered stew of pop songs, comic books, B-movies, and nuclear panic. At the same time, his paranoia is manifested in more violent ways. It seems the only person who Francis can talk to is the Virgin Mary, who appears to him in the form of Sinéad O'Connor.

Amidst all this madness, Jordan keeps the film's rudder straight and never turns it into farce. Francis might be barking mad and a danger to himself and others, but we're never allowed to forget that he's also just a boy who needs help. The result is the devil's own brew of laughter and sadness.

December 9

Spartacus

YEAR RELEASED: 1960
DIRECTOR: Stanley Kubrick
WHO'S IN IT: Kirk Douglas, Tony Curtis, Laurence Olivier

"I am Spartacus!"

At first, the adaptation of Howard Fast's novel about the leader of the doomed Roman slave rebellion was going to be directed by journeyman Anthony Mann. But after shooting about a third or so of the film (less, some say), producer and star Kirk Douglas canned Mann and went with Stanley Kubrick, who had served him so well in *Paths of Glory*. It's possible that if Mann had stayed on, the film might have been stripped of some dragging sections. But without Kubrick (who imparted less personality to this film than just about anything he made) it might not have had its resonant perversity—for example, the unctuous advances of Senator Crassus (Laurence Olivier) on his servant Antoninus (Tony Curtis), or the recumbent cynicism of Charles Laughton as Senator Graccus.

Douglas plays Spartacus—the slave and gladiator who turned his training against his masters—as though his life depends on it. While the film's many thespians recline on the sidelines, continuing the great Hollywood tradition of peopling the upper tiers of the Roman Empire with British stage actors eager to collect an easy paycheck, Douglas is front and center, teeth gritted, every muscle flexed. It would be easy to mock Douglas's commitment to his character (Russell Crowe handled a similar role with more ease in Ridley Scott's *Gladiator*), but without him, this three-hour film would not be half as stirring.

Courting Controversy

With *Spartacus*, Kirk Douglas helped end Hollywood's anticommunist witch hunt by not just hiring blacklisted screenwriter Dalton Trumbo (who shares December 9 with Douglas as a birthday) but also giving him full credit, instead of forcing Trumbo to hide behind a pseudonym as blacklisted writers normally did.

Gunga Din

 LOL!

YEAR RELEASED: 1939
DIRECTOR: George Stevens
WHO'S IN IT: Cary Grant, Victor McLaglen, Douglas Fairbanks, Jr., Sam Jaffe

"Her Majesty's very touchy about having her subjects strangled."

George Stevens directed this swift exercise from a many-authored script that used Rudyard Kipling's ode to a heroic water carrier as the jumping-off point for a colonial-era Western. It comes to the screen with Kipling and the British Raj's condescending racial attitudes firmly in place ("of all them black-faced crew/the finest man I knew"). That said, it's about as entertaining a film as Hollywood ever produced—and in the end, the humble Gunga Din (Sam Jaffe) is the real hero.

Cary Grant, Victor McLaglen, and Douglas Fairbanks, Jr. play a chummy, carousing trio of British soldiers in colonial India. When the death-cult assassins the Thuggees (real-life bandits who supposedly worshipped the Hindu goddess Kali by committing mass murder) start tearing up the countryside, cutting telegraph wires and ambushing military posts, the three are sent out with a detachment of native soldiers to deal with the uprising. The first battle is a dazzler, with the three dashing over rooftops and leaping over walls, sabers in one hand and pistols in the other, hurling orders and sticks of dynamite as the white-robed Thuggees swarm.

Stevens handles the film with quick dispatch, layering the action and comedy in equal measure, erring more toward the latter, with good reason. The three soldiers make for a fantastic slapstick team—particularly Grant's Cockney clown—when not battling against incredible odds in the bright and clear desert landscapes.

In Homage

Steven Spielberg and George Lucas borrowed the Thuggees' elaborate, death-worshipping rituals for the villains in their much bloodier and far less clever *Indiana Jones and the Temple of Doom* (1984).

Goodfellas

YEAR RELEASED: 1990
DIRECTOR: Martin Scorsese
WHO'S IN IT: Ray Liotta, Lorraine Bacco, Robert De Niro, Joe Pesci

"As far back as I can remember, I always wanted to be a gangster."

One of the last classic all-American dramas to achieve near universal acclaim from both critics and the public, Martin Scorsese's hair-trigger gangster film was also the greatest of his collaborations with Robert De Niro and Joe Pesci and the pinnacle of all of their careers.

Based on journalist Nicolas Pileggi's *Wiseguy*, the film is the (mostly) true account of the rise and fall of Henry Hill (Ray Liotta, never better), a footsoldier in New York's Lucchese family during the 1960s and 1970s. Hill narrates the legacy of his crimes with a prideful nonchalance, laying out his criminal enterprises, in particular the multimillion-dollar Lufthansa heist, like he was teaching a class. He introduces us to all the major players, in particular "Jimmy the Gent" Conway (Robert De Niro) and Tommy DeVito (Joe Pesci). That chatty buzz reverberates through the whole story, moved along by Scorsese's frenetic pacing, many wildly improvisational comic scenes, shocks of violence, fizzy soundtrack, and the air of wildly escapist glee.

Unlike most modern Hollywood gangster films—the *Godfather* series, *Bugsy*, *Road to Perdition*—this one wasn't set in a safely nostalgic and glamorous world of mansions and elegance. It followed the wise guys in bad, flashy suits who actually did the dirty business the mob runs on. They were canny, not strategic. Instead of Michael Corleone's calculated assassination sprees, these guys get into stupid fights in bars and gun people down for no good reason. The soundtrack isn't arias; it's pop tunes by the Shangri-Las, Dean Martin, and Tony Bennett.

Historically Speaking

The so-called Lufthansa heist at Idlewild (later JFK) Airport that provides so much of the plot of *Goodfellas* took place on December 11, 1978. One of the largest robberies in American history (some $5 million in cash and jewels was supposedly taken), its aftermath resulted in more than a dozen murders.

Tokyo Story

YEAR RELEASED: 1953
DIRECTOR: Yasujirô Ozu
WHO'S IN IT: Chishû Ryû, Chieko Higashiyama, Setsuko Hara

"I'm afraid we expect too much of our children."

On a hot summer day, two grandparents (Chishû Ryû and Chieko Higashiyama) take a train from their small village to Tokyo to visit their children. Once at the house of their older son, however, things don't go as planned. The conversation is stilted and frequently comes to a halt. Eager to get them out of their hair, the siblings send the parents off to a spa, rationalizing the decision by claiming it will be better for them.

The coldness of the children is thrown into even sharper relief when set alongside the heartbreaking kindness shown by Noriko (Setsuko Hara), the widow of one of their other sons, who died in World War II. Reflecting on the disappointments of life, the grandparents realize that this is the daughter they always wanted.

While the family's mannerisms seem rigorously formal, Yasujirô Ozu's style is unobtrusive in the extreme. With a very few exceptions, like the nicely composed shots of the grandparents' village (a temple, the tranquil harbor), most of the film takes place indoors, with people sitting and talking. Like his roomy story, Ozu likes to sit back and let his actors breathe. In this way, a film that by all rights should be stultifyingly slow or sentimental becomes a living thing, something that you don't watch so much as step inside and have a look around.

In Homage

Hirokazu Kore-eda's great 2008 film *Still Walking* picks up on many of *Tokyo Story*'s themes, particularly in the difficult distances between family members and the quietly astute manner with which the filmmaker tracks their conflicting emotions.

December 13

Mary Poppins

YEAR RELEASED: 1964
DIRECTOR: Robert Stevenson
WHO'S IN IT: Julie Andrews, Dick Van Dyke, Karen Dotrice, Matthew Garber

"That's a pie crust promise. Easily made, easily broken."

Living in a fine house in Edwardian London, the Banks family have all they need but nothing that they want. Mr. Banks (David Tomlinson) is obsessed with work, while Mrs. Banks (Glynis Johns) works for suffragist rights. Acting out in the midst of all this parental neglect, little Jane and Michael (Karen Dotrice and Matthew Garber) send one nanny after another packing. That is, until one Mary Poppins (Julie Andrews) arrives, fluttering down under her umbrella and applying for the job at Number Seventeen Cherry-Tree Lane as though nothing unusual had happened. Before you know it, the kids are behaving, the parents are starting to appreciate their family, and it's time for Mary Poppins to catch the next east wind out of there.

This evergreen musical, Walt Disney's best, is chipper and kid-friendly without being insulting. It's an endearing cast, with Andrews taking center stage not only with her vanilla-sweet voice, but also that brittle and icy authoritative edge, which has her snapping things like "Don't slouch!" in between proffering heartwarming advice. There's Dick Dan Dyke, wonderful as a chimney sweep with possibly the world's dodgiest Cockney accent, and Elsa "Bride of Frankenstein" Lanchester as the nanny we see quitting in the beginning. House Disney director Robert Stevenson herds it all together with the kind of bright cheer that stays intact no matter how many times you watch it.

And the Winner Is . . .

Mary Poppins was nominated for an incredible thirteen Oscars, winning five, including one for Julie Andrews. Ironically, the best picture award went to *My Fair Lady*, which Andrews had performed in onstage.

The Howling

YEAR RELEASED: 1981
DIRECTOR: Joe Dante
WHO'S IN IT: Dee Wallace, Patrick Macnee, Dennis Dugan, Christopher Stone

"Honey, you're from Los Angeles. The wildest thing you've ever heard is Wolfman Jack."

Los Angeles anchorwoman Karen White (Dee Wallace) is having a little problem with a serial killer known as "Eddie the Mangler," who has taken a shine to her. A police sting goes badly enough for her to get a look at Eddie before he's gunned down. A psychiatrist sends Karen and her husband to a rural retreat called the Colony.

Back in the city, Karen's coworkers Terry (Belinda Balaski) and Chris (Dennis Dugan) find strange connections between some of Eddie's drawings and werewolves. At the Colony, Karen is becoming increasingly nervous about the patients' odd, cultish nature; that, and all the howling she keeps hearing. Then Chris shows up with some helpful ancient lore about werewolves and a rifle full of silver bullets.

At a time when horror films mostly followed the slasher template laid down by John Carpenter's *Halloween*, Joe Dante's quick-witted *The Howling* came as a relief. John Sayles's script pitches things just seriously enough to create interest in the mysterious goings-on at the Colony (hints of a broader conspiracy) while simultaneously taking potshots at West Coast pop-therapy trends. Dante plays it mostly for laughs, filling the screen with snort-worthy in-jokes and great casting. Watch for old cowboy great Slim Pickens as well as Dante regular Dick Miller playing the crusty owner of a bookshop specializing in the occult: "Just what you see, buddy."

Auteur, Auteur

John Sayles and Joe Dante both came up through the Roger Corman exploitation-flick factory, first working together on Corman's classic *Piranha* (whose name says all you need to know). Sayles took on *The Howling* while simultaneously writing another deadly-creature flick, *Alligator*.

December 15

Repo Man

YEAR RELEASED: 1984
DIRECTOR: Alex Cox
WHO'S IN IT: Emilio Estevez, Harry Dean Stanton, Tracey Walter, Sy Richardson

"Let's go get sushi . . . and not pay!"

A 1964 Chevy Malibu is driving around Los Angeles with a creepy and slowly dying scientist at the wheel. In the trunk is radioactive material, which in the opening moments of the film vaporizes a highway patrolman. Everyone from government agents to a band of car repossessers tired of the usual chicken feed money is hunting for it. The best (or at least most vocal about his skills) of the repo men is played by Harry Dean Stanton, who brings on a protégé, Otto (Emilio Estevez), a permanently pissed-off punk who doesn't have much else going for him. They drive around town looking for the Malibu while Stanton lectures Otto on the "repo code," life, and politics ("I don't want no Commies in my car . . . no Christians, either!"). Otto also gets an earful from none-to-bright fellow punk Duke ("I blame society. *Society* made me what I am!").

Alex Cox's debut was a low-rent sci-fi comic oddity that achieved cult status both for its nonsensical humor and its street-level view of the punishingly aggressive Southern California punk scene. The raw soundtrack (Suicidal Tendencies, Black Flag, Circle Jerks) stands as a time capsule of a time and place, helped by Cox's filming in the skuzziest parts of the city. Cox includes allusions to everything from *Kiss Me Deadly* to *Grease* and stocks the background with dozens of sight gags, in particular the generic products everybody consumes ("Drink," "Food").

> **Production Notes**
> Sterling punk pedigree aside, *Repo Man* probably wouldn't have existed without the Monkees, whose Michael Nesmith gave Alex Cox the $1.5 million needed to make it.

A Scanner Darkly

YEAR RELEASED: 2006
DIRECTOR: Richard Linklater
WHO'S IN IT: Keanu Reeves, Robert Downey, Jr., Woody Harrelson, Winona Ryder

"What does a scanner see?"

In a near-future that looks suspiciously like a heavily foreclosed suburb of today, a snitch is busy informing to the police about the drug-dealing activities of . . . himself. Bob Arctor (Keanu Reeves, nervier than usual) lives with a houseful of jabbering addicts who don't seem to be much of a threat to anything but each other's patience. But to feed the law enforcement beast, every now and again, Bob puts on something called a "scramble suit" (rendering him a faceless blur) and goes to the cops under the moniker "Fred." There, he watches surveillance footage of his household, where "Bob" seems to be dealing the illegal drug of choice, Substance D. Confusion results.

Richard Linklater lifted much of his verbose script straight from its source, the wordy 1977 Philip K. Dick novel, but the look is all him. Using the same technology (called rotoscoping) that animated his 2001 talkfest *Waking Life*, Linklater layers his chatty performers with a moody rainbow sheen that's in sharp relief to their continual half-baked patter. The haze of paranoia and low junkie comedy hangs over everything. The film has fun at the expense of the tweaked inhabitants of its universe and also speculates that maybe their most off-the-wall fears are true.

Casting Call

Both Keanu Reeves, a fan of Philip K. Dick, and Winona Ryder, whose godfather Timothy Leary was a friend of the author's, agreed to work on *Scanner Darkly* for Screen Actors Guild scale, which worked out to just over $70,000. In contrast, Reeves made over $15 million and 15 percent of the gross for each *Matrix* sequel.

The Thin Red Line

YEAR RELEASED: 1998
DIRECTOR: Terrence Malick
WHO'S IN IT: Elias Koteas, Sean Penn, Adrien Brody, Nick Nolte

"Why does nature contend with itself?"

In adapting James Jones's tough novel about the 1942 Guadalcanal campaign, Terrence Malick—in his first film since *Days of Heaven* (1978)—delivered a war film unlike any other.

Lieutenant Colonel Gordon Tall (Nick Nolte) wants to impress his superiors by having his men assault a deeply entrenched Japanese position. The film then zeroes in on one of the companies in the assault, led by Captain James Staros (Elias Koteas), sick with the thought of losing men pointlessly. The buildup to the assault has a heart-thumping intensity, though interwoven with many curiously beatific interludes where John Toll's camera focuses on the Edenic wildlife while we hear the characters' airy ponderings.

Malick's film is often negatively compared to *Saving Private Ryan*, which came out the same year. But while Malick's vision can sometimes fairly be called pretentious, its furious battle scenes lack none of the savagery of Spielberg's vision. In fact, for all its focus on realistic gore, *Ryan* is the less unsettling picture, because it is structured so much like an action film, with satisfying dramatic payoffs. Malick doesn't impose any false order on the chaos. By keeping his eye on the natural world all around the soldiers, he forcefully reminds viewers of the peaceful existence all these men are being denied.

Lost and Found

As big as the *The Thin Red Line*'s cast was, Terrence Malick sliced some performances out entirely. Among the actors not seen in the final cut: Billy Bob Thornton, Gary Oldman, Martin Sheen, Jason Patric, Bill Pullman, Lukas Haas, Viggo Mortensen, and Mickey Rourke.

December 18

Rififi

🌐 🔗

YEAR RELEASED: 1955
DIRECTOR: Jules Dassin
WHO'S IN IT: Jean Servais, Carl Möhner, Robert Manuel, Jules Dassin

"No rods. Get caught with a rod, it's the slammer for life."

The title is French slang for "tough guy," and that's about the only way one could describe the hero in Jules Dassin's gripping Parisian noir. Tony le Stéphanois (Jean Servais) is a tough-as-nails career criminal with a purgatorial demeanor. He is just out of prison and looking for some payback and money. He gets the first in a shocking scene with his ex-mistress (Marie Sabouret), whom he strips and whips almost without explanation. Then it's back to the job: a big score at a jewelry store.

The brilliant, nerve-jangling twenty-eight-minute sequence in which Tony's crew—assisted by the curious little safe-cracker Cesar the Milanese (Dassin himself, silky and untrustworthy)—robs the store takes place in complete silence so as not to set off alarms. Nearly every heist scene that came after (from *Mission: Impossible* to *Ocean's Eleven*) owes some debt to Dassin. As happens in noirs, well-laid plans fall apart, slowly at first, then with murderous speed.

Dassin made this adaptation of an Auguste le Breton novel for a measly $200,000, shooting the gritty, downbeat Paris locales with his typical crispness and unerring eye for authenticity (supposedly, Dassin scouted locations while wandering around town unemployed). The violence, realistic gangsterspeak, and careful examination of criminal methodology got the film banned in many countries, which didn't stop it from being an international hit.

Everyone's a Critic

François Truffaut singled out *Rififi* for high praise in his book *The Films in My Life*: "One of the worst crime novels I have ever read, Jules Dassin has made the best crime film I have ever seen."

DECEMBER 19

Hearts of Darkness:
A Filmmaker's Apocalypse

YEAR RELEASED: 1991
DIRECTORS: Fax Bahr, George Hickenlooper
WHO'S IN IT: Eleanor Coppola, Francis Ford Coppola, George Lucas, John Milius, Martin Sheen

"Little by little, we went insane."

Apocalypse Now might have been derided as a bloated and pretentious disaster, but that was no problem for director Francis Ford Coppola, since it was a disaster people paid attention to. Coppola has always had a little Orson Welles about him, and this extraordinarily entertaining documentary by Fax Bahr and George Hickenlooper about the troubled making of that film shows what happens when a talented cinematic con artist is given several million dollars, a small army of a crew, and let loose in the jungle.

The stroke of luck was that Coppola's wife Eleanor filmed the entire hellacious shoot. (Coppola also conned the studio into hiring her to shoot publicity material.) All Bahr and Hickenlooper had to do was cut together some of Eleanor's more grueling footage (Coppola ranting about his genius, possibly berating Martin Sheen into a heart attack) with some interviews with most of the major players—more tanned, a little heavier, much happier—many years hence.

If it had been just a portrait of a mad genius at work, that would not have been half as illuminating. What we get instead is an incisive look back at a vanished time in film, when that old crew of California oddities like Coppola, his buddy George Lucas (who was originally supposed to direct), and screenwriter John Milius (who provides some of the film's most resonant, and possibly untrue, tales of excess) could be given the keys to the kingdom.

Lost and Found

Hearts of Darkness was the first place most people saw the footage Coppola cut from *Apocalypse Now*'s first release—such as a long-rumored scene at a ghostly plantation run by French colonials—which he included in the film's 2006 rerelease.

December 20

Walkabout

YEAR RELEASED: 1971
DIRECTOR: Nicolas Roeg
WHO'S IN IT: Jenny Agutter, David Gumpilil, Lucien John, John Meillon

"I expect we're the first white people he's seen."

A father (John Meillon) drives his children into the Australian outback. The girl (Jenny Agutter), an eager-to-please teen with Girl Scout inclinations, sets up a picnic while her younger brother (Lucien John) plays. The father then starts firing at them with a pistol before setting the car on fire and shooting himself in the head. The children head off into the great wilderness.

After its jarring beginning (pointedly contrasting the bleak beauty of the outback with the vacuous chaos of the city), the film looks to be another story about abandoned children forced to survive in the wild, and at first director Nicolas Roeg follows that template.

Then an aboriginal boy (David Gumpilil) appears, likely on his walkabout (the ritual in which sixteen-year-old aboriginals are sent into the wilderness to live off the land). Even with the language barrier, all three are soon walking together, the two boys playing together like brothers. The girl is clearly drawn to their knowledgeable, cheerful new friend. Roeg inserts averted glances, as well as a beautiful dance between the two in an abandoned house—but the girl hides it underneath an increasingly arrogant, colonial attitude.

Roeg's second film, adapted from the James Vance Marshall novella, is an unforgettable visual poem on the clash between nature and modern man. His expansive shots of the outback and the blazing sun are stunning, but it's his attention to the small details of the landscape (bounding kangaroos, scorpions) and the impressionistic way it's woven into the characters' wayward odyssey that makes this such a strange and striking piece of work.

December 21

In the Realm of the Senses

YEAR RELEASED: 1976
DIRECTOR: Nagisa Ôshima
WHO'S IN IT: Tatsuya Fuji, Eiko Matsuda, Aoi Nakajima, Meika Seri

"A girl like you can stab a man's heart without a knife."

Nagisa Ôshima's provocative drama is set in Japan, 1936, where young serving girl Sada Abe (Eiko Matsuda) has eyes for the married Kichizo Ishida (Tatsuya Fuji). Their affair begins casually but turns darker, after he checks them into a hotel so they can make love nonstop. Sada and Kichizo's lust quickly goes beyond the erotic and into a realm of sadomasochistic mania, where they can't bear to be apart from each other for even a moment. It concludes with a scene of horrific violence that is as graphic as the nearly nonstop sex which preceded it.

Whether or not Ôshima's strikingly naturalistic, unforgettable film was pornography has been a source of constant debate ever since its troubled opening. Those on the pro side can easily point to the director's decision not to have his actors simulate the sex scenes. Those who would disagree have a stronger argument, as titillation is clearly not the point. The mood is more desperate than erotic, with its characters caught in an inescapable obsession.

This daring classic is not to everyone's tastes; read up on Sada Abe's status as a demented Japanese folk heroine before viewing. If it wasn't based on a true story, the whole thing might come off as an overelaborate erotica experiment, like Lars von Trier's *Antichrist* (2009) with no theological pretensions or talking animals.

Courting Controversy

Prints of *In the Realm of the Senses* were seized in the United States and Germany, while in Japan the film has only ever played in heavily censored versions.

Eyes Without a Face

YEAR RELEASED: 1960
DIRECTOR: Georges Franju
WHO'S IN IT: Pierre Brasseur, Edith Scob, Alida Valli

"Smile. Not too much."

As far as the world outside is concerned, Doctor Génessier (Pierre Brasseur) has just lost his daughter in a horrible traffic accident, leaving him bereft in his huge estate near Paris. The truth of the matter is that his daughter, Christine (Edith Scob), is actually still alive. Génessier keeps her hidden away in a room without mirrors, a creepy white mask covering her terrible facial injuries. Génessier being not just brilliant, resourceful, and wealthy, but well beyond mad, his solution to the situation is gruesomely logical. Helped by his loyal aide, Louise (Alida Valli), Génessier kidnaps young women and uses their facial tissue to try and reconstruct Christine's face. The procedure is temporary at best, though, requiring a continual influx of new victims. Meanwhile, Christine wanders the halls of her prison-like home, the hideous blankness of her mask the sort of thing that nightmares are made of.

Georges Franju brings a twisted beauty to this simple fable, released years later in America in a sliced and diced version retitled *The Horror Chamber of Dr. Faustus*. Film critic Pauline Kael wrote memorably of seeing the film in a San Francisco theater packed with hopped-up teenagers, who hooted and hollered every time it looked like somebody was about to get killed. Franju's pacing is definitely not for the modern slasher aficionado; this is a film of chilly serenity, not gore.

In Homage

Eyes Without a Face was the inspiration for the 1984 Billy Idol song of the same name. It's also thought that the blank white mask that Michael Myers wears in John Carpenter's *Halloween* was influenced by Christine's in Georges Franju's film.

Cyclo

🌍 👓 🎭

YEAR RELEASED: 1995
DIRECTOR: Tran Anh Hung
WHO'S IN IT: Le Van Loc, Tony Leung

"Eating and sleeping in the street. Pedaling all the time. Some mornings the backaches nail you to the bed."

Starting out as a straightforward neorealist drama of life on the streets of Ho Chi Minh City (formerly Saigon), Tran Anh Hung's blistering film radically shifts gears into a more grandiose crime story. His eighteen-year-old protagonist (Le Van Loc), known as "Cyclo," pedals his cyclo, or bicycle taxi, through the teeming city streets all day, every day. Cyclo's parents are dead, yet the admonishing words of his cyclo-driving father ring in his head ("see if you can find something more worthy"). He lives with his grandfather and two sisters; everybody works.

With nobody to look out for him, Cyclo is ensnared by a crime boss known as the Madam (Nhu Quynh Nguyen), who makes him work with her right-hand man, the Poet (Tony Leung). First portrayed as sensitive—he looks sad and rarely speaks, we only hear his voice in the poetry he recites as narration—the Poet soon shows himself to be a ruthless killer with no qualms about forcing the naive Cyclo, and later one of his sisters, into violently amoral degradation.

Cyclo's tour of an underworld hell starkly contrasts with the sunny and bustling daylight streets, with Tran capturing many poignant details of daily life along the way (shoe-shine children slumped over in exhaustion, the cross-hatching of leaves rustling outside a window). He also creates a scene in a nightclub where Radiohead's "Creep" plays over tinny speakers, acting as prelude to a shocking murder that is simply a knockout, just like the film as a whole.

December 24

Fanny and Alexander

🌐 🎭 👫

YEAR RELEASED: 1982
DIRECTOR: Ingmar Bergman
WHO'S IN IT: Bertil Guve, Pernilla Allwin, Erland Josephson

"Are you sad because you've grown old?"

A vividly colored and magical tale of children, wonder, and imagination, this is on the surface pretty much the last kind of film one would expect to see from Ingmar Bergman. Absent are the stark theological inquiries and world-weary existential ponderings of the films that made his name fairly synonymous with "art" films during the 1950s and 1960s. But the fully imagined performances and smart writing are as much in evidence as ever.

It's Christmas Eve, 1907, in Sweden. There's a party in the Ekdahl clan mansion, and the colorful swirl of conversation is witnessed by ten-year-old Alexander (Bertil Guve) and sister Fanny (Pernilla Allwin). The Ekdahl children's freewheeling days seem to come to an end when their father dies and their mother marries a stern bishop (Jan Malmsjö). Relief comes in the form of Isak Jacobi (Erland Josephson), a Jewish antiques dealer who returns a sense of magic and unpredictability to their lives.

This sprawling, joyful family saga hits all the right notes of childhood fantasy, from the stark evil-stepfather scenes to those of magical-realism in Jacobi's shop. In the end, this film doesn't seem so different from Bergman's earlier, more adult work, in that it's still all about mystery and the unknowability of the universe. It would be his last feature film; the director spent the rest of his career doing theater and films for Swedish television. It's a fitting grace note to end a career on.

Lost and Found

The international theatrical cut of *Fanny and Alexander* was roughly three hours. A television broadcast edit, which Ingmar Bergman apparently preferred, ran to just over five hours.

DECEMBER 25

It's a Wonderful Life

YEAR RELEASED: 1946
DIRECTOR: Frank Capra
WHO'S IN IT: James Stewart, Donna Reed, Lionel Barrymore

"Just remember this, Mr. Potter, that this rabble you're talking about, they do most of the working and paying and living and dying in this community."

The one Frank Capra film that even curmudgeons have a grudging admiration for is a reversed *Christmas Carol*, where instead of a heel being shown how to be a good person, we see a good man learning not to be so down on himself.

George Bailey (James Stewart) is a big-hearted guy who operates a small building and loan in a small town run by the foul old moneybags Mr. Potter (Lionel Barrymore). On Christmas Eve, George's drunk uncle loses their bank deposit, threatening ruination. George is ready to throw himself into the icy river when he spots a man drowning and jumps in to save him. The man is actually an angel, Clarence (an apple-cheeked Henry Travers), who shows George how the town of Bedford Falls would have been without him. It isn't pretty.

A number of factors make the film's sentimentality go down so easily. First among them is the casual perfection of the cast, especially the often underrated Stewart himself, who makes George's suicidal despair just as believable as his good humor. Capra also effectively mines Dickens for his gothic portrayal of Potter and Clarence's slum-ridden alternate universe. This one doesn't get old.

Courting Controversy

An FBI agent reporting on Communist infiltration in Hollywood wrote that *It's a Wonderful Life* was "a rather obvious attempt to discredit bankers by casting Lionel Barrymore as a 'scrooge-type' so that he would be the most hated man in the movie."

Night and the City

YEAR RELEASED: 1950
DIRECTOR: Jules Dassin
WHO'S IN IT: Richard Widmark, Gene Tierney

"Harry is an artist without an art."

Harry Fabian (Richard Widmark) is an American swindler trying to make it in London and getting nowhere fast. A born scammer, he's always trying to figure out the dead-solid con that's going to earn him a bucket of cash with minimal work. So he runs cons wherever he can find them, whether or not they make sense. A particularly ill-considered idea has Harry trying to become a promoter for famous wrestler Gregorious (actual wrestler Stanislaus Zbyszko), which gets him wrapped in tighter than he should be with some local gangsters.

Even without Widmark's wonderfully jangled twitchiness, Jules Dassin's noir would stand tall for its unnerving sense of place. The back alleys and tourist arcades of London have a sharp, nighttime glare whose long, knife-like shadows are more resonantly moody than anything cooked up on a Hollywood backlot. (Since nighttime location filming was still difficult with the technology available at the time, Dassin had to convince many London businesses to leave their lights on.)

Dassin himself was on the lam at the time (troubles back in America with the House Un-American Activities Committee), and so is able to impart a powerful empathy to the scuttling, perennially chased Harry. It says something about the director that a film starring a character so lacking in basic common sense or decency can still evoke such a tug of sympathy when the story's iron jaws come clamping down on him.

Production Notes

Darryl F. Zanuck sent Jules Dassin to London to make *Night and the City* because the director was about to get expelled from Twentieth Century Fox for running afoul of the blacklist.

In a Lonely Place

YEAR RELEASED: 1950
DIRECTOR: Nicholas Ray
WHO'S IN IT: Humphrey Bogart, Gloria Grahame, Frank Lovejoy, Carl Benton Reid

"It was his story against mine, but of course, I told my story better."

In films, writers are usually solitary figures pensively hunched over a silent type-writer—they're rarely depicted as boozing, brawling, potential criminals. (Exception being Charles Bukowski films: witness Mickey Rourke in *Barfly* and Matt Dillon in *Factotum*.)

That's the case with Dixon Steel (Humphrey Bogart) in this cold-blooded Nicholas Ray melodrama. Not long after "Dix" is introduced, we see him starting a knock-down fight for no good reason. He doesn't get into real trouble, though, until he becomes a murder suspect. Having been offered a plum job adapting a lousy bestselling novel, Dix hands it off to a friendly groupie one night at his favorite restaurant, giving her cab fare home and telling her to give him a synopsis later. That morning, the police tell him she's been murdered, and he's a suspect, as the last guy who saw her alive. At that point, his fatally beautiful neighbor Laura Gray (Gloria Grahame) offers to be his alibi, but this doesn't appear to be the whole truth.

Nicholas Ray's reputation depends more on his later work like *Rebel Without a Cause* (1955) and *Johnny Guitar* (1954). But their overheated, neon-colored passions seem far away from this cool, chiseled, noir-ish film, where even Bogart's occasional eruptions of rage seem well calculated

Courting Controversy

At the beginning of production for *In a Lonely Place*, Gloria Grahame was married to director Nicholas Ray. Their marriage ended during filming, supposedly because Ray learned that Grahame was having an affair with his teenaged son, Tony, whom she married in 1960.

Hoop Dreams

YEAR RELEASED: 1994
DIRECTOR: Steve James
WHO'S IN IT: William Gates, Arthur Agee

"People always say to me, 'When you get to the NBA, don't forget about me.' Well, I should've said back, 'if I don't make it to the NBA, don't you forget about me.'"

With eye-opening sensitivity and an awesome dedication, Steve James's documentary follows six years in the lives of William Gates and Arthur Agee. Over the course of the film, they'll grow from kids shooting hoops in the schoolyard to young men with a real chance to make it as professional basketball players. Both are from poor families, so the sports-film clichés of seeing who makes that last shot or who wins the game is given extra weight. The results don't just matter for them as athletes; they matter for their *lives*.

Because William's and Arthur's talents have been recognized, they get the chance to attend an exclusive, largely white prep school in the Chicago suburbs and play for one of the best coaches around. It all sounds like a dream, except that with opportunity comes added pressures. There's the strangeness of new surroundings, that brutally long commute, academic and family pressures, and at the end of it all, the knowledge that no matter how good they are, the chances of them making it to the NBA are minuscule.

Dramatic without being fake and meaningful without being preachy, this is one of the landmarks of documentary filmmaking.

And the Winner Is . . .

Hoop Dreams received one Oscar nomination for editing, but not, oddly enough, for best documentary. It was added to the Library of Congress' National Film Registry—an annual selection of films deemed significant enough to deserve preservation for future generations—in 2006.

Deliverance

YEAR RELEASED: 1972
DIRECTOR: John Boorman
WHO'S IN IT: Burt Reynolds, Jon Voight, Ned Beatty, Ronny Cox

"You play a mean banjo."

Four men from Atlanta take a canoe trip down a soon-to-be-dammed river. There's heavyset and loquacious Bobby (Ned Beatty), quiet and reflective Ed (Jon Voight), nervous Drew (Ronny Cox), and self-proclaimed woodsman Lewis (Burt Reynolds). They're amused by the hillbillies they come across, particularly a banjo-playing boy who looks like he might be inbred. All is fine until they come across a couple of armed locals—one of the four is raped, and they kill one of the attackers with an arrow. Afterwards, the vacation descends into guilt and paranoia, with the men's fears increasing along with the turbulence of the rapids.

On its surface, it's the stuff of a hundred lousy thrillers, where the audience is rewarded for sharing the protagonists' condescending viewpoint after seeing what happens to them. But John Boorman's film of James Dickey's novel uses these stock elements to create something more elementally terrifying. The rape shocks because of its matter-of-fact nature: you can't believe this is about to happen any more than the victim can. Boorman's undermining of certainty in later scenes and chillingly casual way with violence suggests there's no greater reason for what's happening and little that could be done to stop it.

Deliverance is lushly photographed, prefiguring Boorman's evocations of lush green wilderness in *The Emerald Forest* (1985) and *Beyond Rangoon* (1995). It is also deftly acted by a cast who, for the most part (Reynolds and Voight in particular, pushing their characters to the opposite ends of morality), have never done better.

And the Winner Is . . .
Deliverance was a surprise box-office hit and was nominated for three Oscars (director, picture, editing), winning none.

The Man Who Would Be King

YEAR RELEASED: 1975
DIRECTOR: John Huston
WHO'S IN IT: Michael Caine, Sean Connery, Christopher Plummer, Saeed Jaffrey

"Give me a drink, brother Kipling."

Rudyard Kipling (Christopher Plummer) appears as a journalist working in India. In comes an apparent raving lunatic, Peachy Carnehan (Michael Caine, a true rogue's gleam in the eye), who's got a hell of a story to tell. Peachy and his friend Danny Dravot (Sean Connery, agreeably good-humored) are two soldiers who finished their tour of India, con their way into a crateful of modern rifles, and set off for the Khyber Pass. After a lucky accident convinces everybody that Danny is a deity, the two cheats have an unbeatable army. Eventually they come to a glorious city where circumstances make people think Danny is actually Alexander the Great, who'd come conquering through centuries ago and had promised to return. Problems arise when Danny believes his own press, while the down-to-earth Peachy wants to take the gold and run.

Huston's film celebrates the rousing adventurousness of the Kipling original without turning it into a colonialist escapade where the natives are merely extras in the white man's game. The film's stunning locations (it was shot in the mountains of Morocco) and sense of mysterious grandeur stand as rebukes to the imperial con games of Peachy and Danny. They might be charming scamps, but they still have a heavy price to pay when it's all said and done.

Production Notes

The Man Who Would Be King was a twenty-year labor of love for John Huston. It was first to be filmed in 1956 with Clark Gable and Humphrey Bogart, and came close to being started in 1959 and 1964 before languishing for another decade.

December 31

When Harry Met Sally

 ♥

YEAR RELEASED: 1989
DIRECTOR: Rob Reiner
WHO'S IN IT: Billy Crystal, Meg Ryan, Carrie Fisher, Bruno Kirby

"You realize, of course, that we could never be friends."

In Rob Reiner's landmark romantic comedy—equal parts Woody Allen urbanity and therapy session—Billy Crystal plays Harry Burns, a premature burnout who shares a ride from Chicago to New York with Sally Albright (Meg Ryan), the definition of brittle perkiness. Worldviews clash, they have many testy arguments, and part ways. Years later, they meet up again just as their marriages are falling apart and become that rarest of things: a man and woman who are nonromantic friends. Of course, they'll eventually end up together, but the heart of the film lies in the long, spiraling talks they have about dating, sex, dining, and the merits of *Casablanca*.

The script by Nora Ephron serves primarily as a scaffold for Reiner and Crystal to ad-lib various gags, a point backed up by the dreariness of Ephron's later films like *You've Got Mail* (1998). The fall and winter tones of Reiner's New York have a romantic aura that Hollywood had denied the city for so many years. Yes, it reeks of yuppie, and many of the better moments are pulled from *Annie Hall* (1977), but by the time the partygoers sing "should auld acquaintance be forgot" and Harry, beholding a tearful Sally, cracks, "All my life, I've never known what this song means," none of that matters.

Production Notes
When Harry Met Sally grew out of long and frank conversations about relationships between Rob Reiner and Nora Ephron, with the two frankly admitting that Harry and Sally were merely stand-ins for themselves.

Genre Index

 Action

 Animation

 Avant-garde

LOL! **Comedy**

Crime

🎭 Drama. *See also* Crime; Mystery

Family

 Fantasy. *See also* **Science-fiction**

Foreign

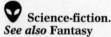 ## Science-fiction.
See also Fantasy

 ## War

 ## Western

Main Index